M. S. Fish

D1738309

OUT OF ORDER

OUT OF ORDER

Russian Political Values in an Imperfect World

ELLEN CARNAGHAN

THE PENNSYLVANIA STATE UNIVERSITY PRESS
UNIVERSITY PARK, PENNSYLVANIA

Library of Congress Cataloging-in-Publication Data

Carnaghan, Ellen
    Out of Order : Russian political values in an imperfect
        world / Ellen Carnaghan
p.   cm.
Includes bibliographical references and index.
ISBN-13: 987-0-271-02973-1 (cloth : alk. paper)
ISBN-10: 0-271-02973-0 (cloth : alk. paper)
1. Political culture—Russia (Federation)
2. Russia (Federation)—Politics and government—1991–
        —Public opinion.
3. Public opinion—Russia (Federation)
I. Title.
II. Title: Russian political values in an imperfect world.

JN6699.A15C38 2007
306.20947—dc22
2006028920

The Pennsylvania State University Press
is a member of the
Association of American University Presses.

It is the policy of The Pennsylvania State University Press
to use acid-free paper. This book is printed on Natures
Natural, containing 50% post-consumer waste, and meets
the minimum requirements of American National
Standard for Information Sciences—Permanence of Paper
for Printed Library Material, ANSI Z39.48–1992.

CONTENTS

LIST
OF
TABLES

To Mark

I started to think about the ideas that inform this book while I was working on another project, at the point when the Soviet Union was seriously beginning to crumble. On one particular day in the fall of 1990, I returned late from the Institute of Sociology and dropped by a nearby bakery to buy bread for dinner. As there was no bread, I bought cookies instead, thinking that the Russian version of that famous phrase could be "Let them eat *prianiki*." I returned to the hotel run by the Academy of Sciences to find that the elevator was not working. I walked up ten flights of stairs with my *prianiki* and opened the door to my room, and the electricity went out. And it struck me: maybe this is what a revolution feels like. Not excitement, not major political changes, but grinding weariness as things slowly fall apart. If ordinary citizens experience political life through a variety of daily occurrences, then in Russia during the 1990s those were often annoying and frustrating occurrences: navigating a subway system dotted with broken escalators, dealing with the sudden disappearance of hot water, and waiting patiently for government officials to do what was supposed to be their jobs. My aim in this book is to examine how the frustrations of daily existence color the political orientations of Russian citizens.

This book is informed by intensive interviews that I conducted with ordinary Russians between 1998 and 2003. I am grateful to all the people who took time out of busy lives to talk with me, in many cases to invite me into their homes and ply me with tea and homemade preserves, and to provide intriguing insights into Russian thinking. I cannot thank them by name without removing their protective cover of anonymity, but each person who spoke with me has made many valuable contributions to this book. Without their willingness to lend their voices to this project, there would be no book.

These interviews would not have been possible without a great deal of assistance. Over the course of these five years, I received funding from Fulbright-Hays (with funds from the U.S. Department of Education), the International Research and Exchanges Board (funds from the National Endowment

ACKNOWL-
EDGMENTS

for the Humanities, the U.S. Department of State, and the U.S. Information Agency), the American Political Science Association, and the Beaumont and Mellon Funds at Saint Louis University. I also received funding to attend the Eurasian Summer Research Laboratory at the University of Illinois during three summers while working on this project (funds provided by the U.S. Department of State Title VIII Program). In the writing stage, I benefited from release time under a Saint Louis University Faculty Research Leave. Of course, none of these benefactors bears any responsibility for the ideas expressed in this book.

I am especially indebted to the people who helped me locate Russian citizens willing to talk about politics with an American scholar. I would particularly like to thank Polina Kozyreva, whose assistance and advice was so valuable that I am not sure this book could have been written without her. Her colleagues at the Institute of Sociology, Mikhail Kosolapov and Marina Chizhova, also gave freely of their time and expertise. Ol'ga Iastrebova, Nina Rostegaeva and Natal'ia Peshkova rounded up a number of the interviewees in Moscow; I am also indebted to them for their friendship and efforts to expand my cultural program. The people who helped me outside Moscow worked under significant time pressure, often finding a large number of interview subjects in a small amount of time. For their yeoman efforts, I would also like to thank Tat'iana Bogomolova in Novosibirsk, Valentina Pervova in Krasnoyarsk, Ol'ga Shcheglova in Voronezh, Andrei Shashenkov in Smolensk, and Arbakhan Magomedov in Ulyanovsk.

I am also indebted to Lisa Pohlman and Mary Santanello, who conducted the American interviews; to Joshua Melton, who examined a variety of Russian public opinion data; and to Shawn Wedel and Maria Grogan, for assistance in preparing the manuscript.

Other people helped in the process of writing the book, whether reading all or parts of it or offering challenging comments. Their assistance has improved the book immeasurably, though of course they cannot be blamed for any remaining error or for my obtuseness in interpreting their remarks. I would particularly like to thank Donna Bahry, who suggested the in-depth interview as a useful portal into the minds of Russian citizens and who provided just the right advice at just the right moments, in her inimitable way. I am grateful to Sandy Thatcher of the Pennsylvania State University Press for his interest in my work. Careful readings of the manuscript by Robert Grey and Eric Shiraev challenged me to write a better and clearer book, and sensitive copyediting by Romaine Perin improved the book further. My department chair in later stages of the project, Wynne Walker Moskop, managed to arrange some release time from teaching, which of course helped a great deal. My colleague Timothy Lomperis read far more of the book than he may have wanted and was a constant source of encouragement and good advice.

A number of people read and commented on either chapters or preliminary papers that later became chapters. They include Eloise Buker, Vicki Hesli, Lisa Pohlman, Richard Rose, Blair Ruble, Jason Wittenberg, and Sharon Wolchik. An earlier version of Chapter 4 was published as "Thinking About Democracy: Interviews with Russian Citizens" in *Slavic Review* (Summer 2001). An even earlier version was published as *Studies in Public Policy* 322 (1999), through the University of Strathclyde Centre for the Study of Public Policy in Glasgow, Scotland. Some paragraphs of Chapter 6 are drawn from "Have Your Cake and Eat It Too: Tensions Between Democracy and Order Among Russian Citizens," *Studies in Public Policy* 352 (2001). This previously published material is reprinted here with acknowledgment.

My most fundamental debt is to my husband, Mark, who, despite an aversion to disorder, has been a beloved and intrepid fellow traveler, in Russia and in life.

In the footnotes and references, I have used the Library of Congress system of transliteration, but in the text itself I have modified that system slightly for the sake of readers who do not speak Russian. I refer to place-names and well-known individuals by the spellings generally used by the news media (e.g., Yeltsin, instead of El'tsin, and Ulyanovsk instead of Ul'ianovsk). I have omitted soft signs in the first names that I assigned to respondents. In an effort to help readers remember the respondents, respondents who were thirty years of age or younger were given diminutive forms of Russian names, and respondents over sixty were given first names and patronymics. For patronymics, I do include soft signs. Where possible, I spell diminutive forms of names with a -*ya* ending, to make them more easily recognized by readers who do not speak Russian.

A NOTE ON TRANSLIT-ERATION

Out of Order

In Russia, many things do not work out as intended. A case in point is the construction of new political and economic institutions after the collapse of Communism. Competitive elections occurred, individual freedoms expanded exponentially, and ordinary people long denied the blessings of liberty embraced new opportunities and in some cases prospered in ways Communists deemed neither possible nor prudent. But under Russia's first president, Boris Yeltsin, what some called "democracy" took the form of a president's ordering the shelling of the parliament, then pushing through a constitution that granted inordinate power to his own office. Yeltsin's successor, Vladimir Putin, worked to strengthen the "power vertical" created by that constitution, moving to end the election of regional officials, closing down critical television networks, and threatening citizens who tried to build the foundations of an independent civil society. Under both men, elites resisted sharing their power, corruption undermined governmental accountability, and citizens had few mechanisms available to influence those who would rule them. In the economic sphere, markets seemed to protect the wealth of the few while providing limited opportunities for the many. Even so, Russia's wealthiest man, Mikhail Khodorkovsky, ended up in jail after challenging Putin's control.

Ordinary people experience these erratic effects of systemic transformation in direct and immediate ways. For the average Russian citizen, the collapse of the Soviet system meant food shortages, electrical outages, and snow piled up in the streets and on sidewalks because municipal services ceased to function. The transition to a market system produced government budget shortfalls, along with delayed paychecks, cutbacks in social services, and a decaying urban infrastructure. Greater freedom for some took the shape of higher crime rates and a steady stream of terrorist acts—including numerous bombs in subways, airplanes, and other public places as well as hostage situations in a Moscow theater and a Beslan grammar school. The outcomes of all these changes—imperfectly functioning institutions with some democratic and some autocratic features—are experienced by ordinary citizens through arcane rules, surly bureaucrats, bribe-collecting traffic police, and offices that remain mysteriously closed during their reception hours. In this book, I show how the sometimes disorderly and unpredictable reality produced by political and economic transformations has shaped the political values of Russian citizens.

In making this case, I challenge the notion that cultural traditions are largely continuous across time and serve as effective limits on the kinds of institutions a country can sustain.[1] A number of scholars have argued that ordinary Russians today drag behind them, if not a thousand-year legacy of serfdom, at least a heavy cultural tradition of autocratic and paternalistic government. Because of that past, the argument goes, Russians were not prepared to become democrats. Rather, they are thought to be fearful of granting freedoms to others, even if they want those freedoms for themselves; overly ready to cede their rights to government, as long as those who rule promise to look after their subjects; and intolerant of the disorder that accompanies democracy. So, for instance, Aleksander Dugin has argued that the ancient and geopolitically rooted values of Eurasia are innately hostile to Western liberalism.[2] Tim McDaniel noticed aspects of a "Russian idea" that remained constant from the time of the czars through the present and that undermined efforts at reform.[3] Frederic J. Fleron Jr. worried that some Westerners might be "attempting to foist off too much democracy too fast onto a society that is striking for its lack of democratic traditions."[4] James Alexander argued that Russian political culture in the 1990s suffered from "formlessness," from political values and beliefs that were "fractured, contradictory and elusive," because Russians were trying to make sense of their changing environment with a set of cultural tools better designed to negotiate the autocratic past.[5]

---

1. See, for example, Samuel P. Huntington, *The Clash of Civilizations and the Remaking of World Order* (New York: Touchstone, 1996); Robert Putnam, *Making Democracy Work: Civic Traditions in Modern Italy* (Princeton: Princeton University Press, 1993); Russell Bova, "Democracy and Liberty: The Cultural Connection," in *The Global Divergence of Democracies*, ed. Larry Diamond and Marc F. Plattner (Baltimore: Johns Hopkins University Press, 2001), 63–77.

2. Aleksandr G. Dugin, *Russkaia Veshch': Ocherki natsional'noi filosofii* (Moscow: Arktogeia, 2001), vol. 1, 35–70.

3. Tim McDaniel, *The Agony of the Russian Idea* (Princeton: Princeton University Press, 1996).

4. Frederic J. Fleron Jr., "Congruence Theory Applied: Democratization in Russia," in *Can Democracy Take Root in Post-Soviet Russia? Explorations in State-Society Relations*, ed. Harry Eckstein, Frederic J. Fleron Jr., Erik Hoffmann, and William Reisinger (New York: Rowman and Littlefield, 1998), 41.

5. James Alexander, *Political Culture in Post-Communist Russia: Formlessness and Recreation in a Traumatic Transition* (New York: St. Martin's Press, 2000), 15, 32.

My approach in this book is different. Rather than looking for origins of present values in geography, distant history, religious traditions, or long-standing cultural norms, I look for more proximate sources in the world that people presently inhabit. Rather than asking whether Russian citizens have the right values to sustain democratic institutions, I examine the values that existing institutions and the reality they create actually encourage. I argue that during the Soviet years, ordinary Russians inhabited an autocratic system, adapted to it, but did not necessarily adopt its values. Similarly, they presently inhabit a political system with some democratic elements, such as elections, and other features that hearken back to Russia's autocratic past, but it is not popular preferences that pull the Russian government away from democracy. For most of their lives, Russian citizens experienced the outputs of their governing system as officially produced disorder—from the unpredictability inherent in a system in which citizens had no rights against the state, to the inefficiencies of state planning that made it difficult to buy toilet paper and soap, to the dislocations of transition and its attendant bouts of hyperinflation and financial collapse. These experiences in their own lives, not the experiences of their forebears centuries ago, have left Russians with a preference for order.

Because of that preference for order, some Russians have little use for the niceties of democratic practice. To them, representative institutions seem too fractious, social disorder appears too threatening, and a market society looks like a dangerous place where ordinary people have few chances and had better be wary of pickpockets and thieves. But not all Russians view the world in the same way. Others, while still attracted to "order," imagine a country where everyone—even the people in charge— obey the law, where rights are respected, and where people are free to pursue their own goals in their own ways. For these Russians, their visions of order are entirely consistent with much more democratic institutions than they have ever enjoyed.

Scholars trying to explain the rapid collapse of Communist institutions that gave way under the pressure of reform have noticed that those institutions inadvertently encouraged the very behavior that led to their demise.[6] Instead of encouraging people to work hard, use resources frugally, and

---

6. Valerie Bunce, *Subversive Institutions: The Design and Destruction of Socialism and the State* (New York: Cambridge University Press, 1999); Stephen Solnick, *Stealing the State: Control and Collapse in Soviet Institutions* (Cambridge, MA: Harvard University Press, 1998); Mancur Olson, *Power and Prosperity: Outgrowing Communist and Capitalist Dictatorship* (New York: Basic Books/Perseus, 2000).

report production outcomes accurately to their supervisors, the incentives built into economic structures encouraged people to shirk, hoard, lie, and steal. Instead of building loyalty to central governmental bodies, political incentives caused all players to seek their own private good at the expense of the community. These observations, though, have focused on elite behavior. I extend the logic of these arguments to the level of ordinary citizens and to the values inadvertently encouraged both in the late Soviet era and the early post-Soviet era. The complex and often disjointed reality of the Soviet and post-Soviet systems has been well described, but scholars of public opinion have paid little attention to the effects of this disorder on popular ideas and values. Instead, most scholars of Russian public opinion have tended to assume that the regime produced what it intended, whether that was relative material security during the Soviet years or political freedom under Boris Yeltsin. I, by contrast, focus more on the immediate reality of what ordinary people experience in their political and economic lives and the effects that immediate reality has on their social and political values.

The result of locating the sources of present values in the daily existence of living citizens provides a more hopeful picture than the one that students of political culture usually draw. If popular values are formed in the present rather than the distant past, no nation, not even Russia, is closed off by culture from the possibility of democracy. No existing historical reality is necessarily immutable. Of course, it may be the case that Russia's leaders no longer intend to move the country closer to democracy. While the early years after the collapse of the Communist regime saw increasing freedoms and greater political competition, under Putin it seemed that progress toward democracy stopped, or even reversed course.[7] Even if the values of Russian citizens favor more democratic elements in their political system, that is no guarantee of a democratic future.

Talking with Russians

In this book, I give ordinary Russians the time and space to describe the sources of their political orientations. My analysis is based on intensive interviews with sixty Russian citizens, interviews that were conducted between 1998 and 2003. I interviewed people in Moscow as well as in two Siberian cities—Krasnoyarsk and Novosibirsk—and three cities in European

---

7. Steven Levitsky and Lucan A. Way, "Elections Without Democracy: The Rise of Competitive Authoritarianism," *Journal of Democracy* 13, no. 2 (2002): 51–65.

Russia's "red belt"—Smolensk, Ulyanovsk, and Voronezh. Russia's red belt is composed of areas that retained Communist Party officials in power well into the 1990s and that tended to elect Communists or nationalists in federal elections. I also traveled to a variety of small towns in the region around Moscow in order to interview people in places where the positive effects of change had been very slow to arrive. The people I interviewed were from all walks of life and displayed a variety of political orientations, from a promarket New Russian with a stunning apartment in the heart of Moscow to an elderly Communist who supplemented her pension by selling *piroshki* at her small-town bus stop. They included a young hairdresser upset about dwindling opportunities, one of the founders of one of Russia's first citizen-based movements, computer operators, electricians, teachers, doctors, and retirees. Respondents were selected to maximize variation in age, education, and region, since these are factors that have been shown to affect political orientations.[8] Although the main focus of this book is the political values of Russian citizens, a smaller sample of interviews with Americans is used to show where Russian interpretations are distinctive and, more often, where they are not.

Where mass surveys provide a very accurate picture of the distribution of ideas across a population, intensive interviews open a window into the logic and operation of a smaller number of minds.[9] It is possible to examine apparent contradictions in people's ideas, to uncover the concerns that lie behind policy preferences, and to tease out why individuals think the things they do. These were open-ended interviews during which the respondents were free to talk at length, to contradict themselves and then to try to explain those contradictions, to tell stories and give examples. From this detail, a richer, if necessarily smaller, picture of the ideas and values of ordinary Russians can be drawn. The large number and high quality of mass-opinion surveys that have been conducted in Russia since the collapse of the Soviet Union have already given the Russian people a chance to speak. The intensive interviews on which this book is based give them a chance to explain what they mean.

8. Timothy J. Colton, *Transitional Citizens: Voters and What Influences Them in the New Russia* (Cambridge, MA: Harvard University Press, 2000); Timothy J. Colton and Jerry F. Hough, eds., *Growing Pains: Russian Democracy and the Election of 1993* (Washington, DC: Brookings Institution, 1998); Richard Rose and Neil Munro, *Elections Without Order: Russia's Challenge to Vladimir Putin* (New York: Cambridge University Press, 2002).

9. Michael F. Schober and Frederick G. Conrad, "Does Conversational Interviewing Reduce Survey Measurement Error?" *Public Opinion Quarterly* 61 (Winter 1997): 576–602.

Studies based on intensive interviews in Russia and elsewhere have been successful in uncovering insights not immediately apparent from large-N surveys (surveys with large numbers of respondents). One of the masterpieces of the genre is Robert Lane's study of the men of "Eastport."[10] Lane explored the social and psychological foundations of the ideas of working-class and lower-middle-class American men and traced some of their political beliefs back to the relationships they had had with their fathers. Jennifer Hochschild was able to use the understanding she gained from intensive interviews with Americans to explain why people in the United States do not support a redistribution of wealth.[11] Intensive interviews were particularly helpful in this context because the answer lay in conflicting ways of thinking about justice, not something that would have been immediately apparent from standardized questionnaires. In the Russian context, one of the most penetrating studies is Nancy Ries's examination of the stories of suffering that Russians tell one another on a daily basis.[12] Ries showed how ever-present litanies of despair and disrepair helped to reproduce the society about which people were complaining. Taking on a topic particularly unsuited to examination through multiple-choice questions, Dale Pesmen used a combination of intensive interviews and participant observation to explore what Russians mean when they talk about the "Russian soul."[13] Using an approach similarly grounded in the logic of letting ordinary people speak for themselves, John Dryzek and Leslie Holmes were able to extract the underlying logic of three political discourses in Russia.[14] Unlike Pesman's and Ries's books, the present study is more focused on political life; unlike the work of Dryzek and Holmes, it plumbs more extensively the social sources of the ideas expressed.

My analysis of intensive interviews with Russians has produced some intriguing findings. For one thing, the interviews show how everyday life and immediate personal experience influence the political orientations of

10. Robert E. Lane, *Political Ideology: Why the American Common Man Believes What He Does* (New York: Free Press, 1962).

11. Jennifer Hochschild, *What's Fair? Americans' Attitudes Toward Distributive Justice* (Cambridge, MA: Harvard University Press, 1981).

12. Nancy Ries, *Russian Talk: Culture and Conversation During Perestroika* (Ithaca: Cornell University Press, 1997).

13. Dale Pesmen, *Russia and Soul* (Ithaca: Cornell University Press, 2000).

14. Dryzek and Holmes use discourse analysis and Q methodology. Q methodology models patterns of subjectivity across a relatively small sample of subjects, who are asked to react to statements developed partly from focus groups. John S. Dryzek and Leslie Holmes, *Post-Communist Democratization: Political Discourses Across Thirteen Countries* (New York: Cambridge University Press, 2002), 92–113.

many Russians. My respondents' assessments of representative institutions, for instance, were based not on an abstract ideal of how democratic institutions are supposed to function, but on the imperfect operation of the institutions of their own experience. Similarly, their reactions to market reform reflected the shortcomings of Russia's markets, not cultural predispositions toward an egalitarian distribution of wealth. For many of my respondents, the immediate social context of their lives was chaotic, threatening, or at the very least unpredictable. And this sense of imminent social disorder had a strong influence on many political orientations. The people most troubled by this social disorder were less likely to support democracy and less likely to have confidence in public officials. However, they were also unlikely to advocate institutional changes, since change itself is an element of the disorder that alarmed them.

But not all Russians shared these concerns. Some of the people I interviewed were strong supporters of democracy. These democrats often were able to perceive patterns in processes that remained incomprehensible to others, among them the internal wrangling characteristic of representative institutions or the interparty strife of elections. They saw democratic institutions as tools by means of which to take control of their environment, not as contributors to social chaos. Even Russia's democrats tend to favor "order" and a "strong state," and analysis of the interviews provides insight into what appear at first to be internal contradictions in their ideas. When the people I interviewed spoke of "order," they often meant a society in which law restrains everyone's behavior—even that of errant government officials—so that freedom may flourish in community. Many of my respondents—democrats and nondemocrats, free-marketeers and market skeptics, pensioners and youth—suffered from passivity in the face of power. As a group, they were highly skeptical about the possibilities of positive change. They have not yet embraced their new roles as citizens because they are not sure that their political context has fundamentally changed. Their passivity may make progress toward democracy dependent on the good intentions of those who govern Russia—probably not the wisest bet.

A Preview

This book proceeds in a number of steps. In Chapter 2, I build the case for examining popular orientations in the context of the immediate circumstances of ordinary people's lives. I argue that those circumstances—

particularly experiences with government institutions, concerns about family economic security, and perceptions of the order and predictability of daily life—color political orientations at least as much as do cultural values inherited from the past. I offer a reinterpretation of Soviet and post-Soviet political culture as a response to current social disorder.

In Chapter 3, I describe the methodology used in the book. Intensive interviews permit respondents to explain their ideas, to clarify the reasoning behind their choices, and to illuminate the logic linking one idea to another. As a result, they provide us with unique opportunities to understand the political and social values of ordinary people. In the Russian context, intensive interviews are especially helpful in untangling apparent contradictions in popular values in a changing society. The Russian respondents are drawn from cities and small towns across Russia, and, also in Chapter 3, I examine the political and economic circumstances in the places where I conducted the interviews, thereby illustrating the variation in circumstances that the respondents—and all Russians—face. In addition, I describe a smaller sample of interviews with Americans that I used for comparative purposes. In some ways, Russian ideas make more sense when we understand how they differ from and how they parallel ideas of people with the great good fortune of living in a much more politically stable and generally prosperous society. Without that comparison, it is too easy to think, say, that imperfect support for democracy is a particularly Russian feature, when it may in fact also be characteristic of populations with more exposure to better-functioning political institutions.

In Chapters 4 through 8, I present findings based on analysis of the interviews. In Chapter 4, I show how imperfections in the operation of Russian political institutions encourage imperfections in citizens' democratic values. Listening to the Russian respondents' comments on the operation of legislative institutions and on the role of law in organizing society makes it clear that what looks like flawed support for democracy can be better understood as a fairly nuanced critique of the flawed operation of existing institutions. My respondents like democracy in the abstract much more than they like what goes by that label in their own experience, and they do not share many of the beliefs that supposedly are characteristic of traditional, undemocratic Russian political culture. My respondents want to see democratic institutions improved, not dismantled. Poorly functioning institutions have left their own mark on popular attitudes, however, and the results may not strengthen democracy overall. Widespread disillusionment regarding the ability of ordinary citizens to influence officials means that citizens are unwilling to work very hard to improve those institutions or to deepen whatever democratic elements those institutions already have.

Many Russians are skeptical about the virtues of free markets, and that includes people who otherwise favor democratic institutions. In Chapter 5, I show that market-skeptical democrats are not profoundly different from liberal democrats in Russia. Based on my sample, both groups think economic life should be governed by principles of desert and that not all people deserve the same things. Neither group favors an equal distribution of wealth. Both groups see a significant role for government in the economy, particularly in establishing the conditions under which people can act for themselves. Both see notable shortcomings in Russian capitalism. Where market-skeptical democrats differ from liberal democrats is in the significance they give to those shortcomings. The problem, as they see it, lies in an economic system that is founded on the strikingly unfair distribution of state property and that rewards criminality and connections more than hard work. Unlike liberal democrats, market-skeptical democrats are not ready to endorse an economic system that does not yet provide opportunities for the majority of Russians. Comparisons with American respondents show that Russians do not seem to have a culturally distinct set of economic expectations. Chapter 5 also illuminates why ordinary Russians—even Russian democrats—support the apparent creeping authoritarianism of the Putin regime. To many of my respondents, Putin seems to be reversing the worst offenses of the Yeltsin years, when regime cronies made vast fortunes, snatched up media outlets, and used their ill-gained wealth to influence political outcomes. By limiting the freedom and taking the property of the very rich, Putin seems to these respondents to be creating the foundation of a political and economic system that might possibly serve the interests of ordinary people.

Chapter 6 looks beyond poorly operating political and economic institutions to broader societal malfunctions and how they affect popular attitudes. Both in the late Soviet period and during the first decade of reforms, the lives of ordinary Russians were marked by considerable unpredictability and social disorder. The end of the Soviet Union meant that the borders of the country constricted, frontier-style capitalism replaced state economic planning, and one set of governmental institutions were replaced by another, which in turn went down in flames in October 1993, to be replaced once again. Inflation soared, real incomes plummeted, and those in power seemed more interested in who would defeat whom than in solving the problems that ordinary people faced. Given this context, it is perhaps not surprising that Russians appear to have a distinctive concern for order: in opinion polls, they often rank order as more valuable than democracy or freedom.[15] In Chapter 6, I examine what the Russian respondents mean when they talk about order and its inverse, disorder, and how concerns about order affect support for democracy. Among my respondents, people who feel they live in the midst of a highly disordered world are more willing to sacrifice democratic procedures and freedoms. People less troubled by social disorder are more supportive of democracy, less willing to sacrifice freedom for other social goals, and more likely to understand a "strong" state in terms consistent with democratic institutions. For these democratic Russians, their desire for both order and democracy is based on an interpretation of order that bears little resemblance to the order provided by past autocratic regimes but that has a lot in common with what is seen in Western democracies. They see order as providing the conditions under which individual freedoms can be realized, and they see a strong government as a mechanism for the accomplishments of popular goals.

In Chapter 7, I examine the degree to which ordinary Russians perceive changes in their political lives. Perhaps surprisingly, given the global significance of the collapse of Communism, not all my respondents perceive significant change in their political status. While respondents with a relatively sophisticated understanding of political life and greater support for democracy tend to see and understand the changes that have occurred in Russian politics, less politically sophisticated and democratic respondents tend not to perceive the same changes. People who do not see how political institutions have changed are unlikely to change their relationships to those institutions. They remain disaffected and apathetic, unable to act as citizens because they still understand themselves to be subjects.

In Chapter 8, I address what Russians want from government and what they would change if they could. I find that support for the existing political system is not related to whether people favor democracy or markets. Nor is support significantly predicted by the demographic attributes of respondents. Support is, however, related to perceptions that the regime has been successful in creating an orderly and predictable environment. Respondents who are troubled by what they perceive as the "disorder" in

15. For instance, vtsiom, "Informatsiia: Nastroeniia, mneniia i otsenki nasleniia," *Monitoring obshchestvennoe mneniia: Ekonomicheskie i sotisal'nye peremeny: Informatsionnyi biulleten'*, no. 1 (1997), 49–58.

their society are more likely to feel that those in power rule in their own personal interest, not for the public good. Although there is considerable dissatisfaction with the existing system among some respondents, there is very little enthusiasm for change. This contrasts with the American sample, where there is a stronger sense that the existing institutions are the right ones and there is more apparent willingness to change them. Given recent political and economic upheavals and continuing material insecurity, change seems to many of my Russian respondents to be too risky. As a result, they are both allegiant to existing institutions—in that they do not want to change them—and alienated from those same institutions, insofar as those institutions fail to serve popular needs.

In Chapter 9, I offer some concluding observations. I summarize the main findings of the previous chapters and extend them in an effort to answer one of the more intriguing questions facing students of Russia today: Why did so many Russians support Vladimir Putin, despite the apparently undemocratic direction in which he tried to take the country? One of the things that is clear from the intensive interviews is that, when Russians are given the opportunity to explain their thinking about democracy, markets, change, the insecurities of their daily lives, what they expect from their government, and how they understand their roles as citizens, many of the apparent contradictions in their ideas begin to dissolve. Russians' political and economic values are formed in the context of a society that is out of order, where government officials are thought to line their pockets at the public's expense, where new economic opportunities appear to be reserved for the few, where a daily subway ride can be a lesson in fear or frustration. The political thinking of ordinary Russians is in many ways a reflection of this disordered world. This book shows, then, that popular political preferences to a significant extent are rooted in the present rather than the past. From the point of view of building democracy in Russia, this finding is encouraging. After all, the present is easier to change than the past. But at least for now the Russian present remains a challenging place, and current political and social structures are not able to meet the needs of most citizens. As a result, popular longing for order creates potential problems for the democratic project. It encourages Russians to look a bit too favorably at energetic individuals who flout rules and democratic procedures to get things done—people such as Vladimir Putin. And it inclines some Russians to accept highly flawed institutions because the dangers of social and political change are too palpable to ignore.

This book, then, treats a number of important themes. In addition to an examination of Russian attitudes toward democracy, markets, order, and change, it offers analysis of what ordinary Russians imagine a good state and a good society to be. And it connects these themes to the issue of social order, a desired but—for many Russians—elusive goal. In short, this book provides a foundation from which to better understand Russia's mix of democracy and autocracy. In a world where many governments mix democratic and autocratic elements and many people suffer under political institutions that do not address their concerns, understanding how ordinary Russians relate to government and to the world it creates illuminates the situation of many citizens in an imperfect world.

The Tangled Web of Culture

In a democracy, the ideas and values of ordinary people matter. But how—and how much—they matter are issues of some debate. On the one hand, it is a rare political system that does not place significant restraints on the power of public opinion or popular mobilization. And many citizens are so uninformed or uninterested in politics that they can have little influence on political decisions. But on the other hand, it matters whether citizens are willing to abide by laws, tolerate the uncertainty that results from shifting electoral majorities, or accept the legitimacy of elections and elected officeholders. At points when representative institutions or individual rights are threatened, it matters whether citizens try to rescue them or, alternately, are indifferent to their fate. Some scholars would go much further and argue that the right popular attitudes and the right culture are essential preconditions for the establishment of democratic institutions. According to this argument, there is not much that aspiring institution-builders can do to make up for missing democrats. Without the correct preexisting political culture, democratic institutions may survive after a fashion, but they are unlikely to thrive. Their failure to find roots in an appropriate cultural and social context will most probably affect their ability to satisfy publics and to govern.

Not surprisingly, this argument is regularly used to explain the relative weakness of democratic institutions in Russia. With the collapse of Communism in Russia, individual freedoms increased, competitive elections occurred, and representative legislatures tried to challenge executive control in a way unimagined under Soviet power. But the promise of the early 1990s seemed to dim with the passing years. Under Vladimir Putin, the range of freedom contracted, and the president developed so much influence over both elections and legislatures that observers questioned how much democracy was left. Were ordinary Russians and their inadequate support for democracy to blame? Was the problem—as some argued—that Russians operated under a set of values more appropriate to their autocratic past, a political culture inherited not only from the Soviet years but also from czarism, Orthodoxy, or maybe even the unalterable destiny of geography?

Russians may be far from perfect democrats, and it is also clear that Russian citizens have not fought hard to save democracy from autocratic encroachments. But these widely shared observations do not in themselves constitute sufficient evidence to conclude that the problem rests in some kind of authoritarian orientation inherited out of Russia's undemocratic past. In this chapter, I address this argument about the roots of Russian political values. I do this, first, by examining the logic of the standard political culture argument that popular political attitudes explain the success or failure of democratic institutions. I argue that this common approach pays insufficient attention to influence in the opposite direction, to the ways institutions affect the ideas of the people who live under them. Then I apply the general argument to the specific case of Russia. I conclude that it makes as much sense to assume that contemporary social conditions, including present political institutions, are an important influence in the creation of popular political attitudes as it does to assume that the order of causation is solely in the opposite direction, or that the prime source of present popular attitudes is something that happened centuries in the past. In the Russian case, I further argue that it is not clear that the past left an unchallenged authoritarian imprint on popular political culture. Instead, ordinary Russians appear to form their social values in the context of a self-contradictory and chaotic society. As a result, Russians are indeed imperfect democrats, but the reason for this seems to be that they live in an imperfectly functioning society, governed by deeply flawed political institutions, not that they inherited undemocratic ideas from previous generations.

In the end, the ideas or values of ordinary people matter in political life. But they are not set in stone, culturally innate and immutable, inherited only from an inhospitable past. And they do not form an insurmountable barrier to the construction of democratic institutions in Russia.

How Does Culture Matter?

The argument that popular attitudes and values influence the success of democratic institutions has a long intellectual heritage. After all, Plato thought that governments varied with the qualities of citizens, and Aristotle believed that the mental habits of the middle class were the foundation of what he considered the most practical form of good government, the polity.[1] Centuries later, Alexis de Tocqueville attributed the viability of American democratic institutions to the popular tendency toward associability, the willingness of Americans to form small groups as mechanisms of civic engagement.[2] Where this social tendency was missing, as in France, the equality of democracy had less sanguine, more sanguinary effects. Gabriel Almond and Sidney Verba likewise suggested that stable democracy depends on the presence of a certain set of attitudes, what they termed a "civic culture."[3] As we enter the twenty-first century, scholars and pundits continue to argue that "culture matters," not only to the stability of democratic institutions, but to economic prosperity as well.[4]

While few would disagree that culture matters, it is less clear exactly what matters, how it matters, and where people's values come from. In terms of *what* matters for the success of democratic institutions, the focus is usually on political culture. Scholars use the term *political culture* to refer to the ideas and values that are widespread across a national population, the "network of meanings" though which political life is lived and understood.[5] Verba, for instance, defined political culture as the "system of empirical beliefs, expressive symbols, and values which define the situation in which political action takes place." He concluded, "It provides the subjective orientation to politics."[6]

Figuring out which values are crucial to democracy is not entirely simple. Democracy can be understood as a political system characterized by highly inclusive participation in the selection of leaders and politics, by competition among individuals and groups for all effective positions in government, as well as by the civil and political liberties essential to make participation and competition meaningful.[7] If this is a fair description of

1. Aristotle, *The Politics,* ed. and trans. Ernest Barker (New York: Oxford University Press, 1958), 179–84.

2. Alexis de Tocqueville, *Democracy in America* (New York: New American Library, 1956).

3. Gabriel A. Almond and Sidney Verba, *The Civic Culture: Political Attitudes and Democracy in Five Nations* (Newbury Park, CA: Sage, 1989).

4. Lawrence E. Harrison and Samuel Huntington, eds., *Culture Matters: How Values Shape Human Progress* (New York: Basic Books, 2000); Francis Fukuyama, *Trust: The Social Virtues and the Creation of Prosperity* (New York: Free Press, 1995).

5. Stephen Welch, "Review Article: Issues in the Study of Political Culture; The Example of Communist Party States," *British Journal of Political Science* 17, no. 4 (1987): 493.

6. Sidney Verba, "Comparative Political Culture," in *Political Culture and Political Development,* ed. Lucian W. Pye and Sidney Verba (Princeton: Princeton University Press, 1965), 513.

7. Georg Sorenson, *Democracy and Democratization* (Boulder, CO: Westview Press, 1993), 13; Robert A. Dahl, *Polyarchy: Participation and Opposition* (New Haven: Yale University Press, 1971), 3–9. Definitions of democracy range from those that focus on a fairly minimal set of

actually existing democracy, then it would seem to follow that democratic citizens should be willing to participate in political activities, should be tolerant of the conflict and instability that may result from competition, and should be ready to defend their own rights as well as respect the rights of others. Indeed, these kinds of values are highlighted in many studies of democratic political culture. Almond and Verba's "civic culture," for instance, was characterized by, among other things, open and moderate partisanship, a sense of obligation to participate, feelings of efficacy and social trust, and membership in voluntary organizations. Likewise, interpersonal trust has been widely recognized as a facilitator of civic participation and hence of a democratic society.[8] A number of studies of new democracies have focused on the "rights consciousness" of citizens in formerly democratic areas, particularly their willingness to extend rights to people and groups they do not like.[9]

But considerable controversy continues to surround these values. For instance, there is disagreement about how avid for participation democratic citizens need to be. Is more activism necessarily better, as students of social capital tend to imply, or can too much activism overload the system, as Almond and Verba suggested? Similarly, does interpersonal trust promote civic participation and democratic values, or is trust the *result* of political activism? Are ordinary citizens anywhere ready to protect the rights of people they do not like?[10] If so, why do constitutional provisions in most democratic countries explicitly remove the protection of

---

institutions, such as competitive elections, to those that require extending equality and rights beyond the strictly political sphere. The understanding of democracy used throughout this book—inclusive participation, meaningful competition, and the protection of individual liberties—is strict enough to exclude political systems that hold elections but that restrict both the opposition and citizen action. It is not so strict that no existing political structures meet its conditions. See Joseph A. Schumpeter, *Capitalism, Socialism, and Democracy*, 3d ed. (New York: Harper and Row, 1950); David Held, *Models of Democracy* (Stanford: Stanford University Press, 1987); Benjamin R. Barber, *Strong Democracy: Participatory Politics for a New Age* (Berkeley and Los Angeles: University of California Press, 1984).

8. Robert Putnam, *Making Democracy Work: Civic Traditions in Modern Italy* (Princeton: Princeton University Press, 1993); Mark E. Warren, ed., *Democracy and Trust* (New York: Cambridge University Press, 1999); Kenneth Newton, "Social and Political Trust in Established Democracies," in *Critical Citizens: Global Support for Democratic Government*, ed. Pippa Norris (New York: Oxford University Press, 1999).

9. For instance, James L. Gibson, "A Sober Second Thought: An Experiment in Persuading Russians to Tolerate," *American Journal of Political Science* 42, no. 3 (1998): 819–50.

10. James W. Prothro and C. W. Grigg, "Fundamental Principles of Democracy: Bases of Agreement and Disagreement," *Journal of Politics* 22 (May 1960): 276–94; Paul M. Sniderman, Joseph F. Fletcher, Peter H. Russell, and Philip E. Tetlock, *The Clash of Rights: Liberty, Equality, and Legitimacy in Pluralist Democracy* (New Haven: Yale University Press, 1996).

individual rights from majority control, on the logic that majorities cannot be trusted to protect the rights of minorities? If it is not empirically clear that democratic citizens need to be enthusiastic about civic participation, willing to trust their neighbors, and ready to defend individual freedoms, it is not immediately obvious what other values it is essential for them to share. Perhaps cynicism and apathy—not uncommon popular tendencies in functioning democracies—are the real values demanded by democratic institutions.

Not only is there only limited agreement on *which* values are characteristic of a democratic political culture, there is disagreement about *whose* values matter. The bulk of recent empirical research in the field of political culture has been based on mass surveys, with the implication that individual attitudes matter and that all individuals matter more or less the same. In practice, however, the attitudes of some people may have more influence on political outcomes. Lucian Pye, for instance, argued that studying individual attitudes will not enable scholars to infer anything about patterns of collective behavior in the political system. He argued that political culture "consists of those 'orientations' that make the system distinctive, not necessarily the ones that may be most distinctive among all the attitudes a population may hold."[11] This approach, however, risks ignoring variations between subgroups in the population, including potentially significant political divisions.

Even if we were certain that we were studying the right attitudes, it is not clear what those attitudes do. Years of study have not produced a generally accepted mechanism describing *how* widely shared attitudes affect the political system.[12] Popular attitudes may affect particular governmental decisions, and in a democracy, they play a role in deciding which candidates will fill which offices; but their impact on institutional structures is less obvious. As long as the candidates among whom citizens may decide to cast their votes do not advocate an overthrow of democratic institutions or mass violation of minority rights, it may not matter if a portion of the citizenry would support exactly those things. While popular attitudes serve as limits on the possibilities of political life, many other factors,

11. Lucian W. Pye, "Culture and Political Science: Problems in the Evaluation of the Concept of Political Culture," in *The Idea of Culture in the Social Sciences*, ed. Louis Schneider and Charles M. Bonjean (Cambridge: Cambridge University Press, 1973), 73.

12. William M. Reisinger, "The Renaissance of a Rubric: Political Culture as Concept and Theory," *International Journal of Public Opinion Research* 7, no. 4 (1995): 328–52; David D. Laitin, "The Civic Culture at 30," *American Political Science Review* 89, no. 1 (1995): 168–73.

including the choices elites make, have a more direct effect on the shape and functioning of political institutions than does the outer boundary of what fringe publics accept or reject.[13]

Where Do Attitudes Come From?

Even more crucial is the question of how popular attitudes are formed. If popular values are supposed to explain the viability of a given set of institutions, then values must be the product of something other than those institutions. And so some scholars have argued that popular attitudes on fundamental political issues such as the value of freedom and how citizens should relate to their governments are products of relatively unchanging cultural tendencies, grounded particularly in religious traditions.[14] At the same time, though, there is considerable consensus that even fundamental values may evolve slowly over time, largely as a result of long-term social and economic changes, especially increasing material security.[15] Whether material security promotes the growth of "postmaterialist" orientations or simply creates an educated citizenry, aware of and interested in the world around it, able to act to protect its interests, but unlikely to push for radical changes that would threaten its property, such security seems to promote the values that support democracy. Prosperous citizens tend to see value in political institutions that protect individual rights, limit the arbitrary power of government officials, and encourage officials to respond to popular concerns.

Yet if economic conditions shape popular attitudes and cause them to change slowly over time, why would other social forces not have a similar effect? In fact, two forces very likely to shape popular attitudes are the political

13. Robert A. Dahl, *Who Governs? Democracy and Power in an American City* (New Haven: Yale University Press, 1961), 325; Philip G. Roeder, "Transitions from Communism: State-Centered Approaches," in *Can Democracy Take Root in Post-Soviet Russia? Explorations in State-Society Relations,* ed. Harry Eckstein, Frederic J. Fleron Jr., Erik Hoffmann, and William Reisinger (New York: Rowman and Littlefield, 1998), 201–28.

14. Samuel P. Huntington, *The Clash of Civilizations and the Remaking of World Order* (New York: Touchstone, 1996); Hans Gerth and C. Wright Mills, eds. and trans., *From Max Weber: Essays in Sociology* (New York: Oxford University Press, 1946), 267–359.

15. Harry Eckstein, "A Culturalist Theory of Political Change," *American Political Science Review* 82 (September 1988): 789–804; Ronald Inglehart, *The Silent Revolution: Changing Values and Political Styles Among Western Publics* (Princeton: Princeton University Press, 1977); Ronald Inglehart, *Culture Shift in Advanced Industrial Society* (Princeton: Princeton University Press, 1990); Seymour Martin Lipset, *Political Man: The Social Bases of Politics* [1959], expanded ed. (Baltimore: Johns Hopkins University Press, 1981).

institutions under which people live and the parameters of public life set by the policies promulgated by those institutions.[16] Political institutions provide a context for action, an incentive structure to which citizens respond. The social world established by political policies similarly encourages some actions and prohibits others. If citizens are presumed to be reasonable enough that what they value responds to changes in their level of material security, then it makes sense to think that they are reasonable enough to respond to the structure of incentives provided by political institutions.

Of course, if institutional structures significantly shape popular attitudes, then it is not entirely reasonable to explain the success or failure of particular political institutions as the result of those same attitudes. Rather than the neat and unidirectional pattern preferred by many students of political culture—in which attitudes affect institutions but influence in the opposite direction is limited—we end up with a more complex picture. Attitudes and values may well shape institutions, but institutions shape attitudes and values as well. This does not diminish the importance of political culture, but it may alter its definition. Rather than a set of ideas and values that can be analytically divorced from presently existing social institutions and the daily reality they create, political culture becomes an integral part of all social relations, a dimension of all political institutions, and a contributing factor in the behavior of people in these institutions.[17] Once we put popular values in this context, it becomes clear that the interesting questions are how values, behavior, and institutional structures influence one another, not simply how values affect the other two.

How political institutions shape the ideas and values of the people who live under them is an undercurrent in a number of arguments purporting

16. Indeed, Gabriel Almond recognized that governmental, social, and economic performance influenced political culture. See Gabriel Almond, *A Discipline Divided: Schools and Sects in Political Science* (Newbury Park, CA: Sage, 1990), 138–56. Also, Edward N. Muller and Mitchell A. Seligson, "Civic Culture and Democracy: The Question of Causal Relationships," *American Political Science Review* 88, no. 3 (1994): 635–52; John Brehm and Wendy Rahn, "Individual-Level Evidence for the Causes and Consequences of Social Capital," *American Journal of Political Science* 4 (July 1997): 999–1023; Michael Burawoy and and Katherine Verdery, Introduction to *Uncertain Transition: Ethnographies of Change in the Postsocialist World*, ed. Michael Burawoy and Katherine Verdery (New York: Rowman and Littlefield, 1999), 1–17.

17. Goodwin and Jasper refer to culture as "a ubiquitous and constitutive dimension of *all* social relations, structures, networks, and practices." Jeff Goodwin and James M. Jasper, "Caught in a Winding, Snarling Vine: The Structural Bias of Political Process Theory," in *Rethinking Social Movements: Structure, Meaning, and Emotion*, ed. Jeff Goodwin and James M. Jasper (New York: Rowman and Littlefield, 2004), 23.

to show the opposite—how popular values shape political institutions. Robert Putnam's research, for instance, points to the importance of social capital, the "norms of reciprocity and networks of civic engagement" that make joint action possible. Without these norms, citizens create "the Hobbesian outcome of Mezzogiorno—amoral familism, clientelism, lawlessness, ineffective government, and economic stagnation."[18] With the right norms and behaviors, people can sustain democratic institutions and economic development. But where do norms of reciprocity and networks of civic engagement come from? In his study of Italy, Putnam argued that the different civic traditions of various regions in Italy could be traced back to social and governmental structures of previous centuries. Strictly autocratic social and political arrangements in the south prevented the growth of mutual assistance and voluntary organizations, while communal republicanism in the north both developed from and then encouraged voluntary groups. According to Putnam, either set of political structures—autocratic or republican—and either corresponding cultural tendency—distrust or trust—were rational responses to the anarchy of medieval Europe. But once cultural patterns were set, they proved sticky. To trust others is an irrational response in a society patterned on distrust, just as a distrustful individual will fail to reap the benefits of a culture based on trust.[19] Putnam may have intended his readers to conclude that attitudinal differences between the north and south of Italy precede and therefore explain the different institutional choices made in the two regions. We might also conclude, however, that political and social institutions shaped popular values. Indeed, Putnam recognized that at least in some cases behavior creates values, not vice versa. For instance, he argued that social trust arises from norms of reciprocity and networks of civic engagement; the trust is the *result*, not the *cause*, of behavior patterns.[20]

In his article on social capital in Britain, Peter Hall made this point even more clearly. To explain why associability has not declined over time in Britain, as it apparently has in the United States, Hall argued that government policy in Britain may have encouraged associability, both directly,

---

18. Putnam, *Making Democracy Work*, 183. Similarly, see Pierre Bourdieu, "The Forms of Capital," in *Handbook of Theory and Research for the Sociology of Education*, ed. John G. Richardson (New York: Greenwood Press, 1986), 241–58; James S. Coleman, "Social Capital and the Creation of Human Capital," *American Journal of Sociology* supplement ("Organizations and Institutions: Sociological and Economic Approaches to the Analysis of Social Structure"), 94 (1988): S95–S120.

19. Putnam, *Making Democracy Work*, 123–27, 177–78.

20. Putnam, *Making Democracy Work*, 171–74.

through the cultivation of the voluntary sector, and indirectly, by expanding education and increasing the size of the middle class.[21] It seems, then, that at least one of the sources of norms of reciprocity and networks of civic engagement is institutional systems that encourage those norms.

What is true for social capital is also true for its sister concept, civil society. Where scholars of social capital focus on the everyday behavior of ordinary people, students of civil society give more attention to larger and more public systems of social organization, such as markets, political parties, churches, a free press, or interest groups. Otherwise their arguments are very similar. Both social capital and civil society are thought to promote democracy. Both social capital and civil society blur distinctions between attitudes, behavior, and institutions. A vital civil society is often posited as a crucial precondition of democracy.[22] Without some kind of independent organization of society, interests cannot be aggregated and articulated in a way that would make democracy meaningful. If not constrained by the countervailing power of civil society, the state could either ignore or invade the lives of its citizens. But the question again is, Where does this civil society come from—and when did it take shape? Cultural attitudes, Tocqueville's "habits of the heart," may play a role. But so do existing political opportunities. Social organizations are unlikely to exist if political conditions do not allow them to. When the independent organization of society is illegal, civil society will be less than vital, no matter the attitudes and values of ordinary people. But once individual rights are protected and opportunities for influence exist, civil society can quickly expand.[23] As with social capital, in the end it may be less the *attitudes* of ordinary people than their *behavior* that matters. And behavior is shaped by many factors, including particularly the limits of what existing institutions allow.

In sum, while the argument is often made that institutions are somehow the product of popular attitudes, the more we push that argument, the more it seems that the reverse is also true: popular attitudes are in part products of political institutions.

21. Peter A. Hall, "Social Capital in Britain," *British Journal of Political Science* 29 (1999): 417–61.

22. John Locke, *The Second Treatise of Government* [1690] (New York: Macmillan, 1985); Francis Fukuyama, "The Primacy of Culture," in *The Global Resurgence of Democracy*, 2d ed., ed. Larry Diamond and Marc F. Plattner (Baltimore: Johns Hopkins University Press, 1996).

23. Steven Fish argues that the character of state power greatly shaped the nature of emerging independent political society under Gorbachev. See M. Steven Fish, *Democracy from Scratch: Opposition and Regime in the New Russian Revolution* (Princeton: Princeton University Press, 1995).

How Institutions Shape Behavior

Various theoretical traditions make the case that, rather than people getting the institutions they socially or culturally deserve, institutions shape behavior within the areas they influence. It was James Madison's argument that institutions had to be designed so that even the baser instincts of men could not undermine them. As Madison famously observed in Federalist Paper 51: "If men were angels, no government would be necessary. If angels were to govern men, neither external nor internal controls on government would be necessary. In framing a government which is to be administered by men over men, the great difficulty lies in this: you must first enable the government to control the governed; and in the next place oblige it to control itself."[24]

According to Madison, that control would be accomplished by institutional checks, not by exhorting men to act like angels. James March and Johan Olsen picked up the essence of Madison's argument in their insistence on the power of institutions to influence individual behavior. They observed, "By providing a structure of routines, roles, forms, and rules, political institutions organize a potentially disorderly political process. By shaping meaning, political institutions create an interpretive order within which political behavior can be understood and provided continuity."[25] In other words, norms and values arise out of institutional structures and the opportunities they provide. Similarly, theories of collective action recognize that groups will be more prone to act to defend their interests when political institutions provide opportunities that make it more likely that action will be successful.[26] The ability of institutions to affect individual behavior can also be expressed in the language of game theory. As Elinor Ostrom noted, "In the most general sense, all institutional arrangements can be thought of as games in extensive form. As such, the particular options available, the sequencing of those options, the information provided, and the relative

---

24. Alexander Hamilton, James Madison, and John Jay, *The Federalist Papers* (New York: New American Library, 1961).

25. James G. March and Johan P. Olsen, *Rediscovering Institutions: The Organizational Basis of Politics* (New York: Free Press, 1989), 52; James G. March and Johan P. Olsen, "The New Institutionalism: Organizational Factors in Political Life," *American Political Science Review* 78 (1984): 734–49.

26. Sidney Tarrow, *Power in Movement: Social Movements, Collective Action, and Politics* (New York: Cambridge University Press, 1994).

rewards and punishments assigned to different sequences of moves can all change the pattern of outcomes achieved."[27]

More directly concerning democracy, whole schools have developed around the idea that institutional choices or the actions of essentially self-interested elites—not inherited values or social structures—are the key factors in determining the successful consolidation of democratic institutions. Institutional choices—whether to create a parliamentary or presidential system, to choose proportionality or majority rule as the guiding principle for elections, or to select the operating rules of legislatures—influence the number and effectiveness of parties, which parties are likely to be more or less successful in elections, and the likelihood of developing gridlock between executive and legislative branches or cycling majorities in parliament.[28] Democratizing elites weigh opportunities to preserve some degree of their power and to promote policies that, while arguably good for the country as a whole, will not hurt themselves too much either.[29] In the end, whether or not democratic institutions can be created may depend more on the balance of power between elites and the choices those elites make than on ideas already in the heads of average citizens.[30]

The obvious importance of institutional choices and the actions of key elites has led some analysts to the conclusion that how citizens think and behave is, at best, of far secondary importance and may even be of little use in understanding the process of democratization. But the theoretical position of focusing on the state instead of society is as problematical as

27. Elinor Ostrom, *Governing the Commons: The Evolution of Institutions for Collective Action* (New York: Cambridge University Press, 1990), 23.

28. See, in particular, the debate originally published on the pages of *The Journal of Democracy* and republished as Juan Linz, "The Perils of Presidentialism," in *The Global Resurgence of Democracy*, ed. Diamond and Plattner, 124–42, as well as the following chapters in the same volume: Donald Horowitz, "Comparing Democratic Systems," 143–49; Arend Lijphart, "Constitutional Choices for New Democracies," 162–74; Guy Lardeyret, "The Problem with PR," 175–80; and Quentin Quade, "PR and Democratic Statecraft," 181–86. See also Josephine T. Andrews, *When Majorities Fail: The Russian Parliament, 1990–1993* (New York: Cambridge University Press, 2002).

29. Adam Przeworski et al., *Sustainable Democracy* (New York: Cambridge University Press, 1995). Similarly, see Jon Elster, Claus Offe, and Ulrich K. Preuss, *Institutional Design in Post-Communist Societies: Rebuilding the Ship at Sea* (New York: Cambridge University Press, 1998), and Guillermo O'Donnell and Philippe C. Schmitter, *Transitions from Authoritarian Rule: Tentative Conclusions About Uncertain Democracies* (Baltimore: Johns Hopkins University Press, 1986).

30. Dankwart A. Rustow, "Transitions to Democracy: Toward a Dynamic Model," *Comparative Politics* 2, no. 2 (1970): 337–63.

its opposite.[31] Even if popular attitudes are not the fundamental constraint that determines the likelihood of democratic stability, in a democracy popular attitudes matter. At minimum, people vote. For governments to work well, people also have to obey the law, respect state authority, and accept the appropriateness of the institutions that exist. If they do not, even the best-designed institutions may function poorly, and the result could be either a collapse into anarchy or a shift toward more autocratic forms of rule. Popular attitudes may affect how officials perceive their interests and their available choices. But if political institutions and other aspects of daily life affect the attitudes that people have, then popular attitudes are not a permanent constraint on the possibilities of political institutions. Institutions help create the attitudes that will in turn influence how well they function. Scholars need to study popular attitudes not as enduring cultural artifacts, formed in the past, insensitive to the demands of the present, but rather as products, at least in part, of that very present. By better understanding how attitudes are constructed, we can better understand how they change and how they can be reconstructed so that they will better fit the institutions that people may want to create.

Russian Political Culture

This is not the approach that students of Russian political culture tend to take. Their question more commonly is whether Russians are democratic enough for their new institutions, not whether Russian institutions encourage people to be democrats. Certainly, Russian history offers little encouragement for democratic tendencies. Russians lived for centuries under autocratic institutions that guaranteed people few freedoms and that were only minimally responsive to popular concerns. Especially in the Soviet period, all independent social organizations were either abolished or co-opted by the state, leaving Soviet citizens with few authentic public places where that they could connect with one another and exchange opinions freely. But does it follow that, because Russians lived under autocratic institutions for centuries, they developed a culturally stable set of ideas supportive of autocracy?

---

31. Joel S. Migdal, *State in Society: Studying How States and Societies Transform and Constitute One Another* (New York: Cambridge University Press, 2001); Michael Mann, "The Autonomous Power of the State: Its Origins, Mechanisms, and Results," in *States in History*, ed. John A. Hall (Oxford, U.K.: Basil Blackwell, 1986), 109–36.

A number of scholars argue just that. Edward Keenan, for instance, contended that the difficult conditions of life in Muscovy during the late fifteenth century mandated both collectivism and conservativism: no one was going to make it alone, and innovation might be fatal.[32] According to Keenan, these ideas changed little in the ensuing centuries and were still present to undermine Mikhail Gorbachev's efforts at democratization. Similarly, Stephen White argued that the authoritarian, collectivist, illiberal political culture that the Bolsheviks inherited in 1917, with its traditions of unlimited state power and only weak representative institutions, persisted largely intact through the Soviet period.[33] Moving forward in time, Kenneth Jowitt thought the legacy of Leninism made the construction of democratic institutions difficult in the post-Soviet era. He said: "That legacy includes a ghetto political culture that views the state with deep-seated suspicion; a distrustful society where people habitually hoard information, goods, and goodwill, and share them with only a few intimates; a widespread penchant for rumormongering that undercuts sober public discourse; and an untried, often apolitical leadership, barely familiar with and often disdainful of the politician's vocation."[34]

Russian scholars also make the case that the Russian people, through time and into the present, held ideas counter to the development of democracy. Such analysts regularly point out societal tendencies toward authoritarianism and cultural discomfort with elements of liberalism.[35] Some of these arguments draw on points made by the Slavophiles, a group of nineteenth-century Russian philosophers and ideologists who

32. Edward L. Keenan, "Muscovite Political Folkways," *Russian Review* 45 (April 1986): 115–81.

33. Stephen White, "Political Culture in Communist States: Some Problems of Theory and Method," *Comparative Politics* 16 (April 1984): 351–65. Also, Zbigniew K. Brzezinski, "Soviet Politics: From the Future to the Past?" in *The Soviet Polity in the Modern Era*, ed. Erik P. Hoffmann and Robbin Laird (New York: Aldine, 1984).

34. Kenneth Jowitt, "The New World Disorder," in *The Global Resurgence of Democracy*, ed. Diamond and Plattner, 28. See also Archie Brown, "Ideology and Political Culture," in *Politics, Society, and Nationality Inside Gorbachev's Russia*, ed. Seweryn Bialer (Boulder, CO: Westview Press, 1989).

35. For instance, Aleksandr S. Akheizer, "Krizis liberalizma v sovremennoi Rossii," *Liberalizm i demokratiia: Opyt Zapada i perspektivy Rossii* (Moscow: International Fund for Socio-Economic and Political Research [Gorbachev Fund], 1992); A. N. Iakovlev, "Ot proshlogo k budushchemu: liberalizm i demokratiia v kontse XX veka," *Liberalizm i demokratiia*; D. Shturman, "Razmyshleniia o liberalizme," *Novyi Mir*, no. 4 (1995): 159–68; Ivan Kachanovskii, "Budushchee liberal'noi demokratii v Rossii," *Obshchestvennye nauki i sovremennost'*, no. 2 (1995): 52–56; Feodor Burlatsky, "Democratization Is a Long March," in *Voices of Glasnost: Interview with Gorbachev's Reformers*, ed. Stephen F. Cohen and Katrina vanden Heuvel (New York: W. W. Norton, 1989).

were convinced that Russia, and not the rationalist, materialist West, held within itself the key to a purer form of community, a new Jerusalem based on Orthodox faith and the true fellowship of the village commune. Victor Sergeyev and Nikolai Biriukov argued that this cultural belief in *sobornost'*, or "harmony," has left Russians uncomfortable with notions of pluralism or competing interests, notions that of course underlie liberal democracy.[36] Other Russian scholars draw from the Eurasianist movement, formed by émigré writers who left Russia after the Bolshevik Revolution. Like the Slavophiles, the Eurasianists stressed the uniqueness of the Russian "ethnos" and the superiority of Russian values compared with the attitudes found in the West. Also like the Slavophiles, the Eurasianists held a messianic view of Russia's destiny, which they believed would lead to a Government of Truth to protect Orthodoxy and counter materialism.[37] Drawing on those ideas, Aleksandr Dugin postulated an intrinsic conflict between Russia and the West, a conflict that incorporated both a geopolitically determined competition between land and sea powers and an innate divergence of cultural values. Whereas the West represented capital, liberalism, and the market, Dugin argued that the ancient and geopolitically rooted values of Eurasia were labor, collectivism, spirituality, hierarchy, and tradition. Despite the fact that the West won the competition in the twentieth century, Dugin believed that Russia was still closer to heaven, an apocalyptic witness on the path to the Divine Jerusalem.[38]

Not everyone looking for the historically rooted beliefs of the Russian people has reached so far back in time. Leonid Gozman and Alexander Etkind argued that the sources of resistance to reform lay in the psychology of people who had lived in Soviet times. According to Gozman and Etkind, many citizens of the Soviet Union adapted to the Soviet regime and accepted the authorities' picture of the world, no matter how implausible. Faced with uncomfortable changes to a world that had

36. Victor Sergeyev and Nikolai Biriukov, *Russia's Road to Democracy: Parliament, Communism, and Traditional Culture* (Brookfield, VT: Edward Elgar/Ashgate, 1993).

37. I. A. Isaev, ed., *Puti Evrazii: Russkaia intelligentsiia i sud'by Rossii* (Moscow: Russkaia Kniga, 1992); Lev Gumilev, *Chtoby svecha ne pogasla: Sbornik esse, interv'iu, stikhotvorenii, perevodov* (Moscow: Airis Press, 2002).

38. Aleksandr G. Dugin, *Russkaia Veshch': Ocherki natsional'noi filosofii* (Moscow: Arktogeia, 2001), vol. 1, 12–70; Shenfield argues that there is no evidence that Dugin's ideas influenced the general public, but they apparently had some influence over the Communist Party leadership and circles of university students. Stephen D. Shenfield, *Russian Fascism: Traditions, Tendencies, Movements* (Armonk, NY: M. E. Sharpe, 2001), 198.

become psychologically satisfying, people resisted reform, including democracy. The authors argue that one characteristic of the psychology of totalitarianism was a belief in a simple world, with simple explanations and simple solutions. In such a world, democracy had no place. They point out, "Democracy—elections, voting, discussion—is needed when the world is complex and the solution has to be ambivalent. When it is clear and there is no alternative all that is needed is a leader whose wisdom will prevent mistakes and whose strength will ensure that decisions are implemented."[39] Older Russians in particular are thought to have clung to the values of the Soviet regime.[40]

There is more agreement on the notion that Russian political culture shows evidence of significant continuity over time than on exactly which ideas are continuously present. Where White and others focus on the autocratic character of Russian ideas, Keenan argues that the czar was more of a figurehead obscuring the reality of collegial or oligarchic rule. Where Keenan described Russian political culture as fundamentally conservative, Alexander Tsipko, as well as the Slavophiles and Eurasianists, focused on messianic elements.[41] More provocatively, some observers have described the "slavishness" of Russian attitudes. In Vasilii Grossman's interpretation, this submissiveness was the consequence of a thousand years of serfdom; Daniel Rancour-Laferriere saw the masochism that results when rage against the mother is turned against the self.[42] Others, especially Russians, remarked on the *absence* of popular ideas, presumably the result of Soviet power's eradication of civil society and of the exchange of opinions that might have occurred with greater freedom. Andranik Migranian went so far as to assert that "during more than seventy years of walking blindfolded, following a guide, [the Russian nation] has lost even that capacity for independent thinking and activity which it used

39. Leonid Gozman and Alexander Etkind, *The Psychology of Post-totalitarianism in Russia* (London: Centre for Research into Communist Economies, 1992), 21.

40. Eric Shiraev and Betty Glad, "Generational Adaptations to the Transition," in *The Russian Transformation: Political, Sociological, and Psychological Aspects,* ed. Betty Glad and Eric Shiraev (New York: St. Martin's Press, 1999), 168–70.

41. Aleksandr Tsipko, "The Roots of Stalinism, Essay No. 3: The Egocentricity of Dreamers," *Nauka i Zhizn* 1 (January 1989): 46–56; Nikolai Berdiaev, *The Russian Idea* (Hudson, NY: Lindisfarne Press, 1992).

42. Vasilii Grossman, *Forever Flowing,* trans. Thomas P. Whitney (New York: Harper and Row, 1972); Daniel Rancour-Laferriere, *The Slave Soul of Russia: Moral Masochism and the Cult of Suffering* (New York: New York University Press, 1995).

to have."[43] Because of this, Migranian argued, Russians had to be ruled by an authoritarian government while they gradually rebuilt the civil society shattered by Communism.[44]

In principle, none of these presumed tendencies of popular opinion would support democracy. If Russians are submissive and habitually obedient, or if they are cynical and prone to feelings of powerlessness before authorities, they will not try to hold their leaders to account. If the "Russian idea" holds proper government to be the embodiment of truth and believes the ruler to be the interpreter of truth, then formal rights, impersonal procedures, laws, and legislative bodies designed to represent multiple points of view have no logical place.[45] Politics will not be about satisfying competing interests, but rather about creating a more ideal world that transforms competition into harmony.

But can we be so certain that the Russian people have the wrong ideas to be democrats? Like any culture, Russia's is varied and contains some strands that exist in apparent contradiction to others.[46] There is, for example, a long history of consultative and representative bodies in Russian political structures, both at the national level and in the effectively self-governing peasant communities. In fact, Pitirim Sorokin once characterized Russian government of the czarist period by saying that "under the iron roof of an autocratic monarchy there lived a hundred thousand peasant republics."[47]

Further, the existence of autocratic institutions does not establish that most Russians shared the values that supported those institutions. Even if popular orientations are formed in a context shaped by existing institutions, institutions do not necessarily produce the ideas they intend. In fact, many people are likely to develop their values in reaction to an unappreciated present. Efforts to construct one orientation may inadvertently encourage another. For instance, Oleg Kharkhordin shows how intensive

---

43. Andranik Migranian, "On Historical Parallels," *Literaturnaia Gazeta*, no. 1 (March 1990): 9; also Mikk Titma, "Videt' dal'she, chem na khod vpered," *Sovetskaia Kul'tura*, interview, 10 November 1990, 4.

44. Andranik Migranian, "Dolgii put' k evropeiskomu domu," *Novyi Mir* 7 (July 1989): 166–84.

45. Tim McDaniel, *The Agony of the Russian Idea* (Princeton: Princeton University Press, 1996), 94–96.

46. Mary McAuley, "Political Culture and Communist Politics: One Step Forward, Two Steps Back," in *Political Culture and Communist Studies*, ed. Archie Brown (Armonk, NY: M. E. Sharpe, 1984), 3–39.

47. Cited in Nikolai Petro, *The Rebirth of Russian Democracy: An Interpretation of Political Culture* (Cambridge, MA: Harvard University Press, 1995), 48.

official efforts to strengthen a collectivist orientation in the Soviet population in fact laid the groundwork for the development of a stronger sense of the individual.[48]

In the Russian case, it is clear that many people held ideas that the government did not intend to encourage. An oppositional segment of the intelligentsia favored democracy and socialism at least from the early nineteenth century.[49] Popular pressure to establish representative institutions, especially in 1905, shows that, whatever the rulers themselves might have preferred, at a number of historical moments the people of Russia wanted a voice in political decisions. For a presumably authoritarian population, a relatively small proportion seems to have mourned either the loss of czarist control after Nicholas II's abdication in 1917 or the end of Stalin's rule. In post-Soviet Russia, it is easy to find someone troubled by the collapse of Soviet-era welfare provisions, but it is much harder to find an advocate of relieving people of recently won freedoms.

Indeed, the argument that traditional Russian political culture was authoritarian is based on the assumption that the ideas and values of ordinary Russians coincided with the institutions they had. There is some reason to imagine that the ideas of ordinary people might fit their political institutions in a democratic context, in which ordinary people have at least some influence on their rulers and the way institutions function. There is much less reason to expect that people who lived under a regime that they did not elect and that would imprison them for criticizing it actually held values that supported that regime.

Under highly repressive conditions, where life itself might depend on avoiding the ire of those who wield arbitrary power, a pose of deference or the appearance of submissiveness can be a calculated strategy of self-preservation. It would have been safer for peasants to affirm their love for the czar and reserve their expressed hatred only for his boyars than for them to suggest that the rule of their little father was not entirely just.[50]

48. Oleg Kharkhordin, *The Collective and the Individual in Russia: A Study of Practices* (Berkeley and Los Angeles: University of California Press, 1999). See also Alexander Lukin, *The Political Culture of the Russian "Democrats"* (New York: Oxford University Press, 2000), 122–33.

49. Boris Kagarlitsky, *The Thinking Reed: Intellectuals and the Soviet State 1917 to the Present*, trans. Brian Pearce (New York: Verso, 1988); Nikolai Berdiaev, Sergei Bulgakov, Mikhail Gershenzon, A. S. Izgoev, Bogdan Kistiakovskii, Petr Struve, and Semen Frank, *Vekhi* [Landmarks], ed. and trans. Marshall S. Shatz and Judith E. Zimmerman (Armonk, NY: M. E. Sharpe, 1994).

50. Abbott Gleason, *Young Russia: The Genesis of Russian Radicalism in the 1860s* (New York: Viking Press, 1980), 6–11.

Similarly, under the Stalin regime, people may have informed on their neighbors and turned a blind eye toward the arrest of apparently innocent acquaintances not because they wanted a ruler who would kill them in the millions while establishing a revised version of the czarist compulsory-service state, but because the alternative to compliance—certain arrest and likely death—seemed worse. Under a repressive regime, the ideas and values of ordinary people and even of some government officials may not fit with the official values of the regime, but people may not be able to express their differences openly.[51] Indeed, Robert Tucker argued that, in both the czarist and Soviet periods, there was such distance between "official Russia" and the population at large that ordinary people saw the state as an alien power, "a bleak elemental force that holds the land in its grasp and is a blight on the life of society."[52] If so, there is little reason to think that the values of ordinary people somehow matched the institutions under which they unhappily lived.

The point is, in the absence of free expression, it is hard to determine whether popular values coincided with the regime or not. We cannot be sure that authoritarianism was a dominant characteristic in the thinking of ordinary Russians or remains a historical legacy even after the collapse of Soviet rule.

What Russians Think

But what *do* Russians think, and what are the sources of those attitudes? Recent studies of Russian public opinion have begun to describe Russian political orientations, but the picture is somewhat contradictory.[53] Early

51. Vladimir E. Shlapentokh, "Two Levels of Public Opinion: The Soviet Case," *Public Opinion Quarterly* 49 (Winter 1985): 443–59; James C. Scott, *Domination and the Arts of Resistance: Hidden Transcripts* (New Haven: Yale University Press, 1990). A number of recent historical studies have used archival sources to make the case that public opinion did not match official propaganda even under Stalin, when pressure for conformity was at its highest. See Sheila Fitzpatrick, *Stalin's Peasants: Resistance and Survival in the Russian Village After Collectivization* (New York: Oxford University Press, 1994); Sheila Fitzpatrick, *Everyday Stalinism: Ordinary Life in Extraordinary Times; Soviet Russia in the 1930s* (New York: Oxford University Press, 1999); Lynn Viola, *Peasant Rebels Under Stalin: Collectivization and the Culture of Peasant Resistance* (New York: Oxford University Press, 1996); Elena Zubkova, *Poslevoenno sovetskoe obshchestvo: Politika i povsednevnost', 1945–1953* (Moscow: ROSSPEN, 2000).

52. Robert C. Tucker, *The Soviet Political Mind*, rev. ed. (New York: W. W. Norton, 1971), 121–22.

53. For a more detailed summary of results of recent survey research, see Frederic J. Fleron Jr., "Post-Soviet Political Culture in Russia: An Assessment of Recent Empirical Investigations,"

results from survey research in post-Communist Russia showed unexpectedly high support for democratic norms, whether they be the *civic culture* attributes of trust and interest in politics, support for elections, or support for individual freedoms and the kind of institutions that defend those freedoms.[54] Even these studies, though, noted some shortcomings, shortcomings that appeared again in later research. For instance, levels of political efficacy, expectations of government responsiveness, and political trust are not particularly high in the Russian population, although they are also not so very much lower than in Western democracies.[55] While popular support for individual freedom is generally high, there seems to be less understanding of the need for certain institutional structures to defend those freedoms. In particular, Russians show little confidence in representative legislatures, neither in the Supreme Soviet nor in the State Duma that replaced it.[56] Russians are reluctant to grant rights to people they do not like and some are willing to surrender liberty for the sake of order.[57] Some scholars have concluded that as many as one citizen in two favors a leader with a "strong hand" capable of solving their country's

Europe-Asia Studies 48 (March 1996): 225–60; and Frederic J. Fleron Jr. and Richard Ahl, "Does the Public Matter for Democratization in Russia? What We Have Learned from 'Third Wave' Transitions and Public Opinion Surveys," in *Can Democracy Take Root in Post-Soviet Russia? Explorations in State-Society Relations*, ed. Harry Eckstein, Frederic J. Fleron Jr., Erik Hoffmann, and William Reisinger (New York: Rowman and Littlefield, 1998), 287–330.

54. On trust and interest in politics, see Jeffrey W. Hahn, "Continuity and Change in Russian Political Culture," *British Journal of Political Science* (October 1991): 393–41. On elections, see Kent L. Tedin, "Popular Support for Competitive Elections in the Soviet Union," *Comparative Political Studies* 27 (July 1991): 241–71. On individual freedom, see especially James L. Gibson, Raymond M. Duch, and Kent L. Tedin, "Democratic Values and the Transformation of the Soviet Union," *Journal of Politics* 54 (May 1992): 329–71.

55. Jeffrey W. Hahn, "Changes in Contemporary Russian Political Culture," in *Political Culture and Civil Society in Russia and the New States of Eurasia*, ed. Vladimir Tismaneanu (Armonk, NY: M. E. Sharpe, 1995), 112–36; Stephen White, "Russia's Disempowered Electorate," in *Russian Politics Under Putin*, ed. Cameron Ross (New York: Manchester University Press, 2004), 80.

56. Richard Rose, "Postcommunism and the Problem of Trust," *Journal of Democracy* 5 (July 1994): 18–30; Richard Rose and Doh Chull Shin, "Democratization Backwards: The Problem of Third-Wave Democracies," *British Journal of Political Science* 31 (2001): 331–54; Timothy J. Colton and Michael McFaul, "Are Russians Undemocratic?" *Carnegie Endowment for International Peace Working Papers*, no. 20 (June 2001), 11.

57. James L. Gibson, "The Struggle Between Order and Liberty in Contemporary Russian Political Culture," *Australian Journal of Political Science* 32, no. 2 (1997): 271–90; James L. Gibson, "Putting Up With Fellow Russians: An Analysis of Political Tolerance in the Fledgling Russian Democracy," *Political Research Quarterly* 51 (March 1998): 37–68; Iurii Levada, "'Chelovek sovetskii' piat' let spustia: 1989–1994 (predvaritel'nye itogi sravnitel'nogo issledovanniia)," *Ekonomicheskie i sotsial'nye peremeny: Informatsionnyi biulleten'—Monitoring obshchestvennogo*

problems.[58] What is less clear is what Russians mean when they talk about a "strong hand." In particular, there is some evidence they do not mean a dictatorship. To many Russians, *strong* may merely mean "competent."[59]

More hopefully from the point of view of establishing democratic institutions, political-activity patterns seem similar to those in the democratic West. Even in early elections, voter choices could be traced to sociological characteristics and issue preferences.[60] As time progressed, clearer patterns developed. Despite the built-in uncertainty of transitional elections, where voters lack the standard clues that are common in established democracies and where the effective power of elected officials is open to question, new Russian voters voted according to some of the same models used to explain voting in Western democracies. As Timothy Colton concluded, "Russian voting is quite highly patterned behavior. Its components and attitudinal underpinnings interrelate in lawful ways that submit to rigorous analysis."[61] Russians have begun to develop partisan identification, and they participate in extensive politicized social networks that approximate civil society, even if at levels somewhat lower than in the West.[62] High levels of distrust for state institutions are balanced by somewhat higher levels of trust in immediate social networks.[63] And democratic attitudes seem to be related

mneniia 1 (January–February 1995): 9–14; Matthew Wyman, "Russian Political Culture: Evidence from Public Opinion Surveys," *Journal of Communist Studies and Transition Politics* 10, no. 1 (1994): 25–54.

58. Igor' Moiseevich Kliamkin, E. Petrenko, and L. Blekher, *Kakim mozhet byt' avtoritarnyi rezhim v Rossii?* Seriia issledovanii "Narod i politika," Vypusk 5/5 (Moscow: Fond "Obshch-estvennoe mnenie," 1993), 10; Grigory I. Vainshstein, "Totalitarian Public Consciousness in a Post-totalitarian Society," *Communist and Post-Communist Studies* 27, no. 3 (1994): 254.

59. William M. Reisinger, "Survey Research and Authority Patterns in Contemporary Russia," in *Can Democracy Take Root in Post-Soviet Russia? Explorations in State-Society Relations*, ed. Harry Eckstein, Frederic J. Fleron Jr., Erik Hoffmann, and William Reisinger (New York: Rowman and Littlefield, 1998), 170.

60. Timothy J. Colton, "Determinants of the Party Vote," in *Growing Pains: Russian Democracy and the Election of 1993*, ed. Timothy J. Colton and Jerry F. Hough (Washington, DC: Brookings Institution, 1998), 75–114.

61. Timothy J. Colton, *Transitional Citizens: Voters and What Influences Them in the New Russia* (Cambridge, MA: Harvard University Press, 2000), 212.

62. Arthur H. Miller and Thomas F. Klobucar, "The Development of Party Identification in Post-Soviet Societies," *American Journal of Political Science* 44 (October 2000): 667–86; Ted Brader and Joshua A. Tucker, "The Emergence of Mass Partisanship in Russia, 1993–1996," *American Journal of Political Science* 45 (January 2001): 69–83; William M. Reisinger, Arthur H. Miller, and Vicki L. Hesli, "Public Behavior and Political Change in Post-Soviet States," *Journal of Politics* 57, no. 4 (1995): 941–70.

63. Rose, "Postcommunism and the Problem of Trust"; Richard Rose, "Russia as an Hour-Glass Society: A Constitution Without Citizens," *East European Constitutional Review* 4, no. 3 (1995): 36–44.

to popular action in defense of democracy, which was particularly the case during the August coup of 1991.[64]

There is also some evidence that Russians do not all agree with one another about the nature of democracy. For instance, while a minority of Russians think that political and economic freedoms go together, political democracy and the market economy are not always linked in the minds of Russians, and a significant number of Russians think that political democracy is compatible with more socialist forms for economic organization.[65] This is truer for ordinary Russians than for elites.[66] Russians who prefer government guarantees for economic well-being tend to understand democracy more in terms of a rule of law than in terms of individual freedom. Yet elites are more likely than ordinary people to emphasize a rule of law, personal responsibility, and respect for others as important aspects of democracy. Ordinary people focus on freedom, especially if they are more educated and politically involved and enjoy improving economic circumstances.[67] At the same time, there is some evidence that the average Russian also has a distinctive view of freedom, understanding it more as material security than in terms of independence or choice.[68]

Generational differences exist on a number of issues. Older Russians are as a group less supportive of democracy and markets than are younger cohorts.[69] They are more likely to be concerned about the preservation of order, more likely to understand democracy as the fulfillment of law and

64. James L. Gibson, "Mass Opposition to the Soviet Putsch of August 1991: Collective Action, Rational Choice, and Democratic Values in the Former Soviet Union," *American Political Science Review* 91, no. 3 (1997): 671–84.

65. Ada Finifter and Ellen Mickiewicz, "Redefining the Political System of the USSR: Mass Support for Political Change," *American Political Science Review* 186 (December 1992): 857–74; Robert J. Brym, "Re-evaluating Mass Support for Political and Economic Change in Russia," *Europe-Asia Studies* 48 (July 1996): 751–66. Some studies find a stronger relationship between support for democracy and support for markets, but even in those studies, many democrats do not support markets. See Arthur H. Miller, William M. Reisinger, and Vicki L. Hesli, "Understanding Political Change in Post-Soviet Societies: A Further Commentary on Finifter and Mickiewicz," *American Political Science Review* 90 (March 1996): 153–66.

66. Judith S. Kullberg and William Zimmerman, "Liberal Elites, Socialist Masses, and Problems of Democracy," *World Politics* 51 (April 1999): 336.

67. Arthur H. Miller, Vicki L. Hesli, and William M. Reisinger, "Conceptions of Democracy Among Mass and Elite in Post-Soviet Societies," *British Journal of Political Science* 27 (1997): 171.

68. M. A. Shabanova, "Obrazy svobody v reformiruemoi rossii," *Sotsiologicheskie issledovaniia*, no. 2 (2000): 29–38.

69. Richard Rose and Ellen Carnaghan, "Generational Effects on Attitudes to Communist Regimes: A Comparative Analysis," *Post-Soviet Affairs* 11 (January–March 1995): 28–56.

the strength of the state, and more likely to vote Communist.[70] Older Russians are also more interested in protecting the collective than the individual good; this includes a readiness to sacrifice the rights of the accused to protect community interests.[71]

Similarly, less-educated people tend to be less supportive than others of democratic values.[72] And masses lag elites in their defense of democratic values.[73] Judith Kullberg and William Zimmerman concluded that "the ideological orientations and values of Russian elites and masses are sharply divided, with masses exhibiting a greater proclivity to socialist and illiberal ideologies."[74] Even elites, though, are not uniformly opposed to the imposition of a "strong hand" regime for the purpose of protecting the private sector of the economy.[75] And, as noted above, although elites support democracy more than masses, their understanding of democracy may contain less room for individual freedom.

Even if Russians are not perfect democrats, recent survey evidence has shown that they are not unremittingly authoritarian, either. Despite various shortcomings in the ways they put ideas together, they still have a great deal more support for individual freedom and even democratic institutions than would be expected if authoritarian values had the penetration and power that some observers imagine. Other evidence that undercuts the argument that past attitudes dictate present ones is the limited differences in attitudes across various post-Communist countries. If past

70. E. B. Shestopal, "Perspektivy demokratii v soznanii rossiian," *Obshchestvennye nauki i sovremennost'*, no. 2 (1996): 45–60; Oksana Viacheslavovna Krasil'nikova, "Politicheskie predpochteniia vozrastnykh grupp," *Sotsiologicheskie issledovaniia*, no. 9 (2000): 50; Timothy J. Colton and Michael McFaul, *Popular Choice and Managed Democracy: The Russian Elections of 1999 and 2000* (Washington, DC: Brookings Institution Press, 2003), 122; Richard Rose and Neil Munro, *Elections Without Order: Russia's Challenge to Vladimir Putin* (New York: Cambridge University Press, 2002), 152.

71. Vladimir Valentinovich Lapkin and V. I Pantin, "Tsennosti postsovetskogo cheloveka," in *Chelovek v perekhodnom obshchestve: Sotsiologicheskie i sotsial'no-psikhologicheskie issledovaniia*, ed. G. G. Diligenskii (Moscow: Institute of World Economics and International Relations, 1998), 12; William M. Reisinger, Arthur H. Miller, and Vicki L. Hesli, "Russians and the Legal System: Mass Views and Behaviour in the 1990s," *Communist Studies and Transition Politics* 13, no. 3 (1997): 24–55.

72. Donna Bahry, "Society Transformed? Rethinking the Social Roots of Perestroika," *Slavic Review* 52 (Fall 1993): 512–54.

73. Miller, Hesli, and Reisinger, "Conceptions of Democracy"; Iurii Levada, "Kompleksy obshchestvennogo mneniia (stat'ia vtoraia)," *Monitoring obshchestvennoe mneniia: Ekonomicheskie i sotsial'nye peremeny: Informatsionnyi biulleten'* 1 (January–February 1997): 7–12.

74. Kullberg and Zimmerman, "Liberal Elites, Socialist Masses," 340.

75. Igor' Moiseevich Kliamkin, Vladimir Valentinovich Lapkin, and V. I. Pantin, "Mezhdu Avtoritarizmom i Demokratiei," *Polis* 2, no. 26 (1995): 57–87.

attitudes were handed down across generations, the varied histories of the many countries that made up the Eastern bloc would lead us to expect different attitude structures in the various countries in the present. But generally this is not the case. In fact, differences within countries, especially generational differences, tend to outweigh difference between countries.[76]

That Russians today are neither the authoritarians many expected nor the democrats some would prefer has led to efforts to understand the sources of Russian attitudes. Some scholars argue that attitudes must have changed over time.[77] Their assumption is that, at some point when Western scholars could not measure Russian attitudes, those attitudes must have been more authoritarian than they subsequently became. It is not clear, however, that Russian popular attitudes were as authoritarian as some scholars assumed, at least in the relatively recent past. Like contemporary surveys, studies conducted in the later Soviet period also show considerable support for some protodemocratic values. For instance, 80 percent of respondents in the 1969 Taganrog survey felt that it was either "quite" or "very" important that local officials know the opinions of wide sections of the population on problems in city life; 80.5 percent believed that people should express their opinions on city problems; 77 percent thought officials should take the opinions of wide sections of the population into consideration when addressing city problems.[78] Results from the Soviet Interview Project of the 1970s and even the Harvard Project from the 1950s showed considerable popular support for greater individual freedoms than

76. Rose and Carnaghan, "Generational Effects."

77. For instance, William Zimmerman, "Synoptic Thinking and Political Culture in Post-Soviet Russia," *Slavic Review* 54 (Fall 1995): 630–41; Shestopal, "Perspektivy demokratii."

78. This survey was part of a much larger project conducted under the direction of Boris Grushin in the southern Russian industrial city of Taganrog between 1967 and 1974. Questions were asked of 1,019 people, a random sample of Taganrog's adult population. The reported results are from direct analysis of the data by the author. "Hard to say" answers are included in the analysis; "quite" and "very" answers are combined. These data were made available to the author with the permission of Boris Grushin and Vladimir Iadov, director of the Institute of Sociology of the (then) Soviet Academy of Sciences. Aleksandr Zhavoronkov's assistance was essential to understanding the coding of the data. See also Boris Andreevich Grushin and L. A. Onikov, *Massovaia informatsiia v sovetskom promyshlennom gorode: Opyt kompleksnogo sotsiologicheskogo issledovaniia* (Moscow: Izdatel'stvo Politicheskoi Literatury, 1980); V. G. Andreenkov and Aleksandr Zhavoronkov, *Katalog peremennykh bazy sotsiologicheskikh dannykh po problemam izucheniia ideologicheskogo protsessa*, 4 vols. (Moscow: Institut Sotsiologicheskikh Issledovaniia AN SSSR, 1988); Aleksandr V. Zhavoronkov, "Nekotorye izmeneniia v strukture informatsionnoi i obshchestvenno-politicheskoi deiatel'nosti naseleniia Taganroga za 10 let (1969–1979 gg.)," *Problemy sovershenstvovaniia deiatel'nosti sredstv massovoi informatsii i propagandy v gorode* (Moscow: Institut Sotsiologicheskikh Issledovaniia AN SSSR, 1988).

the regime provided.[79] Consequently, it is not at all clear that the attitudes first measured by Western scholars in the 1990s were in fact new.

Some analysts found additional evidence of attitude change—presumably the result of social modernization—in the fact that more educated, urban, and younger Russians were less likely than other Russians to have the ideas associated with Russia's authoritarian past.[80] Here again, though, surveys conducted in the Soviet period also provided evidence that younger or more educated Russians were less likely to support many regime values.[81] If social modernization led to attitude change, it did not do so only with the advent of the 1990s. Hence, any legacy of cultural authoritarianism should have been fairly weak by the end of the twentieth century. In any case, there are other ways to explain the demographic distribution of attitudes. Educated and urban Russians had the skills and opportunities to benefit from democracy and markets, and they may have favored those systems out of self-interest. Or maybe educated Russians are simply better at answering survey questions and avoiding undemocratic responses.[82] In any case, we cannot be sure that Russian attitudes have changed over time.

Studies also addressed attitude change under the pressure of political and economic reforms, but again the picture was murky. While some analysts argued that the data showed a decline over time in support for democracy, perhaps as a result of economic distress or negative assessments of progress made, others found popular commitment to democracy to be fairly resilient in the face of economic chaos and largely independent of immediate material benefits.[83] That is to say, scholars

79. Bahry "Society Transformed?"; Ellen Carnaghan, "A Revolution in Mind: Russian Political Attitudes and the Origins of Democratization under Gorbachev," PhD diss., New York University, 1992.

80. William M. Reisinger, Arthur H. Miller, Vicki L. Hesli, and Kristen Hill Maher, "Political Values in Russia, Ukraine, and Lithuania: Sources and Implications for Democracy," *British Journal of Political Science* 24 (April 1994): 183–223; Hahn, "Continuity and Change."

81. Donna L. Bahry and Brian D. Silver, "Intimidation and the Symbolic Uses of Terror in the USSR," *American Political Science Review* 81 (1987): 1061–98; Brian D. Silver, "Political Beliefs of the Soviet Citizen: Sources of Support for Regime Norms," in *Politics, Work, and Daily Life in the USSR: A Survey of Former Soviet Citizens*, ed. James R. Millar (New York: Cambridge University Press, 1987), 116–22.

82. For instance, to score high on many measures of democracy, respondents must be ready to protect the rights of people who would destroy democracy. This may seem counterintuitive to less educated respondents.

83. On declining support for democracy, see Stephen Whitefield and Geoffrey Evans, "The Russian Election of 1993: Public Opinion and the Transition Experience," *Post-Soviet Affairs* 10,

argued both that support for democracy was instrumental—based on the personal benefits it did or did not bring—and that it was not. Here, the difference in findings seems to be at least partly attributable to the focus of the questions respondents were asked. After the experience of the hardships of the reform period, for many people their *normative* commitment to markets and democracy remained high even as their assessments of the performance of their own institutions dipped. Further, economic well-being appears not to have a direct and stable effect on support for democracy: people who have not benefited from new economic opportunities are more hostile to markets than to democracy, and the connection between support for markets and for democracy is far from perfect. In any case, political values seem to be related more to assessments of the economy as a whole than to assessments of personal economic situation.[84] In other words, it does not seem to be strictly self-interest that drives political values.

If neither social change nor narrow self-interest completely explains contemporary social and political attitudes in Russia, then what does?[85] Why are Russian values today neither wholly democratic nor as authoritarian as we would expect if an inherited and comparatively unchanging political culture deeply influenced contemporary attitudes? What makes Russians imperfect democrats? In the chapters that follow, I show that

---

no. 1 (1994): 38–60; Stephen Whitefield and Geoffrey Evans, "Support for Democracy and Political Opposition in Russia, 1993–1995," *Post-Soviet Affairs* 12 (July–September 1996): 218–42. For the argument that support for democracy is relatively stable, see Raymond M. Duch, "Economic Chaos and the Fragility of Democratic Transition in Former Communist Regimes," *Journal of Politics* 57 (February 1995): 121–58; James L. Gibson, "A Mile Wide but an Inch Deep (?): The Structure of Democratic Commitments in the Former USSR," *American Journal of Political Science* 40 (May 1996): 396–420; James L. Gibson, "Political and Economic Markets: Changes in the Connections Between Attitudes Toward Political Democracy and a Market Economy Within the Mass Culture of Russia and Ukraine," *Journal of Politics* 58 (November 1996): 954–84.

84. William Mishler and Richard Rose, "Trajectories of Fear and Hope: Support for Democracy in Post-Communist Europe," *Comparative Political Studies* 28 (January 1996): 553–81; Raymond M. Duch, "Tolerating Economic Reform: Popular Support for Transition to a Free Market in the Former Soviet Union," *American Political Science Review* 87 (September 1993): 600–602. See also Donald R. Kinder and D. Roderick Kiewiet, "Sociotropic Politics: The American Case," *British Journal of Political Science* 11 (1981): 129–61.

85. Some studies have explained one set of attitudes by another, for instance showing the connection between postmaterialist attitudes and support for democracy (for example, James L. Gibson and Raymond M. Duch, "Postmaterialism and the Emerging Soviet Democracy," *Political Research Quarterly* 47 [1994]: 5–39) or, as mentioned earlier, between support for markets and democracy. These studies uncover interesting relationships between attitudes, but they do not tell us much about the sources of those attitudes.

contemporary Russian values to a significant extent can be seen as products of the experienced reality of daily life. The past matters, but not in the way observers usually argue it does. For one thing, what matters is not the very distant past but the more proximate years of the late Soviet Union. Because most Russians who were adults at the turn of the century were born into, raised in, and formed their fundamental values under the Soviet regime, that period can be expected to have influenced the way they think. But that does not mean that people developed attitudes consistent with the realities of Soviet power. People conformed, adapted, and got around, and some rejected the Soviet regime; all those strategies affected their political and social values. They lived under an autocratic regime, but they only imperfectly imbued its values. In fact, some may well have gained a clear picture of what they wanted to avoid. But it is not only the past that influences people's values. People form ideas about social and political life in the context of opportunities and constraints in the world around them. And among those constraints are the social institutions they experience. In Russia, this means a "piratized" market and political institutions with both democratic and autocratic elements.[86]

Generally, public opinion studies in Russia have not examined the effect of deeply flawed social institutions on popular ideas, although there are some exceptions. In explaining the parliamentary elections of 1993, Jerry Hough situated Russian attitudes within the politics of the time, at one point noting that "any sane person" would have negative attitudes about democracy as it developed in Russia between 1990 and 1994.[87] Using data from Russia and Eastern Europe, William Mishler and Richard Rose showed that levels of trust in political institutions were related to satisfaction with the work of those institutions, particularly in terms of their efforts to increase freedom, improve the economy, and fight corruption.[88] When political institutions work well, citizens trust them more.

---

86. Grigory I. Vainshstein, "Obshchestvennoe soznanie i institutsional'nye peremeny," in *Chelovek v perekhodnom obshchestve: Sotsiologicheskie i sotsial'no-psikhologichekie issledovaniia*, ed. G. G. Diligenskii (Moscow: Institute of World Economics and International Relations, 1998), 43–44; Marshall Goldman, *The Piratization of Russia* (New York: Routledge, 2003).

87. Jerry Hough, "The Russian Election of 1993: Public Attitudes Toward Economic Reform and Democratization," *Post-Soviet Affairs* 10, no. 1 (1994): 12.

88. William Mishler and Richard Rose, "Trust, Distrust, and Skepticism: Popular Evaluations of Civil and Political Institutions in Post-Communist Societies," *Journal of Politics* 59, no. 2 (May 1997): 418–51; William Mishler and Richard Rose, "What Are the Origins of Political Trust? Testing Institutional and Cultural Theories in Post-Communist Societies," *Comparative Political Studies* 34 (February 2001): 30–62.

Donna Bahry suggested that when political institutions do not work and government is ineffective, as was the case for at least the first decade of post-Communist Russia's existence, then people should be expected to have less faith in the rules of the democratic game.[89] John Dryzek and Leslie Holmes found the evidence of that lack of faith. Of the three political discourses they located in Russia, only one was somewhat democratic, and it showed considerable disappointment with the way things had turned out in the country.[90] A number of observers have worried that that dissatisfaction with imperfect but supposedly democratic institutions may spill over into dissatisfaction with democracy in the abstract.[91]

I extend this argument by making the case that it is not only political institutions—whether of the near past or of the present—that shape popular ideas. Political institutions are part of the daily reality that ordinary people inhabit and that shapes their points of view. Social attitudes are affected by all the daily experiences of life: by school and work, by shopping and provisioning, by the vagaries of public transport.[92] I further argue that for ordinary Russians in the late Soviet Union or the years just after its collapse, their daily experiences were of a system that did not work very well. Daily life was not only disorderly; in some ways it was surreal. The Soviet system was characterized by a huge gap between reality and the official explanation of reality, between the things people said openly and the truths they kept to themselves. The early post-Communist years provided more opportunities for public complaint but did little to narrow the gap between daily life and official reality. In the rest of this book, I try to show that it is the disorderly nature of social life—not inherited author-itarianism—that best explains the nature of Russian social and political attitudes. While it is impossible to prove that the weight of history has no effect, I think it is possible to show that closer and more proximate sources explain a great deal about observable attitudes. It is not necessary

89. Donna L. Bahry, "Comrades into Citizens? Russian Political Culture and Public Support for the Transition," *Slavic Review* 58 (Winter 1999): 841–53.

90. John S. Dryzek and Leslie Holmes, *Post-Communist Democratization: Political Discourses Across Thirteen Countries* (New York: Cambridge University Press, 2002), 100–102.

91. Vainshstein, "Totalitarian Public Consciousness," 255.

92. Social attitudes are also likely influenced by many aspects of family life and personal development, but those influences are outside the scope of this study. See Denise V. Powers, "Understanding Reactions to Post-Communist Transitions: Conception of Self, Political Attitudes, and Democratic Consolidation," prepared for the annual meeting of the American Association for the Advancement of Slavic Studies, Boca Raton, Florida, 1998; Harry Eckstein, Frederic J. Fleron Jr., Erik Hoffmann, and William Reisinger eds., *Can Democracy Take Root? Explorations in State-Society Relations* (New York: Rowman and Littlefield, 1998).

to reach deep into Russian history, back to the fifteenth century, to find the roots of contemporary attitudes. Many of those roots lie much closer to the surface, in people's reactions to a disordered present.

Culture Grounded in Chaos

Many students of Russian political culture think they can understand the nature and sources of present Russian attitudes by looking back into history. Since the history of Russia is one of unrelieved authoritarianism, the assumption goes, that authoritarianism must be reflected in the ideas and values of ordinary Russians. As products of their own past, Russians can at best be imperfect democrats. At worse, they cannot be democrats at all.

But we may come to a different conclusion if we focus instead on the duality of Russian existence: the permanent split between the state and the people, between the elite and the masses, between word and deed, and between public profession and private belief. With this focus, it is clear that Russians lived under authoritarian regimes, adapted to them, and found ways to survive under them, but it is not as clear that they adopted authoritarian values as their own. It is also not clear that Russians experienced their authoritarian past—here, particularly, the one that most of them lived through—as a system characterized by order. At the level of daily life, the Soviet regime produced more chaos than carefully organized control. And perestroika and its aftermath did little to improve the predictability of life. My argument is that this pervasiveness of instability can help us to better understand Russians' social and political attitudes. As future chapters will show, that does not mean that Russians are perfect democrats. Indeed, some of their values support democracy and some do not. But if experienced reality shapes attitudes, attitudes may be relatively fungible. People committed to building democratic institutions may have more room than they think to create the citizens that well-functioning democracy needs.

As a whole, the study of political culture has stumbled over the question of what political culture explains. Scholars have tried to argue that popular values influence the shape institutions take, but it is not clear how this influence occurs. In any case, it is just as likely that influence is equally at work in the reverse direction: present institutions affect popular values. Scholars who want to show how popular values shape institutions in Russia have the additional problem that ordinary Russians did not apparently have much effect on institutions, certainly in the past and probably in the present as well. I address part of this problem by turning the question around. Rather than asking what popular political values explain, I hope to answer what explains political values. What are the sources of the popular attitudes and values of ordinary Russians?

To ask this question, though, implies that the answer matters, that it is worth knowing what ordinary Russians think. While the political culture approach has come in for considerable criticism in this chapter, none of that criticism suggests that the ideas and values of ordinary Russians do not warrant our attention or that popular attitudes have no impact on the shape of institutions. If politics is the way collectivities make decisions, make the rules that will enable those decisions to reshape the world, and implement and enforce the rules they make, then people who study politics—and people who are simply interested in politics—should be interested in the entire collectivity, and not just in those few officials who inhabit key institutions, and not just in the institutions themselves. If it matters whether Russians manage to establish democratic institutions, which by their nature must bear some relationship to the popular will, then it matters what Russian citizens think. While Russian democracy may not stand or fall because of the ideas that ordinary citizens hold, even in restricted and imperfect electoral democracy citizens cannot be ignored. To the extent that popular ideas reflect present circumstances—and not just a distant past—understanding the population and the roots of their ideas is an important tool in constructing a different future. The more citizen attitudes are consistent with institutional structures, the easier it is for government to be based on consent. The more, then, that democracy is possible.

Russians in Their Own Words

Since the *glasnost'* years, ordinary Russians have been meta-phorically poked and prodded, examined and appraised by myriad public opinion surveys. Successive surveys conducted by Western scholars have provided abundant information on Russian attitudes toward democracy and markets, emerging patterns of voting and partisanship, popular assessments of the past, and hopes for the future. Once freed from Soviet-era restrictions, professional Russian polling organizations have also expanded their work exponentially, and Russian scholars now can research questions that formerly were out of political bounds. As a result of all this work surveying the Russian population, we know a great deal about what ordinary Russians think.

There is also a great deal that we do *not* know. We know, for instance, that Russians are imperfect democrats. Their strong support for some democratic values is mixed with weak support for others. But we do not know *why* Russians have this mixture of attitudes. The usual explanation—that Russians inherited nondemocratic attitudes from their own cultural past, but long-term social change is now changing some of those ideas—does not cover all the facts. It is not only older and less educated Russians who worry about democracy and markets. It is not clear that popular attitudes have been changing over time, even under the influence of a highly turbulent present. Explanations that divide the Russian population into supporters and denigrators of democracy also do not help. In Russia, it is often not the case that some people hold consistently democratic attitudes while others are more authoritarian. Instead, many individuals seem to hold a mix of apparently contradictory ideas.

Opinion surveys can tell us a great deal, but they cannot tell us why many Russians hold what seem to be inconsistent ideas about political life. For that explanation, it is helpful to allow ordinary Russians to speak in their own words. Intensive interviews, in which respondents can speak at length, tell stories, give examples, and generally explain the logic of their ideas, are a valuable tool in sorting through some of the conflicting findings and contradictory images that survey research in Russia has produced. In this chapter I explain the intensive interview method and compare what we can learn from intensive interviews with what we can learn from standardized opinion surveys. While surveys are essential in drawing the big picture of attitude distribution across a countrywide population, intensive interviews can help determine what that big picture means.

Drawbacks of Standardization

Standardized public opinion surveys provide outstanding data for a number of purposes, including, particularly, generalizations to the wider population and multivariate data analysis. But at the same time, these data have certain limitations. Some of the limitations stem from the standardization inherent in a large-sample survey. In order to be able to analyze the answers of a thousand of people or more, survey researchers have no choice but to transform their research concerns into multiple-choice questions. Even the responses to open-ended questions must be grouped into a relatively small number of categories if the goal is to conduct statistical analysis. Respondents cannot talk with the interviewer as if the two were involved in a normal conversation. Rather, they must respond to predetermined questions with a choice of preset answers. In most survey protocols, respondents cannot reframe the questions, elaborate on or explain their responses, or even receive substantial clarification about confusing items. So as not to influence results, interviewers must ask the same questions, in the same order, with the same neutral inflection, of all respondents.

This standardization makes it possible to summarize the answers of thousands of respondents and to examine statistical relationships between the various answers. Just as there are benefits, though, there are also costs of such standardization. Respondents may find the artificiality of the interview experience off-putting. Some researchers worry that respondents may psychologically withdraw from the interview process once they realize that only small pieces of their opinions are of interest to the interviewer.[1] If the artificiality of the interview situation stunts conversation, it can also limit the information that researchers get from survey respondents. The short answers respondents are allowed to provide may

---

1. Lucy Suchman and Brigitte Jordan, "Validity and the Collaborative Construction of Meaning in Face-to-Face Surveys," in *Questions About Questions: Inquiries into the Cognitive Bases of Surveys,* ed. Judith M. Tanur (New York: Russell Sage Foundation, 1992), 244.

be misleading if they leave out the reasoning that led to the answer or the qualifications that substantially moderate the recorded response. The answers will also be misleading if the respondent has lost interest in the interview process and is answering questions by rote.

The accuracy of standardized survey responses also depends on respondents and survey researchers sharing the same interpretations of words. But we cannot be certain that respondents' understanding of words and concepts matches the intention of the researcher. Public opinion research has shown that even words such as *children, you, weekend,* and *generally* do not have a universally shared meaning.[2] Certainly the same is true for *government, trust,* or *extremist,* words commonly used in questions about democratic values or responses to political institutions. The difficulty of knowing what words mean is compounded for American researchers interviewing Russians. Some words in English do not have direct equivalents in Russian. Others have similar meanings to those of a variety of Russian words, which in turn do not all mean the same thing to Russians. In recent surveys of Russians by Western scholars, the word *government* has been variously translated as "pravitel'stvo" (the cabinet ministries), or as "gosudarstvo," literally *state,* as in Moscow *State* University. Similarly, *people* is variously translated as the neutral "liudi" or as "narod," a word that may designate the common people or the ethnically Russian people, but that probably does not include everyone in the country.[3] These differences most likely influence results and can explain some of the variation in findings between surveys.

Another problem that stems from the standardization of large-N surveys is that respondents have to be able to select the answer that most closely reflects their own opinions. That may not be too difficult if the respondent understands all the alternative responses and has a precisely articulated opinion that nearly matches one of the alternatives provided. But it is far from obvious that this is normally the case. Inspired by the instability of survey responses over time and their sensitivity to phenomena such as question order, some public opinion researchers have concluded that much of the public does not actually have opinions.[4] Russian researchers have echoed this concern, on the logic that people who for decades were

2. William Belson, *Validity in Survey Research* (Aldershot, U.K.: Gower, 1986).

3. Nancy Ries, *Russian Talk: Culture and Conversation During Perestroika* (Ithaca: Cornell University Press, 1997).

4. Philip E. Converse, "The Nature of Belief Systems in Mass Publics," in *Ideology and Discontent,* ed. David E. Apter (New York: Free Press, 1964), 206–61.

not allowed to voice opinions may not ever have developed them.[5] These concerns are probably exaggerated, but evidence suggests that most people possess multiple and often conflicting opinions that do not fit easily into the narrow framework of a standardized questionnaire.[6] The answers that respondents provide to closed-choice questions seem to depend on what words are used, what questions occurred earlier in the interview, and the attributes and mannerisms of the interviewer. Confronting respondents with counterarguments or other information often induces them to change their minds.[7] Survey responses are thus snapshots of reality, but the reality they describe may have seemed quite different had the shot been taken from a slightly different angle.

That reality may also be distorted in the process of interpreting the results of the survey. Once the ideas of the respondent are split apart into the answers to scores of multiple-choice questions, only the power of statistics can put those pieces together again. It is, of course, easier to lie without statistics than with them, but the statistics reported from most survey research hardly emerge from the raw data untouched by human intention. Reported findings reflect a series of decisions about which questions capture what underlying attitudes, as well as the analyst's understanding of what statistical relationships may mean. Analysts often can do brilliant work making sense of survey data, but it is not clear that their explanations of how attitudes fit together or what answers mean are necessarily more accurate than the ones respondents themselves might have provided, if only they had been allowed to talk a bit more.

The Intensive Alternative

There is an alternative. Intensive or in-depth interviews allow respondents to do the things that standardized surveys rarely permit. Respondents can

5. Boris Andreevich Grushin, "Est' li u nas obshchestvennoe mnenie?" interview with Boris Balkarei, *Novoe Vremia*, no. 30 (1988): 29–31.

6. John Zaller and Stanley Feldman, "A Simple Theory of the Survey Response: Answering Questions Versus Revealing Preferences," *American Journal of Political Science* 36 (1992): 579–616; Donna Bahry, "Comrades into Citizens? Russian Political Culture and Public Support for the Transition," *Slavic Review* 58 (Winter 1999): 841–53.

7. James L. Gibson, "A Sober Second Thought: An Experiment in Persuading Russians to Tolerate," *American Journal of Political Science* 42 (July 1998): 820; Paul M. Sniderman, Joseph F. Fletcher, Peter H. Russell, and Philip E. Tetlock, *The Clash of Rights: Liberty, Equality, and Legitimacy in Pluralist Democracy* (New Haven: Yale University Press, 1996), 65; R. Michael Alvarez and John Brehm, *Hard Choices, Easy Answers: Values, Information, and American Public Opinion* (Princeton: Princeton University Press, 2002).

give examples and tell stories. They have the opportunity clarify their meaning and to describe how they came to their answers. They can express their opinions with all their complexity and inner contradictions intact and even try to explain those contradictions. As a result, we can know more about what people think and why they think it.[8] The problem, of course, is that we necessarily have to know it about fewer people. It is standardization that permits the analysis of hundreds or even thousands of answers at a time. When we study people talking in paragraphs rather than giving machine-readable responses, we can only make sense of a smaller number of answers.

This is not a trivial trade-off. On the one hand, we have nationally representative surveys that may not accurately capture the whole thinking of respondents, but that permit quantitative analysis and provide considerable confidence that the answers analyzed are not substantially different from the answers the rest of the population would have given under the same circumstances. On the other hand, we have a smaller number of intensive interviews. Intensive interviews may provide a broader and more nuanced picture of respondents' thinking, but they are cumbersome to analyze. Because the sample size is small, we cannot confidently generalize the results to the wider population, even though we may be more confident about the accuracy of an individual's responses. Neither method is without both drawbacks and advantages. The choice between them is dictated partly by the research agenda.

Standardized surveys are somewhat blunt instruments. They tackle complex concepts with short statements and simple alternatives. People answer many questions in a short amount of time, offering the first answer that comes to mind, rather than a considered opinion. Intensive interviews, by contrast, provide an opportunity for respondents to talk at length. As Jennifer Hochschild has noted, given the opportunity to talk, "people do not make simple statements; they shade, modulate, deny, retract, or just grind to a halt in frustration."[9] This makes intensive interviews particularly useful in studying the internal contradictions in people's ideas. Using intensive interviews, for instance, Hochschild was able to

8. David J. Elkins, *Manipulation and Consent: How Voters and Leaders Manage Complexity* (Vancouver: University of British Columbia Press, 1993); Michael F. Schober and Frederick G. Conrad, "Does Conversational Interviewing Reduce Survey Measurement Error?" *Public Opinion Quarterly* 61 (Winter 1997): 576–602.

9. Jennifer Hochschild, *What's Fair? Americans' Attitudes Toward Distributive Justice* (Cambridge: Harvard University Press, 1981).

show how Americans use different norms in evaluating justice in different spheres. For instance, they apply egalitarian norms in the political sphere, but differentiating norms in the economic sphere. Where issues—such as the political distribution of economic goods—straddled two domains, contradictions arose that Hochschild's respondents tried to repress or ignore. Hochschild concluded that her small group of interviews provided insight into why Americans do not support a downward distribution of wealth even though arguably a majority would benefit from such a thing. The political redistribution of economic wealth raises two conflicting justice norms, and it is psychologically easier for people to ignore the problem.

Similarly, Olga Shevchenko used intensive interviews to capture contradictory impulses in the ways in which Russians are adapting to a changing social environment. Her respondents were highly discontented with many of the effects of the transition away from Communism. Other elements in their ideas, however, kept that discontent from turning into action. Because people did not expect to be well off and could easily imagine things getting worse, they dealt with their dissatisfactions stoically, instead of through social action. As one of Shevchenko's informants commented, "So what should we do, rebel? I think our history is packed with evidence that rebellions never improve the situation, but only make it worse. . . . Anything is better than civil war, and that's what will happen if people get militant."[10]

Where standardized surveys show us that contradictions in people's attitudes exist, intensive interviews can help us begin to make sense of why those contradictions are there and what their effect is likely to be. Understanding internal contradictions is particularly important when studying attitudes under conditions of social change, as in Russia in the decades after the collapse of Communism, where we cannot suppose that people's ideas will be as stable and internally unchallenged as they might be in simpler times and places.

Just as intensive interviews are more helpful than standardized surveys in plumbing contradictory attitudes, intensive interviews are also better than standardized surveys at capturing things respondents do not mean to reveal or possibly do not even know themselves. The classic example of this is Robert Lane's study of the men of "Eastport." Lane was able to use intensive interviewing to plumb the social and psychological foundations

---

10. Olga Shevchenko, "Bread and Circuses: Shifting Frames and Changing References in Ordinary Muscovites' Political Talk," *Communist and Post-Communist Studies* 34, no. 1 (2001): 86.

of the ideas of working- and lower-middle-class American men. Among other things, he rooted political beliefs back to the relationships the men of Eastport had with their fathers.[11] Nancy Ries used intensive interviews to study the stories of suffering that Russians tell one another in describing and explaining their social reality. She was able to show how these ever-present litanies of despair and disrepair helped to reproduce suffering. She concluded, "To put it bluntly, this national story of victims, villains, and saviors, performed through litanies, has been a discursive mechanism that facilitated authoritarian social relations. . . . By making the hierarchy of social categories 'natural' and inevitable, and by asserting that they are undone only through the magical intercession of persons like Sakharov, litanies reaffirmed hierarchy, exploitation, and structural violence. By essentializing powerlessness, the iteration of litanies had the reflexive, unintended consequence of reproducing powerlessness."[12] It would be hard for standardized surveys to uncover such unintended consequences of behaviors that people may not even be aware they have.

Similarly, intensive interviews may get closer to the "hidden transcripts" of a culture than standardized surveys usually do. Observers have long worried that people respond to standardized surveys according to cultural myths—what they think they are supposed to think—instead of according to the ideas and values that actually guide their behavior. This tendency is probably even greater under repressive regimes, where people regularly adopt a public pose to hide private truths and to protect themselves from the vagaries of the powerful.[13] While repression has diminished in Russia, habits of hiding truths may not have entirely disappeared. And, in any case, ordinary Russians still find themselves comparatively powerless

---

11. Robert E. Lane, *Political Ideology: Why the American Common Man Believes What He Does* (New York: Free Press, 1962); Robert E. Lane, *Political Man* (New York: Free Press, 1972), 63–75.

12. Ries, *Russian Talk*, 120.

13. Vladimir E. Shlapentokh, "Two Levels of Public Opinion: The Soviet Case," *Public Opinion Quarterly* 49 (Winter 1985): 443–59; Václav Havel, "The Power of the Powerless," in *Without Force or Lies: Voices from the Revolution of Central Europe in 1989–90*, ed. William M. Brinton and Alan Rinzler (San Francisco: Mercury House, 1990); Valentine Turchin, *The Inertia of Fear and the Scientific Worldview*, trans. Guy Daniels (New York: Columbia University Press, 1981). For instance, during collectivization Russian peasants obscured their resistance behind drunkenness, feigned compliance, and anonymous group action. See Lynn Viola, *Peasant Rebels Under Stalin: Collectivization and the Culture of Peasant Resistance* (New York: Oxford University Press, 1996); Sheila Fitzpatrick, *Stalin's Peasants: Resistance and Survival in the Russian Village After Collectivization* (New York: Oxford University Press, 1994); Elena Zubkova, *Poslevoenno sovetskoe obshchestvo: Politika i povsednevnost', 1945–1953* (Moscow: ROSSPEN, 2000).

against an arbitrary and sometimes capricious state. As a way of penetrating to private truths, James Scott suggests examining the hidden transcripts that exist at sites where subordinates speak freely.[14] While intensive interviews do not necessarily capture drunken honesty or the license of carnival, they can reach to the grumbling, gossip, rumors, and jokes that make up a lot of ordinary political discourse. Also, given the amount of time that respondents talk in intensive interviews, it is harder for them to continue to answer with ideas they do not really hold. It is harder for them to mistakenly select a response alternative with which they would not have agreed had they understood all the implications.

In that way, intensive interviews may begin to equalize the participation of people from a variety of backgrounds. Research in survey methods has made it clear that some kinds of questions often used in standardized surveys, such as those that ask respondents to rank preferences, are particularly hard for people to answer.[15] Some categories of people are less likely than others to answer questions and are more likely to provide a "don't know" response. Females, the less educated, and the poor are less likely to answer questions in standardized surveys. The same is true for people with feelings of low political efficacy and little interest in politics.[16] This implies that some people can more comfortably negotiate the artificiality of the standardized survey interview than can others. Some of this disparity is addressed by intensive interviews, in which respondents need only to be able to talk. They do not need to talk well or concisely or to fit their answers into a prearranged framework. In the interviews I conducted, I noticed a tendency for some people—especially less educated women—to preface all their responses with "I don't know." In standardized surveys, that might be the only response recorded. In my interviews, these people often continued to talk at length, sometimes elaborating on the various

14. James C. Scott, *Domination and the Arts of Resistance: Hidden Transcripts* (New Haven: Yale University Press, 1990).

15. Jean M. Converse and Stanley Presser, *Survey Questions: Handcrafting the Standardized Questionnaire* (Newbury Park, CA: Sage, 1986), 29.

16. Ellen Carnaghan, "Alienation, Apathy or Ambivalence? 'Don't Knows' and Democracy in Russia," *Slavic Review* 55, no. 2 (1996): 325–63; Jean M. Converse, "Predicting No Opinion in the Polls," *Public Opinion Quarterly* 40 (1976): 515–30; Joe D. Francis and Lawrence Busch, "What We Know About 'I Don't Knows,'" *Public Opinion Quarterly* 39 (1975): 207–18; Stephen E. Bennett, "Know-Nothings' Revisited: The Meaning of Political Ignorance Today," *Social Science Quarterly* 69 (1988): 476–90. Fran Markowitz used intensive interviewing and participant observation to examine the responses to change of teenagers, a group usually excluded altogether from standardized surveys. See Fran Markowitz, *Coming of Age in Post-Soviet Russia* (Urbana: University of Illinois Press, 2000).

ideas that made a single, simple answer difficult.

In the end, at least for some research agendas, the fact that intensive interviews may not be representative of the wider population is not as significant a barrier as it might at first seem. Certainly, if our goal is to tally up responses and uncover what proportion of the population favors one or another position, intensive interviews are not the way to go. Results from such a small respondent set could easily be misleading. But if our goal is to begin to uncover the logic that binds a culture together, to understand how people within a given culture interpret their experiences and make sense of the world around them, to allow informants to teach us what they know but we can only guess about their understandings of the world, then the fact that intensive interviews take us deeper in the minds of the individuals with the knowledge we seek makes up for the fact that we cannot visit as many minds.[17] As Jennifer Hochschild commented, "Intensive interviews may find results where surveys find only noise."[18] In any case, interview data are not replacements for survey data. Given the large number and high quality of nationally representative surveys that have been conducted in Russia since the early 1990s, we already have a fairly good idea about which Russians favor what positions and about which ideas have majority support. We are on shakier ground when it comes to knowing what those answers mean. If we let Russians speak for themselves, they may help us make sense of the sometimes conflicting messages sent by survey results.

Talking with Russians

In this book, I rely primarily on more than sixty intensive interviews I conducted in Russia between 1998 and 2003, after the chaotic changes of the early 1990s, but before a stable new social order had been established. The interviews consisted of a directed discussion about a variety of political institutions, starting with the president and the State Duma, and moving to local mayors and police forces. The early part of the discussion was fairly concrete. As the interview progressed, I tried to elicit more abstract responses, including definitions of democracy and "strong state power" and indications of how respondents would make trade-offs

17. James P. Spradley, *The Ethnographic Interview* (New York: Harcourt Brace Jovanovich, 1979), 3–8.
18. Hochschild, *What's Fair?* 24.

between individual freedom and community control. The interviews ended with a discussion of economic changes in Russia and evaluations of the major political parties. The aim of the interview was to get a discussion going that would allow the respondent to reveal more complex thoughts and methods of organizing concepts.

The interviews took place in large and small cities in Russia with people of a variety of ages and educational backgrounds.[19] Most took place in the respondent's home or workplace. A smaller number occurred either in the apartment I was renting in Moscow or in my hotel room in cities I visited for a shorter amount of time. Some interviews occurred in the home of the person who served as a point of contact between the respondent and myself. Although the interviews proceeded along a series of prearranged topics, they were relatively informal affairs. Respondents talked for as long or as little as they liked. I used the planned questions more as a guide than as something that had to be accomplished. I provided nodding encouragement, occasional clarification, and some short comments, but I was far from an equal participant in the conversation. In fact, I made every effort to limit the effect I might have on respondents' comments. Other than asking questions and trying to elicit clarifications or expansions of comments, I was largely silent during the interviews. I refrained from registering either agreement or disagreement with the comments the respondents made. I found that nodding to show that I understood the meaning of what was being said was sufficient to keep most people talking. Since the opinions of interest to me were those of the respondents, I did not interject my own.

Some interviews were punctuated by interruptions from others in the home or office. Many included breaks for snacks, most often tea and homemade preserves. Because so many interviews took place in locations where I would not normally have been granted entry, more than the respondents'

---

19. All interviews were conducted in Russian. Most were conducted by the author; four, by a Russian colleague, Ol'ga Iastrebova. Interviews ranged in length from a minimum of about forty-five minutes to a maximum of more than three hours. The interviews were taped, with the permission of the respondent. I also took copious notes, both in case the tape recorder failed and to distract the respondent from the tape recorder. The tape recorder did not seem to influence the willingness of respondents to talk. The only times respondents asked me to turn it off were when they offered me food or were interrupted by phone calls, visitors, or wayward children. A native speaker transcribed the tapes in Russian, except for two cases in which recording difficulties made that impossible. In those cases, I rely on the notes I took during the interview. Translations are my own. Most interviewees were offered a small stipend, although many of them refused it in 1998. Most accepted the stipend in 2000 and 2003.

words have informed this study. In addition to what these people thought, I was able to observe a great deal about their lives: their apartments; their family life; the condition of public places around their homes; the difficulties they faced on a daily basis negotiating mass transit, finding a working pay phone, or deciphering the meaning of Russian addresses.

The sample of respondents is not formally random. Indeed, even if it were, it would still be too small to allow generalization to the population of Russia as a whole. In any case, given the small size of the group of respondents, a random sample was not ideal: characteristics that are relatively uncommon in the population as a whole might not show up in a small random sample; common characteristics might show up so frequently as to result in many respondents who were essentially the same.[20] One "uncommon" characteristic is particularly important to this study. In order to examine the underlying contradictions and commonalities in the political and social thinking of ordinary Russians, it was necessary to speak with Russians who were willing to talk about politics at some length. They did not have to be especially articulate or well informed, but they had to be at least minimally garrulous. They also had to have time to talk: a respondent constantly checking her watch would be as little help as someone with very little to say. It was also essential that respondents felt comfortable talking with an American researcher. Even though the interviews were conducted in Russian, potential respondents with very limited contact with foreigners might have felt inhibited in circumstances that were, for them, highly unusual. Consequently, for a number of reasons, a formal random sample was not appropriate.

At the same time, a pure convenience sample was not ideal either. Public opinion studies have made it clear that political attitudes vary with a number of personal characteristics, but particularly with age, education, and location within Russia. Older Russians, for instance, seem to have different conceptions of what democracy entails. They are also more likely to support Communist Party candidates in elections, and the party's supporters

---

20. Robert S. Weiss, *Learning from Strangers: The Art and Method of Qualitative Interview Studies* (New York: Free Press, 1994), 22.

21. E. B. Shestopal, "Perspektivy demokratii v soznanii rossiian," *Obshchestvennye nauki i sovremennost'*, no. 2 (1996): 45–60; Jerry F. Hough, Evelyn Davidheiser, and Susan Goodrich Lehmann, *The 1996 Russian Presidential Election* (Washington, DC: Brookings Institution, 1996), 56–57; Ralph S. Clem and Peter R. Craumer, "A Rayon-Level Analysis of the Russian Election and Constitutional Plebiscite of December 1993," *Post-Soviet Geography* 36 (October 1995): 459–75.

seem to have distinctive policy desires.[21] Urban, better-educated voters are more likely to support democratic parties and to have promarket views.[22] Observers talk about a "red belt" that extends across the south of Russia. Voters in the red belt regularly return Communist or nationalist candidates to the State Duma and kept Communists in power locally through the 1990s.[23] In attitude surveys, red-belt respondents tend to lean against reform. In order to capture these systematic differences in political attitudes, I used a quota sample, based on desired combinations of age, education, and gender.[24] After establishing the characteristics I wanted to see in my informants, I enlisted a variety of assistants to find potential informants of a talkative nature.[25] Less than a third of the sample is from Moscow. I also interviewed people from small towns around Moscow and from four cities either in or near Russia's red belt.[26]

22. Timothy J. Colton, "Determinants of the Party Vote," in *Growing Pains: Russian Democracy and the Election of 1993*, ed. Timothy J. Colton and Jerry F. Hough (Washington, DC: Brookings Institution, 1998), 87.

23. See Timothy Colton, *Transitional Citizens: Voters and What Influences Them in the New Russia* (Cambridge, MA: Harvard University Press, 2000), 69–102; Ralph S. Clem and Peter R. Craumer, "The Regional Dimension," in *The Russian Parliamentary Elections of 1995: The Battle for the Duma*, ed. Laura Belin and Robert W. Orttung (Armonk, NY: M. E. Sharpe, 1997), 137–59.

24. David Nachmias and Chava Nachmias, *Research Methods in the Social Sciences*, 3d ed. (New York: St. Martin's Press, 1987), 186. Relying on an even smaller sample of Russians, Dryzek and Holmes also chose respondents in order to maximize variation on similar social characteristics. Their goal, like mine, was to identify patterns in how people's ideas fit together. John S. Dryzek and Leslie Holmes, *Post-Communist Democratization: Political Discourses Across Thirteen Countries* (New York: Cambridge University Press, 2002), 27–28.

25. I am particularly grateful to the following people for their help in locating respondents: Polina Kozyreva, Mikhail Kosolapov, Marina Chizhova, Nina Rostegaeva, Ol'ga Iastrebova, and Natal'ia Peshkova in Moscow; Tat'iana Bogomolova in Novosibirsk; Valentina Pervova in Krasnoyarsk; Ol'ga Shcheglova in Voronezh; Andrei Shashenkov in Smolensk; and Arbakhan Magomedov in Ulyanovsk.

Although there were a couple of exceptions, most interviewees were happy to talk at length and did not seem constrained either by the context of the interview or by the fact that they were talking to an American researcher. The hardest part about conducting the interviews was convincing respondents to set a specific time for the interview in advance. See also Sharon Werning Rivera, Polina M. Kozyreva, and Eduard G. Sarovskii, "Interviewing Political Elites: Lessons From Russia," *PS: Political Science and Politics* 35, no. 4 (2002): 683–88.

26. Analysts disagree on the exact borders of the red belt, and I opt for a fairly wide application of the term. In its narrow application, the term includes Voronezh and Smolensk *oblasti*, two of the interview regions. Ulyanovsk Oblast lies on the eastern border of Penza, a widely accepted member of the red belt even in its narrowest definition. As I discuss below, the politics of the region justify the label *red*, even if the Volga region is not always considered formally part of the red belt. Some observers would not extend the red belt over the Urals into Siberia. Even so, Novosibirsk is a region that regularly returned Communist candidates. Krasnoyarsk Kray is interesting less because of its Communist leanings than because its citizens elected Aleksandr Lebed, a key figure in the national-patriotic movement, to the governorship in 1998.

Another characteristic that seems to affect at least some political attitudes is whether people think they have been faring well economically under the changing economic system. Unfortunately, it was difficult to know enough about my respondents before the start of the interview to be able to select on that characteristic. But informally, the people helping me find informants tried to maximize the variation in material welfare as well as a variety of other characteristics, such as political activism or ethnic heritage.

In research based on intensive interviews, the size of the sample is considered sufficient when the topic is saturated, that is, when additional interviews provide little new information.[27] By 2003, the final year in which interviews were conducted, I found myself able to predict responses before they were provided. The only responses that were sometimes surprising at that time were from people in smaller towns. Consequently, in 2003 I concentrated on interviewing respondents in small towns in Moscow Oblast and in the comparatively small city of Smolensk.

Unlike a snowball sample, in which the early informants suggest other potential informants, this was a sample of people who mostly did not know one another. Indeed, they traveled in very different social circles. Some were members of the cultural intelligentsia; others worked manual jobs. Some lived in Stupino, a small town south of Moscow; others lived in Siberia. Nor were respondents merely a group of politically interested and well-educated people. A number of them were obviously only motivated by the stipend offered for participation. A few others—from a wealthy "New Russian" stay-at-home wife to most of the pensioners—seemed to consider themselves well compensated simply by the company of an attentive listener. Aside from the people from small towns in Moscow Oblast and a resident of the collective farm of Elita in Siberia, this is a primarily urban sample. While it might have been desirable to talk with people in the Russian "depths," as one researcher who specializes in rural Russia put it, logistical difficulties and the relative infrequency of American researchers in isolated Russian villages made that impossible. I was unable to stay long enough in a Russian village to earn the trust that would have made meaningful interviews possible. It is fortunate, then, that most of the attitudinal differences between urban and rural Russians can be explained by differences in education, age, and economic situation, attributes on

27. Kathleen M. Blee and Verta Taylor, "Semi-structured Interviewing in Social Movement Research," in *Methods of Social Movement Research,* ed. Bert Klandermans and Suzanne Staggenborg, Social Movement, Protest, and Contention, vol. 16 (Minneapolis: University of Minnesota Press, 2002), 100.

which there is considerable variation in my sample.[28] Although those in my sample are somewhat more educated than the population as a whole, the age breakdowns do roughly match the wider population.

A decade after the collapse of Communism, most Russians were in difficult economic circumstances, and that was also true of my respondents. The sample includes a number of pensioners who had been forced to take on additional ways of earning money to survive, either through formal jobs, by taking in boarders, or by selling items at bus stops and markets. Some of the young men were unemployed, having lost jobs variously in defense industries or private sales. Others were still working at enterprises that were collapsing. A small number of interviewees had tested the waters of entrepreneurialism, usually with some success. Based on such characteristics as computers in the home or foreign vacations, around six of the respondents could be described as relatively well off by Russian standards. One was an objectively wealthy New Russian, with not only foreign vacations, but also properties in Spain and Greece, a child in boarding school in England, and a stunning apartment in central Moscow. Given their variety of economic circumstances, it is not surprising that the respondents also had a variety of political orientations. While some preferred democratic parties, many others liked the Communists, and more than a few had good words to say about Vladimir Zhirinovskii, one of Russia's radical nationalists. In 1998, the bulk of the respondents greatly disliked then president Boris Yeltsin. Yeltsin's successor, Vladimir Putin, acting president at the time of the 2000 interviews, was impressively popular with the respondents at that time. By 2003, Putin's luster had dimmed somewhat, but he remained much more popular than Yeltsin had been.

Although most of the respondents identified themselves as ethnic Russians, a smattering of other nationalities was also represented: two Tatars, one individual from Dagestan, an ethnic Armenian, and a variety of people of mixed descent, usually Russian and another former Soviet republic nationality. The result is a sample that, while smaller and also less representative than would be the case in a standardized survey, is also

28. See William M. Reisinger, Arthur H. Miller, and Vicki L. Hesli, "Political Norms in Rural Russia: Evidence from Public Attitudes," *Europe-Asia Studies* 47 (September 1995): 1025–42. Clem and Craumer conclude that, even though leftist parties remained relatively strong in rural areas, as of 1999 Edinstvo had begun to erode the Left's support in rural areas. Ralph S. Clem and Peter R. Craumer, "Urban and Rural Effects on Party Preferences in Russia: New Evidence from the Recent Duma Election," *Post-Soviet Geography and Economics*, 43, no. 1 (2002): 1–12.

quite a bit larger and more varied than is often the case for ethnographic work. Ethnographers regularly rely on samples from a quarter to half the size of the one used here, and they do not necessarily make the effort to systematically capture the variety of respondent characteristics the sample used here contains.[29] The demographic characteristics of the Russian respondents are summarized in Appendix A.

Analyzing the Interviews

Conducting the interviews led to a diverse set of adventures. In the course of this project, I got profoundly lost in neighborhoods where building numbers seemed to follow no discernable pattern and none of the pay phones worked; I figured out how to find the bus to Shakhovskaya, a small rural town on the far edge of Moscow Oblast, when no buses bore any signs indicating their destination. (Ask everyone; no one else knew either.) And I negotiated the seemingly mysterious system to purchase train tickets. I drank a lot of tea and ate delicious preserves, cookies, and chocolates. I met a Russian Orthodox nun in the lobby of a hotel in Siberia in order to hand over a care package from her mother in Moscow. Strangers trusted me to carry their money from one city to another; a previously unknown American suddenly became more reliable than either banks or the post office.

Analyzing the interviews produced new adventures. Once all the interviews were transcribed, I had more than a thousand pages of text. While there had been some consistency in the order in which I asked questions, there was much less consistency in the answers, and relevant pieces of information arrived at different points in the various interviews. My goal was not to impose my interpretation on the respondents' answers, but to draw out patterns already present within the answers. To that end, I had not asked questions that forced respondents to provide answers that would fit the argument I intended to make. On the contrary, my primary argument about how contemporary Russians' values are a product of the experienced social and political reality of daily life emerged after this project was well under way. It was not an idea I deliberately intended to prove when I began this project. Indeed, had it been, I probably would have asked some different questions.

---

29. Spradley, *The Ethnographic Interview.*

Obviously, though, I am unable to present in this book everything that each of the respondents said. In order to persuade readers that my selections do not misrepresent the respondents' own words, I have followed a number of strategies. For one thing, I provide fairly extensive quotations from the interviews throughout the subsequent chapters. This is the key evidence that will allow readers to judge the value of my interpretation. I try to provide a sense of the variety of perspectives present within the responses. Although most of my analysis rests on the words my respondents spoke, I occasionally provide some simple quantitative analysis using answers from the entire sample. This analysis is not meant to show trends that can be generalized to the whole of Russia. Rather, it is intended to provide evidence that the tendencies I identify in the answers really are present in the sample. Through the quantitative analysis and some of the tables that show how responses were distributed across the sample, readers can see roughly how many and what types of people made various sorts of comments and how different ideas relate to one another. Generally, I do not provide counts of the number of respondents who made a particular comment, since the only reason to do so would be to imply that the same proportion of the entire Russian population would be likely to say similar things. The size of my sample does not support that conclusion. It does, however, allow us to better understand the variety of ways that Russians make sense of their political world, as well as some of the reasons they think the things they do. That is the goal of this book.

In addition to the Russian interviews, from time to time I also make use of a smaller group of American interviews. The American respondents were also selected using a quota sample to maximize variation on age, education, and gender. All the American respondents lived in the Midwest.[30] The demographic characteristics of the American respondents are described in Appendix B.

I use the American sample to demonstrate what is and is not distinctive about the ways Russians think about political life, not to draw conclusions about American attitudes and values. For instance, one of the features of the Russian respondents' comments is that they mix democratic and undemocratic statements. With no point of comparison, readers might come to the conclusion that Russians are oddly authoritarian. For that reason, it is helpful to compare Russians with citizens elsewhere so that

---

30. For the American interviews, I am grateful for the assistance of Lisa Pohlman and Mary Santanello.

the parts of Russian ideas that are distinctive emerge in higher relief and the parts that are fairly common to ordinary people in other parts of the world gain that perspective.

It is helpful to compare the Russian respondents to *Americans,* specifically, because Russians and Americans differ so greatly in the social context in which they form their political orientations. Russians would characterize life for most Americans as "orderly," or what amounts to the same thing, "civilized," qualities they rarely use to describe their own lives. In the United States, jobs are comparatively stable and most pay enough to cover at least necessities. Inflation is fairly low. Government is largely effective at making and enforcing laws, collecting taxes, and restraining its officers from abusing ordinary citizens. The country's constitution has been in place for centuries, and it successfully informs how political institutions interact with one another and with citizens. If the social context in which political attitudes are formed matters, then the different contexts in which Americans and Russians form political values should produce some traceable attitudinal responses. If there are no differences between American and Russian responses, then that would indicate that social conditions do not carry much weight in the formation of political values.

Of course, differences between the American and Russian respondents could be explained in various ways. For one thing, Americans are thought to differ greatly from Russians in the cultural values they extract from their history, not just in the conditions of their mundane lives. As a result of their unique history—democracy without a feudal predecessor—Americans are presumed to be more democratic, individualistic, and hopeful about the possibilities of political life.[31] Here, again, the intensive nature of the interviews is crucial. The different ways in which the Russian and American respondents *explain* their ideas should provide insight into the reasons Russians hold the ideas they do.

Interview Locations

In this section, I provide background information about the political conditions in each of the Russian cities or regions where interviews were conducted. This information is helpful in appreciating the variety of life circumstances of the Russian respondents.

---

31. For instance, Louis Hartz, *The Liberal Tradition in America* (New York: Harcourt Brace Jovanovich, 1955).

The largest group of the Russian interviews—nearly a third of the sample—took place in the city of Moscow. Moscow, of course, is the largest city in Russia, with an official population of more than 8 million in the late 1990s, although informal estimates put the real population higher. Around 90 percent of the city's population is composed of ethnic Russians. As the capital of the Russian Federation, the home of many of Russia's largest corporations, and a relative magnet for foreign investment, Moscow has weathered the economic changes that followed the collapse of the Soviet Union better than most of the rest of Russia. For instance, in 1997 Muscovites enjoyed the second-highest gross regional product per capita in Russia.[32] In the mid-1990s, recorded personal incomes were three times as high in Moscow as the Russian average, but the cost of living in Moscow was not especially higher than average, leaving Muscovites comparatively better off.[33] Muscovites also are more likely than other Russians to hold higher-status professional jobs and to have completed a higher education. All these advantages do not mean, of course, that the economic benefits enjoyed by the city as a whole have reached all Muscovites. Between 1992 and 1995, industrial production in Moscow declined by 52 percent. As a result, many people either lost jobs or lost regular paychecks while their jobs in theory remained. The banking sector experienced considerable growth in Moscow up until the 1998 financial crash but was slow to recover after that. While the average Muscovite has more opportunity than most Russians to get a better-paying job in the private sector, relatively few make a great deal of money, while most people remain comparatively poor as some of their neighbors prosper.

Moscow is considered one of the most democratic places in Russia.[34] Democratic parties and candidates tend to do well in Moscow both in local and national elections, and nationalist parties or Communists do relatively worse than in the rest of Russia. The Democratic Russia movement was founded in Moscow and won 45.6 percent of the vote in the

---

32. *The Territories of the Russian Federation*, 2d ed. (London: Europa, 2001), 262. The petroleum producing Tyumen Oblast was first.

33. Grigory Ioffe, Olga L. Medvedkov, Yuri Medvedkov, Tatiana Nefordova, and Natalia Vlasova, "Russia's Fragmented Space," in *Fragmented Space in the Russian Federation*, ed. Blair A. Ruble, Jodi Koehn, and Nancy E. Popson (Washington, DC: Woodrow Wilson Center Press, 2001), 42.

34. Aleksei Titkov, "Obrazy Regionov v Rossiiskom Massovom Soznanii," *Polis*, no. 3 (1999): 72. According to Titkov, experts consider Saint Petersburg, and the Nizhegorodskaya and Sverdlovskaya oblasts, to be more democratic than Moscow.

second round of Moscow municipal elections in 1990.[35] In the 1993 Duma elections, the promarket Russia's Democratic Choice received 34.7 percent of the Moscow vote, its highest plurality in any region of Russia. By contrast, the populist-nationalist Liberal Democratic Party of Russia earned only 12.8 percent of the Moscow vote, its fourth-worse showing in all areas.[36] In the 1997 municipal elections, Russia's Democratic Choice won a majority of seats in the city duma.

The democratic tendencies of Moscow's citizens are not always reflected in the operation of city government. During all the years in which interviews for this project were conducted in Moscow, the mayor of that city was Yurii Luzhkov. Under Mayor Luzhkov, city government was characterized by overwhelming executive power, a subservient city legislature, control of local mass media by the mayor's office, persecution of opposition groups, and recurrent efforts to restrict immigration into Moscow by people who were not ethnic Russians, particularly people from the Caucasus region.[37] Luzhkov, a former manager in the chemical industry, was a deputy to the Moscow city soviet and a member of the city executive (Mosgorispolkom) in the declining years of Communism. Yeltsin appointed Luzhkov mayor in 1992, at the resignation of the previous mayor, Gavril Popov. At first, Luzhkov supported both Yeltsin and reform more generally. He backed Yeltsin in the 1991 coup attempt and in Yeltsin's 1993 battle against the Supreme Soviet. After winning nearly 90 percent of the popular vote in the 1996 mayoral election, Luzhkov became more critical of central government policies and advocated government intervention in the economy to reduce the cost of economic reform for ordinary Muscovites. These policies, along with efforts to improve the physical infrastructure of Moscow, endeared Luzhkov to much of his electorate.

35. Timothy J. Colton, *Moscow: Governing the Socialist Metropolis* (Cambridge, MA: Belknap Press of Harvard University Press, 1995), 623.

36. Judith S. Kullberg, "Preserving the Radical Stronghold: The Election in Moscow," in *Growing Pains: Russian Democracy and the Election of 1993*, ed. Timothy J. Colton and Jerry F. Hough (Washington, DC: Brookings Institution, 1998), 311. In 1993, Russia's Democratic Choice received 15.5 percent of the vote nationally; the LDPR received 22.92 percent of the national vote. Laura Belin and Robert W. Orttung, *The Russian Parliamentary Elections of 1995: The Battle for the Duma* (Armonk, NY: M. E. Sharpe, 1997), 114–17.

37. James Alexander, Andrei A. Degtyarev, and Vladimir Gel'man, "Democratization Challenged: The Role of Regional Elites," in *Fragmented Space in the Russian Federation*, ed. Blair A. Ruble, Jodi Koehn, and Nancy E. Popson (Washington, DC: Woodrow Wilson Center Press, 2001), 161–87.

The popular perception that Luzhkov had done a lot for Moscow while in office tempered criticism that he had also done a lot for himself. By the end of the 1990s, the Moscow city government owned controlling stakes in a television station and a bank, as well as a chain of convenience stores and gas stations. The "czar" of Moscow lived in an exclusive high-rise. Along with former prime minister Evgenii Primakov, Luzhkov founded the Otechestvo–Vsia Rossiia (Fatherland–All Russia) party to compete nationally in the 1999 Duma elections. The party won limited support outside Moscow, which crushed Luzhkov's hopes for a successful run at the presidency in 2000. While Luzhkov remained popular in Moscow, he had to grapple with a series of terrorist attacks, including the 2002 theater takeover that resulted in more than 150 deaths.

Eleven interviews occurred either in small towns in Moscow Oblast, the region surrounding Moscow, or in Moscow with people who normally live in these towns but were visiting relatives. Like the city of Moscow, Moscow Oblast is relatively prosperous, with a variety of industries, including mechanical engineering, radio electronics, chemicals, light manufacturing, and textiles. The respondents from Korolev, a center of aerospace research, fit this image, but the respondents from Stupino, Staraya Kupavna, Shakhovskaya, Lukhovitsky *raion,* and Il'inskaya were not a very prosperous group. One had lost his job in the military aerospace industry and was hoping to get a new one in the Mars candy factory. Another had left behind a good job in Latvia because she felt Russians were no longer welcome in that country. One pensioner spent summers growing vegetables in the village where she had inherited a house and winters peddling *piroshki* at a bus stop. In the 1990s, citizens and local government officials in Moscow Oblast tended to support the policies and candidates of the central government. But Moscow Oblast was not a particularly liberal area. In his 1999 study, Aleksei Titkov listed Moscow Oblast as among the least democratic regions in the country. In the 1995 State Duma elections, Communists received more than 50 percent more votes than Nash Dom Rossii, the party of then prime minister Viktor Chernomyrdin.[38]

The rest of the interviews were conducted in cities where, compared with Moscow, democrats had a weaker presence. These cities were either in or near Russia's red belt, but not all of them were equally "red." The most unreformed for much of the 1990s was probably Ulyanovsk, named

---

38. Titkov, "Obrazy Regionov," 72. Titkov excludes non-Russian regions from the comparison. *The Territories of the Russian Federation,* 184.

for its most famous son, Vladimir Lenin. Ulyanovsk is a city of fewer than seven hundred thousand on a bend in the Volga River, 441 miles east of Moscow. Bordered by Tatarstan, Mordovia, and the Chuvash Republic, Ulyanovsk Oblast is more ethnically diverse than some of the other areas where interviews were conducted. The largest ethnic minority is the Tatars. Although the Ulyanovsk region has oil fields, fertile land and forests, and a variety of industries, it suffered economically in the post-Communist era. The city of Ulyanovsk was hit both by the collapse of the local aviation and automobile industries and by the great decline in tourists visiting the birthplace of Lenin. Politically, the region was considered a holdover from the Soviet era during much of the 1990s. While many areas dropped names derived from illustrious Bolsheviks, Ulyanovsk did not. In the 1995 State Duma elections, Communists won 37 percent of the regional vote, higher than the national average. In the first round of the 1996 presidential elections, the Communist candidate Gennadii Ziuganov won twice as many votes as Yeltsin. The first regional elections were held only in 1995. Before then, government officials were a mix of Communist-era holdovers and Yeltsin appointees.

One such appointee, Iurii Goriachev, was elected governor of Ulyanovsk Oblast in 1996. A former first secretary of the *oblast'* Communist Party, Goriachev was supported by the Communist Party and rural residents of the *oblast'*. In both style and substance, his regime seemed more suited to the Soviet period than the era of reform. Goriachev resisted "shock therapy" economic policies imposed by the central government and adapted traditions of bureaucratic paternalism to maintain the ruling group's control over economic resources.[39] He banned local privatization and collective farm

39. Arbakhan Magomedov, "Ul'ianovskaia oblast': Khronika politicheskikh sobytii (1990–1998)," in *Nizhegorodskaia oblast', Ul'ianovskaia oblast'*, Regiony Rossii: Khronika i rukovoditeli, ed. K. Matsuzato and A. B. Shatilov, vol. 6 (Sapporo, Japan: Slavic Research Center, Hokkaido University, 1999); Vladimir Shlapentokh, Roman Levita, and Mikhail Loiberg, *From Submission to Rebellion: The Provinces Versus the Center in Russia* (Boulder, CO: Westview Press, 1997), 193–94. Gel'man et al. attribute Goriachev's success in resisting economic reforms demanded by the center to high levels of elite unity in Ulyanovsk, highly concentrated economic resources, and the successful manipulation of clientelistic relations developed during the Soviet period. See Vladimir Gel'man, Sergei Ryzhenko, and Michael Brie, with Vladimir Avdonin, Boris Ovchinnikov, and Igor' Semenov, *Making and Breaking Democratic Transitions: The Comparative Politics of Russia's Regions* (New York: Rowman and Littlefield, 2003), 193–98. In her broader study of Russia's regions, Kathryn Stoner-Weiss agrees that such conditions tend to produce coalitions between political and economic elites that are often beneficial in terms of government performance, but that may undermine political pluralism and economic efficiency in the long run. See Kathryn Stoner-Weiss, *Local Heroes: The Political Economy of Russian Regional Governance* (Princeton: Princeton University Press, 1997).

reforms, imposed restrictions on regional imports and exports, and subsidized bread prices until early 1997. Food was rationed until July 1996.
Local industries were protected through government subsidies, and a system
of small businesses was created under state patronage.

Goriachev complained about the bad press his policies earned in Russia's
more reform-oriented media. He said, "I don't understand what's so bad
about a person who has managed to save the region from complete price
collapse, especially since our financial potential was enough to support
the subsidies. . . . The region is not subsidized, it pays taxes conscien-
tiously, and coupons have helped us prevent the market from collapsing.
And 'vodka' taxes have helped us keep our prices in check."[40] Goriachev
lauded the results of his policies: rent costs, public transportation fares,
and the prices of essential food items were the lowest in Russia. Because
of these low costs, citizens of Ulyanovsk in the later 1990s enjoyed a
standard of living higher than the national average.[41] Those, however,
were not the only results. The region racked up enormous debts, industry
developed slowly, and teachers undertook hunger strikes to protest delayed
wages.[42] In 2000, Goriachev lost a reelection bid to Vladimir Shamanov,
former commander-in-chief of Russia's ground forces. By the time Goriachev
left office, the Russian government considered Ulyanovsk to be one of
Russia's least fortunate regions. In the winter of 2001–2, Ulyanovskenergo
reduced the amount of publicly provided heat, claiming that local officials
failed to pay for public energy supplies. The lack of heat forced the closing
of schools and kindergartens.

By contrast with the *oblast'* administration, public officials in the city of
Ulyanovsk tended to be more reform oriented and were sometimes in
open conflict with regional government. The mayor of Ulyanovsk at the
time at which interviews were conducted there was Vitalii Marusin. By
1998, the city of Ulyanovsk gave some appearance of changing with the
times. New, consumer-oriented businesses were developing. There was
something of a building boom in parts of the city dominated by single-
family houses. The city was not turning its back on its heritage, though.
The "Lenin sites" were in immaculate condition, and the guides still
spoke affectionately of Vladimir Il'ich. Despite having grown up wholly in

40. Quoted in Guzel Fazullina, "Ulyanovsk Hovers on the Brink of Change," *Moscow
News*, no. 39 (9–15 October 1996): 3.
41. John Helmer, "Communist Reform: A Success Story," *The Russian*, November 1997, 40.
42. Rustam Muratovich Bikmetov, "Izbiratel'nyi protsess, vlast' i oppozitsiia v Ul'ianovskoi
oblasti," *Polis: Politicheskie Issledovaniia*, no. 3 (1999): 126.

the post-Communist period, schoolchildren visiting the sites could relate with great accuracy and detail the facts of Lenin's childhood.

The interview city that appeared least changed from the Soviet period was Voronezh. Located 250 miles south of Moscow, Voronezh is the largest city in Russia's Central Black Earth region and an important administrative and cultural center of the area. Regionally significant industries include agriculture, aerospace, radio electronics, and machine building. Just under a million people live in the city of Voronezh, with another million and a half in Voronezh Oblast, though low birthrates have been causing population levels to decline. Compared with Ulyanovsk, in Voronezh in 2000 there were fewer private restaurants, stores continued to use the arcane "kassa" system that market reform had largely eliminated in the rest of Russia's cities, and customers still suffered under the arbitrary closings and surly sales help of the Soviet era. During the administration of Mayor Aleksandr Tsapin, running water was shut off for a few hours at midday in the city center. When the water did run, it was rusty red.

To a degree, *red* also describes the region's politics. In the immediate post-Soviet years, the Communists continued to control the regional duma and won 27 percent of the regional vote in the 1995 State Duma elections. Communist candidate Gennadii Ziuganov won by a wide margin in Voronezh Oblast in the 1996 presidential election, even though he lost in the country as a whole. As governor of Voronezh from 1992 to 1996, Aleksandr Kovalev tried to hold down agricultural prices and prevent the export of goods out of the *oblast'*. After the 1992 reorganization of collective farms, grain production plummeted and this very fertile region was forced to import food.[43]

In an expression of popular dissatisfaction with the Kovalev regime, Ivan Shabanov was elected governor of the *oblast'* in late 1996. Although a Communist, Shabanov marked a change from the old regime. By 1997, some sectors of the economy, particularly light industry, food processing, and construction materials, were almost entirely privatized. Foreign investment increased dramatically after 1995. By 1999 there were more than twice as many small businesses in Voronezh Oblast as in Ulyanovsk Oblast.[44] Shabanov's administration, however, was characterized by considerable corruption, which seems to have undermined support for the

43. Jessica Allina-Pisano, "Reorganization and its Discontents: A Case Study in Voronezh Oblast," in *Rural Reform in Post-Soviet Russia,* ed. David J. O'Brien and Stephen K. Wegren (Washington, DC: Woodrow Wilson Center Press, 2002), 309.

44. *The Territories of the Russian Federation,* 248, 257.

Communist Party in the region. In the 1999 State Duma elections, the progovernment Edinstvo bloc outpolled the Communist Party in Voronezh Oblast. In December 2000 Shabanov lost his reelection bid to Vladimir Kulakov, a Federal Security Service (FSB) general endorsed by Putin who ran on a platform of honesty and accountable power.[45] By 2001, left representation in the *oblast'* duma had shrunk to five seats. It seemed that holes were developing in Russia's red belt.

Smolensk, too, was less red after 2002 than it had been earlier. A city of about 350,000 located close to Russia's border with Belarus, Smolensk is capital of the Smolensk region. One of Russia's oldest cities, Smolensk sat astride the trade route from the Baltic Sea to Constantinople. It is also on the main route between Moscow and Warsaw and hence has been subject to repeated invasion. Napoleon passed through Smolensk on his way into and out of Russia, and Smolensk was occupied and virtually razed by the Nazis between 1941 and 1943. Smolensk Oblast has few natural resources and most of its industries suffered during the reform period, but its location remains significant for overland trade with Europe. Gazprom's natural gas pipelines go through Smolensk Oblast, and many European consumer goods travel through by train. In the 1990s, Kristall, Russia's only diamond-cutting factory, accounted for 70 percent of the export income of the *oblast'*.[46] Income for most people in the region was below the national average.

Throughout the 1990s, Communist or national-patriotic candidates won nearly all elections in Smolensk Oblast. For instance, Communist presidential candidate Gennadii Ziuganov received 56 percent of the vote in 1996, compared with Yeltsin's 32 percent. Locally, in the 1990s the region was ruled by former members of the Komsomol, the Communist youth organization, strongly influenced by a tightly interconnected group of directors of large Soviet-era factories.[47] The governorship of the *oblast'* was held by candidates backed by the Communist Party until 2002, when Aleksandr Prokhorov lost to the Kremlin-backed candidate, General Viktor Maslov, head of the regional FSB. The 2002 election received some attention because, days before voting took place, the car carrying Vice Governor

---

45. Christopher Marsh, *Russia at the Polls: Voters, Elections, and Democratization* (Washington, DC: CQ Press, 2002), 125–28. The Federal Security Service is the successor to the Soviet-era KGB.

46. Jean-Charles Lallemand, "Who Rules Smolensk Oblast," *EWI Russian Regional Report* 3, no. 40 (8 October 1998), 1, http://www.ceri-sciencespo.com/archive/october/artjcl.pdf.

47. Lallemand, "Who Rules Smolensk Oblast," 2–3.

Anatoly Makarenko was ambushed. The driver was killed, and Makarenko's bodyguard was wounded. Earlier, two dachas belonging to Prokhorov's election staff had burned, a bomb exploded in Prokhorov's election headquarters, and Prokhorov's lawyer's son was beaten. The Prokhorov team complained about intimidation by Maslov's camp, but federal law enforcement authorities thought it more likely that Makarenko's illicit business dealings were at the heart of the matter. In 2002 regional duma elections, the Communists lost all representation, after having held more than a third of the seats previously. In March 2003, after Mayor Ivan Averchenkov died in office, Maslov apparently strong-armed the deputies of the Smolensk city soviet into selecting as mayor his preferred candidate, Vladislav Khaletskii, former Kristall commercial director.[48]

The rest of the interviews took place in Siberia, either in Novosibirsk or Krasnoyarsk. Although both cities are in south-central Siberia, economically and politically they are rather different from each other. Novosibirsk Oblast is in the southeast of the Western Siberian plain, between the Ob and Irtysh rivers. The city of Novosibirsk was founded in 1893, during the construction of the Trans-Siberian Railway. In the 1990s, Novosibirsk was the third largest city in Russia, with an estimated population of just under a million and a half. The Novosibirsk region is sometimes considered part of Russia's red belt, and Communists dominated regional government in the 1990s.[49] The interviews took place outside Novosibirsk, in the suburb of Akademgorodok, home of the Siberian branch of the Academy of Sciences.

The political and economic development of the Novosibirsk region in the post-Communist era is considered typical of many industrial areas far from Moscow.[50] The region is not especially rich in natural resources, although it does produce coal, petroleum, natural gas, peat, marble, limestone, and clay. Nor is it home to significant ethnic tensions or armed conflicts. It receives some foreign investment, though not as much as local officials would like. The region is unusual, however, in containing forty-three Russian Academy of Science institutes, more than one hundred industrial research institutes, and thirteen private and nineteen state institutes of higher education. The leading industry is machine building. With the collapse of the Soviet economy, the region was hit hard by the loss of

48. *Radio Free Europe/Radio Liberty Newsline*, vol. 7, no. 47, 12 March 2003.
49. *The Territories of the Russian Federation*, 196.
50. Grigory L. Olekh, "Novosibirsk Oblast: Problems of Globalization and Regionalization," *Regionalization of Russian Foreign Policy and Security Policy*, Working Paper no. 9 (Zurich: Center for Security Studies and Conflict Research, 2001), 7.

subsidies from Moscow. In their efforts to become more self-sufficient, regional authorities clashed with Moscow about the distribution of tax receipts. Regional authorities argued that a fair distribution of income would give more to the regions and less to the center, especially since the center had been transferring responsibilities to the regions. They further complained that even funds legally appropriated for the Novosibirsk region often never actually arrived. In addition, the federal government accumulated debts to the *oblast'* because of failure to pay for heat, electricity, and deliveries made to the defense industry.

Vitalii Mukha, governor of Novosibirsk Oblast for much of the period between 1991 and 1999, has the distinction of having been fired by Yeltsin twice. After clashing with Yeltsin over regional interests, he was fired in March 1993 and reinstated a few days later. He was fired again after he sided with Yeltsin's opponents in the October 1993 conflict with Supreme Soviet. At that time, he refused to disband the regional parliament and local soviets, as Yeltsin ordered, and he threatened to blockade the Trans-Siberian Railway if Yeltsin did not give in to the demands of the Supreme Soviet and the regions it claimed to represent. After Mukha was reelected to the governorship in 1995, he followed somewhat more pragmatic policies, remaining neutral in the 1996 presidential campaign.

Mukha rose to power in the Communist Party, achieving the position of first secretary of the party *oblast'* committee before the collapse of the Soviet Union, and the Communist Party supported his candidacy for governor in 1995. Even so, Mukha tried to find a third way between Communism and Yeltsin's market reforms. In February 1996, the regional administration agreed to a "social contract" with labor unions and employers. The agreement stipulated that pay for workers on the public payroll would be maintained at no less than 85 percent of the average wage in industry, and unemployment would be kept below 6 percent. Along with Moscow mayor Yurii Luzhkov, Mukha is among the founders of the Otechestvo Party. Mukha argued that the methods of implementing market reforms had to "change radically," with the government taking greater responsibility for the standard of living and life expectancy of the people, for the country's safety, and for the protection of people's rights and freedoms.[51]

After elections in December 1999, Mukha was replaced by Viktor Tolokonskii, former mayor of the city of Novosibirsk. Tolokonskii, who continued many of Mukha's policies, presented himself as a reformer, but

---

51. Olekh, "Novosibirsk Oblast," 18.

he advocated generous social support for the region's poorest citizens, regardless of the effect on the regional budget. While he was mayor of the city of Novosibirsk, Tolokonskii worked for a change in tax policy, so that taxes would stay in the city rather than move to the budget of the *oblast'*.[52] He was also rumored to be close to the oligarch Boris Berezovsky, himself an opponent of Putin's.

In the midst of continual conflict between the center and the region, the standard of living of the population in Novosibirsk Oblast declined. In 1995, about 40 percent of the population had an income lower than their cost of living. In 1999, 60 percent of the population was in this position. In the second half of the 1990s, the average wage was 19.4 percent lower and the purchasing power of income was 58.8 percent lower than for Russia as a whole. More than a third of business enterprises in the *oblast'* were unprofitable. Protesting arrears in wages, teachers went on strike in January 1999. In rural areas of the *oblast'*, people also reported declining welfare in the late 1990s.[53]

Likewise, people in Krasnoyarsk Kray reported declining material welfare. Whereas in 1995, 45 percent of the region's residents identified themselves as poor, by 1999 64 percent did. By contrast, 2 percent considered themselves wealthy, up from 1 percent in 1995.[54] Krasnoyarsk Kray was the site of Russia's largest strike of teachers protesting wage arrears in 1999.[55] The economic distress of the majority of residents of Krasnoyarsk contrasts with the wealth of the region as a whole. Krasnoyarsk Kray is one of Russia's richest regions, with huge deposits of minerals, gold, and petroleum; abundant hydroelectric power; and a still-functioning aluminum industry. The region's riches have attracted some of Russia's less savory *biznesmen,* and my tour of the city of Krasnoyarsk included visits to various businesses and homes burned down by the presumed mafia. Krasnoyarsk Kray is the second-largest federal unit in Russia and stretches along the

52. R. F. Turovskii, "Otnosheniia 'tsentr-regiony' v 1997–1998 gg.: Mezhdu konfliktom i konsensusom," *Politiia,* no. 1, issue 7 (1998): 15.

53. Olekh, "Novosibirsk Oblast," 11; Tat'iana Iu. Bogomolova and Vera S. Tapilina, "Mobil'nost' naseleniia po material'nomy polozheniiu: Sub"ektivnyi aspekt," *Sotsiologicheskie issledovaniia,* no. 12 (1998): 28–37.

54. Sergei Vasil'evich Grishaev, "Dinamika sotsial'noi struktury Krasnoiarskogo regiona," *Sotsiologicheskie issledovaniia,* no. 2 (2001): 118. The category *bednye* was not at the bottom of the social spectrum. Another 12 percent identified themselves as *nishchie,* or "destitute," in 1999 (up from 7 percent in 1995). Grishaev defined *poor* to mean being able to buy few things and having hardly enough money for food. The destitute did not have even enough money for food.

55. Viktor Krasnikov, "Krasnoiarskii krai," in *Regiony Rossii v 1999 g,* ed. Nikolai Petrov (Moscow: Gendal'f, 2001), 372.

Yenisei River from the Arctic Ocean south to the Republic of Tyva. It formally includes the Khakasiia Autonomous Republic, the Taimyr Autonmous Okrug, and the Evenk Autonomous Okrug. The two *okrugi* border on the Republic of Sakha (Yakutia), the largest unit in the Russian Federation. Because of the preponderance of defense industries and nuclear reactors, the region was closed to foreigners during the Soviet period. The city of Krasnoyarsk, the largest city in eastern Siberia, had an estimated population of just under nine hundred thousand in 1999. The mayor of Krasnoyarsk when interviews were conducted there was Petr Pimashkov.

Popular dissatisfaction with economic conditions seems to be one of the reasons why Valerii Zubov failed in his effort to be reelected governor of Krasnoyarsk Kray in 1998. Zubov, a university economics professor, had been elected governor in 1993 with more than 70 percent of the popular vote.[56] An economic reformer and supporter of Boris Yeltsin, Zubov proved an ineffectual leader. In 1997, the provincial administration collected less than half the taxes owed and regularly failed to pay wages to public employees.[57] The victor in the 1998 election was Aleksandr Lebed, the former general in the parachute troops who did not deploy his troops against the defenders of the White House in the 1991 coup attempt and who negotiated the end of the first Chechen war. Yeltsin chose Lebed to be his running mate in the second round of the presidential elections of 1996, but Lebed was later fired from Yeltsin's government and seemed to have seen the governorship of one of the richest regions of Russia as a potential stepping-off point for future presidential ambitions.

Lebed's stated positions marked him as no friend to democracy. During the 1996 presidential campaign, he explicitly attacked democracy and praised authoritarian alternatives, particularly the Augusto Pinochet model of economic reform directed from above by a dictator. In terms of the economy, he supported job creation and deficit spending and linked the growth of crime in Russia to privatization. He has also been hostile to the West, criticizing the presence of the North Atlantic Treaty Organization (NATO) in Bosnia and accusing the West of funding the war in Chechnya.

There is some evidence that the population of Krasnoyarsk Kray became gradually more authoritarian in its political orientations during the 1990s.[58]

56. V. G. Sukhovol'skii, "A. Lebed' v Krasnoiarskom krae: Elektoral'nye uspekhi i politicheskie porazheniia," *Politiia*, no. 1, issue 116 (1999): 95.

57. *The Territories of the Russian Federation*, 123.

58. V. G. Nemirovskii, "Sibiriaki: Dinamika Sotsial'no-politicheskikh orientatsii," *Sotsiologicheskiie Issledovanii*, no. 8 (1999): 25–31.

Even so, Lebed's victory may not have been an endorsement of his stated positions. Instead, Lebed seems to have benefited from the economic protest vote. While Zubov won in the city of Krasnoyarsk, Lebed did better in economically depressed regions of the *krai,* including poorer districts of the city of Krasnoyarsk. Lebed was also successful in part because he had substantial support from wealthy sources. In fact, some observers comment that Lebed's lasting legacy may not be his counterdemocratic tendencies but the lesson that big money used well wins elections.[59] Lebed's supporters included oligarch Boris Berezovsky, who apparently was interested in positioning Lebed for a run at the presidency. Another major campaign contributor was Anatolii Bykov, who reportedly used criminal methods, including assassinations of business competitors and government officials, while taking over a large part of the region's aluminum industry. Lebed's alliance with Bykov was short-lived, though, and turned into open conflict when Lebed tried to assert the government's authority over regional economic concerns.[60] After two years of relative prosperity, the regional economy suffered from falling world prices for metals and fell into crisis after Lebed's death in a helicopter crash in April 2002. The highly contested victory in the ensuing gubernatorial elections of Aleksandr Khloponin, director of Norilsk Nickel, seemed to confirm the takeover of the *krai's* government by regional business interests.

Conclusion

The intensive interviews upon which this book is largely based, then, provided the opportunity for Russians from many different backgrounds and many different regions in Russia to speak in their own words. Rather than answering multiple-choice questions, they could speak at length and explain the possible inconsistencies in their ideas. Consequently, they could begin to explain what about democracy is attractive to Russians and what is not, how Russian citizens see their relationship to changing political structures,

59. Laura Belin, "Lebed's Presidential Campaign: His Most Enduring Legacy," *RFE/RL Russian Political Weekly* 2 (29 April 2002); Nikolai Petrov, "Vybory gubernatora Krasnoiarskogo Kraia," in *Regiony Rossii v 1998,* ed. Nikolai Petrov (Moscow: Gendal'f, 1999), 223–32. Lebed's campaign spending is alleged to have far exceeded electoral regulations. See Andrew Yorke, "Business and Politics in Krasnoyarsk *Krai,*" *Europe-Asia Studies* 55, no. 2 (2003): 244.

60. David Satter, *Darkness at Dawn: The Rise of the Russian Criminal State* (New Haven: Yale University Press, 2003), 182–93; Krasnikov, "Krasnoiarskii krai," 368–74; Yorke, "Business and Politics."

and why Russians exhibit the mix of attitudes they do. Whereas standardized surveys break complex ideas into easily manipulated data points, these intensive interviews allowed respondents to present their ideas as a whole. As a result, the interviews can help us begin to make sense of the picture already drawn by the results of mass surveys.

Abstract Notions of Democracy Versus
Current Experiences

The path toward democracy in Russia has been bumpy, and blame for uncertain progress often has been placed on ordinary citizens. Because Russians suffer under the weight of long traditions of authoritarianism, government paternalism, and popular passivity, some observers fear that Russian citizens must not have the right ideas to be democrats. In this chapter, I use evidence from the in-depth interviews with ordinary Russians to begin my analysis of what Russians think about democracy. I start with what they find troubling about their new political institutions and how they think citizens should relate to their government.

The results suggest that Russians are bothered by the ways that existing institutions fail to reflect the views and protect the interests of ordinary citizens, their tendency toward unproductive conflict, and their overcentralization. While many citizens support democratic values, they are less certain that their institutions do the same. But they want to see democratic institutions improved, not dismantled. Thus, there is little evidence of historically rooted cultural antipathy to democratic institutions, and there is much more evidence that people object to problems they see in existing institutions. However, poorly functioning institutions have left their own mark on popular attitudes, and the results may not strengthen democracy overall. Many of my respondents are more interested in beneficial outcomes than in careful attention to democratic processes, more tolerant of effective individuals than of representative bodies, and so disillusioned with the political process that they are unwilling to take action to defend or advance the imperfect democracy they have. Ordinary Russians are quick to criticize the institutions they have, but they may also be slow to change them.

In this chapter, I focus on two sets of attitudes whose significance stems from their importance to democratic theory, their relevance to supposed tendencies in Russian political culture, and the insight they offer into how institutional arrangements affect ordinary people's political values. The first of these subjects concerns what Russians think about political institutions, particularly the representative legislature as a key structure of democracy, but also strong executives, as the most authoritarian element within nominally democratic institutions. The second set of ideas focuses on Russians' conceptions of the role of citizens in relation to those institutions, the expectations of ordinary people in a democracy.

By examining these attitudes, it is possible to assess whether Russian ideas fit badly with democratic institutions or whether Russians think their institutions badly serve democratic values. By rooting Russian popular attitudes in the specific context of the institutions under which Russians live, it becomes clear that at least some of what looks like flawed support for some aspects of democracy can be better understood as a fairly nuanced critique of the flawed operation of those institutions. This, of course, is not to say that ordinary Russians are exemplars of a democratic citizenry or that they have no responsibility for the shortcomings of their present institutions. Russians are more critical of their institutions than they are of themselves. If one of the jobs of democratic citizens is to pressure institutions to serve the public good, it is not clear that Russians are yet up to the task.

The Course of Democratic Change in Russia

The first decade after the collapse of the Soviet Union saw the development in Russia of institutions that mixed democratic and authoritarian elements, with the unsteady support of apparently imperfectly democratic citizens. On the one hand, competitive elections occurred on a regular basis, and both incumbents and the general population abided by their results. Individual freedoms expanded exponentially, and the barriers that had isolated Soviet citizens from the rest of the world dissolved. But at the same time, Russia's new rulers did not always play by the new rules. The first institutions of an independent Russia suffered a fatal stalemate that ended only when Russia's first elected president, Boris Yeltsin, ordered the shelling of the parliament in October 1993. The 1993 constitution failed to create any kind of balance between institutions. The president clearly dominates over the State Duma: he can call for new elections if the Duma refuses his candidate for prime minister three times; he can ignore a single vote of no confidence in the government and can dissolve the Duma if it votes no confidence a second time; and he can make executive decrees with the force of law.[1] Many of the most controversial policies of the Yeltsin regime, in particular the sale of state property and the first war on Chechnya, were conducted largely by executive decree.[2]

Even so, Yeltsin seemed to dislike the few limitations the constitution put on his actions. When it looked as though he might lose his bid for reelection in 1996 because of the severe economic hardships his policies had caused, Yeltsin's administration talked of declaring a state of emergency and calling off the election. Instead, strategic transfers of state assets to certain "oligarchs" with power over the mass media enabled Yeltsin to win.[3] In 1999, Yeltsin resigned in order to give his handpicked successor, Vladimir Putin, all the advantages of incumbency rather than submit Russia to the unpredictability of an unmanaged election. Putin in turn has scared both Russians and Western observers with his talk of strengthening the state and reestablishing order in society. His efforts to muzzle the independent press and silence his political rivals, to bring regional leaders more directly under his authority, and to manage the competition and uncertainty inherent in democracy look uncomfortably like a return to the past.[4]

The popular response to Russia's irregular democracy can best be described as muted. Ordinary Russians have not made much of an effort to push the government to be more accountable to the public or even to follow its own laws. Nor have their electoral choices always encouraged development in a democratic direction. In many local elections and in

---

1. Constitution of the Russian Federation, articles 111, 117, and 90. See also Philip G. Roeder, "Varieties of Post-Soviet Authoritarian Regimes," *Post-Soviet Affairs* 10, no. 1 (1994): 61–101; M. Steven Fish, "The Dynamics of Democratic Erosion," in *Postcommunism and the Theory of Democracy*, ed. Richard D. Anderson Jr., M. Steven Fish, Stephen E. Hanson, and Philip G. Roeder (Princeton: Princeton University Press, 2001), 54–95.

2. Russell Bova, "Political Culture, Authority Patterns, and the Architecture of the New Russian Democracy," in *Can Democracy Take Root in Post-Soviet Russia? Explorations in State-Society Relations*, ed. Harry Eckstein, Frederic J. Fleron Jr., Erik Hoffmann, and William Reisinger (New York: Rowman and Littlefield, 1998), 189. In many respects, Russia is a delegative democracy. See Guillermo O'Donnell, "Delegative Democracy," *Journal of Democracy* 5 (January 1994): 55–69.

3. Peter Reddaway and Dmitri Glinski, *The Tragedy of Russia's Reforms: Market Bolshevism Against Democracy* (Washington, DC: United States Institute of Peace Press, 2001), 477–81.

4. Michael McFaul, Nikolai Petrov, and Andrei Ryabov, *Between Dictatorship and Democracy: Russian Post-Communist Political Reform* (Washington, DC: Carnegie Endowment for International Peace, 2004); Michael McFaul, *Russia's Unfinished Revolution: Political Change from Gorbachev to Putin* (Ithaca: Cornell University Press, 2001), 362–63; Timothy J. Colton and Michael McFaul, *Popular Choice and Managed Democracy: The Russian Elections 1999 and 2000* (Washington, DC: Brookings Institution, 2003), 214–23.

elections to the State Duma throughout the 1990s, significant numbers of Russians chose Communists, near-fascist nationalists, or others of questionable democratic credentials to represent them. Democratic parties fared poorly in many elections, and in the 2003 Duma elections failed to win a single seat. Russians rarely questioned the right of incumbents to manipulate election results.[5] At crisis moments, such as the 1991 showdown between Boris Yeltsin and Communist hard-liners hoping to keep the Soviet empire alive or the 1993 battle between the president and the Supreme Soviet, most Russians stayed home. Although the majority of the population opposed early efforts to subdue rebel Chechnya, after several bombs in public places and private apartment houses in the fall of 1999 many ordinary Russians rallied around the government, parroting the government line that the problem was just a few terrorists acting without support of the Chechen population even as cities were destroyed and the countryside laid waste. That is to say, ordinary Russians have not been especially quick to defend democratic institutions or to force them to work better, nor have they been ready to protect the rights of others in their society, particularly others who are not ethnic Russians.

At the same time, though, in many respects ordinary Russians have acted more or less like the citizens of more established democracies. They have voted in relatively high numbers, and they have countenanced the results of elections even if they did not think much of the people selected. They have made use of their new freedoms to criticize the government. Once Gorbachev loosened up social controls, Russians created the social and political organizations that form the backbone of civil society quickly and in great number even before they were legalized.[6] If anything, Russians have created too many political parties, not too few. Even in highly contentious times during which many people have suffered severe economic hardship and dislocation, public demonstrations have been mostly orderly and citizens have allowed the government ample time to address problems. In short, while Russians may not be perfect democrats, they often act as though they are. As we saw in Chapter 2, in public opinion surveys as in life, Russians demonstrate that they support many democratic values, but

5. Richard Rose and Neil Munro, *Elections Without Order: Russia's Challenge to Vladimir Putin* (New York: Cambridge University Press, 2002); Stephen White, Richard Rose, and Ian McAllister, *How Russia Votes* (Chatham, NJ: Chatham House, 1997).

6. V. N. Berezovskii and N. I. Krotov, *Neformal'naia Rossiia: O neformal'nykh politizirovannykh dvizheniya i gruppakh v RFSFR (opyt spravochnika)* (Moscow: Molodaia Gvardiia, 1990).

not in all contexts, not always in the hard cases, and not necessarily more than other social values, such as order.

Measures of Democracy

In this chapter, I investigate the sources of ordinary Russians' imperfect support for democracy. The intensive interviews are well suited to this project because they allow lines of questioning that are difficult to undertake in standardized surveys. In particular, they allow a different kind of conversation about institutions.

For a number of reasons, support for democracy is tricky to measure. For one thing, the word *democracy* itself is a problem. It refers to an abstract and complicated concept and may have a number of real-world referents. We cannot be certain that both researchers and respondents—or even different respondents—mean the same thing when they talk about "democracy."[7] The distance between possible meanings is probably particularly broad in Russia, since the word *democracy* has been used so loosely there. After all, the Soviet regime presented itself as a "people's" democracy, and the reform period's so-called democrats were more faithful to free markets than to political equality. The result is that it is hard to know what Russians mean when they use the word *democracy*. In their study, for instance, John Dryzek and Leslie Holmes interpret agreement with the statement "Democracy and the situation in Russia in general are a mess" as evidence of authoritarian leanings.[8] But that may be an inaccurate conclusion if by democracy respondents meant the political institutions that existed in 1997, when the study was conducted. To avoid these potential problems, survey questions rarely use the word *democracy*, and if they do, they immediately follow the word with a more specific explanation.[9] Survey questions tend instead to deal specifically with a variety of aspects of democracy, rather than the abstract concept or the specific word.

7. Damarys Canache, Jeffrey J. Mondak, and Mitchell A. Seligson, "Meaning and Measurement in Cross-National Research on Satisfaction with Democracy," *Public Opinion Quarterly* 65, no. 4 (2001): 506–28.

8. John S. Dryzek and Leslie Holmes, *Post-Communist Democratization: Political Discourses Across Thirteen Countries* (New York: Cambridge University Press, 2002), 105.

9. For instance, Stephen Whitefield and Geoffrey Evans asked, "How do you feel about the aim of building democracy in the country, in which political parties compete for government?" Stephen Whitefield and Geoffrey Evans, "Support for Democracy and Political Opposition in Russia, 1993–1995," *Post-Soviet Affairs* 12 (July–September 1996): 218–42.

But what are the important aspects of democracy? Scholars usually think of democracy as having at least three main elements.[10] First, there should be mechanisms for a large proportion of the population to *partici- pate* in the selection of leaders and policies, if not also in more specific decisions. Second, there should be meaningful *competition* between people and groups for those offices. That is to say, it is not enough to offer citizens the opportunity to participate in elections but then refrain from giving them a choice among candidates, as of course was the case in the Soviet Union. Nor is it enough to hold a competition that one side always wins. In a democracy, the hold on power of any individual or group is necessarily uncertain.[11] The third main element in most understandings of democracy is the *protection of civil and political liberties*. Without these protections, it is too dangerous for individuals to freely discuss their preferences with other citizens or work together with them to advance their interests. It is also too dangerous for alternative candidates to put their names forward, since they are more likely to end up in jail than in office.

One can, of course, hold democracy to an even higher standard. David Held has argued, for instance, that it is not enough to provide equal voting rights without also providing "equal rights to enjoy the conditions for effective participation, enlightened understanding and the setting of the political agenda." He concludes that democratic autonomy requires that individuals be "free and equal in the determination of the conditions of their own lives."[12] That is to say, there may be no effective upper limit to the power that democracy implies people should have over their lives. But there is a lower limit. Without inclusive participation, competition for offices, and protections of individual rights, citizens do not have even the possibility of influencing the conditions that affect their lives. Indeed, some definitions set the bar even lower, using elections as the sole criterion of democracy, with little attention to the conditions under which those elec- tions occur.[13] This standard is too low, if by democracy we mean some

10. Georg Sorenson, *Democracy and Democratization* (Boulder, CO: Westview Press, 1993), 13; Robert A. Dahl, *Polyarchy: Participation and Opposition* (New Haven: Yale University Press, 1971), 3–9; Guiseppe Di Palma, *To Craft Democracies: An Essay on Democratic Transitions* (Berkeley and Los Angeles: University of California Press, 1990), 16.

11. Adam Przeworski, "Some Problems in the Study of the Transition to Democracy," in *Transitions from Authoritarian Rule: Comparative Perspectives*, ed. Guillermo O'Donnell, Philippe C. Schmitter, and Laurence Whitehead (Baltimore: Johns Hopkins University Press, 1986).

12. David Held, *Models of Democracy* (Stanford: Stanford University Press, 1987), 285, 290.

13. Joseph A. Schumpeter, *Capitalism, Socialism, and Democracy*, 3d ed. (New York: Harper and Row, 1950).

meaningful power of the part of citizens to affect political decisions and to live securely even when in the minority.

Standardized surveys that focus on democratic values usually ask questions about aspects of political participation, competition, or individual liberty. Questions about the utility of elections, the extent to which individual freedoms should be protected, and whether citizens should be able to influence the decisions made by their leaders are common. Soft questions about democracy—whether people should enjoy individual freedoms or be able to influence decision makers—tend to have high levels of support even in countries, such as Russia, that have had little prior experience of democracy.[14] Consequently, survey questions tend to focus on the hard cases: whether people should have so much freedom that they may harm the community, or whether members of political parties that aim to overthrow democracy should be allowed to take part in elections.[15] Questions such as these are problematic for a number of reasons. For one thing, it is not obvious that the success of democracy depends on whether ordinary citizens understand the hard issues of democratic life. In many working democracies, courts and constitutions—not the will of the majority of citizens—protect the rights of unpopular minorities. Further, such questions may force respondents to make choices between two unpalatable extremes, neither of which reflects the circumstances in which people hope to live.[16]

The difficulty in devising survey questions to measure support for democracy lies in the fact that that the ideas and values that we aim to measure are quite abstract. We want to know whether respondents think that ordinary people should be able to control their lives and the decisions of those who govern them; what the responsibility of the governors is to the governed; whether the difficulties of democracy in practice—delays, confusion, and conflict—are worth the potential benefits. We want to know how respondents think citizens should relate to the state, and vice

14. Timothy J. Colton and Michael McFaul, "Are Russians Undemocratic?" *Carnegie Endowment for International Peace Working Papers,* no. 20 (June 2001), 10.

15. Timothy J. Colton, *Transitional Citizens: Voters and What Influences Them in the New Russia* (Cambridge, MA: Harvard University Press, 2000), 248; Whitefield and Evans, "Support for Democracy."

16. Survey researchers consider forced-choice questions superior to many of the alternatives, particularly to asking respondents whether they agree or disagree with a particular question. Particularly in polite cultures, respondents tend to say they agree. See Debra Javeline, "Response Effects in Polite Cultures: A Test of Acquiescence in Kazakhstan," *Public Opinion Quarterly* 63, no. 1 (1999): 1–28.

versa. We ultimately want to understand what people think about the possibilities of collective action to achieve a communal goal. Unfortunately, problems arise when abstract questions are asked in standardized surveys. For people who do not spend a lot of time thinking systematically about political life, abstract questions are hard to answer. Even if respondents do answer, analysts cannot be certain what respondents have in mind when they answer very abstract questions. Indeed, respondents could have been thinking about very different things from what the people who wrote the survey questions meant to imply. So in public opinion surveys, abstract questions are translated into specific terms. Questions about elections replace more abstract questions about citizen influence over government. Questions about whether extremists should be able to hold open meetings stand in for more abstract questions about the proper limits of liberty in community.

These more specific questions, however, can be misleading. Rather than answering them in terms of what *should* be true in an ideal democracy, respondents may answer in terms of their own experiences. In new democracies, those experiences are often with imperfectly functioning institutions. So, for instance, when respondents are asked to agree or disagree with the statement "Any individual or organization has the right to organize opposition or resistance to any governmental initiative," they might answer in terms of what they think is practically possible in their own country, not according to what democracy requires or what they might personally prefer.[17] When they agree that elections are a waste of money, they may not wish to imply that citizens should give up the option of selecting their leaders. Instead, they may be indicating that the conditions under which elections are held in their country do not actually give people that ability.

The tension between the abstract ideal we want to measure and the concrete referent of the question is particularly strong in questions about

17. This question is from Arthur H. Miller, William M. Reisinger, and Vicki L. Hesli, "Understanding Political Change in Post-Soviet Societies: A Further Commentary on Finifer and Mickiewicz," *American Political Science Review* 90 (March 1996): 153–66. Miller and his colleagues may have intended respondents to focus on whether a "right" to assembly exists, on the logic that democrats would defend the existence of such a right even if the right is denied in practice. In established democracies, or at least in the United States, people might believe rights of assembly and opposition to be inalienable, endowed by their Creator rather than dependent on the will of the governors. In new democracies where exactly these rights were formerly missing, citizens are more likely to imagine that the only rights they effectively have are the ones their governments are willing to recognize.

institutions. A number of institutions are vitally important in a working democracy. For instance, representative legislatures or parliaments hold a particularly central role in democratic theory.[18] Such bodies are best able to represent the various interests and ideas of a diverse public. Hence, they are among the places where the competition between alternative outcomes that is at the heart of democracy becomes most visible. By electing representatives to legislatures, citizens participate indirectly in the choices that will affect their lives. Citizens are also more likely to be able to meet and talk with legislators than with presidents; hence legislatures provide more accessible and more numerous points of access to decision makers. Historically, legislatures have been the source of limitations on the power of kings. They continue to play a key role in limiting executive power and the potential for tyranny.[19] Popular support for democracy, then, necessarily must include support for representative institutions and the way they function. Without representative institutions, it is hard to imagine a democratic system for a reasonably large group.

But how can standardized surveys measure such support? Questions about ways to reconcile competing interests are too abstract. Questions about the institution of the respondent's own experience may, once again, elicit a response that measures satisfaction with that particular and probably imperfect institution, instead of support for the concepts of representation and competition. Similar problems arise with questions about other institutions: courts that may not currently be doing a particularly good job of protecting the rights of citizens, a "free press" that peddles the opinions of its owners, political parties that do not survive from one election to the next. Because of the difficulties involved in asking about institutions, measures of democracy developed in standardized surveys often avoid institutional questions and depend heavily on items related to individual rights, an important aspect of democracy, but far from the only one.

18. For instance, Robert A. Dahl, *Democracy and Its Critics* (New Haven: Yale University Press, 1989), 28–30; Alexander Hamilton, James Madison, and John Jay, *The Federalist Papers* (New York: New American Library, 1961), no. 48; Irving Leonard Markovitz, "Constitutions, the Federalist Papers, and the Transition to Democracy," in *Transitions to Democracy*, ed. Lisa Anderson (New York: Columbia University Press, 1999), 42–71.

19. Jean-Jacques Rousseau, *The Social Contract and Discourses* [1762], trans. G. D. H. Cole (repr., London: J. M Dent and Sons, Everyman's Library, 1973); Charles Montesquieu, *The Spirit of the Laws* (Birmingham, AL: Legal Classics Library, 1984); Matthew Soberg Shugart and John Carey, "Presidents and Assemblies," in *The Democracy Sourcebook*, ed. Robert A. Dahl, Ian Shapiro, and Jose Antonio Cheibub (Cambridge, MA: MIT Press, 2003), 272–76; Dahl, *Polyarchy*.

The open-ended nature of intensive interviews addresses some of these problems. In the more normal conversational context of intensive interviews, respondents can explain what democracy means to them. In intensive interviews, it is possible to ask forced-choice questions without forcing respondents to actually make a choice. Respondents can explain their reasoning and their difficulties in placing themselves between alternatives. In an ongoing conversation, it also is possible to talk both about specific institutions and about the abstract principles that underlie those institutions. It is clearer which of those things the respondent is thinking about when making specific remarks. It is possible to proceed naturally from the institutions of the respondent's own experience to institutions that might exist under more ideal conditions. The fact that these complex ideas do not need to be broken down into short and easily understood questions allows for a greater focus on institutional aspects of democracy than is usually the case in standardized surveys.

Representative Institutions

Although theoretical treatments consistently place representative institutions among the most important in a working democracy, the representative institution fits uneasily with standard descriptions of Russian political culture. Nearly all discussions of Russian political culture argue that Russians, culturally or traditionally, do not like political arrangements that divide up power and introduce too much conflict. Some scholars point to the Slavophile notion of *sobornost'*, a supposed symphonic unity in which the diversity of individual concerns is resolved in a harmonious whole.[20] *Sobornost'* contains no recognition of competing interests, no concept that the goods individuals pursue might be varied and might conflict. Others point to autocratic tendencies in Russian political thinking. Edward Keenan, for instance, has argued that the difficult conditions in Russia—from the huge size of the country to its challenging weather to the prevalence of human-eating wolves—made the creation of any kind of political order difficult.[21] The solution was to concentrate authority as a bulwark against encroaching chaos. Whereas representative institutions might have other virtues, their tendency toward endless debate and decisions that change with shifting

20. Tim McDaniel, *The Agony of the Russian Idea* (Princeton: Princeton University Press, 1996), 32–46; Victor Sergeyev and Nikolai Biriukov, *Russia's Road to Democracy: Parliament, Communism, and Traditional Culture* (Brookfield, VT: Edward Elgar/Ashgate, 1993), 22–34.
21. Edward L. Keenan, "Muscovite Political Folkways," *Russian Review* 45 (April 1986): 115–81.

majorities were deemed too risky for Russian conditions. According to Keenan, it seemed safer to concentrate authority in relatively few hands. Leonid Gozman and Alexander Etkind argued that Russian discomfort with differences of opinion had more proximate causes: under Soviet rule, Russians lacked knowledge about lifestyles other than their own, had little experience making independent decisions or choices between two views that were both presented as correct, and had been educated in schools that suppressed any kind of difference.[22]

In any case, concentrated authority certainly describes the institutions that Russia has endured, not only in the fifteenth century that Keenan described but also under both the czars and the commissars. It is often assumed that the concerns that made their forebears reluctant to disperse authority still weigh heavily on Russians today. For instance, Yuri Zarakhovich has argued, "Every nation has the leaders it deserves, but I have the uneasy feeling that we have the leaders we want. . . . If our leaders are liars, it is because we the people take lying for granted. . . . If our leaders are oppressive, it is because too many people in this country are wailing for the *khozyain,* the autocratic boss."[23] Indeed, considerable survey research has shown that most Russians did not trust the old Supreme Soviet, and they do not think more highly of the State Duma that replaced it.[24]

In this section, I try to determine whether Russian reactions to representative institutions are the result of cultural preferences for less democratic alternatives or, alternatively, are produced by dissatisfaction with the way actual institutions function. If cultural preferences are key, then we would expect as much criticism of democratic ideals in the abstract as of operating institutions. We would expect Russians to advocate replacing representative institutions with something more autocratic, with fewer limits on executive authority and less room for the compromise and conflict inherent in democracy. Alternately, if the dissatisfaction of ordinary Russians stems from the failure of new political institutions to function democratically, then the criticisms should focus on those failures, the alternative offered should aim to move the institutions closer to a democratic ideal, and cynicism

22. Leonid Gozman and Alexander Etkind, *The Psychology of Post-totalitarianism in Russia* (London: Centre for Research into Communist Economies, 1992), 83–85.

23. Yuri Zarakhovich, "Viewpoint: A Russian's Lament," *Time,* 21 September 1998, 76.

24. Richard Rose, "Postcommunism and the Problem of Trust," *Journal of Democracy* (1994) 5 (July): 18–30; Richard Rose and Doh Chull Shin, "Democratization Backwards: The Problem of Third-Wave Democracies," *British Journal of Political Science* (2001) 31: 331–54; VTSIOM, "Informatsiia: Resul'taty oprosov," *Monitoring obshchestvennoe mneniia: Informatsiia analiz,* no. 1, issue 51 (2001): 67.

should not extend much past the institutions themselves. Specifically, we would expect people to continue to support democracy in the abstract even as they criticize it in practice.

Few of my respondents had anything good to say about the State Duma. A couple compared it to a television soap opera or a puppet theater. They echoed Lenin's famous critique of "bourgeois" parliamentarianism in accusing Duma deputies of talking a lot but accomplishing little. Those who were more satisfied with the Duma were either largely satisfied with their material situation (the deputies must be doing something right) or more explicitly aware of the role of a representative legislature in balancing the power of the executive. When respondents were asked to define democracy, few volunteered answers that noted the importance of the legislature as a representative of the variety of popular ideas.

Still, my interviewees' complaints about representative bodies were clearly aimed at their own legislative body and not legislatures in general. For instance, the respondents who were most critical of the State Duma wondered not only whether deputies wasted too much time in the making of decisions, but also whether they reached any decisions at all. They complained about the slowness with which deputies were filling the large holes left in the legal codex by the collapse of Communism. Ruslan, a skilled worker in Moscow, remarked, "The Duma pays too much attention to their own affairs, their friends, and very little to law. They need to make us laws. Now, unfortunately, several years have passed, but we still don't have normal laws. Structures have changed in general, but we still live under the old laws."[25] Five years later, Dima, a local government official, allowed that some decent laws had been adopted but still felt that deputies

25. All respondent names are pseudonyms. To help readers keep track of the respondents, candidates were given different kinds of names depending on their age. Respondents up through thirty years of age were given diminutive names (ending in –ya for women and –a or –ya for males). Respondents over sixty years old were assigned not only a first name but also a patronymic, since people in that age range are more commonly addressed with such respectful politeness. To make it harder to identify individual respondents, I identify the interviewees only as being residents of Moscow, of Moscow Oblast, of Siberia (Krasnoyarsk, Novosibirsk, Elita), or of European Russia (Smolensk, Ulyanovsk, and Voronezh). See Appendix A for demographic characteristics of the respondents.

A word on quotations: All quotations are direct translations from the taped interviews. In translating, I attempted to re-create the original idea in conversational English, which, given the peculiarities of conversational Russian, meant changing word order and sometimes sentence structure as well. I did not attempt to capture every oral hesitation, and I have sometimes smoothed disjointed phrases into a more grammatical form. I also add words in the English translation where the exactness of Russian grammar permitted conveying more meaning than did the directly equivalent English. Occasionally, I have turned partial responses into complete "should provide more attention to legislation than to conjecture that does not influence—as they say—that contains no concrete levers to impact the situation. That is, it is only declaratory statements, with nothing behind them, in general, that affect nothing, but only provoke political games in society." Some of the most politically aware respondents observed that the Duma sometimes made perfectly good laws but did not bother to provide the financing necessary to implement them.

Aside from the tendency for talk to outweigh action, much of what the respondents disliked about the Duma were not features inherent in its nature as a representative institution. Rather, they thought that the Duma failed to function as a representative institution should: to serve the public interest, represent the will of the majority, and provide opportunities for ordinary people to have an impact on decisions. Alla, an economist, said of the deputies, "They don't defend the interests of the people. They don't know how to talk with the people; they don't know how to conduct a dialogue. . . . They are independent from the people." In mass surveys, few Russians identify their government as democratic, and my respondents were the same.[26] Apparently, my respondents' distain for the Duma was linked to its failure to perform as a democratic institution.

Perhaps the most common complaint about the Duma was that it was full of self-interested, self-serving individuals; Tatiana Mikhailovna commented that the Duma functioned as a "feeding trough" for people trying to grab public goods for themselves. Like many others, Boris Borisovich called the deputies mercenaries. He said, "The Duma has divided itself into party factions, but the thing is that they're not parties. They're gangs of swindlers pursuing only their private, mercenary interests, which push necessary public activities into the background." Lev observed simply, "Well, you choose a deputy at the elections, but then he only enjoys his own benefits." These findings echo the results of mass surveys conducted at about the same time as the interviews: substantial majorities report that, in their opinion, the Russian government is corrupt at all levels.[27]

---

sentences, adding in enough of the question to make the response have meaning by itself. Ellipses indicate excerpts, not conversational pauses.

26. In a ROMIR poll conducted in September 2000, Natal'ia Laidinen found that 6.5 percent of respondents fully agreed that Russia was a democratic country; another 21.3 percent agreed somewhat. Natal'ia Valer'evna Laidinen, "Obraz Rossii v zerkale Rossiiskogo obshchestvennogo mneniia," *Sotsiologicheskie issledovaniia,* no. 4 (2001): 28.

27. Laidinen, "Obraz Rossii v zerkale Rossiiskogo obshchestvennogo mneniia," 29; Leontii Georgievich Byzov, "Pervye kontury 'postperekhodnoi epokhi,'" *Sotsiologicheskie issledovaniia,* no. 4 (2001): 8.

Other respondents were startled by the Duma's incompetence. Zinaida, a worker in a disintegrating aviation factory, said: "It's a peasant women's bazaar. I am simply amazed that it is possible for people with higher education to sink so low. They don't have any concrete suggestions. . . . It is staggering, honestly staggering. Is it possible that people with advanced economic, political, humanitarian educations cannot develop an understanding? Each of them has a home, right? They have families. They have a family budget. Do they organize their family budgets like they run the country?"

At the same time that many of my respondents wished that Duma deputies did a better job representing the public, they also worried that there was too much conflict in the Duma, that the deputies were too much immersed in politics and too little involved in the purer business of writing law. That the writing of law might require hashing out conflicting interests, that it was a political and not just a technical process, was not something all my interviewees recognized. Tolya, for instance, complained about lobbyists who pushed the Duma to pass laws they favored. He said, "I consider that laws should be made in the interests of the whole society, of all people, and not in the interests of a particular group or some kind of oligarchic formation." While Tolya's apprehensiveness about laws favoring the wealthy is understandable, he did not temper his criticisms of the Duma with any appreciation of the fact that the interests of "the whole society, of all people" may be hard to identify, never mind satisfy all at once.

Others suggested that the deputies should simply write laws and not try to call the government or president to account for various policies, or they recommended that the deputies stay out of "political" issues not of their concern, such as the war in Chechnya. Aleksandra Antonovna, a retired government bureaucrat, commented, "It seems to me that the Duma has not yet learned how to act. There is too much emotion. I would prefer that they really did more work there. It needs to create a base of laws. That's all very undeveloped in Russia. It's necessary to create all that and not to occupy themselves with any political things." Respondents interviewed during the Yeltsin years were concerned that there was too much conflict between the Duma and the president and wished that the leaders of the Duma more readily recognized their proper role of "helping" the president.

People who were fonder of Yeltsin's policies in 1998 were more likely to see the Duma as an unwelcome brake on forward progress; those who disliked Yeltsin's policies were occasionally less unhappy with the Duma, though they were dissatisfied with the Duma's inability to hold Yeltsin to account. Although conflict between the president and the Duma diminished during the Putin years, complaints about the Duma did not. Instead, they shifted focus. Respondents interviewed in 2003 were more likely to complain that the Duma was overly servile, too ready to compromise with the president or wealthy constituents, too little independent.

There was little recognition that the Duma enjoys few constitutional powers and consequently is dependent on the will of the president. In fact, one respondent commented that the Duma did not need any power to write laws, which after all was its "proper" function. Since the 1998 interviews took place during or immediately after the period when Yeltsin threatened to call for new Duma elections if the deputies failed to approve Sergei Kirienko as prime minister, it is perhaps surprising that more people did not recognize the constitutional vulnerability of the Duma, its inability to effectively challenge the president on personnel or policy issues. A few people did comment that perhaps they did not have enough information to judge the day-to-day activities of the Duma. If they knew more, they might appreciate its work more fully.

Despite their complaints about their own Duma and despite a limited understanding of the various roles parliaments play, my respondents were largely agreed that the Duma or some body like it continue to exist. There were exceptions. Vladimir Il'ich, an elderly man from Moscow Oblast, defined democracy as "demonstrations by idlers" and decreed the Duma a useless weight on the backs of the pensioners and the nation. He was also largely satisfied with Yeltsin and therefore less likely in general to welcome the balancing role of the Duma. Some of the respondents who noted the ineffectiveness of the Duma also remarked that its absence would hardly be missed. People who were dissatisfied with the Duma did mention that all would be fine if better people were elected into office, but most were ready to countenance the existence of the Duma in any form. In fact, when pushed to try to explain *why* an institution such as the Duma should exist, many even got to the point of arguing that a parliament is necessary to balance the power of the president and to represent the diversity of Russia's regions and peoples in a way no single individual can.[28] Arkadii, a Siberian academic, commented, "There are people in the Duma who oppose the president, don't give him full power. In that sense,

---

28. By contrast, many respondents were more willing to see city dumas abolished, at least in smaller cities where it was not obvious to them that there were conflicting interests that needed to be represented.

I'm happy with the Duma. That it is some kind of counterweight to the president." Lev, a factory worker, said more simply, "If there was no Duma, as they say, we would have a dictatorship. The president alone would be like a dictator." Other respondents thought that the representative nature of the Duma brought government closer to the population. Vasya said, "The Duma is needed in any case because it is the connecting link between the summit of power and those below."

In sum, my interviewees had a fairly conflicted view of the State Duma and through it of representative institutions in general. And that conflict was not especially between different individuals but rather within each person. Almost everyone complained about some aspect of the Duma's work—or what most perceived as its lack of work—and yet almost everyone could articulate a reason why the Duma should exist. In articulating those reasons, respondents often displayed a more nuanced understanding of the role of representative institutions in a democracy than they had tended to at the beginning of the conversation. Certainly, many respondents had an oversimplified view of the ease with which laws agreeable to all can be written and conflicting interests can be defended, but in this way they are certainly not culturally unique.

This is a place where it can be useful to compare the Russian respondents to Americans. Without some point of comparison, it is hard to know whether Russians are unusual in their discomfort with some of the conflict inherent in representative institutions, or whether this is a trait they share even with citizens of stable democracies. As it turns out, Americans do not seem to be much more tolerant of political conflict than were the Russian respondents. They do not like democratic procedures any more than the Russians did. Americans tend to be hostile to Congress, to see its work as inefficient and unnecessarily conflictive. They seem to believe that citizens agree; it is just government officials who introduce clashing interests.[29]

My own American respondents complained about the partisanship of Congress, of the "bickering and holding out," and of the tendency for representatives to focus a great deal of attention on matters that apparently did not much affect the citizens of the country. Not unlike the Russian respondents, they thought their representatives served their parties and

29. John R. Hibbing and Elizabeth Theiss-Morse, *Congress as Public Enemy: Public Attitudes Toward American Political Institutions* (New York: Cambridge University Press, 1995); John R. Hibbing and Elizabeth Theiss-Morse, "Democrats or Anti-Democrats? Americans' Preferences for Governmental Processes," paper presented at the annual meeting of the Midwest Political Science Association, Chicago, April 1999.

the interests of wealthy lobbyists instead of trying to reflect the views of constituents. Caroline asked, "Is any member of Congress really interested in the people they represent? Or do they worry about the chess game they play?" More so than the Russian respondents, though, the Americans tended to see Congress through their own partisan eyes. Democrats complained about the Republicans; Republicans complained about the Democrats. And in the process, the institution itself seemed a bit less at fault. Bill concluded, "Congress I trust. A lone Congressman maybe not so much, but Congress as a whole, I trust them. I think in Congress there're checks and balances. People kind of set each other off. I think in the long run you're going to get the best side of people." In any event, nearly all the American respondents could clearly articulate the vital role a representative legislature plays in a democratic system and, hence, they saw the institution as essential. Much more than the Russians, they understood that the relationship between legislatures and executives is often conflictive, and that conflict can serve the interests of ordinary people.

Overall, the reasons for my Russian respondents' unhappiness with the Duma seem to stem somewhat from inexperience and the failure, so far, of public education to instill understanding of the iconic principle of checks and balances. More than that, though, the source of difficulty seems to be the Duma's failure to adequately represent ordinary people, not cultural preferences to avoid the disorder of representative institutions. As Misha summarized, "In the ideal, the Duma as it should be should limit the cabinet, the president, and act in defense of the interests of the nation. But so far this is not what we have." But tolerance of the kind of disorder inherent in representative institutions was not without limit. My Russian respondents wanted concrete accomplishments from their Duma: they wanted to know the laws that would govern their new society. If the Duma could not fulfill this direct duty, some of my Russian respondents saw little reason for its continued existence.

Wailing for the *Khoziain*?

In any case, the predictions of the political culture school are not only that Russians are unsympathetic to representative institutions, but also that they prefer strong centralized power. How then do ordinary people respond to Russia's constitutionally powerful president? Here, the fact that interviews were conducted in Russia at three different points in time is useful. The 1998 interviews were conducted near the end of Yeltsin's time in office, after he had been president for almost seven years. The 2000 interviews occurred while Vladimir Putin held the title of acting president, between his temporary appointment by Yeltsin and the March elections. The 2003 interviews took place after Putin had held the presidency for more than three years, giving people ample time to form an assessment of him.

Near the end of his time in that office, Yeltsin had more fans than the State Duma, but not many more. Those who spoke well of Yeltsin tended to be among the strongest supporters of the marketization of the Russian economy. They were willing to overlook Yeltsin's shortcomings because of the importance of his goals. Kolya, a young worker in the south of Russia, commented, "So, personally, I think Yeltsin certainly made mistakes. No one is perfect, and of course there are going to be mistakes. . . . Sooner or later, there will be blunders, but in my opinion the policies are correct." Many people were generally positive about Yeltsin's early years and his efforts to make Russians freer, but they had many complaints about the later years of his regime. Yeltsin's economic policies came in for much criticism, often on the argument that it could not be in the majority's interests to have factories standing idle while a small group close to government and the old power structure grabbed what they could.

More to the point of the present discussion, most of the respondents who were unhappy with Yeltsin criticized what they perceived as Yeltsin's autocratic behavior. Slava, an unemployed young man in Moscow who was generally sympathetic to Yeltsin, remarked that Yeltsin "conducts such hard politics. He doesn't bargain with anyone, not with the deputies. Even all the TV broadcasts remark on that." Nikolai, a less friendly reviewer, said of Yeltsin, "He's deceitful, he's unpredictable. He's a petty tyrant—there is such a word *samodur*. He doesn't obey even those laws that he establishes." Others likened Yeltsin's leadership style to that of a senior Communist Party official. In particular, they thought he made decisions without any discussion. Focusing on the topic of Kirienko's appointment as prime minister, a number of the 1998 interviewees remarked that Yeltsin did not even think that he had to explain to the Duma deputies why Kirienko was good candidate, a legitimate question given Kirienko's youth and rapid elevation from relative obscurity. Anna Pavlovna, an elderly woman in Moscow Oblast, commented, "[Yeltsin] conducts himself so tactlessly. . . . He said, 'I say Kirienko—and that's all! There is nothing else!'. . . If I were president, I would go to the Duma and discuss, well, my reasons for supporting Kirienko."

In form reminiscent of traditional peasant views of the czar, some blamed Yeltsin less than the circle around him. Many of the 1998 respondents felt that Yeltsin was too sick to work effectively and consequently had slipped out of touch with the people. But only one respondent criticized Yeltsin for too weak leadership at a time when conditions demanded decisive action. Iosif said, "Yeltsin has a great deal of authority. He has many powers. But he displays passivity in the conduct of decisive policies, which are necessary for Russia in this transition period. Therefore Russia is losing time, and the Russian people are losing faith in democracy. As a result, the leadership of Yeltsin is dangerous for democracy." But even this respondent's concern was that Yeltsin's government was too weak to control corruption or to defend the interests of citizens. Despite a positive reference to Stalin at one point, he was not advocating the kind of strong leadership that would take away the democratic rights that were widely seen as the singular accomplishment of Yeltsin's years in power.

In their evaluations of Yeltsin, then, my interviewees do not look like reflexive authoritarians. They criticize both Yeltsin's autocratic behavior and the unpopular policies his powers permitted him to establish. What they liked best about Yeltsin were the ways individual freedoms expanded under his leadership. The Western press tended to present Yeltsin's successor, Vladimir Putin, as cut from a more authoritarian cloth than Yeltsin, since he was a former KGB agent and the prosecutor of a brutal war in Chechnya. Did Putin's relative popularity stem from those traits?

The February 2000 respondents tended to agree that Putin was different from Yeltsin, but the traits they stressed were his energy, vitality, youth, education, experience, and decisiveness. A member of a work collective interviewed as a group liked the fact that Putin was capable of putting more than two words together, whereas Yeltsin was regularly caricatured as speaking in one-word sentences. Svetlana, a member of the Moscow intelligentsia, liked the way Putin handled the press, argumentative but unflappable. A number complimented his human touch in interpersonal relations, as displayed in numerous television appearances prior to the 2000 election. Gennadii, who expected to vote "against all" in the then upcoming election, criticized Putin for his lack of an authoritarian image. He said, "Putin doesn't fit the image of a Russian ruler. . . . Despite all his flaws, Yeltsin better fit the monarchical aspect of Russian leaders."

Gennadii also wondered whether Putin was trying to construct a tougher political image as a fighter against terrorism through the war in Chechnya. Respondents who were more sympathetic to Putin, however, tended to see the war as a necessarily evil, even a humanitarian act comparable to the NATO intervention in the former Yugoslavia. Scared by terrorist acts in the heart of Russia and what they saw as criminal disorder in Chechnya itself, they thought that Putin had at least conducted an unhappy war well, setting goals, taking responsibility, and moving from chaos toward something that might one day be peace. Galina Grigor'evna, an elderly women who had lived though her city's occupation by the Nazis during World War II, remarked: "I am satisfied with his decisiveness and courage. Why? Because where others started in Chechnya and then threw it off, afraid, he bravely went to it. He took it upon himself, young, energetic, and said, 'I will go to the end. There. That's how it will be.' Everyone says that Stalin was such an old so-and-so, but under him we lived without being afraid of anything. We were under a kind of large defense. I would hope Putin will be like that."

There was a longing in many of the early comments on Putin, a hope that he would prove a better president than Yeltsin, listen to people, fight corruption, and improve the economy. But the expectations were muted. In 2000, my interviewees did not anticipate that Putin would transform Russia or their own lives, much as they might have wanted him to. Their tolerance for actions that abridged other people's rights, such as the Chechen war or memories of Stalin's umbrella of safety, might be taken as a readiness to follow a strong leader away from democracy. But most respondents did not think Putin was an autocrat or a savior, just a competent man with a sense of responsibility toward his people. That seems to be what appealed to them. This interpretation is borne out by national surveys. In 1998, while Yeltsin was still president, a majority of respondents thought Russia was headed toward a dead end. But by 2001, after a year with Putin, a majority considered that Russia's path was likely to lead to positive results.[30]

By 2003, Russians had had quite a bit of experience with Putin. They had watched as he arrested oligarchs, tried to bring regional leaders under central control, and built up a commanding power base at the center of Russia's political spectrum. Did they see him as a potential dictator and, more important, approve of that potential? By 2003, many respondents were somewhat less hopeful about what Putin could do for them. Some felt Putin had not fully lived up to his potential and that the lives of ordinary

---

30. M. K. Gorshkov, *Rossiiskoe obshchestvo v usloviiakh transformatsii: Mify i real'nost' (Sotsiologicheskii analiz)* (Moscow: ROSSPEN, 2003), 413.

people had not improved enough under his reign. As Sofiia succinctly said, "Putin doesn't do enough. That's clear from how people live." Svetlana, who was interviewed in all three years, had been quite a supporter of Putin's in 2000 but by 2003 no longer thought that he was really in control of the government; rather, she felt he was acting on the orders of others. On the whole, respondents were more likely to criticize Putin for being ineffectual and too soft than for any authoritarian leanings. Like that held by people interviewed earlier, their image of Putin was still of an energetic and intelligent man, not a dictator. Comparing Putin to Yeltsin, Tolya said, "I like Putin more. First, without doubt he is an educated person, erudite. A sportsman. He always thinks sensibly, argues reasonably. I am never ashamed of him when he participates in some kind of international arrangements, whether he receives an international delegation or participates himself in a visit. In general, I consider that today Vladimir Putin is the optimal head of government." Some of the respondents would have been willing to give Putin even more power than he enjoyed under Russia's permissive constitution, but that was less because they wanted an autocratic government than because they trusted Putin's intentions—and his goodwill for Russia—more than they trusted either the circle around him or the deputies of the Duma.

There was another energetic leader who pleased the Moscow respondents: Mayor Yurii Luzhkov.[31] While they varied in their level of enthusiasm, all Muscovites had at least some good things to say about Luzhkov. Some were positively effusive. Ekaterina, a materially comfortable woman, remarked, "I adore him! There are not words to say how I love him. . . . There's no need to change anything about him. He is splendid, our mayor!" Like Robert Lane's men of Eastport, Muscovites credited their mayor with apparently trivial accomplishments. Many mentioned that Luzhkov had repaired streets and cleaned up the city; pensioners were grateful that he had found a way to supplement their pensions from the city coffers. In other words, where federal authorities were credited mostly with creating harm, Luzhkov was seen to accomplish things of palpable use to most Muscovites. For that reason and not because of particularly democratic procedures, most Muscovites were willing to credit him with working in the interests of the majority.

---

31. Except in Voronezh, where the water supply is erratic, interviewees outside Moscow tended to have better things to say about their mayors than they did about Yeltsin, but the contrast was not nearly as sharp as for Luzhkov.

Many of the interviewees also praised Luzhkov's manner, proclaiming it energetic, businesslike, and effective. A number called him the good *khoziain* for whom Russians are presumed to be looking, although their meaning seemed to be more that he was a good manager.[32] There also were criticisms. Some of the respondents pointed to projects that cost a great deal of money and did not seem to directly benefit residents of Moscow. Boris Borisovich commented: "I don't like his unilateral decisions on various questions that should be decided by the population, particularly the construction of the cathedral, the monument to Peter, and similar questions." A few respondents remarked that nothing, not even mass demonstrations, would change Luzhkov's mind once he decided what he wanted. On the whole, though, it is hard to imagine a group of people more satisfied by their government than my Moscow respondents were with Yurii Luzhkov.

Being satisfied with an energetic manager in a city with a good tax base, though, is not the same as wanting to be delivered from the messiness of democracy by an authoritarian leader who will whip the city into shape against its will. The Moscow sample was impressed with Luzhkov not merely because he was decisive and got things done, but because he got done the things *they* thought needed to be done, one very large cathedral and an ugly monument to Peter I possibly aside. The interviewees who liked Luzhkov were convinced not only that Luzhkov was working in the interests of the majority of Muscovites—whether he intended to or not—but they were also more likely to think that local government was comparatively open to their influence. For many, the way they could tell that they had influence was that things worked in the city the way they wanted them to. Iurii remarked, "But, really, the need to influence city government does not arise. It's as if we had a *dvornik*. How does the *dvornik* work? She works well when things are clean. This means the duma works well. . . . The snow is cleared from the streets."[33] Others remarked on the opinion polls that were conducted by the mayor's office and the fact that local officials were relatively more accessible than national-level officials, though nobody in the sample had tried to contact them.

32. *Khoziain* can mean "master," "manager," or "host." When my respondents wanted to convey a more authoritarian relationship, they tended to use *barin*. This word was used regularly in talking about authorities in the abstract, but not about Luzhkov.

33. A *dvornik* is a person whose job is to keep sidewalks around buildings clean and clear of snow and otherwise manage public spaces.

No matter how much people liked Mayor Luzhkov, few wanted to give him any more power, and most were unwilling to let him run the city without the city duma, even though they had little idea what the city duma did. Ruslan remarked, "Well, my view is that the city duma is necessary in order generally to have some control over the mayor." That is to say, Muscovites were happy to support an effective and decisive leader, and in that sense they favor "strong" leaders. But they were not willing to let even a popular leader rule the city single-handedly. And they had no intention of sacrificing either their freedom or their influence over government just because they had an effective leader. Nikolai noted, "The mayor's power should be under controls because someone else might come to office later who will do what he wants and make a mess. And again it will be impossible to change anything, like with Yeltsin."

In sum, it is clear that my Russian interviewees tend to respect effective leadership. They think that the State Duma has failed to accomplish much, and as a result popular support for it is limited. Putin and Luzhkov are credited with being relatively effective. In this way, the Russian interviewees are very similar to the Americans. My American respondents were more likely to express satisfaction with the president, even presidents from parties they did not normally support, if they could identify a useful accomplishment: a war on terrorism or a flourishing economy. That Russians praise effective leaders does not indicate that they are craving an autocratic boss who will take away their newly found freedoms. For many of them, the "order" they want seems to be that the snow is cleared off the streets and the potholes repaired. Few were waiting for a man on a white horse to save the country in ways the country did not chose for itself to be saved. It emerged in interview after interview that many Russians were waiting for leaders who were competent, intelligent, professional, honest, businesslike, and respectable. It also emerged again and again that, as far as my Russians interviewees were concerned, they mostly did not yet have these leaders. As Grigorii remarked, "Here, it is like another planet."

From the perspective of what Russians expect of their institutions, then, the problem appears to be less a set of culturally skewed expectations than a set of institutions and incumbents that, so far, have mostly failed to fulfill a reasonable desire for a predictable environment. That desire for predictability and a tendency to value outcomes over procedures, however, could undermine democratic institutions in certain circumstances. If an effective politician delivered many of the things that people want, satisfied

Russians could well ignore any compromises of democratic procedures it may have taken to produce tangible achievements. Indeed, given that Russian knowledge of the ordinary procedures of democracy is somewhat underdeveloped, many citizens might not even notice that compromises had occurred. Here again, though, it is not obvious that Russians are worlds away from Americans, who were apparently ready enough to sacrifice some civil liberties to George W. Bush's war on terror.

Individuals and the State

The Russians in my sample were largely disappointed with the accomplishments of those who govern them, but what do Russians expect of themselves? Democratic theory does not tend to presume that democratic institutions stand by themselves. In an idealized participatory democracy, citizens are supposed to care enough to devote considerable time to discussion of public problems.[34] Similarly, a vital civil society can be a key force in adjusting the behavior of errant institutions and elites.[35] Even in the less extensive liberal model of democracy, citizens must respect the laws that will leave them secure enough from others that they can pursue their own private interests.[36] In a democracy, law is the vehicle through which rights are protected, government institutions are kept within bounds, and the majority will is made the rule for all. By contrast, less democratic societies are more likely to rely on forced submission to whatever the autocrat decrees, instead of voluntary obedience to a rule presumed to be just. Russians are ready enough to complain about shortcomings in their political institutions. But are they ready themselves to act in ways that would sustain or improve those institutions?

Those who assert a distinctive Russian political culture would say no. Keenan, for instance, argued that Russians rely on external authority to control society because of a cultural belief that individuals cannot be relied on to control themselves: if people will not voluntarily play by the

34. Benjamin Barber, *Strong Democracy: Participatory Politics for a New Age* (Berkeley and Los Angeles: University of California Press, 1984).

35. John Keane, *Democracy and Civil Society: On the Predicaments of European Socialism, the Prospects for Democracy, and the Problem of Controlling Social and Political Power* (London: Verso, 1988).

36. George H. Sabine, "The Two Democratic Traditions," *Philosophical Review* 61 (October 1952): 451–74.

rules, they must be kept in line by force.[37] That Russia missed being incorporated into the Roman Empire is thought to mean that Russians never developed a clear sense of the power of law to regulate social relations.[38] Russians are presumed to be cynical and indifferent to law and too passive to take action to defend their rights.[39]

Some of my educated respondents echoed these concerns. Tatiana Mikhailovna, a former librarian said, "But maybe our institutions can't work the same as everyone else's. All Western countries came out of the tradition of Roman law, the laws of the Roman Empire. And all of them are extremely law abiding. But we, excuse me, are never going to wait for a green light when there is not one car on the road. We have our own heads. No cars—what in the devil am I waiting for? Naturally, I'm going to cross the street. Therefore laws aren't all that important for us. To produce and observe laws—it's just another culture. Like cockroaches, we try to creep away to some chink where the law won't reach us." She went on to argue that the creation of the kinds of internal limits that would lead people to obey laws "is probably the spiritual work for several generations." Others among the well-educated interviewees also bemoaned the low level of "culture" in the common people (*narod*), presumably not among themselves personally. That well-educated Russians complain about the same deficiencies in Russian political culture that some specialists do, though, does not mean that those deficiencies actually exist. Do the interviews show that Russians are ready to obey laws established by representative institutions and to try to hold their government to account?

There are some indications in the interviews that Russians do not have a lot of confidence in the power of law. Many thought it would make more of a difference to have better *people* in office than to have better laws. A surprising number thought that there was no way laws could control corruption. They were not all convinced that people should pay the

37. Keenan, "Muscovite Political Folkways."

38. Andrzej Walicki, *A History of Russian Thought: From the Enlightenment to Marxism*, trans. Hilda Andrews-Rusiecka (Stanford: Stanford University Press, 1979).

39. Frederic J. Fleron Jr., "Congruence Theory Applied: Democratization in Russia," in *Can Democracy Take Root in Post-Soviet Russia? Explorations in State-Society Relations*, ed. Harry Eckstein, Frederic J. Fleron Jr., Erik Hoffmann, and William Reisinger (New York: Rowman and Littlefield, 1998), 36; Zinaida T. Golenkova, Viktor V. Vitiuk, Iurii V. Gridchin, Alla I. Chernykh, and Larisa M. Romanenko, "Stanovlenie grazhdanskogo obshchestva i sotsial'naia stratifikatsiia," *Sotsiologicheskie issledovaniia*, no. 6 (1995): 14–24. Also published in *Sociological Research* 35 (March–April 1996): 6–22.

taxes the law prescribed, especially when it came to taxes on small businesses, which were widely perceived as being too high. Some of the reluctance to rely on law, however, was based in a reluctance to rely on the enforcers of law. That is to say, once again, the problem was the form institutions took in Russia, not the abstract idea of what the institutions were supposed to accomplish.

Many people were highly unsatisfied with the police. They considered them corrupt and unprofessional, people you would not want to meet on a dark street. Nikolai commented, "The police have a lot of power, but they use it for their own ends. Their own mercenary ends, you could say. That is, they are simply some kind of large gang, an official gang. That's all." More commonly, people complained that the police simply did not do enough. Sofiia said, "I am completely unsatisfied with the activities of our police. Because terrible things sometimes happen on our streets, and the police don't respond in any way. That is, they can burglarize in broad daylight, and the policeman will stand somewhere on the side and say that he doesn't have a telephone to report it. There are very many burglaries of apartments and other crimes that aren't solved."

While few people had opinions about the court system—since they had had no direct contact with it—those who did have opinions were uniformly negative. Polina summed up the legal system: "We're not afraid of judges, trials, prison—nothing scares us. You can kill someone and get out in two years. And maybe never even go to prison if you know the right people. Justice here is still at a low level." Overall, the impression was that without adequate enforcement it did not much matter what the law said. After all, as Grigorii remarked, Lenin had a nice constitution, too.

Despite the unreliability of legal enforcement, many interviewees did express an understanding that good laws, well and fairly applied, were the important missing element in Russian political life and the key to a working democracy. Boris Borisovich noted, "Democracy is the strict execution of laws in the interests of every person." Ekaterina said, "Democracy for me is above all that the laws work normally, all laws. That's the very first thing. Everything follows from that." Natalia, a member of the Moscow intelligentsia, summed up democracy succinctly: "Democracy is the interaction of the authorities and the population, when the authorities respect the population and the population respects the authorities and all together they respect the law, which is the same for both." Similarly, "strong" governmental power was widely understood to be power that could enforce laws, protect rights, and not only demand respect but also deserve it. On the subject of strong power, Ivan Ivanovich commented, "Strong power is the fulfillment of all laws, regardless of rank: whoever, minister, procurator, policeman, ordinary worker, *kolkhoznik*. All should be under the power of law." This idea was repeated frequently.

In arguing for law, as a feature either of democracy or of effective government, my respondents did not seem to think that they or even most of their fellow citizens needed to be kept in better control. Their focus was more on the power of law to restrain government officials and "bandits," overlapping categories of people in their eyes. In the minds of the respondents, a world without law was one where criminals could operate freely and ordinary people were at the mercy both of them and of unpredictable state officials. One member of the Siberian work collective remarked that, because laws were not adequately enforced in Russia, people's homes had become fortresses, with steel doors and reinforced windows. She relayed her son's comment when she called him at home to see how he was doing on his birthday. "Yes," he said, "everything is fine. All the criminals celebrate their birthdays in restaurants, but I'm behind bars." Like model democratic citizens, a large number of my respondents saw uniformly enforced law as the instrument that would defend their rights, property, and freedom in a more ideal world than the one in which they actually lived.

Using mass-opinion data from Russia and the Ukraine from 1992 and 1995, Arthur Miller, Vicki Hesli, and William Reisinger found that elites were more likely to understand democracy in terms of law and order, while masses emphasized freedom.[40] The people described here, by contrast, while not an elite sample, mentioned law at least as often as freedom. And those comments were not limited to the more educated members of the group of interviewees. It would not be surprising if an understanding of the importance of law had grown over time in Russia, as the early excitement over new freedoms wore off and the price of social disorder began to wear heavily. For instance, S. V. Patrushev and his coauthors found that between 1996 and 2002 an increasing percentage of Russians considered that Russian society *should* be based on the principle of law, while at the same time a decreasing percentage thought that it actually was.[41] Similarly,

---

40. Arthur H. Miller, Vicki L. Hesli, and William M. Reisinger, "Conceptions of Democracy Among Mass and Elite in Post-Soviet Societies," *British Journal of Political Science* 27 (1997): 157–90.
41. S. V. Patrushev, S. G. Aivazova, G. L. Kertman, L. Ia. Mashezerskaia, T. V. Pavlova, and A. D. Khlopin, "Vlast' i narod v Rossii: Povsedevnye praktiki i problema universalizatsii institutsional'nogo poriadka," *Politia*, no. 2, issue 29 (2003): 59.

G. M. Denisovskii and Polina Kozyreva found that the number of respondents saying that citizens could break laws with which they disagreed declined steadily between 1996 and 2000, from 10.1 percent to 8.6 percent.[42]

In their reliance on law to organize society, my respondents seemed to be rejecting chaos, which many felt they were already experiencing. They also seemed to be rejecting the idea that arbitrary rulers should be free to do whatever they please. Against the predictions of most descriptions of Russian political culture and despite a lack of confidence in the present enforcers of law, many of my respondents seemed to think law could organize society, restrain the powerful, and protect the weak. In that sense, they were ready to play by the rules of democratic citizenship. They just did not think those rules yet applied in their country.

Indeed, comparison with the American respondents makes it even clearer how Russians' attitudes toward the law reflect the immediate circumstances of their lives. My American respondents did not talk about law in describing democracy; they talked about freedom or, less frequently, the fact that people's voices were reflected in government decisions. When they tried to define what constituted a strong state, law enforcement did not loom large. Instead, people talked about bipartisanship, cooperation, and effectiveness. The Americans also had more confidence in their police forces, although with some exceptions. They felt generally safe and not overly worried that the police would arbitrarily exercise their authority. Most of the American respondents contacted the police to report relatively minor problems—like keys locked in cars—and were satisfied with the attentive response. Leo commented, "Well, I haven't been robbed lately. I haven't been beat up. And I have had an incident where I had to call the police just to report to them that somebody drove over my signs in the front yard, and they came out immediately. It was, to me, a minor thing and I really hated to bother them with it. But just to let them know it happened in the neighborhood, that's all I really do. And, oh yeah, a hundred percent, and I trust them." Living as they did in a more orderly world, Americans were much less conscious than Russians of the role of law in creating that world.

So Russians were ready to obey the law. But they were not particularly ready to take much other action in order to defend their rights or force

---

42. G. M. Denisovskii and Polina M. Kozyreva, *Politicheskaia tolerantnost' v reformiruemom Rossiiskom obshchestve vtoroi poloviny 90-kh godov* (Moscow: Institut Sotsiologii Rossiiskoi Akademii Nauk, Tsentr Obshchechelovecheskikh Tsennostei, 2002), 72.

improvements in the way their government worked. With very few exceptions, the interviewees were happy to vote and thought it was important to do so. One was a founding member of a local chapter of one the earliest national "unofficial" organizations. Another was active in a popular journal aimed at influencing public opinion. A couple mentioned mostly failed attempts at trying to get problems solved by contacting local officials. Some described their activities under the Communist system: memberships in the Komsomol or the party itself, an enthusiastic volunteer policeman, and one former *ispolkom* (city executive committee) member. On the whole, though, they did not want to do more than vote.

When pushed, some respondents acknowledged that the behavior of citizens mattered in a democracy. One member of the Siberian work collective remarked, "Naturally, no one is going to hand us democracy on a saucer with a golden border." But much of the helpful behavior they had in mind was not directly political. They suggested that people should try to influence public opinion; start businesses; get off the government's neck; and "in the end, . . . live honestly, according to the law, you understand" (Oleg). The reluctance to undertake political action was more notable in older than in younger members of the sample, that is among people who had experienced the Communist system as adults.[43] Tatiana Mikhailovna, a woman in her seventies, remarked, "We ran to elections when these changes were just beginning. But now we understand our role and are reluctant even to watch television." Another pensioner, Vilen Nikolaevich, said that he had bought his wife headphones, so that he would not have to listen to the news. Svetlana, a woman in her forties, wished the Duma would do its job better, so that she could ignore it. Many middle-aged people said they were more worried about immediate material aspects of their lives. One of the women in the Siberian work collective said, "Much depends on us. But many people are simply tired of everything. . . . There is no faith in the future; therefore, to some extent we're all depressed, disappointed. And we have become a bit more passive. It wasn't like this before. You know, we were quite active women."

43. By comparing survey results from 1989 and 1999, Iurii Levada similarly noticed a substantial increase in the number of respondents who said that "the government gives us so little that we are not obliged to it in any way." In 1989, 6 percent of the respondents chose this answer; in 1999, 38 percent did, with older respondents more likely to feel they owed nothing to the government. Iurii Levada, "Koordinaty cheloveka i itogam izucheniia 'cheloveka sovetskogo,'" *Monitoring obshchestvennoe mneniia: Informatsiia analiz*, no. 1, issue 51 (2001): 7–15.

In their unreadiness to undertake political action, my interviewees do not necessarily look like the vital citizenry that will keep democracy alive in Russia. In fairness to them, though, they look pretty much like the citizens of most functioning democracies. Most Americans do not want to devote more time to political action; indeed, many do not even vote. In Western democracies, it is rare for wide sections of the population to participate in political activity beyond voting.[44] My Russian respondents did not sound so different from American respondents such as Bill, who said, "I think all people whether you're in a democracy or not have a responsibility to act a certain way. I think we should vote. I think, personal accountability among all of us, we shouldn't rely on the government. We should do things for ourselves and for our family. Be honest. Not be criminals, I guess. That's bad. And be involved, be intelligent, get an education. That's the best way to help out with everything, just to be honest, to be a good person, and to be an intelligent as you can be." For many American citizens as for Russians, it is enough to vote, obey the laws, and live an exemplary private life. Intensive political participation is widely considered optional for the democratic citizen.

More important, most of the Russian respondents were reluctant to become engaged politically because they doubted that their actions would have much effect: present institutions did not provide effective avenues for popular action. Although some Russians thought they might be able to influence local government officials, few thought they could influence the central government in any way other than by voting. Boris Borisovich remarked, "They don't worry about my opinion in the least. Even the labor strikes and hunger strikes which the miners have undertaken have practically no influence on those in power." Pelageia spoke at length about the problems of one of her acquaintances, whose grandson's murder had not been solved and who had written to Putin in despair. Pelageia said, "How many letters did she write? Putin answers to our local authorities: Look it over. And they are looking it over. They called her and said, 'You should write fewer letters. Bye!' That's how it is here." Most respondents refused to label central political institutions in Russia "democratic."[45]

---

44. Hibbing and Theiss-Morse, "Democrats or Anti-Democrats?"; Sidney Verba, Norman H. Nie, and Jae-On Kim, *Participation and Political Equality: A Seven Nation Comparison* (New York: Cambridge University Press, 1978), 46–62.

45. See also Miller, Hesli, and Reisinger, "Conceptions of Democracy," 195. There was some change on this point over time, with respondents in 2003 more likely to think that their central governmental institutions might be democratic.

Indeed, some found new institutions less responsive than the ones that existed under Communism.[46] Anna Pavlovna remarked, "It seems to me that, when I was working and drew the attention of the boss to something, he would say to me, 'Oh, you find a lot to talk about!' Now, if you raise an issue, they say, 'You're fired.' The boss can do what he likes. Then there were trade unions. Now I have no place to complain." Interviewees outside Moscow commented that it was difficult to contact deputies to the State Duma, since the latter were often in Moscow.

In sum, as a group the Russian respondents were willing to play by the minimal rules of democratic citizenship, in particular to vote and to obey laws created by representative legislatures. Few were ready to do much more than that. Even if the reason they are unwilling to challenge imperfect officials and institutions is that they are convinced that the institutions are so imperfect they will not respond to the challenge, the effect is still that these unhappy citizens are unlikely to be a force for change. If Russian political institutions eventually become more responsive, it probably will not be because they were pushed in that direction by a motivated citizenry.

Conclusion

In sum, most of my Russian interviewees do not share many of the particular beliefs supposedly characteristic of traditional, undemocratic Russian political culture. Most of them are ready to vote; to obey the law; and, save exorbitant tax rates on private businesses, to pay their taxes. Similarly, most are ready to countenance the disorder of representative government, even under conditions in which they have practically no faith that their so-called representatives care a whit about the people they are supposed to represent. Few were willing to sacrifice newly found freedoms to autocratic leaders who could get things done. However, the Russian respondents had limited confidence in the presidency, less in the State Duma, and none in the police. Many of my respondents so despaired of well-functioning political institutions that they were unwilling to take action to improve the ones they had. Many also were more impressed with results than the processes used to achieve them. They valued effective leaders more than argumentative legislatures. While my Russian respondents did not seem to be actively looking for an autocratic boss who would set things straight,

---

46. See similar views in Sarah Ashwin, "'There's No Joy Any More': The Experience of Reform in a Kuzbass Mining Settlement," *Europe-Asia Studies* 47 (December 1995): 1376.

it seems plausible that, under the right conditions, they might tolerate such an autocrat, were one to come to power and actually get useful things done. That my respondents share their democratic imperfections with many of the citizens of a functioning democracy may not matter: citizens of functioning democracies are likely to face fewer challenges to their institutions.

In many respects, my Russian interviewees' opinions seemed to be reflections of the institutions under which they lived, rather than cultural predispositions that made democracy suspect. My respondents were reluctant to undertake political action, because they perceived little potential payoff from such action. They did not trust most political officials, because they thought those officials had done little to earn their trust. This feeling was particularly sharp in regard to the State Duma. That these opinions were reflections of a flawed reality can be seen especially in instances in which they changed. In 2000, respondents were largely willing to give Putin the benefit of the doubt, because in their estimation he had not done anything wrong yet. Even in 2003, people found Putin vastly superior to his predecessor, if only because people were receiving their paychecks on time and the economy was showing some improvement. Muscovites made an exception for Mayor Luzhkov because Moscow showed the beneficial results of his activity. Given a political figure who appeared to act in the public good, even if that only meant plowing the streets or raising pensions a fraction, people were ready to give that person the benefit of the doubt. For most, though, their confidence was limited: respondents wanted neither Luzhkov nor Putin to rule without their respective dumas or existing constitutional restrictions. If the cynicism of my Russian respondents is largely the product of their own institutions, and not culturally determined, then that cynicism need not be permanent. Russian evaluations of the possibilities in political life would be likely to become more positive if those possibilities improved in fact.

My Russian interlocutors tell us things we would not otherwise know. They tell us why surveys show little willingness on the part of most Russians to defend their legislatures: it is less that Russians do not like the institutions of democracy than that they do not like the institutions they have. They also tell us why Russians rank so poorly on personal efficacy and political trust: again, it does not seem that the problem lies in culturally inherited tendencies but rather in governmental institutions that provide few opportunities for citizens to affect policies. The interviewees may even tell us one reason why Russians are comparatively reluctant to extend rights to their political enemies: without a legal system that can be trusted to preserve the fundamentals of social order, the risk of extending rights to some groups may simply be too great. In general, these interviews show the vital importance of being absolutely certain that the questions in mass surveys that are used to gauge Russians' support for democracy in the abstract do not in any way reflect on the imperfect democratic institutions of their own experience. At minimum, interpretations of results should not draw general conclusions from questions rooted in immediate historical experience.

The analysis so far also leaves many questions unanswered. In particular, how do Russians vary among themselves in their political values and assessments of democratic institutions? How are their evaluations of democracy related to evaluations of emerging market systems and some of their social consequences, such as social inequality? Will widespread concerns for "social order" undermine support for democracy, particularly since Russians seem more concerned with the effectiveness of their government than with the procedures it follows? How do Russians interpret the changes in their political and economic systems? And, in the end, what do Russians want from government? These are the questions examined in subsequent chapters.

Views of Markets: Russians Confront Inequality

In the industrialized West, most citizens do not see severe contradictions between democracy and markets: to them, the inequality produced by markets does not conflict with the egalitarian principles behind democracy. In post-Communist Russia, by contrast, many citizens are less convinced. Recent public opinion research has shown that ordinary Russians are less than enthusiastic about market structures and are more likely to support democracy than they are markets.[1] That many of Russia's *democrats* do not support market institutions presents a particular puzzle. In this chapter I examine the reasons some Russians who value democracy quite highly have little good to say about capitalism. By focusing on this puzzle, we can begin a deeper investigation of Russian understandings of democracy, capitalism, and the interrelationships between the two.

The conventional wisdom is that Russians are insufficiently liberal. Whether as a result of an overly Byzantine traditional culture or the recent history of Soviet economic paternalism, the presumption is that Russians are too committed to an egalitarian distribution of economic goods, too reliant on government as a vehicle to promote the general welfare, and too ready to sacrifice the freedom of the individual to the collective good to be democrats in the Western liberal mode.[2] To many, the illiberal tinge of Russian democracy is confirmed by the continued popularity of President Vladimir Putin despite his apparent attacks on personal freedom, despite in particular

1. For instance, Grigory I. Vainshtein, "Obshchestvennoe soznanie i institutsional'nye peremeny," in *Chelovek v perekhodnom obshchestve: Sotsiologicheskie i sotsial'no-psikhologicheskie issledovaniia,* ed. G. G. Diligenskii (Moscow: Institute of World Economics and International Relations, 1998), 35; James L. Gibson, "The Russian Dance with Democracy," *Post-Soviet Affairs* 17, no. 2 (2001): 101–25; Boris Dubin, "Zapad, granitsa, osobyi put': Simvolika 'drugogo' v politicheskoi mifologii sovremennoi Rossii," *Monitoring obshchestvennoe mneniia: Informatsiia analiz,* no. 6, issue 50 (2000): 28.

2. Judith S. Kullberg and William Zimmerman, "Liberal Elites, Socialist Masses, and Problems of Democracy," *World Politics* 51 (April 1999): 323–58; Francis Fukuyama, *Trust: The Social Virtues and the Creation of Prosperity* (New York: Free Press, 1995), 40.

his efforts to curb the power of the most successful of Russia's entrepreneurs—"oligarchs" such as Mikhail Khodorkovsky, Boris Berezovsky,
and Vladimir Gusinsky.[3]

But are Russian democrats really insufficiently liberal? Is their dislike of
markets and oligarchs the product of an alternative set of nonliberal values,
or do the sources of discontent lie elsewhere? In this chapter, I show that
the suspicion of markets among some of Russia's democrats has more to
do with how markets function in Russia than with preferences for greater
egalitarianism or government control of the economy. Market-doubting
democrats in Russia embrace the ideals of liberal economic freedom as
readily as do most liberals. They are simply unconvinced that the markets
developing in their country provide most people with those freedoms. As
we saw in the previous chapter with representative institutions, the problem
lies not in the ideal but in the highly imperfect reality. That imperfect reality
also lies behind support for Putin. To many Russians, Putin's attacks on the
few who have benefited from economic reforms look less like assaults on
markets than like efforts to make markets work better for ordinary people.

I begin this chapter by examining logical tensions between democracy
and capitalism and by addressing ways those tensions can be reconciled.
I then review what we already know from mass surveys about how ordinary
Russians assess the relationship between democracy and capitalism, and
I develop hypotheses to explain why some Russians fail to reconcile conflicting elements of democracy and capitalism. I test those hypotheses
using the intensive interviews with Russians.

Democracy and Inequality

The idea that democracy and capitalism are intimately linked is partly based
on the joint historical origins of the two systems and on the empirical
tendency for democratic polities also to have capitalist economies. Democracy "sprang from the womb of the capitalist economy": the rise of the
bourgeoisie provided the impetus for restrictions on traditional power
structures and the repudiation of anachronistic restraints on individuals.[4] In
the contemporary world, democracy seems to function best in higher-income

3. Rudra Sil and Cheng Chen, "State Legitimacy and the (In)significance of Democracy in
Post-Communist Russia," *Europe-Asia Studies* 56, no. 3 (2004): 358–62; Ol'ga Kryshtanovskaia,
"Vybor patriotov: bednost' ili rakety?" *Argumenty i Fakty*, no. 30 (July 2003): 3.

4. Kyung-won Kim, "Marx, Schumpeter, and the East Asian Experience," *Journal of
Democracy* 3 (July 1992): 24.

countries, which is to say, countries with flourishing market economies, with a large middle class and an affluent and secure working class.[5]

The connection between democracy and capitalism, however, is generally argued to be not only empirical, but also logical. The key logical connection is that both systems rest on the shared value of individual freedom.[6] Both democracy and capitalism are supposed to leave us as free as possible to pursue "our own good in our own way."[7] Democracy does this by limiting the arbitrary power of governments over citizens, thereby protecting rights given by "Nature" or the "Creator." These rights include free speech, assembly, and the unfettered exercise of religion, and they also prominently include rights of property and individual initiative in the economic sphere. Some would argue that citizens must have property to defend if they are to take seriously democracy's precept that they keep the government in check.[8] Capitalism, similarly, is based on the individual's freedom to pursue happiness in whatever form it takes, particularly in forms that can be counted, stored, and saved against a rainy day. Capitalism further enhances individual freedom by limiting government's role in the economy, thereby shrinking the possible size of the state as well as protecting a private sphere outside government direction.

To many Americans, democracy and capitalism are so tightly intertwined that the features of one get mixed up with those of the other. For instance, one of my American respondents, Ted, defined democracy as "certain inalienable rights. Freedom. You know, we must always have some laws. Freedom to make your own choices—where you want to work, where you want to live, what you want to do with your life. I love having those choices. I couldn't stand being told what I was going to do with my life. Having four thousand deodorants to choose from, I mean that's great. I like it." In an affluent liberal democracy, the pursuit of happiness may look a lot like consumer choice.

But there are also tensions between democracy and capitalism. Chief among these tensions is different treatment of the value of equality.

5. Seymour Martin Lipset, *Political Man: The Social Bases of Politics* [1959], expanded ed. (Baltimore: Johns Hopkins University Press, 1981); Adam Przeworski, Michael E. Alvarez, Jose Antonio Cheibub, and Fernando Limongi, *Democracy and Development: Political Institutions and Well-Being in the World, 1950–1990* (New York: Cambridge University Press, 2000).

6. Karl R. Popper, *The Open Society and Its Enemies*, 4th ed. (Princeton: Princeton University Press, 1963); Friedrich Hayek, *The Road to Serfdom* (Chicago: Chicago University Press, 1944).

7. John Stuart Mill, *On Liberty* (New York: Penguin, 1985), 72.

8. Andranik Migranian, "Dolgii put' k evropeiskomu domu," *Novyi Mir* 7 (July 1989): 166–84.

Democracy rests on the ideas that citizens have equal rights and equal dignity, that they can expect equal treatment from government, that they all have an equal ability to assess their own interests, and hence that their votes are equal. Capitalism, by contrast, accepts inequality as a basic premise. If people are not equal in their skills, luck, starting positions, and determination to succeed, then some will prosper while others do not. Employees and consumers have little direct power over corporate decisions, despite their often vital interests in the outcome. Even equality of opportunity is difficult to guarantee in a society characterized by strong class differences. In fact, before democracy demonstrated through practice its ability to coexist with capitalism, observers worried that political empowerment of the poor would necessarily threaten the property of the few.[9] More recently, scholars have suggested that, in a democratic context, public demands for immediate material welfare could undercut efforts at market reform.[10]

There are a variety of ways to downplay the significance of this tension between democracy and capitalism. One way is to take aim at some of the gauzier pretensions of democratic theory. John Mueller, for instance, argues that democracy in its worldly form falls far short of the ideals of equality on which it is theoretically based. Rather than equality, democracy in practice is "about the freedom to become politically unequal."[11] Some interests are better protected than others; some people have better access to power; some voices are louder or their owners can afford better amplification. In real-world democracy, "minorities rule."[12] The inequality built into existing democracy makes democracy more consistent with capitalism partly through protecting wealth from redistribution, since the wealthy have a strong incentive to use whatever political advantages they can create to defend their economic interests. Mueller concludes, "Democracy, it seems to me, is built not on political equality, but on political inequality; not on majority rule, but on minority rule and majority acquiescence; not on enlightened consensus, but on apathy and distraction; and

9. Marc F. Plattner describes Thomas Babington Macauley's views on this subject in "From Liberalism to Liberal Democracy," in *The Global Divergence of Democracies*, ed. Larry Diamond and Marc F. Plattner (Baltimore: Johns Hopkins University Press, 2001), 83–84.

10. Adam Przeworski, *Democracy and the Market: Political and Economic Reforms in Eastern Europe and Latin America* (New York: Cambridge University Press, 1991).

11. John Mueller, *Capitalism, Democracy, and Ralph's Pretty Good Grocery* (Princeton: Princeton University Press, 1999), 137.

12. Robert A. Dahl, *A Preface to Democratic Theory* (Chicago: University of Chicago Press, 1956), 132.

not nearly so much on elections as on the frantic and chaotic interweavings and contestings of isolated, self-serving, and often tiny special interest groups and their political and bureaucratic allies." Democracy works because it requires people, "on average, to be no better than they actually are or are ever likely to be: flawed, grasping, self-centered, prejudiced, and easily distracted."[13]

But publics may be so easily distracted that they might never learn the lesson that Mueller is trying to impart. Certainly Americans have had enough experience with actually existing democracy to know about minority rule, apathy, and self-serving interest groups, but they still see these things as *distortions* of the democratic process and not its essence.[14] That is to say, Mueller could be right in his description of the values that really underlie democracy, but his argument, even so, might give us little purchase into the minds of ordinary citizens and the ways they reconcile apparent tensions between democracy and capitalism because ordinary citizens are not convinced that he is describing democracy as it is supposed to be.

Another way to deal with the tension between democracy and capitalism is to fall back on Barrington Moore's observation that there is no democracy without a strong middle class.[15] Although Moore's argument had more to do with the historical origins of democratic institutions, the existence of a large middle class has other benefits as well. In particular, a large middle class reduces the tension between democratic equality and capitalist inequality. If most people are relatively materially secure and fairly satisfied with their lot, the political significance of inequality is diminished. This is particularly true if people tend to think that other people are like themselves, leading to an "illusion of justice" in societies where people assume that everyone is a member of the middle class.[16] The theoretical tension still exists—and what is judged "fair" in one context seems unfair in another—but people have little reason to dwell on the problem because most

13. Mueller, *Capitalism, Democracy,* 161.

14. John R. Hibbing and Elizabeth Theiss-Morse, *Congress as Public Enemy: Public Attitudes Toward American Political Institutions* (New York: Cambridge University Press, 1995).

15. Barrington Moore Jr., *Social Origins of Dictatorship and Democracy: Lord and Peasant in the Making of the Modern World* (Boston: Beacon Press, 1966).

16. James R. Kluegel, Gyorgy Csepeli, Tamas Kolosi, Antal Orkeny, and Maria Nemenyi, "Accounting for the Rich and the Poor: Existential Justice in Comparative Perspective," in *Social Justice and Political Change: Public Opinion in Capitalist and Post-Communist States,* ed. James R. Kluegel, David S. Mason, and Bernd Wegener (Hawthorne, NY: Aldine De Gruyter, 1995), 179–207.

people are doing OK. Indeed, Jennifer Hochschild's research on American attitudes toward wealth redistribution gives credence to this argument.[17] Her respondents relied on egalitarian norms of distributive justice in the political sphere but differentiating norms in the economic domain. Faced with an issue that bridged the two domains, such as the political distribution of economic goods, respondents preferred to let the issue drop rather than to find a way to reconcile the contradictions in their own ideas.

The third way to address the tension between democracy and capitalism is to argue that it is not, in fact, a problem for people to apply different justice norms in different circumstances. David Miller argues that the demands of justice differ in terms of the various kinds of relationships people have with one another. In a solidaristic community, such as a family, the operative principle of justice is distribution according to *need*. In an instrumental association—most economic organizations—justice demands distribution according to *desert*, while the distributive principle of *equality* rules in terms of citizenship.[18] The problem is not a philosophical one of reconciling conflicting standards of justice. Rather it is a political problem of determining which standard of justice applies in which context. Do people relate to one another as citizens, in which case equality is the appropriate distributive norm, or as economic competitors? How can claims for one kind of distribution be balanced against claims for another kind?[19]

Empirical studies provide evidence of some of this tension between various justice claims. Herbert McClosky and John Zaller, for instance, found that Americans who are highly supportive of democracy display the least support for capitalism, even though they still favor capitalism over more collectivist alternatives. Likewise, strong proponents of capitalism show comparatively low support for democracy.[20] Translating these findings into Miller's terms, it seems that people who are strongly attached to

17. Jennifer Hochschild, *What's Fair? Americans' Attitudes Toward Distributive Justice* (Cambridge, MA: Harvard University Press, 1981).

18. David Miller, *Principles of Social Justice* (Cambridge, MA: Harvard University Press, 1999), 25–30. *Desert* and *need* can also be understood as alternative formulations of equality based on equal treatment for, respectively, equal worth or equal utility. See Amartya Sen, *Inequality Reexamined* (New York: Russell Sage Foundation, 1992), 12–16.

19. Miller, *Principles of Social Justice*, 36, 62.

20. Herbert McClosky and John Zaller, *The American Ethos: Public Attitudes Toward Capitalism and Democracy* (Cambridge, MA: Harvard University Press, 1984), 161–88. Experimental studies show that people apply multiple principles of distributive justice when making judgments about income distribution. See Philip A. Michelbach, John T. Scott, Richard E. Matland, and Brian H. Bornstein, "Doing Rawls Justice: An Experimental Study of Income Distribution Norms," *American Journal of Political Science* 47, no. 3 (2003): 523–39.

democracy see more relationships as falling into the category of citizenship and hence demanding that all people be treated as equals. Consequently, these democrats suggest ways to modify capitalism so that it can better address demands of equal citizenship. By contrast, Americans most strongly attached to capitalism apparently see more relationships as governed by criteria of desert. There is no injustice in inequality if the losers seem to deserve no more.

Empirical studies also show that apparently unjust outcomes are acceptable to people if they are reached by just means. To Miller, just procedures provide equal treatment, not favoritism or arbitrariness; they are accurate, relying on all relevant information; they are public, with the rules and criteria clear to all; and they do not violate the personal dignity of the recipients.[21] Some research indicates that Americans have more confidence in the fairness of market procedures than in political ones, explaining an apparent preference among Americans for market over political justice.[22]

The Russian Public on Democracy and Capitalism

Russians, in this regard, seem to be different from Americans. The former are less confident about the justice of markets and, apparently, less convinced that conflicting elements in capitalism and democracy can be reconciled. A number of studies have addressed the relationship between support for democracy and capitalism among Russian citizens, but the conclusions are not entirely consistent. A positive relationship between support for markets and support for democracy shows up in some datasets but not others, with some measures but not others, and in bivariate analysis more often than when other relevant variables are controlled.[23] There is also disagreement about how elites differ from the rest of the population.

21. Miller, *Principles of Social Justice,* 99–102.

22. See Robert E. Lane, "Market Justice, Political Justice," *American Political Science Review* 80 (1986): 386.

23. Ada Finifter and Ellen Mickiewicz, "Redefining the Political System of the USSR: Mass Support for Political Change," *American Political Science Review* 186 (December 1992): 857–74; Arthur H. Miller, Vicki L. Hesli, and William M. Reisinger, "Reassessing Mass Support for Political and Economic Change in the Former USSR," *American Political Science Review* 88 (June 1994): 399–411; Arthur H. Miller, William M. Reisinger, and Vicki L. Hesli, "Understanding Political Change in Post-Soviet Societies: A Further Commentary on Finifer and Mickiewicz," *American Political Science Review* 90 (March 1996): table 4, 163; Raymond M. Duch, "Tolerating Economic Reform: Popular Support for Transition to a Free Market in the Former Soviet Union," *American Political Science Review* 87 (September 1993): 590–608; Gibson, "The Russian Dance with Democracy," 115–16.

Miller, Hesli, and Reisinger found that elites who strongly supported democracy preferred a *controlled* economy.[24] But Kullberg and Zimmerman found that elites were significantly more likely than ordinary people to be liberal democrats, supporting *both* markets and democracy.[25]

Much of the disparity in these findings is attributable to the fact that the various studies employ very different measures, based on differently worded survey questions. But it is also clear that, for Russians, support for democracy and support for markets do not always go hand in hand. Some proponents of markets are skeptical about democracy. Under the Yeltsin regime, for instance, supporters of markets sometimes favored undemocratic policies or procedures for political reasons: governors appointed by the president and a weak parliament might provide fewer obstacles to unpopular market reforms.[26] By contrast, some of Russia's democrats are skeptical of the results of unregulated markets and favor a strong social and economic safety net.[27] These trends seem to apply across Central and Eastern Europe as well: proponents of markets often but not always support democracy, and not all democrats support markets.[28]

It is also clear that the first decade of economic transition was extraordinarily hard for most Russians. From the hyperinflation of 1992, to the wage arrears of the mid-1990s, to the currency collapse of 1998, economic reform produced many by-products that left people worse off than they had been before. Surveys showed that many Russians perceived a decline in their welfare and a rise in the inequality of society in the 1990s and that they worried about impoverishment and unemployment.[29] The fear among

24. Arthur H. Miller, Vicki L. Hesli, and William M. Reisinger, "Conceptions of Democracy Among Mass and Elite in Post-Soviet Societies," *British Journal of Political Science* 27 (1997): 182.

25. Kullberg and Zimmerman, "Liberal Elites."

26. Jerry F. Hough, "The Russian Election of 1993: Public Attitudes Toward Economic Reform and Democratization," *Post-Soviet Affairs* 10, no. 1 (1994): 16–19.

27. Robert J. Brym, "Re-evaluating Mass Support for Political and Economic Change in Russia," *Europe-Asia Studies* 48 (July 1996): 751–66; David S. Mason and James R. Kluegel, "Introduction: Public Opinion and Political Change in the Postcommunist States," in *Marketing Democracy: Changing Opinion About Inequality and Politics in East Central Europe*, ed. David S. Mason and James R. Kluegel, with Ludmilla Khakhulina, Petr Mateju, Antal Orkeny, Alexander Stoyanov, and Bernd Wegener (New York: Rowman and Littlefield, 2000), 13.

28. Mary E. McIntosh, Martha Abele MacIver, Daniel G. Abele, and Dina Smeltz, "Publics Meet Market Democracy in Central and East Europe, 1991–1993," *Slavic Review* 53 (Summer 1994): 483–512; David S. Mason, "Attitudes Toward the Market and Political Participation in the Post-Communist States," *Slavic Review* 54 (Summer 1995): 385–406.

29. Iurii Levada, Vladimir Shubkin, Grigoriy Kertman, Veronika Ivanova, Vladimir Yadov, and Eric Shiraev, "Russia: Anxiously Surviving," in *Fears in Post-Communist Societies: A Comparative*

many observers has been that the hardships of the transition period might undermine support not only for markets but also for democracy. Here again, though, research results are mixed. Some scholars have found that economic hardship seems to reduce support for democracy, while others have not.[30] Some studies have shown that people whose personal economic situation deteriorated were less likely to favor markets or more likely to vote Communist.[31] Others have concluded that people with qualities that made them more likely to benefit from market opportunities—particularly, youth and education—were more likely to favor markets.[32]

Leaving aside for a moment the relationship to democracy and just looking at popular attitudes toward markets, consistent tensions are still evident. Researchers who participated in the International Social Justice Project surveys in seven Eastern European and five capitalist countries noticed what they called "split-consciousness": people in post-Communist countries, like people in capitalist countries, often hold two sets of ideas that appear to contradict each other. For instance, Russians focus on qualities of individuals to explain why some people are rich and others poor, but they are also ready to argue that social factors limit the opportunities of some individuals.[33] Similarly, Russians are open to the idea that social inequality might be justified, but they are also persuaded by arguments supporting social equality.[34] Overall, even while Russians support markets

Perspective, ed. Eric Shiraev and Vladimir Shlapentokh (New York: Palgrave, 2002), 19; Leontii Georgievich Byzov, "Pervye kontury 'postperekhodnoi epokhi,'" *Sotsiologicheskie issledovaniia*, no. 4 (2001): 10.

30. On the point that economic hardship reduces support for democracy, see Stephen Whitefield and Geoffrey Evans, "The Russian Election of 1993: Public Opinion and the Transition Experience," *Post-Soviet Affairs* 10, no. 1 (1994): 38–60. For the opposite view, see Raymond M. Duch, "Economic Chaos and the Fragility of Democratic Transition in Former Communist Regimes," *Journal of Politics* 57 (February 1995): 121–58; James L. Gibson, "A Mile Wide but an Inch Deep (?): The Structure of Democratic Commitments in the Former USSR," *American Journal of Political Science* 40 (May 1996): 396–420; Gibson, "The Russian Dance with Democracy," 118–20; William Mishler and Richard Rose, "Trajectories of Fear and Hope: Support for Democracy in Post-Communist Europe," *Comparative Political Studies* 28 (January 1996): 553–81.

31. Miller, Hesli, and Reisinger, "Understanding Political Change," 404–5; Vicki L. Hesli and Elena Bashkirova, "The Impact of Time and Economic Circumstances on Popular Evaluations of Russia's President," *International Political Science Review* 22, no. 4 (2001): 379–98.

32. Terry D. Clark, Ernest Goss, and Larisa B. Kosova, "Economic Well-Being and Popular Support for Market Reform in Russia," *Political Development and Cultural Change* 51, no. 3 (2003): 753–68; M. K. Gorshkov, *Rossiiskoe obshchestvo v usloviiakh trasnformatsii: Mify i real'nost' (Sotsiologicheskii analiz)* (Moscow: ROSSPEN, 2003), 382.

33. Kluegel et al., "Accounting for the Rich and the Poor."

34. James R. Kluegel and Petr Mateju, "Egalitarian vs. Inegalitarian Principles of Distributive Justice," in *Social Justice and Political Change: Public Opinion in Capitalist and Post-Communist*

in a general sense, they are very critical about some of the ways in which markets function in their own country. In the International Social Justice Project, for instance, Russians were more likely than people in almost all the other twelve countries sampled to think that wealth was the product of dishonesty and having the right connections, not of hard work and good ideas.[35] M. K. Gorshkov reports on polls showing that 77.5 percent of Russian respondents had a negative opinion of the process of privatizing government property, and 53.5 percent had a negative opinion of the start of radical economic reforms.[36]

What Makes Russians Different?

Why are some Russian democrats hesitant to support markets? For people who argue from political culture, the answer is that Russians give priority to the distributive principle of equality instead of desert, and the roots of this preference lie in both religious traditions and the practice of Soviet socialism.[37] So, for instance, Viktor Sergeyev and Nikolai Biriukov argue that the Orthodox idea that all abilities, skills, and talents are gifts from God militates against notions that the talented deserve greater material rewards for exercising those gifts. Further, if a peasant's work is seen as *consumption* of God-given resources, then work is no particular virtue and efforts to work more efficiently and effectively are simply "ruses of a thief anxious to grab even more."[38]

States, ed. James R. Kluegel, David S. Mason, and Bernd Wegener (Hawthorne, NY: Aldine De Gruyter, 1995), 209–38; Svetlana Stephenson and Ludmila Khakhulina, "Russia: Changing Perceptions of Social Justice," in *Marketing Democracy: Changing Opinion About Inequality and Politics in East Central Europe,* ed. David S. Mason and James R. Kluegel, with Ludmilla Khakhulina, Petr Mateju, Antal Orkeny, Alexander Stoyanov, and Bernd Wegener (New York: Rowman and Littlefield, 2000), 87.

35. Only Estonians ranked higher in regard to the dishonesty behind wealth. See Kluegel et al., "Accounting for the Rich and the Poor," 190.

36. Gorshkov, *Rossiiskoe obshchestvo,* 391.

37. Edward L. Keenan, "Muscovite Political Folkways," *Russian Review* 45 (April 1986): 115–81; Grigory I. Vainshtein, "Totalitarian Public Consciousness in a Post-totalitarian Society," *Communist and Post-Communist Studies* 27, no. 3 (1994): 247–59; E. Z. Basina, "Individualizm i kollektivizm v postsovetskom obshchestve: Differentsiatsiia sotstial'nykh ustanovok," in *Chelovek v perekhodnom obshchestve: Sotsiologicheskie i sotsial'no-psikhologicheskie issledovaniia,* ed. G. G. Diligenskii (Moscow: Institute of World Economics and International Relations, 1998), 88–112. Nina F. Naumova, "Sotsial'naia politika v usloviiakh zapazdyvaiushchei modernizatsii," *Sotsiologicheskii Zhurnal,* no. 1 (1994): 6–21; trans. in *Sociological Research* 34 (March–April 1995): 12.

38. Victor Sergeyev and Nikolai Biriukov, *Russia's Road to Democracy: Parliament, Communism, and Traditional Culture* (Brookfield, VT: Edward Elgar/Ashgate, 1993), 128–29.

Traditional preferences for an egalitarian society in which extra work did not translate into extra rewards were altered but not overturned by Soviet efforts to glorify the working class, to downplay the contributions of intellectual labor, and to moderate income differentials across society. In Russian culture in the 1990s, material success was not an indication of desirable personal traits or God's favor, but rather of "immorality, loss of sacredness, and disconnection from ones' peers."[39] Dale Pesmen adds that wealth was even a way for ethnic Russians to lose their claim to having a "Russian soul." One of Pesmen's informants argued, "Our politicians with American bents are going to break their heads on this one. Russia will not. To force her to live according to the idea of the market is impossible. *Give her a worthy idea! The market cannot be a goal!* 'Get rich!' you say to the people. The people will answer you: 'Go screw yourself!' That never was the basis of life."[40] Accordingly, public opinion researchers sometimes interpret survey findings in light of these cultural values. So they see nostalgia for the socialist past, a tendency to view wealth as illegitimate, or a cultural disinclination to distribute goods according to the principle of desert.[41]

But the problem for capitalism in Russia may lie less in the past than in the present. For one thing, it is not self-evident that ordinary Russians would be nostalgic for all aspects of their socialist past, even if they liked parts of it. After all, the Soviet regime did not create a workers' utopia of equality and abundance. As a joke popular in Eastern Europe described it, "What is socialism? Socialism is the dialectical synthesis of the various stages in the history of humankind. From pre-history it takes the method. From antiquity, slavery. From feudalism, serfdom. From capitalism, exploitation. And from socialism, the name."[42] Or there is the Russian joke that Adam and Eve were Communists: "Were they not barefooted? . . . Were they not naked? Did they not sleep under a hedge? Was not their only food a

39. Nancy Ries, *Russian Talk: Culture and Conversation During Perestroika* (Ithaca: Cornell University Press, 1997), 129.

40. Dale Pesmen, *Russia and Soul* (Ithaca: Cornell University Press, 2000), 128. On the pursuit of private interest as a worthy social goal, see also Tim McDaniel, *The Agony of the Russian Idea* (Princeton: Princeton University Press, 1996), 26.

41. See particularly Irina Boeva and Viacheslav Shironin, "Russians Between State and Market: The Generations Compared," *Studies in Public Policy*, no. 205 (Glasgow, U.K.: University of Strathclyde, Centre for the Study of Public Policy, 1992); Levada et al., "Russia: Anxiously Surviving," 13.

42. John Keane, *Democracy and Civil Society: On the Predicaments of European Socialism, the Prospects for Democracy, and the Problem of Controlling Social and Political Power* (London: Verso, 1988), 197–98.

measly apple? And were they not constantly told that they were in Paradise?"[43] From their experience with "actually existing" socialism, ordinary Russians could well have concluded that efforts to foster equality do not work and productive members of society should be rewarded materially. The difficulties of maneuvering through a planned economy that consistently put too few consumer goods in the stores and provided resources for production on an unpredictable schedule could as easily lead to self-reliance and entrepreneurial creativity as to a tendency to wait for benefits from a paternalistic state.[44]

And the capitalism that developed in Russia in the first decade since the collapse of the Soviet regime was hardly a system that cleanly rewarded merit. Certainly some people got very rich, very fast, but they did so largely through abuse of their connections to power, not because they made a better mousetrap. Their methods were not always savory. Successful entrepreneurs often could not avoid connections with criminals, either because wealthy entrepreneurs were likely targets of thugs offering "protection" at a price or because they sought out thugs to enforce their own contracts.[45]

The case of Mikhail Khodorkovsky, one of the oligarchs targeted for legal prosecution by Putin, is instructive. Khodorkovsky's ties to the Communist Youth League, the Komsomol, earned him permission to start one of the first banks during the perestroika years. Later Khodorkovsky's bank, Menatep, was rewarded with the opportunity to run the auction that put Yukos, Russia's largest oil company, under Menatep's control. At that auction, Khodorkovsky and five partners paid $309 million for a 78 percent stake in Yukos; two months later Yukos was trading at a market capitalization of $6 billion. By 2002, Yukos had a capitalized value of approximately $15 billion.[46]

Khodorkovsky's climb to wealth is hardly unusual. It is widely believed that Boris Yeltsin used the second round of privatization to reward campaign

43. John Kolasky, ed., *Laughter Through Tears: Underground Wit, Humor and Satire in the Soviet Russian Empire* (Bullsbrook, Australia: Veritas, 1985), 102.

44. On this point, see Elizabeth Dunn, "Slick Salesmen and Simple People: Negotiated Capitalism in a Privatized Polish Firm," in *Uncertain Transition: Ethnographies of Change in the Postsocialist World*, ed. Michael Burawoy and Katherine Verdery (New York: Rowman and Littlefield, 1999), 125–50. Dunn finds that Polish workers felt that socialism prepared them to be flexible and independent because production inputs were so uncertain.

45. Vadim Volkov, *Violent Entrepreneurs: The Use of Force in the Making of Russian Capitalism* (Ithaca: Cornell University Press, 2002.

46. Paul Klebnikov, "The Khodorskovsky Affair," *Wall Street Journal*, 17 November 2003; Marshall I. Goldman, *The Piratization of Russia: Russian Reform Goes Awry* (New York: Routledge, 2003), 147.

contributors with chunks of Russia's natural resources.[47] Yegor Gaidar, the architect of privatization, seems to have believed that giving away state property, and thereby turning the Communist era *nomenklatura* into a propertied class that would support the new regime, was the only way to avoid civil war. He said, "I consciously preferred to buy power from them, rather than to declare a crusade against them."[48] Once they received Russia's riches at fire sale prices, Russia's new oligarchs did not worry about investing in and building up the Russian economy; rather, they sent their capital to safety abroad.[49] They also cultivated their connections to government power, contributing to the spread of corruption across Russian society and undermining democracy. One commentator argued that it hardly mattered which party won elections in Russia; what mattered was which oligarch controlled deputies' votes.[50] In the first decade after the collapse of Communism, the fair procedures that help overcome the tension between democracy and capitalism were missing in Russia.

So were the large middle class and the affluent and secure working class. Most ordinary Russians had few opportunities to prosper under conditions of economic reform.[51] While Khodorkovsky and his ilk accumulated billions, Russia's teachers, doctors, and others on the public payroll did not receive their wages for months in the late 1990s, as the government tried to balance its budget on their backs. Savings were destroyed by the hyperinflation of 1992 and again by the banking and currency collapse of 1998. Entrepreneurship was strangled by prohibitive taxes and criminal intervention. Opportunities for well-paid work were limited.

---

47. Rose Brady, *Kapitalizm: Russia's Struggle to Free Its Economy* (New Haven: Yale University Press, 1999); Svetlana P. Glinkina, Andrei Grigoriev, and Vakhtang Yakobidze, "Crime and Corruption," in *The New Russia: Transition Gone Awry*, ed. Lawrence R. Klein and Marshall Pomer (Stanford, CA: Stanford University Press, 2001), 240–42.

48. From an interview excerpted in Vladimir Mau and Irina Starodubrovskaya, *The Challenge of Revolution: Contemporary Russia in Historical Perspective* (New York: Oxford University Press, 2001), 149.

49. L. I. Nikovskaia, "Politika i Ekonomika v Sovremennoi Rossii: Konflikt na pereput'e (Kruglyi Stol)," *Sotsiologicheskie issledovaniia*, no. 2 (2000): 88–89.

50. Dmitry Oreshkin, "The Silence of the Oligarchs," *Moscow News*, no. 28, 23–29 July 2003, 5.

51. V. E. Guliev, "Rossiikaia gosudarstvennost': Sostoianie i tendentsii," in *Politicheskie Problemy Teorii Gosudarstva*, ed. N. N. Deev (Moscow: Institut Gosudarstva i Prava RAN, 1993), 6; Vladimir Mikhalev, "Poverty and Social Assistance," in *The New Russia: Transition Gone Awry*, ed. Lawrence R. Klein and Marshall Pomer (Stanford: Stanford University Press, 2001), 251–68; Tat'iana Iu. Bogomolova and Vera S. Tapilina, "Ekonomicheskaia stratifikatsiia naseleniia Rossii v 90-e gody," *Sotsiologicheskie issledovaniia*, no. 6 (2001): 32–43.

Grigorii Yavlinskii, one of Putin's critics and head of the Yabloko Party, complained that "the huge mass of the able-bodied population not only lacks normal, well-paying work, but they also lack the chance of gaining such work before the end of their working lives."[52] Yavlinskii argued that Russia had become a peripheral economy—a raw material exporter in which a small number of people profited from externally oriented trade, while the government lacked the resources either to revive the economy or to address the immediate needs of the poor majority. Russia's new capitalism, he said, was wasteful of human resources, denying most people productive work, the education they wanted, and adequate medical care. Devastated by the effects of economic reform, ordinary Russians focused on their own survival and failed to organize politically to protect their usually ignored interests.[53]

I argue that Russians' attitudes toward markets and hence their understanding of how compatible democracy is with capitalism arose in this immediate context, in which the vast majority enjoyed few benefits and competition was far from free and equal. My first hypothesis is that *the more Russians base their assessments of markets on the way markets operate in Russia, the less likely they are to support markets and, hence, the less likely they are to think that markets and democracy are compatible.* That is to say, the reason some Russians show relatively weak support for markets is not a culturally distinctive understanding of social justice that admits little appreciation of inequality. Instead, it is the product of how markets operate in Russia. If this hypothesis is correct, then I would expect to find that Russians do not differ from people who live in better-functioning capitalist systems in terms of the *standards* by which they judge the outcomes of the system. Rather, with similar standards they come to different conclusions about the desirability of the economic system because of differences in the way that system actually functions.

But there is no reason to anticipate that all Russians come to the same conclusions when they examine economic life around them. If Russians'

52. Grigorii Yavlinskii, "Periferiinyi kapitalizm," *Moskovskie Novosti,* no. 18, issue 1187, (13–19 May 2003): 10. Even Russia's staunchest liberals criticize the Russian economy. Boris Nemtsov, one of the founders of the Union of Rightist Forces, called Russia's "administrative-oligarchic capitalism" a "monstrosity." See Boris Nemtsov, "Boris Nemtsov o presidentstve, bogatstve i Chubaise," *Argumenty i Fakty,* no. 12 (March 1998): 3.

53. Graeme Gill and Roger D. Markwick, *Russia's Stillborn Democracy? From Gorbachev to Yeltsin* (New York: Oxford University Press, 2000); Mau and Starodubrovskaya, *The Challenge of Revolution,* 162.

economic values more or less rationally reflect their immediate reality, then it is likely that people who think they can succeed under present conditions will tend to assess those conditions more favorably. In general, the people who have managed to take advantage of the opportunities offered by Russian markets have been relatively young, either well educated or with a salable technical skill, and inhabitants of regions where there are more opportunities available, particularly around Moscow or other larger cities.[54] Based solely on immediate self-interest, these are the people we might expect to evaluate Russian capitalism more favorably. But considerable research indicates that immediate self-interest is not a major influence on standards of justice or voting. Instead, ideologies are more important than incomes in affecting people's attitudes toward income distributions.[55] And sociotropic evaluations of the overall health of the economy play a greater role in voting decisions than do pocketbook issues.[56] It is likely to be more crucial, then, whether people *think they can* succeed in Russian markets than whether they actually have succeeded. Consequently, my second hypothesis is that *the more people think markets offer opportunities for people like themselves, the more likely they are to think markets are consistent with democracy.*

To see whether my respondents' comments confirm these two hypotheses, I first examine the patterns of support for democracy and markets in the Russian sample. I find that for many of the respondents greater support for markets is linked to greater support for democracy, but not for all. A significant chunk of Russia's democrats are fairly hostile to markets, and some market supporters are not particularly consistent democrats. I use comparisons between groups of respondents to examine the reasons for their varying assessments. I focus particularly on the standards my respondents use to evaluate emerging income inequalities in Russia, their impressions of the opportunities available under changed conditions, and opinions of the proper role of government in economic life.

54. Stephenson and Khakhulina, "Russia: Changing Perceptions."
55. Lane, "Market Justice," 398.
56. Donald R. Kinder and D. Roderick Kiewiet, "Sociotropic Politics: The American Case," *British Journal of Political Science* 11 (1981): 129–61; Timothy J. Colton, "Economics and Voting in Russia," *Post-Soviet Affairs* 12, no. 4 (1996): 289–317; Timothy J. Colton, *Transitional Citizens: Voters and What Influences Them in the New Russia* (Cambridge, MA: Harvard University Press, 2000), 96.

Support for Democracy and Markets

In order to examine patterns of attitudes, it is necessary first to group respondents according to similarities in their general political orientations. Patterns are unlikely to emerge from a group of sixty respondents unless we can compare them to one another, noting both the attitudes they share and the views that differ. In order to examine differences in respondents' degree of support for democracy, I categorized the Russian respondents according to their answers to a set of questions asked of all respondents. The questions touched on a number of important aspects of democracy, in particular the key factors mentioned earlier: participation, competition, and individual rights.[57]

To measure the respondent's evaluation of the importance of *participation* in the political system, I used answers to questions on whether the authorities *should* care about the opinions of ordinary people and whether it is important for citizens to vote. For most citizens in most democratic countries, participation is limited to voting, so it is appropriate to ask about that common act. The purpose of participation is to ensure that popular voices and preferences are heard and presumably acted upon; the responsiveness of authorities to the opinions of ordinary people touches on that aspect of participation. To measure the respondent's evaluation of the importance of *competition* in the political system, I rely again on the question about voting, since multiparty elections are one of the main vehicles for citizens to make choices between alternative political visions, and also on a question about the need for representative institutions.[58] As we saw in Chapter 4, Russian citizens perceive their legislature in part as an arena of competition between the various delegates, and some are quite uncomfortable with the messiness that results. To capture the aspect of *individual rights*, I used a question that asked respondents whether they

---

57. See particularly the discussion in Chapter 4, pp. 78–79. For more information and the exact wording of questions, see Appendix C. These three factors emerge from Robert A. Dahl, *Polyarchy: Participation and Opposition* (New Haven: Yale University Press, 1971), 3–9; Guillermo O'Donnell and Philippe C. Schmitter, *Transitions from Authoritarian Rule: Tentative Conclusions About Uncertain Democracies* (Baltimore: Johns Hopkins University Press, 1986), 7–14; Georg Sorenson, *Democracy and Democratization* (Boulder, CO: Westview Press, 1993), 13.

58. Competition in democratic systems is often understood as competition between political parties. Unfortunately, I did not ask all respondents whether it was necessary to have a choice of parties in elections. Nonetheless, they did think that the ability to express their *choice* was what made elections meaningful, even if they did not explicitly identify that choice as a choice between parties.

thought there was too much freedom in Russia at the time of the interview. Since the general tendency of the Russian respondents was to think they were not free enough, worries that there was too much freedom seemed to indicate uneasiness with the whole idea of individual liberty and its social costs. As a more overarching measure of support for democracy, I also included my assessment of the depth of understanding reflected in answers that respondents gave when asked to define democracy. My logic here was that, to really support democracy, it is necessary to know what it is.

Overall, in their responses to these questions, my Russian respondents mostly showed considerable support for democratic values. Nearly all the Russians thought that government officials should be attentive to people's opinions and that it was important to vote. For my respondents, these were not controversial points. There was more variation on the perceived need for representative bodies, the comfort level with the amount of freedom democracy delivered, and the depth of articulated understanding of democracy. The nature of that variation will be described as the chapter progresses.

Based on their answers to these questions, I divided the respondents into four groups of varying support for democracy. People with low support for democracy had little good to say about democratic institutions and held a number of values or ideas that openly conflicted with the way democratic institutions work and the purposes they are supposed to serve. People with mixed support for democracy exhibited contradictory ideas: they were positive about some aspects of democracy, but hostile toward others. Some unwittingly demonstrated opinions at odds with what democrats tend to believe. Compared with the "mixed" group, people with moderate support for democracy were mostly positive about democracy, but sometimes they simply did not have much to say. They did not show evidence of much sophistication or depth in their thinking. Their understanding of how democracy functions often stopped short of a complete picture, but they liked democracy as far as they understood it. In their definitions of democracy, for instance, they tended to fall back on standard formulations, such as "rule by the people," without much indication of what the stock phrase might mean in practice. People with high support for democracy showed extensive understanding of democratic processes, and their support was unmixed with reservations or contradictory attitudes. In this chapter, people with moderate support for democracy are combined with the "high support" group, since the two groups were similar on relevant issues.

Table 5.1 shows demographic characteristics of the Russian respondents in the various categories of support for democracy. The oldest respondents

were most likely to show mixed support for democracy; more highly educated respondents tended to show greater support. There were not especially strong gender or regional differences. Too much attention should not
be paid to the *number* of people in each category, since the answers of
people in adjacent categories are not highly different from one another.
Nonetheless, it is interesting that so few of the respondents end up in the
low-ranking group. However, combining the "low" and "mixed support"
groups, more than half the sample exhibited imperfections of one degree
or another in their support for democracy. While these results are similar
to those of mass surveys, my intention in presenting this information and
the information in subsequent tables is to provide more information about
my sample, not to imply that the distribution in my sample is identical to
the distribution in the population at large. I hope that information about
the sample as a whole will help readers see that I am not focusing on the
comments of a few unrepresentative respondents.

I tried to devise a similar measure of support for democracy to group
the American respondents. For a number of reasons, it did not work. For
one thing, only half the American sample had been asked the question
about freedom, and that was the question on which answers tended to
vary most for the Russians. On the other questions, there was not enough
variation to divide the Americans into clearly different categories. Further,
to the degree that some Americans ranked lower in their support for
democracy than others, it seemed to be an artifact of the tendency for the
oldest and least educated respondents to do the worst job answering the
questions. Consequently, in the subsequent discussion I do not categorize
the American respondents by their support for democracy.

Table 5.1 also provides information on levels of support for markets
among Russians in the various democratic categories. To gauge support
for market reform, I used the respondents' answers to a question asking
how they felt about the economic changes that had occurred in Russia
over the past few years. More specific elements of support for markets are
examined later in this chapter; this question captures overarching support
or hostility to economic reforms.[59] There is a tendency for people who
favor the market reforms that occurred in Russia during the 1990s to also

59. Similarly holistic measures are used in standardized surveys. See, for instance,
Stephen White, Richard Rose, and Ian McAllister, *How Russia Votes* (Chatham, NJ: Chatham
House, 1997), 287. For more information on the measure of support for market reform used
in this chapter, see Appendix C. Americans were not asked a similar question and, consequently, are not categorized according to their support for markets.

Table 5.1 Characteristics of the Russian respondents, by their support for democracy

Low support for democracy	Mixed support for democracy	Moderate support for democracy	High support for democracy
Total: 6 respondents 3 female, 3 male	Total: 26 respondents 16 female, 10 male	Total: 16 respondents 9 female, 7 male	Total: 12 respondents 4 female, 8 male
1 under 30, 2 over 60	5 under 30, 8 over 60	6 under 30, 2 over 60	2 under 30, 3 over 60
4 Muscovites, 2 from Moscow Oblast	6 Muscovites, 5 from Moscow Oblast, 5 from Siberia	6 Muscovites, 3 from Moscow Oblast, 1 from Siberia	3 Muscovites, 1 from Moscow Oblast, 2 from Siberia
1 with higher education	7 with higher education	11 with higher education	9 with higher education
Support for markets: 5 low, 1 mixed	Support for markets: 10 low, 11 mixed, 5 high	Support for markets: 4 low, 4 mixed, 8 high	Support for markets: 4 low, 4 mixed, 4 high
Aleksei, Evgenii, Inna, Tatiana Mikhailovna, Valya, Vladimir Il'ich	Anna P., Boris B., Elena, Grigorii, Irina L., Ivan I., Katya, Klara, Kollektiv, Lena, Liuba, Nadya, Nikolai, Olga I., Pavel, Pelageia, Polina, Ruslan, Sergei, Sofiia, Valentina, Vasya, Vilen N., Yegor Y., Zinaida, Zoia I.	Aleksandra Antonovna, Alla, Anya, Ekaterina, Galina Grigor'evna, Iurii, Kolya, Lev, Mikhail, Raisa, Raya, Slava, Sonya, Svetlana, Tolya, Vitya	Andrei Viktorovich, Arkadii, Dima, Gennadii, Iosif, Konstantin, Liudmilla Vladimirovna, Marina Aleksandrovna, Misha, Nadezhda, Natalia, Oleg

rank high in support for democracy, but that connection is not particularly strong. The relationship between support for democracy and markets can be seen even more clearly in Table 5.2. Table 5.2 shows the regression line with favorable attitudes toward market reforms as the dependent variable and support for democracy as the independent variable. Although the variables are positively related, the regression line is not particularly steep and the strength of the relationship is significant only at the .05 level. As Table 5.2 also shows, a fair proportion of the sample falls fairly far from the line. People with negative attitudes to markets show up at all degrees of support for democracy, and there are market advocates among people with relatively less support for democracy. Again, my purpose here is to show how attitudes are distributed in my sample, in order to get a sense of overall patterns of attitudes, before focusing on the respondents' individual remarks.[60]

That there are a number of respondents for whom support for democracy and markets do not go hand in hand is also clear from Table 5.3, which shows how the individual respondents are distributed in terms of these attitudes. A large portion of the sample falls more or less on the diagonal running from lower left to the upper right. I will call the people on the lower left of Table 5.3 "skeptics" because they are skeptical about both markets and democracy. The second group, on the upper right, is composed of the "liberal democrats," with high support for both markets and democracy. The people on this diagonal appear to organize their ideas in the way Western observers expect, either supporting *both* markets and democracy or neither. But about a third of the sample is not on this diagonal, and how these people organize their ideas is of particular interest in this chapter. One group is made up of the people in the upper-left-hand part of the table. They are highly supportive of market reforms while less than perfect in their support for democracy. The other interesting group consists of the people in the lower-right-hand corner: strong democrats skeptical of markets. These last two groups defy easy labels. Although not strong proponents of democracy, people in the first group are not necessarily hostile to democracy and certainly not "authoritarians," as low supporters of democracy are sometimes labeled. And the market-skeptical democrats are not necessarily socialists, or at least we do not know that about them yet. So they will need to make do with awkward, hyphenated names.

---

60. For mass-survey results on this relationship, see, for instance, Kullberg and Zimmerman, "Liberal Elites"; Brym, "Re-evaluating Mass Support."

Table 5.2   Relationship between support for markets and support for democracy (linear regression, $N = 60$)

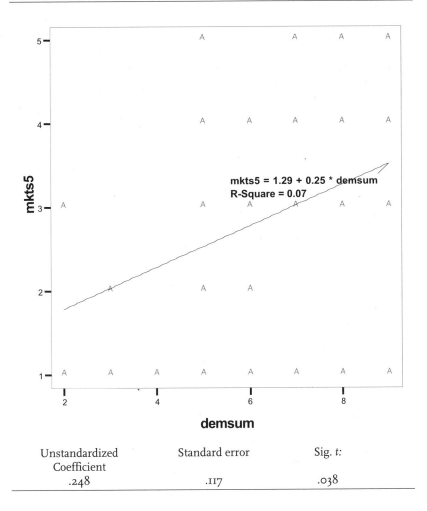

Unstandardized Coefficient	Standard error	Sig. t:
.248	.117	.038

In the discussion of individual respondents' comments that follows, readers may want to refer back to Table 5.3 in order to remember which respondents fall into which groups. Appendix A is a useful resource as well, providing demographic information about each of the respondents.

The measure of support for markets is based on a question that asked people to describe how they felt about the economic changes that had occurred in Russia over the past several years. It is clear from what people

Table 5.3   Distribution of respondents by support for democracy and markets

High support for markets, mixed support for democracy	Middle (mixed support for both democracy and markets)	Liberal Democrats (high support for democracy and markets)
Liuba, Vasya, Polina, Sofiia, Boris Borisovich *(5 respondents)*		Kolya, Misha, Slava, Vitya, Svetlana, Ekaterina, Iurii, Oleg, Raisa, Aleksandra Antonovna, Ludmilla Vladimirovna, Marina Aleksandrovna *(12 respondents)*
	Katya, Lena, Grigorii, Klara, Nikolai, Valentina, Pavel, Ruslan, Sergei, Vilen Nikolaevich, Zoia Igorevna *(11 respondents)*	
Skeptics (low markets, low or mixed democracy)		High support for democracy, low or mixed support for markets
Valya, Nadya, Evgenii, Zinaida, Aleksei, Inna, Kollektiv, Elena, Pelageia, Anna Pavlovna, Irina L'vovna, Ivan Ivanovich, Olga Iur'evna, Vladimir Il'ich, Yegor Yegorovich, Tatiana Mikhailovna *(mixed market, low democracy)* *(16 respondents)*		Dima, Raya, Sonya, Tolya, Anya, Gennadii, Iosif, Mikhail, Nadezhda, Alla, Arkadii, Konstantin, Lev, Natalia, Andrei Viktorovich, Galina Grigor'evna *(16 respondents)*

said when they answered the question that some people were offering ideas about economic reform in the abstract, while others were responding to the actual results of Russian reforms. In fact, people who were more supportive of market reform seemed to be thinking about how markets were *supposed to* function more than how they actually worked in Russia. They talked about the objective necessity of eliminating the planned economy and expressed certainty that the future would bring prosperity, even if the present had not yet. If they acknowledged problems that had occurred in Russia in the course of economic reform, they were more likely to blame those problems on insufficient reform than on markets themselves. Kolya, for instance, called market reform "an exit to a higher level" and expressed the opinion that any mistakes Yeltsin may have made were inevitable and temporary.

People *less* supportive of markets, however, were more likely to express dissatisfaction with the *actual* course of reform in Russia. Anna Pavlovna complained that it had become harder to live. She said, "Here the factories practically all stand idle. People work very little. . . . Now everything is there, everything is in the stores. But there isn't much money. We cannot buy everything, not everything, not even close. We get only what is necessary. . . . The directors of enterprises run things for themselves, it seems to me, and not for the people." The others in the sample who were hostile to markets echoed her litany of complaints. Among the strong democrats in the sample, people who were doubtful about markets tended to be the ones who focused on the particulars of how market reform had proceeded in Russia. Arkadii said, "It was necessary to try to get our products up to a world level, and not to obliterate everything that was. But this wasn't done." Gennadii explicitly drew the distinction between Russian and Western markets. He said, "The contemporary market did not bring economic freedom such as exists, for example, in the West. In fact, now there is even worse economic unfreedom than in the Soviet period."

So far, then, my first hypothesis seems to be supported, at least for people who are skeptical about market reform: people who look negatively at markets are more likely to assess them in terms of the actual practice of Russian markets. People who favor market reform, however, support the *idea* of markets, not necessarily exactly what has occurred in Russia. In order to further investigate differences in the thinking of people who do and do not favor markets, I now turn to an examination of how market advocates and market skeptics differ from each other in terms of evaluations of income inequality.

Income Inequality

One of the standard ways that researchers study popular attitudes toward economic arrangement is by examining evaluations of society-wide income distributions.[61] Approval of the existing income distribution is taken to

61. Miller, *Principles of Social Justice*, 61.

indicate that people think the economic system operates fairly and according to the appropriate standard of justice. Generally, researchers have found that people in capitalist countries accept inequality on the rationale that people who work harder or have greater ability should earn more, although some would prefer a bit less inequality than actually exists.[62] That is to say, people in capitalist countries apply a standard of justice based on desert. They think that some people deserve higher incomes, even if they are less convinced that higher incomes always go to the right people.[63] If my first hypothesis is correct, Russians will use the same standards even if they come to different conclusions about the justice of their own markets.

I asked the Russian respondents to choose between two abstract alternatives: a society characterized by material equality or one in which there are rich and poor people. Answers to this question and the explanations that accompanied them can help us extract the understandings of social justice that underpin attitudes toward markets. At first glance, it appears that Russia's market doubters apply different standards of justice from those of market proponents. In particular, we can see that skeptics prefer different principles of distribution from those of liberal democrats. For instance, Valya, a skeptic, clearly preferred equality to differentiation. She said, "When there is money, it is easy, nose in the air, not to notice even other people. To think the whole time that this is a lower rung, well, lower than me on the ladder. It seems to me it is better if people are identical, if there is material equality." Elena added that a more equal society was preferable because then she would not need to feel embarrassed about her unremodeled home, in which we were at the time cozily ensconced. Equality was not the preference of the majority in the skeptical corner, but people in this group were more likely to express preferences for equality than were people in any other group. Even when they accepted the justice of inequality, they tended to favor a relatively small gap between rich and poor. Nadya, for instance, defended a generally equal society that allowed some opportunity to accumulate wealth. She said, "I consider that there should not be poor people. There should be wealthy people. Equality, also.

---

62. McClosky and Zaller, *The American Ethos*, 84; Everett Carll Ladd and Karlyn H. Bowman, *Attitudes Toward Economic Inequality* (Washington, DC: American Enterprise Institute Press, 1998); James R. Kluegel and Eliot R. Smith, *Beliefs About Inequality: Americans' Views of What Is and What Ought to Be* (Hawthorne, NY: Aldine de Gruyter, 1986); Jonathan Kelley and M. D. R. Evans, "The Legitimation of Inequality: Occupational Earnings in Nine Nations," *American Journal of Sociology* 99, no. 1 (July 1993): 75–125.

63. Miller, *Principles of Social Justice*, 71–72, 83.

All the same, many of the wealthy help, undertake philanthropy. They help orphanages. It is necessary to have such wealthy people, who don't send their capital abroad but keep it here, who invest in Russia."

At the other end of the spectrum, liberal democrats clearly applied a principle of desert to evaluations of income distribution. They tended to think that an equal society is impossible to accomplish because it is unnatural: it fails to recognize the distinctions that exist between people. Oleg felt equality was an offense against those who work hard. Vitya focused on the injustice of rewarding a slacker the same as someone who put in more effort. Raisa added, "Whoever works more, who is more knowledgeable, brighter, should live better." Misha commented on the inevitability of inequality. He said, "Historically, it turns out that in society there exists both poor and rich. It's clear this will always be. Everyone has different wants, different desires. Everyone strives for something. Equality did not exist even under socialism. It simply was less sharply manifested. There was the government. Alongside them, there were the bosses, who lived better. Well, there should not be equality. Everyone should receive what he wants or desires for himself, what he strives for, what he deserves."

Generally, liberal democrats were not overly sensitive to the plight of the poor. Kolya commented, "In my opinion, the poor are just those who don't want to work. They are accustomed to receiving their ration. They are satisfied with that. And those who want to receive some kind of increase, so that they grow in their own eyes, society cannot make them equal. One way or another, there will be some kind of disparity."

People in the middle of this spectrum—neither strong proponents nor strong critics of both markets and democracy—seem to be more like liberal democrats than like the all-around skeptics. They did not favor social equality, although a few did worry about the welfare of the poor. In a comment that was representative of this middle group, Pavel said, "Material equality never was, no, and won't be. That's what I think. It is my personal opinion. Everybody gets what they work for." Lena expressed the softer side, more concerned with the situation of people who do not get much. She said, "Well, material equality can't exist on the whole. And the poor also should be relatively poor. Poor, but not starving. They should be able to dress themselves and study. That kind of poverty, yes. But again, I can't say lower than that, no. A person should be able to provide for himself." Her concern for the poor was consistent with distribution according to a principle of desert: poor people deserved the opportunity to work to improve themselves. She seemed to imply that they might also benefit from the negative incentives that their poverty provided. Similarly, Vilen Nikolaevich thought the government was obligated to help people with "deficiencies of the mind," that is people who in his view deserved help from the wider society.[64]

It seems, then, that people who favor markets and also democracy—even if only to a moderate degree—think social justice is determined by a principle of what people *deserve*, while people skeptical of both markets and democracy are more likely to be guided more by a principle of *equality*. But what about Russia's market-skeptical democrats? What principle do they use? Like Russia's liberal democrats, democrats who were more skeptical about markets tended to think that an equal society was a practical impossibility, and they were ready to reward deserving individuals with greater wealth. Where they differed from the liberal democrats was not in their view that social justice was based on desert but rather in their assessments of whether emerging inequality in Russia was the product of rewarding desert. They thought that in Russia too few people were benefiting to too great a degree, and that illegal methods produced undeserved wealth. Raya said, "Because it turned out that those who want to work, who don't want to steal, but want to work, they don't have the possibility to survive. People who work receive very little pay. And at the same time we see that people who are able to steal and take live very well. That's bad." The source of Raya's concern was not the *fact* that Russia was becoming a less equal society, but rather the *way* the inequality was arising. She continued, "Well, in society of course there needs to be both rich and poor people so that the poor will strive to live better. But this wealth should not be received by dishonest methods. That is, a person should earn it, display wit, some kind of ideas, in order to have a lot of money."

Natalia agreed with Raya's assessment of the kind of inequality developing in Russia. She said, "But when a small group of people takes all the national wealth, well, it's hard to resign yourself to that. No one can like that. All the same, work is not rewarded according to effort. Not according to physical, moral, or psychological effort, not by the level of knowledge or experience. Nothing like that. Unfortunately, it turns out that people who devoted many years to education, to the acquisition of some kind of professional experience—if they only have one job, they'll be paid badly."

64. Interestingly, these assessments of the justice of income inequality are also consistent with the Rawlsian notion that social inequality must benefit the least advantaged members of society. John Rawls, *Justice as Fairness: A Restatement,* ed. Erin Kelly (Cambridge, MA: Belknap Press of Harvard University Press, 2001), 42–43.

Some of the market-skeptical democrats were willing to accept inequality at the upper edges of society, but were more troubled by inequality at the bottom of society. Here, though, they did not necessarily abandon principles of desert: they were simply unconvinced that the poor deserved to suffer. Galina Grigor'evna said, "Let there be rich people. Let them be—those who can do something and improve our lives. But so that there would not be poor people. Very rich and very poor, far from each other in their views and in their lives, do not understand each other. I want to say, let the intelligent person—well, he invented something, like rockets—be wealthy. He's intelligent. Let him live well. But he lives on the improvement of our country. He produces something. He doesn't just grab it, like so many." Generally, democrats skeptical about markets also tended to be committed to social efforts to improve the welfare of those who did not prosper in market systems. They could see where some people might deserve to be wealthier than average, but none made a strong argument in defense of why others deserved to be poorer.

It seems, then, that a generalized commitment to an egalitarian society is not very common in Russia. Although some of the skeptics expressed such a preference, most did not. And very few others did at all. Based on this sample, most Russians seem fairly comfortable with a society in which some people earn more than others; they are comfortable with distributing wealth and income according to a principle of desert. And the more they favor markets, the more likely they are to hold these views. What distinguishes Russia's market-skeptical democrats is not that they would apply a different standard to evaluating the distribution of income in Russia. Rather, they look closely at the markets they know and think that the standard of desert does not apply to them. They doubt that those who have reaped rewards in the new Russia actually deserve them. The distinctiveness of the market-skeptical democrats is especially clear if we compare them to the other outliers in Table 5.3: people whose admiration for markets seems disproportionate given their comparatively low support for democracy. These people were strong defenders of the principle of desert. Polina, for instance, proclaimed, "Because it is always the realization of the person. Because where there is equality, it is not possible to have that realization. . . . But here everyone chooses his fate for himself. It is possible to sink to the bottom or to live decently." People with disproportionately high support for markets were satisfied enough that markets distributed rewards to the people who deserved them. Market-skeptical democrats believed Russian markets failed to observe the justice of desert.

Comparison with the American respondents is useful here to see whether Russia's market-skeptical democrats are unusually skeptical about the likelihood that markets would reward the deserving. If they are much more skeptical than Americans, that could indicate a culturally ingrained preference for other forms of economic organization. The comparison with the Americans shows that both Russians and Americans use the principle of desert to evaluate markets in similar ways.[65] Like Russian liberal democrats, many of the American respondents feared that government handouts to the poor would destroy incentives to work. Some added that people who lacked what they needed in America probably also lacked initiative. Many Americans agreed with Bill when he said, "If you work hard, and this is why I love America, if you work hard, you get what you deserve." Grace, for instance, said, "Well, I guess I would rather see a society where everybody has somewhat of a comfortable life, to a degree. I think you should only get it, though, if you deserve it. I don't believe in people getting things for nothing, so I think you should have to work for what you get. . . . I don't really feel you deserve it just because you're here breathing air."

But other of the respondents implied that there are things people deserve, not because they work for them, but just because they are human, because they breathe air. Rick said, "All people deserve the necessities of life." Ernest added, "Oh, well, I don't think we can any longer tolerate a society where people don't have the necessities of life. I mean, yes, individual initiative has to be rewarded, but it's scandalous that we have homeless people and undernourished children and things of that sort." These things seemed scandalous to Ernest because he thought all Americans deserved better, not because he thought all Americans should be equal. That is to say, Russia's market-skeptical democrats seem not unlike some Americans. Like Americans, Russians speak a language of desert, and they are not always convinced that markets provide people with the things they deserve. And they are not convinced that work is the only criterion that establishes desert.

Market Justice

It seems, then, that Russians who favor democracy but have doubts about markets apply the same standards when judging market outcomes as do

---

65. American respondents were asked a slightly different question. They were asked to choose between a society in which everyone has the material things they need, even if that

liberal democrats; they just come to different conclusions. Is this simply because market-skeptical democrats are more hostile to the way capitalism operates in Russia? Apparently not. Although market-skeptical democrats more regularly decried the injustice of Russian markets in their assessments of a preferable social distribution of wealth, they were far from alone in their criticisms of capitalism in Russia. I asked the Russian respondents whether they thought the distribution of wealth and income in Russia was fair. Unlike the question in the previous section, this question focused attention specifically on *Russian* conditions. Here, it turns out that respondents made similar assessments whether they favored market reforms or not. Very few respondents considered Russian market outcomes just.[66] Even proponents of markets found much to criticize. Similar complaints about the inequities of pay, for instance, occurred in all groups. Common complaints were that directors of enterprises had the power to set their own salaries and thus were able to set them disproportionately high, that the gap between the rich and the poor was too wide, that people at the mercy of the government budget suffered no matter how hard they worked, that pensions were too low, and that people did not have the money they needed to survive.

Russians of all degrees of market and democratic sympathy were particularly incensed about the way state property had been privatized. While they were happy that people could own their apartments and buy plots of land, they were unhappy with the way natural resources and industrial enterprises had been sold. Here, the common complaint was that whoever had greater power at the start of the privatization process had been able to grab more for themselves. Even the same words occurred in each group: *theft, plundering, grabbing, usurpation, deception.* Businessmen or any wealthy people were regularly characterized as "bandits." Nikolai, in the middle group, observed, "Voucher privatization proceeded with such deception that it was simply evident. Cynicism, simply, that it was all given away.

---

entailed moderating higher incomes, and a society where individual initiative is rewarded, even if it meant that some people could not afford the necessities of life.

The American sample was not divided into groups based on levels of support for markets or democratic values. This was primarily because, on measures parallel to the ones used to categorize the Russians, the Americans were not very different from one another. It was also troubling that the few individuals who showed up as marginally less democratic than the others were also the oldest and least educated people in the sample, raising suspicions that they simply answered the questions less well.

66. Twelve percent of the Russian sample thought the existing income distribution was just, versus 39 percent in the American sample.

Whoever was close to power took everything for themselves." Even the liberal democrats were critical. Misha said, "From the beginning, privatization was conducted unjustly. We were simply plundered, using some kind of connections or power. At the present time, there is practically no more to distribute. The best is always seized by whoever can." Among market-skeptical democrats, these comments were particularly strong. Sonya remarked, "Now it seems we are going through the stage of the primitive accumulation of capital. Earlier we had common property, which belonged to no one. And now—whoever had power, maybe whoever was smart, they tried to grab what they could from this big country and all its resources. It was a usurpation of property."

Although very few respondents were uncomfortable with the *idea* of private property, even private property in significant concentrations, very few were satisfied with the way Russia's resources had ended up in private hands. Raisa, a liberal democrat, said, "The wealth of the country—forests, oil, gas—ended up in the hands of individuals, even though this was social wealth, that belonged to the whole nation. Now those resources are in the hands of individuals, who have become practically the richest people in the world. On the national wealth, they receive more dividends. You could say, they don't grow with the nation, but live by themselves. I consider this unjust. And there are many such cases here now. During perestroika there was this unjust redistribution and it has been retained until now. The government lacks something—I don't know what they lack—to change this, even though everyone thinks it is unjust."

Raisa exaggerated when she said that "everyone thinks" the distribution of property in Russia is unjust. There were some people in the sample who defended the justice of the present situation and considerably more who had trouble figuring out how "justice" applied to economic conditions. We can gain further insight into the values that animate Russia's market-skeptical democrats by looking at what they say about the justice of market outcomes.

Liberal democrats and people in the middle group—with neither high nor low support for markets and democracy—were more likely than people in any other groups to see some kind of justice in the distribution of incomes in Russia. But even in these groups most respondents considered outcomes unjust. Comments typically revolved around the idea that justice is served when people who work get paid and people who do not work suffer. So, for instance, Sergei, an unemployed factory worker in the middle group, said, "Someone who knows how to earn money will earn money. Someone who doesn't know how won't earn anything. If you want to have an income, . . . you have to look." Sergei also defended the privatization of property in Russia as "probably just," since it was unrealistic for him to think he would share in the products of his labor.

This kind of comment was widely echoed in the American sample. For instance, Ted said, "Well, those who take the risks get rewarded. I don't believe . . .'the rich won the lottery of life.' You take a risk, sometimes it succeeds, sometimes it don't. Yeah, the rich get richer and poor get poorer. Yeah, it's tough, but if you have enough drive you can succeed." Among Russians, people who approved the existing distribution of property and incomes either had done rather well for themselves in the first years of reform or focused less on the privatization of factories and natural resources and more on the ability of ordinary citizens to buy apartments and cars, an opportunity favored even by people who had little good to say about markets. Other Russian respondents thought that economic outcomes could not be called just, but that did not trouble them. They did not consider that justice was often a product of the economic sphere. Boris Borisovich said, "Justice in this area is a fantasy of Marx, Engels, Lenin, Stalin. It never existed, does not exist now, and never will." Similarly, Sofiia said, "Well, if you notice that now property is sold and anyone who has money can acquire it, then it seems to me that it is not possible to speak of justice or injustice. It is simply fact." Marina Aleksandrovna, a liberal democrat, commented that the distribution of income was never just anywhere in the world: owners of factories make a lot of money because they can. Might may not make right, but it clearly shapes the distribution of income under market conditions.

Interestingly, Marina Aleksandrovna was not wholly convinced that *democratic* outcomes were always just either. Her interview included a long discussion about the questionable justice of letting the guilty go free because the government could not adequately prove their guilt. She concluded, "Is the economy bad now? Yes. Maybe capitalism isn't the best economic structure. Yes, maybe there are costs. Democracy, also, maybe isn't the best. But, as Churchill said, no one has yet thought up anything better. You understand, it's not an ideal. . . . Yes, democracy is difficult, because you let criminals go free. This is good. If you know they killed someone but you can't prove it, it's also bad. But you can't prove it, and that's it. And you know that a killer is walking the streets. This is also a cost, isn't it?" For Marina Aleksandrovna, democracy and capitalism were consistent in that neither promised just outcomes.

A few respondents also remarked on the existence of multiple standards of justice and admitted confusion about which one should apply in market conditions. Tatiana Mikhailovna, a skeptic about both markets and democracy, noted that from a socialist point of view, market outcomes were unjust, but from the point of view of people who had profited those outcomes seemed just indeed. One of those people who had profited, Ekaterina, made the same observation. She said, "For me, the distribution of income is just, but for others it's not."

Some observers have argued that Russian attitudes in the transition period suffered from "formlessness": Russians were trapped between two conflicting value systems and could not always figure out which one applied.[67] Tatiana Mikhailovna's and Ekaterina's comments seem at first to support this interpretation. But comparisons with people in the American sample show some of the same difficulties applying standards of justice. Leo, for instance, interjected "Well, what the hell's just?" before concluding that "you should not be prevented from earning it, but doggone it, you should not be given it." Bill's belief in markets and personal accountability conflicted with religious beliefs that gave him an obligation to care for the poor. He waffled, "Well, *just* is, I think, the wrong word to use. Because it's not just for anybody to be poor, but I think it's fair. I believe that most people are intelligent enough to be successful." That is to say, it is not only Russians, new to market discipline, who have trouble figuring out what is just when it comes to market outcomes.

Market-skeptical democrats were different from other Russians—and from some Americans—in that they were consistently able to articulate standards of justice that might be relevant to markets, apply them, and come to the conclusion that markets as they operated in Russia did not produce just outcomes. The standard of justice that they most commonly applied was a standard of desert, although respondents varied somewhat on what they based desert. For instance, Andrei Viktorovich thought income should be proportional to work. He said, "It seems to me that the distribution of incomes would be just if it were related to work, either current work or past work, but work all the same. It turns out that for people who worked their whole lives, their pensions don't permit them to live. For people who are working today, their real income does not depend at all on their real work. The income of people in business depends not on whether they are good businessmen. . . . It depends of whether they can bribe some bureaucrats or use other illegal methods." Nadezhda, by

---

67. James Alexander, *Political Culture in Post-Communist Russia: Formlessness and Recreation in a Traumatic Transition* (New York: St. Martin's Press, 2000).

contrast, was more willing to evaluate desert in a way that rated some work as more valuable than other work. She particularly decried the low wages for intellectual labor in Russia.

Tolya thought people deserved what they had attained by legal means. He said, "That property that people own legally and that they acquired by legal methods, consistent with existing law, is just. That property that people own illegally, that was acquired through graft, that's unjust, correspondingly. This property should be confiscated."

Less commonly, some people among the market-skeptical democrats applied a standard of need. Galina Grigor'evna thought that everyone should have the things that were necessary for a decent life. She said, "We don't what to live in clover. We want that our life would be real—not vegetative, but real life. That there would be no mansions, that everyone would have housing, that everyone would have food, that every person would have the same, and every person could study, could increase his qualifications and could live humanely. I only want a little. And of course that everyone could have medical treatment."

Liberal democrats, then, do not differ profoundly from market-skeptical democrats in their evaluations of Russian markets: both groups find much to criticize in the way capitalism works in Russia. Liberal democrats are different not in that they think markets operate more justly but in their willingness to suspend standards of justice when evaluating markets. That markets produce outcomes they themselves consider unfair does not seriously undermine their support. Market skeptics, however, are more likely to keep justice standards in their minds when they evaluate markets and to be more concerned when markets fail to operate according to those standards. While there are some exceptions, most democrats apply some form of a standard of desert. That is to say, market-skeptical democrats accept the principle of an unequal society, but not the practice of such inequality in Russia.

Thus, my first hypothesis seems to be confirmed. Market skeptics, no matter what their support for democracy, seem to form their assessments of markets in the immediate context of Russian markets. By and large, they apply standards of justice that are largely similar to those used by market proponents, with a heavy emphasis on the idea that work should be rewarded. Applying those standards, they judge Russian capitalism to be highly flawed. Proponents of markets, however, seem to try to downplay conditions in Russia in their assessments of markets or of justice. This may indicate a belief that markets, though flawed, represent the best available alternative to improve conditions in Russia. It could also represent something of an ideological component to faith in markets: liberal democrats are so certain that capitalism will produce a preferable society that they are willing to ignore the factual evidence and let considerations of justice slide. Ideological thinking also shows up in a minority of market skeptics: these people are still guided by standards of the socialist past and the equality it proclaimed.

Markets and Opportunities

Of course, self-interest could also be at work separating market-skeptics from market advocates. It is after all easier to overlook the injustice of others' circumstances than one's own. In this section, I examine evidence that proponents of markets, and particularly liberal democrats, think markets offer opportunities for people like themselves. In the Russian sample, people who favored market reform tended to be moderately better off than those who did not.[68] Many of the people who were relatively hostile to markets were pensioners who were earning money to supplement inadequate pensions by working as doormen, selling plastic bags in open-air markets, or renting out rooms in already crowded apartments. Others were doctors, teachers, college professors and others paid from the state budget, people who had considered themselves middle class under the Soviet system, but who were now clearly poor. Market supporters were more likely to live in Moscow or in cities and towns comparatively close to Moscow, where there were more opportunities than deep in the Siberian hinterlands.

Even though market supporters were *more* likely to have done comparatively well in changed conditions, only one could be categorized as "wealthy"

68. The correlation between support for markets measure and a measure of personal economic situation is .54, significant at the .001 level. The measure of personal economic situation was based on the respondents' own assessments of how they had been managing over the years of economic reform, a specific question asked of all respondents, as well as on other comments made in the course of the interviews. There was a tendency for respondents to evaluate their own economic situation as "fine," even after, for instance, a twenty-minute diatribe about how pensions were too low to secure survival or the admission that the family had become vegetarians because they could no longer afford meat, so attention to other comments was a necessary correction for stoical self-assessments. Multinational surveys have also produced evidence of a correlation between support for markets and personal economic well-being. See James R. Kluegel and David S. Mason, "Market Justice in Transition," in *Marketing Democracy: Changing Opinion About Inequality and Politics in East Central Europe,* ed. David S. Mason and James R. Kluegel (Lanham, MD: Rowman and Littlefield, 2000), 172–81.

even on a Russian standard. Among the market supporters were a number of people who were not doing especially well. Slava was unemployed at the time of his interview. Kolya, a clearly intelligent young man, had been forced to cut his schooling short after high school because his family needed another income. Overall, the promarket part of the sample was a hard-working group of people, with as many skilled workers as professionals and a number of people who had found creative ways to put their skills and resources to work in the new Russia.

There have been suggestions that the elderly have had particular difficulties adjusting to changed conditions in Russia, but that tendency was not borne out in this sample.[69] There were four pensioners among market supporters. Marina Aleksandrovna, for instance, had joined with other fellow teachers to form a private music school, putting her talents to use and earning more than she would in a state-run school. There were also many young people among the market critics. Valya, for instance, was one of the youngest respondents in the sample. She hardly remembered the Soviet system and was nostalgic only for perestroika-era rationing, when her family could get the things they needed, even if only at the price of standing in line for hours.

I asked the Russian respondents whether, in current conditions, a person who knew how to work well could make money, maybe even become rich. People who favored markets tended to answer this question positively. Ekaterina replied, "Certainly, and I call upon all." Other market supporters echoed her confidence and brevity. Vitya said, "Yes, exactly." Slava said, "Without doubt. If a person strives for something in general, then he will certainly achieve it." Polina affirmed, "If you work, you can live well." Boris Borisovich agreed, "Today everything depends on the individual, on his opportunities. He can earn money as he likes."

Only a few market supporters questioned whether all people had the opportunity to improve their material situation. Marina Aleksandrovna suggested that some people were closed out of opportunities because of their age, energy, or where they lived. Liudmilla Vladimirovna thought an honest nature might keep some people from getting rich. Sofiia commented, "Well, here, of course, it is hard to say yes or no, because many factors influence it. Simply there are examples where people are sufficiently educated and have

---

69. The correlation between age and support for markets was not statistically significant. This is likely an artifact of the small sample, which gives disproportionate weight to the small number of promarket elderly respondents.

specialties but cannot find applications for their abilities. There are quite a few examples."

Market doubters were more likely to focus on those examples where hard work was not enough, but even among those who showed little support for markets there were quite a few people who thought significant opportunities existed. Among skeptics, people were more likely to think that opportunities existed than that they did not. Pelageia, for instance, felt that as a pensioner she had few opportunities, but she seized the ones she could find and admonished others to do the same. She supplemented her pension by selling plastic bags in the market, and spoke with some heat about the necessity for young people to look for better jobs. She said, "Young people stand with us—young people, around twenty years old, selling shopping bags. We tell them, 'Girls, you can go to work. Well, OK, we stand there, pensioners. They already won't take us anywhere. . . . But you are young. Go and work. Why are you standing here? You need a steady job. You need to work for your interests. But you stand here with the old women, stand with these plastic bags. . . . Why aren't you ashamed?'" Even Zinaida, a stressed, overwhelmed employee of a barely operating defense-related factory, thought that people could improve their own material positions by selling privately the goods produced in their factories.

Among market skeptics, it was particularly those of a more democratic leaning who saw severe limits in the opportunities markets provide. While a couple of market-doubting democrats thought hard work was enough to push the ambitious ahead, most noted the importance of other qualities: working outside the public sphere, being able to see opportunities as well as being young enough to seize them, having an ability to do something that someone needed, living in an area where good jobs existed. Nadezhda commented, "Doctors are poor, no matter how hard they work. Well, that's the government budget sphere. Everything depends on where you work." Asked whether a person could improve his or her material situation through hard work, Dima replied, "Well, theoretically yes, of course. Theoretically. But at the same time, the majority of people who don't know how to work well may earn more than this person. And society doesn't always help him. Sometimes it gets in the way." Anya noted that "it is not enough to know how to work. It is necessary to have other qualities: assertiveness, maybe, and impudence."

The kinds of doubts expressed by market-skeptical democrats tended to be broader and more systemic than the ones expressed by less democratic market skeptics. For instance, the less democratic skeptics often complained about the limits of their own particular jobs or the injustice of their own situations. Nadya noted that she worked well but nonetheless was paid less than the government-calculated minimum for survival. Inna complained, "I have worked twenty-seven years. I want to work further, but all the same my financial situation does not improve through my work." Market-skeptical *democrats,* by contrast, complained about the state of the economy as a whole. They wondered how people could improve their situation through work if they could not find work, or if they had jobs but did not receive paychecks. Raya commented, "Even the intelligentsia, people like me, work well but in principle it is not possible to improve our material situation. And the same is true for workers, I know. I have some acquaintances, ordinary workers. They haven't been paid for several months." Tolya argued that, short of moving their families to Moscow, people in the provinces enjoyed few opportunities. As it turned out, within a year he had moved to Moscow, leaving wife and baby temporarily behind.

Some of the differences between people who saw opportunities in markets and those who did not seemed to lie in their own experiences. Where Lev, a market skeptic, complained that pay scales were equal across whole industries, Raisa, a market defender, extolled the virtues of the more sensitive pay scales where she worked. She said, "In our case, mine and my husband's, earlier we worked. It was the same kind of work, but there was equalization. You worked well; someone beside you drank the whole day; but you both received the same thing. But not now. Now we have mechanisms so that if you work—well, come to work, let's say, on Saturday, sometimes on Sunday, and stay late—if you work, you will be paid accordingly. Now whoever works badly receives little, so there is the possibility to earn." Raisa described hard times in the early years of Yeltsin's reforms, when her husband had searched through harvested fields, hoping to find potatoes that had been left behind so that the family would have enough to eat for the winter. But conditions for her family had improved over the years, and it is perhaps not surprising that she looked favorably on market reforms as a result.

By and large, though, market skeptical democrats were not concerned only about the limitations of their own situations. They clearly believed that the Russian economy did not provide very many people with meaningful opportunities. A useful contrast can be drawn here with the American respondents. While not all Americans believed that hard work alone would suffice for success, the other necessary quality that Americans tended to mention was luck. Jean, for instance, said, "You know, the luck of the draw. I think it's unjust sometimes, because one person could still be just as hard of a worker as another, but the other person with an education may have more money, just because they were lucky enough to be blessed with a good brain and go to college."

That is to say, Americans seem to see markets as rewarding hard work but also something of a game of chance. Market-skeptical Russians see a stacked deck. My second hypothesis, then, also seems to be confirmed: Russians who think that they and others like them can benefit from market opportunities are more likely to have confidence in markets and hence to think that markets and democracy can work together. Democrats who think markets benefit only the few are more mindful of the potential conflict between democracy and markets.

The Role of Government in the Economy

What are the political implications of these findings? Does the fact that many of Russia's democrats doubt the glory of markets make a return to some kind of authoritarian socialism more likely? How do the attitudes described so far help us understand popular support for Vladimir Putin's government?

Russians are thought to favor a paternalistic government that takes responsibility for the welfare of the population.[70] And indeed, in the Russian sample, many people at all levels of support for markets and democracy envisioned a significant role for the government in the economy. Among skeptics, the most common suggestion was that the government should guarantee jobs. Ivan Ivanovich said, "That's the direct responsibility of the state—to guarantee work at respectable pay." Aleksei agreed that the government "should take full responsibility for conditions in the country and the material position of the people." But advocates for a strong state role in the economy extended to people more supportive of markets. Grigorii, for instance, said, "Everyone now is looking for a way to earn money by some method so he can live better, not understanding that the whole ship

---

70. Vainshstein, "Totalitarian Public Consciousness;" Leonid Gozman and Alexander Etkind, *The Psychology of Post-totalitarianism in Russia* (London: Centre for Research into Communist Economies, 1992), 100–106; Zinaida T. Golenkova, Viktor V. Vitiuk, Iurii V. Gridchin, Alla I. Chernykh, and Larisa M. Romanenko, "Stanovlenie grazhdanskogo obshchestva i sotial'naia stratifikatsiia [The Formation of Civil Society and Social Stratification]," *Sotsiologicheskie issledovaniia*, no. 6 (1995): 14–24, translated in *Sociological Research* 35 (March–April 1996): 13

on which we are located is quietly sinking. Therefore, now it is necessary to create those conditions, it is necessary to limit opportunities for economic parasitism. . . . The state gives nothing to the family."

The feeling among many Russians was that the problems facing the Russian economy were too big for the individual to solve. Individual initiative would have limited effect hoisting up a sinking ship. Even many strong market supporters argued that the state needed to limit corruption, ensure the long-term viability of Russian industries, look after those who could not help themselves, and pay wages and pensions on time. Aleksandra Antonovna said, "It seems to me that the government should play a direct role in efforts to improve the material situation of the people. Quite a bit depends on the government. Quite a bit depends on the resolution of problems they are obligated to solve: like the payment of pensions, salaries, and so on." Vasya added, "The government should take care of its people. It should create new jobs, consistently increase the level of pay and the immediate survival minimum." Vasya's point was that the government should create the conditions that would enable people to take advantage of the opportunities that markets provide.

There were, of course, some market supporters who imagined a very minimal role for government in the economy. Polina thought the government's role was to get out of the way and not mess things up for ordinary people. Ekaterina said, "Of course, before everything else it is necessary to improve the material position of pensioners, before everything else. But the rest depends on us." Kolya thought the government should lower taxes to promote industry and help pensioners and students, but otherwise people should shoulder the responsibility for building up the economy. But these were minority views even among market supporters.

In most cases, market supporters and skeptics sounded a lot alike. Like liberal democrats, market-skeptical democrats thought the government was obligated to take care of the young, the old, the sick, and the disabled. They also imagined similar, and not necessarily highly intrusive, ways for the government to improve the economy. Iosif, for instance, suggested, "The state should stimulate the activity of people through wise laws, through wise tax policy. Naturally, to defend the most economically active part of the population." Similarly, Arkadii said, "The government should create the conditions by which the country can move ahead, improve. As a consequence, the government should support precisely those people who create this development and movement ahead. More than anything else, stimulate their activities." Andrei Viktorovich thought that the correct role of the government in the economy was to "make reasonable laws and enforce them." Anya suggested that maybe the role of the government was simply "to grant more freedom."

That is to say, market-skeptical democrats do not sound like a bunch of old socialists, eager to return to a planned economy. A few did suggest a reversal of the worse offenses of privatization. Some mentioned efforts to moderate income differences, particularly so that teachers and doctors were not among the worst-paid members of the population. But market supporters made similar suggestions. By and large, market-skeptical democrats wanted to see the distortions in Russia's markets fixed, not the markets themselves eliminated. And they were not waiting for government handouts, although they did think that government should take care of people who could not take care of themselves.

In this regard, the Russian respondents seem not all that different from the Americans. As with the Russians, among the Americans there were some in the sample who thought that government should simply stay out of the economy. Leo said, "It's not the responsibility; see, the government *does not create one damn thing*. It does not make a widget or any other item that you can see. The government strictly sits back and collects taxes and sets regulations. The hardworking people of the country have made it what it is, and the best thing the government can do, like I said earlier, is lead, follow, or get the hell out of the way." Of the president, Leo said, "I mean, he's not our dad, he's not our uncle, he's not Santa Claus or anybody like that." But many others in the American sample, like the Russians, envisioned a constructive role for government in stabilizing the economy; making sure people had good jobs; managing monopolies for the public good; providing welfare, jobs programs, and social security. Speaking about important parts of the president's job, Adam said, "I think that jobs for everyone in the United States [is] important. I think education and health care, I think those are the biggest things." The range of opinions in Russia pretty much matched the range in the United States, even though the American economy is doing a far better job of serving the interests of large segments of the population.

That Russian market skeptics do not advocate a return to socialism is clear as well from the political parties they favor. Table 5.4 shows the number of respondents who expressed some sympathy for Russia's various parties; respondents could make positive assessments of as many parties as they wanted. As Table 5.4 shows, there was notable support for liberal parties not only among liberal democrats in the sample, but also among people skeptical of markets. According to this table, market-skeptical democrats in the sample show greater sympathy for liberal parties than do disproportionate market proponents: 63 percent of market-skeptical democrats expressed some sympathy for liberal parties, while only 40 percent of disproportionate market proponents did.[71]

Obviously, not all these people vote for liberal parties: liberal parties have consistently fared poorly in parliamentary elections and did not receive enough votes in the party-list portion of the 2003 Duma election to win any seats.[72] But the reason for the poor showing of liberal parties seems to be that most people who expressed some sympathy for liberal parties also supported Putin's mainstream party—Edintsvo or Edinaia Rossiia, depending on the year—and apparently voted for the party they thought could win.[73] As Vitya said, "At one time I really liked Yabloko, but now I like Edinaia Rossiia more." He was particularly concerned that Yabloko was too small and had too few supporters to make a difference. Many others simply did not like Yavlinskii's personality or considered him more interested in self-promotion than in the good of the country.

People in the sample who were skeptical about both markets and democracy were more likely to support Zhirinovskii's Liberal Democratic Party than they were the Communists, but they preferred Edintsvo to either of those groups. In fact, the largest number of Edintsvo supporters comes from this skeptical group.

Putin is sometimes accused of wanting to take Russia back toward authoritarian practices and, in his attacks on Russia's oligarchs, of wanting to return to government control of the economy. Is this why the Russian people support him and the Edinaia Rossiia party? Not according to my respondents. As noted earlier, few of the respondents reported any sympathies for the oligarchs, who are widely believed to have stolen the national wealth with the complicity of Yeltsin's architects of privatization.

71. Disproportionate market supporters make up only a small group in this sample, and it is risky to base any firm conclusions on such a small number of individuals. It seems, though, that this group is somewhat politically disconnected: they expressed sympathy for fewer parties and not particularly the parties closest to their promarket position. One person favored the nationalist LDPR; sympathies for liberal parties tended to be for Yabloko, the best known but least promarket of the parties included in this category. This is consistent with findings that proreform constituencies are less politically active. See Donna L. Bahry and Lucan Way, "Citizen Activism in the Russian Transition," *Post-Soviet Affairs* 10, no. 4 (1994): 330–66.

72. Steven Lee Myers, "Putin Revels in Election, but Others Cite Flaws," *New York Times*, 9 December 2003, A1, A8.

73. Edintsvo (Unity) became Edinaia Rossiia in December 2001 when it united with the Yuzhkov-Primakov bloc, Otechestvo–Vsia Rossiia (Fatherland–All Russia).

Table 5.4   Party sympathies, 1998–2003

	KPRF[a]	LDPR[b]	Any liberal[c]	Edintsvo[d]	Total/(For Edintsvo)
Market and dem skeptic	4 / 25% / *31%*	6 / 38% / *50%*	4 / 25% / *13%*	5 / 46% / *33%*	16/(11)
Neither high nor low support	5 / 46% / *38%*	2 / 18% / *17%*	6 / 55% / *19%*	3 / 60% / *20%*	11/(5)
Liberal Democrat	0	1 / 8% / *8%*	9 / 75% / *30%*	3 / 60% / *20%*	12/(5)
Promarket, low democracy	0	1 / 20% / *8%*	2 / 40% / *6%*	1 / 33% / *7%*	5/(3)
Prodemocracy, low market	4 / 25% / *31%*	2 / 13% / *17%*	10 / 63% / *32%*	3 / 50% / *20%*	16/(6)
	13 / 22% / *100%*	12 / 20% / *100%*	31 / 52% / *100%*	15 / 50% / *100%*	· 60/(30)

NOTE: The top number represents the number of people in that category who expressed some sympathy for the party. The upper percentage is the percentage of people in that category who expressed some sympathy for the party. Numbers add up to more than the total for the category (or 100 percent) because people could express sympathy for as many parties as they wanted, and most chose more than one. The lower (italicized) percentage is the percentage of total support for that party provided by people in this category.

[a]Communist Party of the Russian Federation (Kommunisticheskaia Partiia Rossiskoi Federatsii).

[b]Liberal Democratic Party of Russia (Liberal-Demokraticheskaia Partiia Rossii).

[c]Includes support for Russia's Democratic Choice (Demokraticheskii Vybor Rossii), which existed in 1998, but not after that; Yabloko, which existed throughout the whole period of 1998–2003; or the Union of Rightist Forces (Soiuz Pravikh Sil), which did not exist in 1998.

[d]Includes support for Edintsvo (in 2000) and for Edinaia Rossia (in 2003). Respondents from 1998 are excluded, since neither party existed at that point.

Hence, taking back what seemed to be ill-gained wealth hardly troubled most of the respondents. Tolya explained, "Where people break the law, it is cataclysmic for the economy. Well, for example, the case of the oligarchs, of Berezovsky. People, having broken the law, created—that is, knocked together, let's say it like that—a big fortune. It's illegal. It must be stopped. But the course of reforms themselves, toward a market economy, I of course support."

By limiting the freedom of the very rich—or, as my respondents might put it, by curbing the licentiousness of the oligarchs—Putin seems to them to be reversing the worst offenses of the Yeltsin years and creating the foundation of an economic system that might provide opportunities for ordinary people.

Yegor Yegorovich provides the perspective of someone who has suffered much in the new Russia. Of peasant background, he nearly starved during World War II only to find that conditions in the countryside did not improve quickly after the war. By the time reforms started, he was too old to take advantage of them, and his wife and daughter were invalids. He complained that his pension was shamefully small: his family could buy only food, not clothes, and could not always afford the medicines they needed. But he proclaimed himself wholly satisfied with Putin. He said that Putin "started to give us something to live, he started to give us something to live, do you understand? The first president, Gorbachev, and the same with the second—they gave us absolutely nothing ever. They only—how can I tell you?—took everything to the devil's mother. Not far from here, there was an aviation factory, a large, good factory, an all-union enterprise. Under Gorbachev, everything was simply stolen. And now Putin gives us a little to live, a little, yes. The pension isn't much, but it helps. It helps a little. Well, Putin is a just man, a fine man."

Raisa provided the perspective from a different social strata; she is a member of the scientific intelligentsia. She said that before Putin, all state institutions "were in decline. We received miserly pay. We didn't have anything. For a year, they didn't pay us. We worked on sheer enthusiasm. . . . With the arrival of Putin, these questions began to receive attention. Resources began to be allocated for science, for the army. My sister is a teacher. She doesn't live badly now. My mom—she's already elderly—she was a doctor before she retired. Well, after leaving work, she also started to live better. . . . Well, and in general I like that Putin is modest in life. I feel that he doesn't steal, that he is honest. I like how he talks. I understand all his views, positions. That's what appeals to me. A serious consideration for our country has begun."

Dima was somewhat more critical of Putin but still considered him a vast improvement over the recent past. He said of Putin, "The president has very significant levers of influence on the situation in the country—both political and economic. And, as far as I can see, in my opinion not all these levers are being used, first, as much as they really can and, second, in a way that would help the population, although in comparison, if you compare with his predecessor, then of course it's like heaven and earth. Then the situation was simply catastrophic. Now it doesn't seem catastrophic, but I'm not fully satisfied."

In all, my respondents saw Putin as someone who, in Bill Clinton's words, felt their pain. And they thought he might be leading the way to a less painful economic reality, without abandoning markets, but also without abandoning citizens to dysfunctional markets. Mass surveys reinforce this finding. Whereas in the year 2000, at the start of Putin's reign, 13 percent saw the Russian economy improving, by 2002 almost 44 percent of respondents thought things were looking up.[74]

Conclusion

In this chapter, I set out to test two hypotheses: first, that the more Russians base their assessments of markets on the way markets operate in Russia, the less likely they are to support markets and the less likely they are to think that markets and democracy work well together and, second, that the more people think markets offer opportunities for people like themselves, the more likely they are to think that markets are consistent with democracy. Both hypotheses were supported by analysis of the intensive interviews, particularly for the group of respondents who were positive about democracy but negative toward markets.

According to the analysis presented here, market-skeptical democrats in Russia are not profoundly different from liberal democrats. Like liberal democrats, they do not favor an equal distribution of wealth. Like liberal democrats, they think that economic life should be governed by principles of desert and that not all people deserve exactly the same things. Like liberal democrats, they question whether Russian markets operate according to these principles. Like most liberal democrats, they think it is the job of government to care for the least fortunate within society. Where market-

74. Gorshkov, *Rossiiskoe obshchestvo*, 461.

skeptical democrats differ from liberal democrats is in the significance they give to the problematical nature of Russian capitalism. Given the outcomes of market reform in Russia, market-skeptical democrats are less convinced than liberal democrats that markets hold the answers Russia seeks. They see fewer opportunities for most people to prosper and more threats to the general welfare. Despite those differences, they favor similar parties to the liberal democrats and, like liberal democrats, they support Putin because he seems to be making it possible for more people to live well in the new Russia.

Even all-around skeptics, people who favor neither democracy nor markets, have a lot in common with liberal democrats. Although this is the group most likely to advocate an equal distribution of wealth, many in this group are ready to embrace principles of desert and the inequality they imply. Even though skeptics provided nearly a third of Communist Party supporters in the sample, they also provided a third of the supporters for the centrist Edinstvo party, also favored by liberal democrats.

The Russian respondents also showed a fair amount in common with the Americans in the way they organized their political and economic values. Like Russia's market-skeptical democrats, many in the American sample believed that the poor deserve the help of the wider society. Like some Russians, some Americans were confused about which principles of justice could be used to evaluate markets. Like most of the Russians, many Americans saw a constructive role for government in stabilizing the economy and promoting growth. All in all, Russians do not seem to have a culturally distinctive way of organizing their economic and political values. They use the same standards and reach many of the same conclusions that Americans do.

Where Russians are very different from Americans is in their assessment of their own economic system. While Americans in the sample seemed to have economic prosperity on their minds when they declared, like Leo, that the United States is "the greatest country on the face of the earth," where "you can do anything you damn well please," most Russians saw their own economic system as one riddled with favoritism, corruption, and criminality, with opportunities for the few and dangers for the many. Given the similarity in how they otherwise organize their ideas, this difference in the ways Americans and Russians assess their own economic systems does not seem to be rooted in different assessments of capitalism in the abstract. Instead, it appears to be rooted in different manifestations of capitalism in the two countries. Russians, especially market skeptics, seem to have their own economic system in mind and the opportunities it appears to offer them when they formulate their opinions of markets.

In some ways, this is good news. While there were many critics of the market reforms that had occurred in Russia, only a small fraction of those critics were ideological opponents of markets. Only a fraction of critics advocated equalization of wealth or the elimination of risk in economic life. But it is also a challenge to the Russian government to transform the present economy into one that better serves the needs of more people.

My respondents were fairly clear about what they wanted to see happen in the near future. They wanted people to live better, closer to the Western European standard. They wanted their immediate problems addressed: problems such as the rapidly rising costs of utilities, housing shortages, unemployment worries. They wanted a greater focus by government on, as Vasya said, "the undefended strata of the population: pensioners, children, well, the homeless." Some had grander hopes, among them Liuba, who said, "I would hope that money wouldn't be the key to happiness, whether you have money or not. That apartments be provided freely, that it would be possible to find work without difficulty, that paying for the education of children would be easier, that they would give out school-books so that parents didn't have to always be buying." But others wanted only that conditions not get worse, and even high hopes were tempered by difficult realities. Dima said, "I would like, first, that there would be no poor people, so that all of our citizens in the country were provided with minimal material welfare and social protections. Well, second, that, say the average level of life got closer to—well, later of course."

Market-skeptical democrats among my respondents are not convinced that a capitalist Russia can never provide for the general prosperity of the population; they are only worried that it has not yet and does not always seem to be moving in that direction. World practice seems to show that capitalism works best to serve the needs of the majority when it is combined with a political system that respects individual rights and averts predation by narrow interests, that is to say, when it is combined with democracy.[75] The Russian government, of course, still has much work ahead of it in this regard. But to many of my respondents, containing the oligarchs was a step toward reducing the role of predatory interests in the Russian state.

---

75. Mancur Olson, *Power and Prosperity: Outgrowing Communist and Capitalist Dictatorship* (New York: Basic Books, 2000).

In pushing for a capitalism that benefits the population broadly as well as for a political system that protects individual rights and provides security from criminals, from business unbounded by law, and from arbitrary authorities, Russia's market-skeptical democrats may be the key to the future of liberal democracy in Russia. Unlike Russia's liberal democrats, they are not ready to endorse a system still floundering at finding its path.

Views on Order, Disorder, and Democracy

Russians seem to have a distinctive concern for order. Order—along with security, conscience, and lawfulness—is among the values that Russians tend to rank as more important than democracy.[1] Indeed, in surveys conducted by the All-Russia Center for the Study of Public Opinion, consistently close to 80 percent of the respondents say that order is more important than democracy.[2] Some Russians think that greater social order is sufficient cause for limiting individual freedoms.[3] And studies have shown that perhaps half the Russian population favors a leader with a "strong hand" capable of solving their country's problems and bringing, presumably, order.[4] There appear to be reasons, then, to think that this Russian concern for order might undermine democracy, or that Russians might have a cultural preference for an autocrat reminiscent in some ways of rulers from their past. In this chapter, I use the interviews with Russians to examine what Russians mean when they talk about order and its inverse, disorder. And I use their explanations to explore further how they think about democracy.

I find that while it is certainly true that some Russians have something like Stalin's image in mind when they praise order,

1. Vladimir Valentinovich Lapkin and V. I Pantin, "Tsennosti post-sovetskogo cheloveka," in *Chelovek v perekhodnom obshchestve: Sotsiologicheskie i sotsial'no-psikhologicheskie issledovaniia,* ed. G. G. Diligenskii (Moscow: Institute of World Economics and International Relations, 1998), 29.

2. vTSIOM, "Informatsiia: Nastroeniia, mneniia i otsenki naseleniia," *Monitoring obshchestvennoe mneniia: Ekonomicheskie i sotsial'nye peremeny; Informatsionnyi biulleten',* no. 1 (1997): 52.

3. James L. Gibson, "The Struggle Between Order and Liberty in Contemporary Russian Political Culture," *Australian Journal of Political Science* 32, no. 2 (1997): 271–90; James L. Gibson, "Putting Up With Fellow Russians: An Analysis of Political Tolerance in the Fledgling Russian Democracy," *Political Research Quarterly* 51 (March 1998): 37–68.

4. Igor' Moiseevich Kliamkin, E. Petrenko, and L. Blekher, *Kakim mozhet byt' avtoritarnyi rezhim v Rossii?* (Moscow: Fond "Obshchestvennoe mnenie," 1993), 10; Grigory I. Vainshstein, "Totalitarian Public Consciousness in a Post-totalitarian Society," *Communist and Post-Communist Studies* 27, no. 3 (1994): 254; Boris Dubin, "Zapad, granitsa, osobyi put': Simvolika 'drugogo' v politicheskoi mifologii sovremennoi Rossii," *Monitoring obshchestvennoe mneniia: Informatsiia analiz,* no. 6, issue 50 (2000): 25–34.

most apparently do not. They refer instead to an end to the raw unpredictability of their daily lives, racked as they are by economic upheavals, capricious authorities, and social disintegration. For many Russians, democracy is not order's opposite, and democratic mechanisms may be a means to construct greater social order.

To understand what Russians mean by order, it helps to try to mentally inhabit the day-to-day world in which Russians live. In the declining years of the Soviet system, this was a difficult and unpredictable world where the behavior of individuals bore little resemblance to the selfless ideals of Communist dogma or official propaganda. Instead, as some of the best explanations for the rapid collapse of Communist regimes have pointed out, the presumed order of the Soviet system unintentionally set in motion a number of disintegrative processes that ultimately provided both incentives and opportunities for lower-level officials to "steal the state," for nationalist leaders to undermine the foundations of Soviet empire, and for enterprise managers to appropriate the patrimony of struggling workers.[5] Behind the facade of Communist control, there was an alternate reality of incipient chaos. With Communist power now gone, that chaos has emerged into full view. Government officials use their power for private ends, apparently going so far as to spend money earmarked to pay for public utilities to build themselves elegant homes.[6] Business executives take out murder contracts on their competitors. Workers sell their factories' products on street corners to make up for their own missing or diminutive wages.

While the systemic dysfunction of Soviet-style Communism and of the "bandit capitalism" that followed it have been well described, studies of Russian public opinion have given little attention to the impact on ordinary citizens of living in a dysfunctional universe. Many public opinion scholars seem to assume that, at least as long as the Soviet Union existed, Russians inhabited a system that lived up to its hype: a system that provided order, security, and a predictable if not free existence. The assumption seems to be that, while government bureaucrats sold their services and enterprise

5. Jerry F. Hough, *Democratization and Revolution in the USSR, 1985–1991* (Washington, DC: Brookings Institution, 1997); Steven L. Solnick, *Stealing the State: Control and Collapse in Soviet Institutions* (Cambridge, MA: Harvard University Press, 1998); Valerie Bunce, *Subversive Institutions: The Design and Destruction of Socialism and the State* (New York: Cambridge University Press, 1999); Mancur Olson, *Power and Prosperity: Outgrowing Communist and Capitalist Dictatorship* (New York: Basic Books (Perseus, 2000).

6. Michael Wines, "In Russia's Far East, a Region Freezes in the Dark," *New York Times*, 12 February 2001, A6.

managers stole their factories, ordinary citizens went about orderly lives and absorbed the values of an adequately functioning authoritarian regime. Hence, their preference for order must reflect these values. But if, like people closer to institutional sources of power, ordinary citizens also experienced the chaos behind the facade, then it is less clear that they would understand order in authoritarian terms.

In this chapter, I use the interviews to explore the connections between a disordered daily existence, a yearning for order, and the meaning of democracy for ordinary Russians. The interviews show that Russians are less likely to support democracy and more likely to understand *order* in authoritarian terms if they are troubled by the chaotic conditions of their daily lives. More democratic Russians, however, understand order as providing the conditions under which individual freedoms can be realized, and they see strong government as a mechanism for the accomplishment of popular goals. For these more democratically oriented Russians, order is intimately linked to a rule of law and is potentially compatible with democracy.

The Disordered Soviet Union

The leaders of the Soviet Union meant to create a new world order. A rationally planned economy would free people from the unpredictability of capitalism. A powerful regime guided by the Communist Party's understanding of the true path of history would organize the citizenry for its pursuit of social justice and global power. However, none of this quite came off. As the country lurched from revolution to civil war and from forced industrialization to world war, the lives of ordinary people were beset by turmoil.[7] In the years after Stalin's death, as gulags began to shrink and stagnation replaced rapid social change, conditions became less overtly chaotic, and the regime managed to provide stable prices and guaranteed jobs. Beyond these benefits, though, life for ordinary Russians lacked elemental predictability.

The practical results of central planning, for instance, are well known. Lines in stores were long, goods were scarce, and supplies erratic. Both

7. Russian polls show that while Russian citizens considered the 1990s to be a difficult time, they thought those years were not as difficult as World War II or the period of Stalin's repressions. See Petr-Emil Mitev, Veronika Alekseevna Ivanova, and Vladimir Nikolaevich Shubkin, "Katastroficheskoe soznanie v Bolgarii i Rossii," *Sotsiologicheskie issledovaniia*, no. 10 (1998): 114.

consumers and producers hoarded resources against the day when they would not be available. In an economy designed for anything but their convenience, consumers found provisioning a family to be a difficult, time-consuming, and unpredictable chore. As one Soviet-era joke pointed out, "The Russians have absolute proof that the Bible is wrong. According to the holy book originally there was chaos, and then there was order. The Russians know from experience that this is not so. *First* there was planning, and *then* there was chaos."[8]

From the point of view of ordinary citizens, the political realm was no easier than the economic to comprehend and outmaneuver. The Soviet regime declared itself a socialist democracy but gave citizens no choice in elections and no rights of free speech or assembly. Citizens suffered the capriciousness of government officials, with little hope for recourse. Red banners proclaimed the government's commitment to the workers, while government officials shopped at special stores filled with the goods that workers wanted but were not allowed to buy. Tim McDaniel commented, "Word did not correspond to deed, professed belief to actual practice. Society acquired surreal qualities; every word and act had to be interpreted, not according to face value, but in terms of the hidden meaning of events."[9]

In an effort to adapt to political and economic incoherence, Russians developed personal and social networks that provided needed goods and protection in an unpredictable environment. Some of these networks were legal and institutionally encouraged, such as the workplace *kollektiv* or the provision of goods through enterprise-level social programs.[10] Others were more informal, such as groups of acquaintances that traded scarce goods and services or understandings between enterprise directors that secured needed but elusive resources. Some, of course, were directly criminal. What all these networks had in common was that they made it less likely that hierarchical structures would actually work, that commands would be obeyed, that decisions would be implemented. The crucial role of personal networks as survival mechanisms meant for many people that the needs of the network superseded any commands from higher up a

---

8. John Kolasky, ed., *Laughter Through Tears: Underground Wit, Humor and Satire in the Soviet Russian Empire* (Bullsbrook, Australia: Veritas, 1985), 135.

9. Tim McDaniel, *The Agony of the Russian Idea* (Princeton: Princeton University Press, 1996), 14.

10. Sarah Ashwin, "Endless Patience: Explaining Soviet and Post-Soviet Social Stability," *Communist and Post-Communist Studies* 31, no. 2 (1998): 187–98.

hierarchy perceived to be both dangerous and ineffective.[11] Workers "pretended" to work and stole from their factories what they could not find on store shelves. By underreporting production, enterprises could keep some of their products for themselves and sell them on the side. Bribes and other illicit payments to secure favors and goods were hidden in deceptive accounting practices. Even party and state officials, by exacting the tribute that forced others into illegal activity, contributed to a cycle of self-seeking behavior that ensured that few knew exactly what was going on and fewer still could control it.[12]

Perestroika deepened the dysfunction faced by ordinary people and provided new opportunities for self-seeking behavior across Soviet society. Goods disappeared from stores; local laws contradicted federal laws; and the main aspects of stability that had been provided by the Soviet system—constant prices and guaranteed employment—evaporated. As citizens faced empty shelves and declining material security, they remarked with some disappointment that perestroika meant "the truth, only the truth, and nothing but the truth."[13] One of Nancy Ries's informants went so far as to call Russia of the perestroika period the anti-Disneyland, "a gargantuan theme park of inconvenience, disintegration and chaos."[14] For government officials trying to protect their own interests, perestroika presented expanded opportunities to put state resources to private use. By the end of the Soviet period, Soviet society suffered from a massive "principal-agent" problem. The principals—higher-level party officials— had few mechanisms to ensure that their agents—everyone else—were

11. McDaniel, *The Agony of the Russian Idea*, 124; Leonid Gozman and Alexander Etkind, *The Psychology of Post-totalitarianism in Russia* (London: Centre for Research into Communist Economies, 1992), 49.

12. Konstantin M. Simis, *USSR: The Corrupt Society; The Secret World of Soviet Capitalism* (New York: Simon and Schuster, 1982); Arkady Vaksberg, *The Soviet Mafia*, trans. John and Elizabeth Roberts (New York: St. Martin's Press, 1991); Brian Kuns, "Old Corruption in the New Russia," in *The Russian Transformation: Political, Sociological, and Psychological Aspects*, ed. Betty Glad and Eric Shiraev (New York: St. Martin's Press, 1999), 119–24.

None of this is to imply that the Soviet system was destined to collapse. It could, perhaps, have continued in this dysfunctional pattern for a number of years, had not Gorbachev decided to implement reforms that changed what people could get away with. See Vladimir E. Shlapentokh, *A Normal Totalitarian Society: How the Soviet Union Functioned and How It Collapsed* (Armonk, NY: M. E. Sharpe, 2001).

13. Iurii Borev, *Istoriia gosudarstva sovetskogo: V predaniiakh i anekdotakh* (Moscow: RITTOL, 1995), 221.

14. Nancy Ries, *Russian Talk: Culture and Conversation During Perestroika* (Ithaca: Cornell University Press, 1997), 42.

performing their appointed tasks. Adequate supervision depended on accurate information, but the only source of information were the agents themselves. And just as the regime lied to the people, the people had every incentive to lie in return.

Ultimately, all this self-seeking behavior undermined Soviet political institutions and established the foundations of an oligarchic capitalism. But as we saw in the previous chapter, most ordinary people reaped few benefits from the collapse of the command economy and were subject to increasing unpredictability, particularly when their employers failed to pay wages due. In the three years after 1991, average consumer prices increased by several thousand times, while the population's real income declined by approximately 150 percent.[15] By spring 1993, more than half the population had incomes below the subsistence minimum.[16] A few years later, Russian sociologists estimated that about a third of the population lived in extreme poverty and only a sixth lived under good conditions.[17] After almost ten years of economic reform, E. I. Stepanov of the Institute of Sociology of the Russian Academy of Sciences estimated that 65 to 80 percent of the inhabitants of Russia were poor, while the wealthy made up only 1.5 to 5 percent of the population.[18]

As ordinary Russians suffered, criminals prospered. According to data from the State Duma Committee on Security, by the late 1990s organized crime controlled around 40 percent of private and 60 percent of state enterprises, and between 50 and 85 percent of banks.[19] Even if Russians could accumulate money beyond their subsistence needs, they would have trouble finding a safe place to put it. And its value might vanish in the next fiscal emergency. It was not lost on the Russian population that that fiscal emergency would likely have all the earmarks of deliberate

15. Tatiana I. Zaslavskaia, "Biznes-sloi rossiiskogo obshchestva: Sushchnost', struktura, status," *Obshchestvennye nauki i sovremennost'*, no. 1 (1995): 17–32.

16. Aleksandr Kazintsev, "Na pereput'e: Vybornoe shou i glubinnaia zhizn' Rossii," *Nash sovremennik*, no. 2 (1994): 112–28, translated in *Russian Social Science Review* 36 (July–August 1995): 28–65.

17. S. M. Khenkin, "Potensial massovogo protesta v usloviiakh protivorechivykh peremen," *Politiia*, no. 2, issue 8 (1998): 129–46. Khenkin cites Leonid A. Gordon, A. Terekhin, and Ie. Bubilova, *Monitoring obshchestvennoe mneniia: Ekonomicheskie i sotsial'nye peremeny; Informatsionnyi biulleten'*, no. 2 (1998): 18.

18. E. I. Stepanov, "Politika i Ekonomika v Sovremennoi Rossii: Konflikt na pereput'e (Kruglyi Stol)," *Sotsiologicheskie issledovaniia*, no. 2 (2000): 87–100.

19. Aleksei Aleksandrov, "Korruptsiia trebuet zhertv," *Argumenty i Fakty*, no. 9 (February 1998): 2. See also David Satter, *Darkness at Dawn: The Rise of the Russian Criminal State* (New Haven: Yale University Press, 2003).

government policy. R. V. Ryvkina observed, "The logic in these conditions is this: the economic policies of the government lower the living standard of the population, give rise to mistrust toward those in power, contribute to a growth in crime, and create disorganization in society."[20]

During the 1990s, citizens and the news media commonly categorized political events as theater of the absurd or, as time progressed, as a circus or a zoo.[21] With good reason. So-called democrats regularly called for the imposition of authoritarian rule, while the remnants of the old Communist Party advocated the rights of a free opposition.[22] While Yeltsin was president, he maintained control over a wayward system by shelling his parliament, threatening to forego elections, and regularly firing his own government for having the temerity to follow his lead. The institutions and individuals of government were in direct conflict with each other, often ignoring each other's decisions.[23] Caught in an ideological vacuum, many individual politicians pursued their own selfish goals, intensifying corruption while undermining public confidence.[24] The result was a series of scandals involving suitcases full of money being carried out of the Kremlin and videos of sexual indiscretions. In such an atmosphere, even the most outrageous interpretations—that, for instance, the government was setting bombs in apartment buildings in Moscow to build support for intensifying the attack on Chechnya—might begin to seem plausible.[25]

20. R. V. Ryvkina, "Politika i ekonomika v sovremennoi Rossii: Konflikt na pereput'e (kruglyi stol)," *Sotsiologicheskie issledovaniia*, no. 2 (2000): 94–95.

21. Elena Iur'evna Meleshkina, "Perspektivy i ogranicheniia politicheskoi reformy," *Polis: Politicheskie Issledovaniia*, no. 4 (1999): 85; Olga Shevchenko, "Bread and Circuses: Shifting Frames and Changing References in Ordinary Muscovites' Political Talk," *Communist and Post-Communist Studies* 34, no. 1 (March 2001): 87.

22. Leonid Nikitinskii, "'Million terzanii' zabludshego intelligenta (popravki k paradigme)," *Obshchestvennye nauki i sovremennost'*, no. 2 (1995): 120.

23. Ivan Kachanovskii, "Budushchee liberal'noi demokratii v Rossii," *Obshchestvennye nauki i sovremennost'*, no. 2 (1995): 55–56; Vladimir Valentinovich Lapkin, "Prezhde chem vypisyvat' retsept, trebuetsia utochnit' diagnoz," *Polis: Politicheskie Issledovaniia*, no. 4 (1999): 75–76.

24. Archie Brown, "From Democratization to 'Guided Democracy,'" *Journal of Democracy* 12, no. 4 (2001): 37–38.

25. Victor Pelevin's novel *Homo Zapiens* takes political outrageousness to its logical conclusion and posits that Russian politicians only exist as 3-D computer graphics, with special public relations workers trying to convince an unwitting public that their leaders really exist. "There's a special service for that called The People's Will. More than a hundred of them, former state security agents, and all Azadovsky's men. That's their job: to go around telling people they've seen our leaders. One at his three-storey dacha, one with an under-age whore, one in a yellow Lamborghini on the Rubliovskoe Highway." Victor Pelevin, *Homo Zapiens* (New York: Viking, 1999).

Is this an environment likely to create a preference for autocratic order? Some observers have argued that it was Russia's *rulers* who were inclined to suppress the danger of instability through total control, while ordinary Russians developed a high tolerance for chaos.[26] Indeed, the cultural image of the Russian male/nation as "a powerful, menacing, mischievous hooligan, wrecking havoc on the societies and economies he/it touches, contaminating and spoiling everything along the way," shows some perverse pride in disorder.[27] Semen Faibisovich argued that "in a situation of permanent cataclysm and in an atmosphere of total absurdity," pragmatic behavior was difficult. People in more orderly societies could plan for a knowable future, but Soviet citizens had to let matters they could not control take a course they could not predict. Faibisovich continued, "We assume in advance that life in the Russian whorehouse (or, on the other hand, on the Procrustean bed of totalitarian daily existence) is 'stupid and inconvenient,' but the absence of individual deliberate planning only deepens the chaos."[28]

Even so, Russians complained about the unpredictability of their lives. A survey conducted by Vladimir Lapkin and Vladimir Pantin showed that by 1996, only 1 percent of respondents thought there was order in Russia. Lapkin and Pantin's respondents mostly blamed the government for the disorder they observed: 21 percent felt the government lacked the power to prevent lawbreaking, 37 percent observed that the government itself broke laws, 25 percent blamed bad laws, while only 8 percent thought that the problem lay in the fact that citizens did not obey the laws.[29] Ordinary Russians had little faith that social institutions would perform correctly. According to surveys conducted by Richard Rose, in the late 1990s less than half believed that the police would protect a home from burglary; only one in six would borrow a week's wages from a bank; 80 percent grew food for family consumption.[30] The rise in crime was consistently near the top of the list of things that worried Russians, at the same time

26. Aleksandr S. Akheizer, "Dezorganizatsiia kak kategoriia obshchestvennoi nauki" [Disorganization as a Category of Social Science], *Obshchestvennye nauki i sovremennost'*, no. 6 (1995), 42–52. Also published in *Sociological Research* 35 (September–October 1996): 65–81.

27. Ries, *Russian Talk*, 78–79.

28. Semen Faibisovich, *Russkie novye i nenovye: Esse o glavnom* (Moscow: Novoe Literaturnoe Obozrenie, 1999), 43.

29. Vladimir Valentinovich Lapkin and Vladimir I. Pantin, "Russkii poriadok," *Politicheskie issledovaniia*, no. 3 (1997): 76–77.

30. Richard Rose, "Living in an Antimodern Society," *East European Constitutional Review* 8, nos. 1/2 (1999): 72.

that confidence in the police plummeted.[31] Throughout the late 1990s, a majority considered the economic situation either poor or very poor; after the financial collapse of 1998, they considered the situation unbearable.[32] People yearned for greater confidence in what tomorrow would bring.[33]

The disordered reality of the late Soviet and post-Soviet world has been convincingly described on an institutional level and clearly has been recognized by ordinary Russians, but it has not yet been well integrated into the study of Russian public opinion. Instead, students of Russian public opinion, while basing their assessments of present attitudes on the data at hand, have tended to assume that the Soviet regime successfully inculcated in its citizens authoritarian attitudes and an appreciation for government economic paternalism. If these are not the orientations present in their data, then the reason must be that attitudes have changed over time, perhaps as a result of widespread social change or the growth of an increasingly urban, educated population.[34] Even studies that recognize the disordered present facing Russian citizens contrast this new disorder with an older order lost in the transition and imply that it is the newness of disorder that makes it hard for citizens to cope.[35] Continued popular commitments to order, as a result, are usually interpreted as holdovers from the past and thus as obstacles to support for democracy.

My approach in this chapter is different. I look to the unpredictability—the disorder—of daily life both in the late Soviet Union and in post-Communist Russia to illuminate Russians' imperfect support for democracy, particularly their apparent longing for order. This chapter, then, extends the argument of previous chapters. Where Chapter 4 showed how some imperfections in support for democracy could be traced to the actual functioning of democratic institutions in Russia, and where Chapter 5 showed how suspicions of

31. N. I. Lapin, *Puti Rossii: Sotsiokul'turnye transformatsii* (Moscow: Rossiiskaia Akademiia Nauk, Institut Filosofii, 2000), 124–26.

32. VTSIOM, "Informatsiia: Resul'taty oprosov," *Monitoring obshchestvennoe mneniia: Informatsiia analiz*, no. 1, issue 51 (2001): 66.

33. Iurii Levada, "Koordinaty cheloveka i itogam izucheniia 'cheloveka sovetskogo,'" *Monitoring obshchestvennoe mneniia: Informatsiia analiz*, no. 1, issue 51 (2001): 7–15.

34. For instance, William M. Reisinger, Arthur H. Miller, Vicki L. Hesli, and Kristen Hill Maher, "Political Values in Russia, Ukraine, and Lithuania: Sources and Implications for Democracy," *British Journal of Political Science* 24 (April 1994): 183–223; Jeffrey W. Hahn, "Continuity and Change in Russian Political Culture," *British Journal of Political Science* (October 1991): 393–41.

35. James Alexander, *Political Culture in Post-Communist Russia: Formlessness and Recreation in a Traumatic Transition* (New York: St. Martin's Press, 2000).

markets and their compatibility with democracy stemmed from experience with the imperfect markets of early Russian capitalism, this chapter shows how a generalized sense of social dysfunction expressed in daily unpredictability affects support for democracy and interpretations of the meaning of political order. Specifically, I demonstrate that the more Russians perceive disorder as a characteristic of their social world, the less consistently they support democracy and the more likely they are to interpret "order" in nondemocratic ways. But for Russians less troubled by social disorder, democracy appears to be less problematical and more often consistent with the order they imagine for Russia.

Of Bandits and Incompetence

To examine how perceptions of social disorganization might affect support for democracy, I categorized the Russian respondents according to their sense of social disorder. I divided respondents into three groups: people with a strong, moderate, and minimal sense of social disorder.[36] For ease of reference, we can call these people the worried, the wary, and the relaxed citizens of Russia. People with a strong sense of social disorder— the worried—were those who thought crime was out of control and were doubtful of the competence or determination of the police to protect them. They felt that the Russian economy had fallen apart, leaving few options for ordinary people to improve their material situations. And they believed that government institutions were suffused with criminal

---

36. I used responses to questions about satisfaction with the work of local policeman, the president, and the State Duma. If people were worried about social order, they tended to express those concerns in their initial assessments of these government bodies, as explanations for why they were dissatisfied. I also coded respondents' evaluations of the economic situation in Russia. Over the time period during which interviews were conducted, the economic situation was objectively difficult for most of the respondents, but some perceived the transitional economy in much more cataclysmic terms than did others. This sense of economic chaos—and attendant difficulties providing for mundane security—was a crucial part of a disordered reality for many respondents. See VTSIOM, "Informatsiia," *Monitoring obshchestvennoe mneniia: Informatsiia analiz*, no. 2, issue 58 (2002): 70.

The questions upon which the "disorder" measure is based capture the three most widespread sources of fear among Russian citizens. According to the 1999 Homo Sovieticus survey, Russians fear unemployment (85 percent of the population), the arbitrariness of authorities (76 percent), and criminal attacks (74 percent). See Iurii Levada, Vladimir Shubkin, Grigoriy Kertman, Veronika Ivanova, Vladimir Yadov, and Eric Shiraev, "Russia: Anxiously Surviving," in *Fears in Post-Communist Societies: A Comparative Perspective*, ed. Eric Shiraev and Vladimir Shlapentokh (New York: Palgrave, 2002), 20. For more detailed information on the measure, see Appendix C.

behavior or flagrant incompetence. People with a minimal sense of social disorder—the relaxed—had greater confidence in the police; saw more opportunities to survive economic challenges; and, while often still critical of those who governed them, were less likely to accuse them of criminal misconduct, pursuit of conflict for its own sake, or raw self-enrichment. Wary people fell between the two extremes, with a tendency both to recognize that sources of disorder existed and to think that there were knowable ways to navigate those problems successfully.

Table 6.1 shows that respondents were more likely to be worried about social disorder if they were older, less educated, and in worse economic circumstances. Worried Russians in the sample were somewhat more likely to support the Communist Party.[37] As it turned out, they were also somewhat more likely to be residents of Siberia, perhaps partly a reflection of apparently cozy relations between government officials and organized crime figures in Krasnoyarsk, one of the two Siberian cities where interviews took place.[38] As in previous chapters, my point in presenting these statistics is to provide readers with evidence about the overall contours of the sample, not to imply that these relationships can be generalized to the wider population.

Table 6.2 shows which respondents were more or less worried about social disorder, along with their corresponding support for democracy. From Table 6.2, we can see that the expected relationship between disorder and democracy held in the Russian sample as a whole.[39] Worried citizens as a group were less supportive of democracy; relaxed citizens were more supportive. The relationship was not perfect, of course, but it is strong enough to merit further investigation. Examining the respondents' comments should illuminate the ways in which concern with social disorder

37. And as Donna Bahry and Lucan Way show, losers in the economic transition are more likely than the winners to vote. See Donna L. Bahry and Lucan Way, "Citizen Activism in the Russian Transition," *Post-Soviet Affairs* 10, no. 4 (1994): 330–66.

38. See Alexei Tarasov, "'Legal Corruption' Deeply Rooted in Krasnoyarsk," *Moscow News*, no. 27 (16–22 July 2003): 5.

39. The correlation between perceptions of social disorder and support for democracy is -.341, significant at the .01 level. I use the measure of support for democracy first introduced in Chapter 5 and described in Appendix C. The measures of democracy and disorder were based on different questions. While both measures use questions about the State Duma, the disorder measure uses a question about how people respond to the actual functioning of the Duma (a point of great dissatisfaction), whereas the democracy measure is based on a question about the need in the abstract for a body like the Duma. Answers to these two questions tended to be quite different. Even people who were highly critical of the Duma in practice often supported the idea of a representative body in the abstract.

Table 6.1   Determinants of disorder

	Strength of feeling of disorder
Sex	−.12
(high = male)	.36
Age	.28*
(high = older)	.03
Education	−.29*
(high = more)	.02
Economic situation	−.46**
(high = better)	.00
Resident of Siberia	.27*
(high = yes)	.04
KPRF supporter	.26*
(high = yes)	.05

NOTE: Russian respondents, $N = 60$; bivariate correlation coefficients, 2-tailed significance.

may undermine support for democracy. In this part of the chapter, I focus mostly on the two extremes, people who think their world is falling apart and people with a fair amount of confidence that it is holding together. Members of the wary group resurface later in the chapter. As the discussion proceeds, Table 6.2 may continue to prove helpful to readers having trouble keeping track of which respondents fell into which categories. I start with the worried group.

When people who felt that their world was strongly disordered spoke at length, they described a society that had come apart at the seams. Valentina summarized the views of many when she said, "Everything has gone to pieces." The sense of widespread dysfunction came through clearly when people spoke about the economic changes they had recently experienced. Iosif said, "Economic transformation occurred under conditions of chaos and disorder. Therefore the result was that we have a poor, ruined economy. This is the consequence of this destruction." Ivan Ivanovich spoke in balder terms. He said, "They pilfered and plundered the whole economy. The common people call privatization prikhvatizatsia. 'Grabbing.' Whoever was nothing became everything. They completely plundered the government, the whole economy." People in this category took issue with the idea that there had been economic "reforms," since nothing had

Table 6.2   Distribution of support for democracy and feelings of social disorder (Russian respondents)

	Low disorder	Moderate disorder	High disorder
High (or moderate) support for democracy	Anya, Dima, Kolya, Misha, Slava, Vitya, Arkadii, Ekaterina, Iurii, Mikhail, Nadezhda, Natalia, Oleg, Raisa, Marina Aleksandrovna *(15 respondents)*	Raya, Sonya, Tolya, Alla, Gennadii, Konstantin, Lev, Svetlana, Aleksandra Antonovna, Andrei Viktorovich, Liudmilla Vladimirovna *(11 respondents)*	Iosif, Galina Grigor'evna *(2 respondents)*
Mixed support for democracy	Katya, Liuba, Nadya, Sergei, Ruslan, Klara, Pavel, Olga Iur'evna *(8 respondents)*	Vasya, Grigorii, Nikolai, Polina, Sofiia, Anna Pavlovna, Irina L'vovna, Boris Borisovich, Vilen Nikolaevich *(9 respondents)*	Lena, Elena, Kollektiv, Valentina, Pelageia, Zinaida, Ivan Ivanovich, Yegor Yegorovich, Zoia Igorevna *(9 respondents)*
Low support for democracy		Valya, Evgenii, Tatiana Mikhailovna *(3 respondents)*	Aleksei, Inna, Vladimir Il'ich *(3 respondents)*

improved for the better. Inna said, "I would like to know, what is this economic change? That they took everything out of our wallets and left us without money? That some banks closed and left us without money? Is that economic change? . . . Generally, what is the economy? I don't understand. Factories are not operating. Businesses are closing. I don't know, what do we produce? I don't know."

In such an economic climate, it is hard for ordinary people to manage. People with a strong sense of social disorder particularly doubted their ability to do so. They were worried about prices that climbed faster than their pay could keep up, about finding the money to pay for a child's education or medicine needed by an invalid wife, about whether the cost to raise livestock was more than the price that meat would command, about how to support children on a paycheck that was half the government's estimated survival minimum. Members of the work collective interviewed as a group felt that they had been raised under one set of rules and now had to live under another. One remarked, "We knew that if we raised our children well, as patriots, they'd be able to . . . achieve success through work, on their merits. And now there's no money. You can't achieve anything without money." Most of the people in this group felt that the economic disorder to which they were subject was of relatively recent provenance. Generally, they thought life had been better under the Communists. There had been government assistance for single mothers. Wages and pensions were paid on time. Education had been free and parents had been able to save for old age. Zinaida thought that under Communism there had not been such problems with daily life: people were happier and sang more.

For people with a strong sense of social disorder, their sense of economic unpredictability was compounded by the conviction that government only made things worse. They felt either that the government was directly responsible for the distress of their daily lives or that government was incapable of making anything better. Iosif remarked, "The government is weak and corrupt. It does not defend the interests of the citizens, and citizens do not want to defend the government." Valentina noted that she was so distressed by Yeltsin's economic policies that she would not even watch him on television. Galina Grigor'evna, like others in this group, suggested that the government was directly linked to criminal figures. Of Yeltsin, she said, "I had a feeling he wasn't the master of the country. He was—I'll say it crudely—someone's puppet. Whose? A criminal, I think. And he did everything they wanted. So, in a way he was decisive and all. . . . But in the country little changed for us, for the better. It changed for the worse, but little for the better."

People interviewed in 2000 had some hope that Putin would do a better job than Yeltsin and maybe, as Inna remarked, "finally end the plundering of our country by Yeltsin's 'family.'" Only four of the 2003 respondents were among this worried group, and in their comments they were much kinder to Putin than earlier respondents had been to Yeltsin, but even so they had little confidence that Putin had helped people substantially. In none of the interview years did the respondents have any faith that the legislative branch could keep a wayward and grasping executive in line or contribute constructively to the welfare of the nation. Vladimir Il'ich said simply about the State Duma, "It doesn't work." Alexei and Zinaida compared it to a bazaar. Inna called deputies parasites. Valentina suggested that deputies suffered from personal disorders that made them unable to do constructive work. And again there were suggestions of links to criminals. Zinaida said, "Here, who comes to power? Whoever has money. . . . In Russia, now money is not all clean. Clean work doesn't provide that kind of money." She continued that citizens knew very little about candidates, where they came from, why they had money. Clearly, she suspected the worst.

Perhaps if the disorders of government were limited to the upper reaches of power, people could have coped. They could have imagined that the problems were far away and did not directly touch their lives. But at least for these worried Russians, the problems in government reached deep into their local police force, leaving ordinary citizens at the mercy of a criminal class that seemed to them to be the real source of all power. People with a strong sense of social disorder complained about rampant corruption, arguing that justice was for sale in Russia. They were fearful of going out at night, afraid that policemen stuck to well-lit and safe streets, convinced that the police had little interest in preventing or solving crimes.

Yegor Yegorovich tearfully complained about the police investigation of his grandson's murder: "My grandson was killed, eighteen years old. For nothing. And now nobody knows anything. They are not looking. We wrote. We even wrote a letter to Putin so they would investigate. But Moscow sent it here, and they are also silent here. They only sent a form letter." Zoia Igorevna's complaint about the police was more mundane, but also more common. She called the police to report "hooligans" making noise in the entryway to her apartment building. "You telephone. Do you think they came? No. No. And what can an old person do? Go out in the square and express her opinion? They said, 'Close the door,' and we closed it." Rather than making the world safer, the police seemed to contribute to the disorder people perceived.

When these worried citizens began to talk more directly about democracy, it became clear how their worries about the unpredictability of life undermined their support for democratic values. As far as they were concerned, supposedly democratic institutions were not working very well to solve the real problems of their lives. Consequently, as far as they could see, there was little reason to support the principles behind democracy. If elections put criminals in power, then the logic of open competition for power seemed unconvincing. Inna commented, "Of course it's important to participate in elections because we are not indifferent to who will be president. But in principle we don't know these people. Well, we see them on television, but what people say about them is completely different: that they are corrupt, that they take bribes. That they take money from it's not clear where. It turns out that they extort money out of our very pockets. . . . And there's nowhere for us to turn, because it's our own government that is fleecing us."

Similarly, if legislative bodies could not make the laws that might begin to create social order, then perhaps an individual with a surer grasp of the situation should take over that responsibility. Vladimir Il'ich commented, "The Duma is unnecessary. It's on the back of the pensioners, of the people. Given the kind of people who are there, it would be better to dissolve it." Members of the work collective agreed. They characterized the Duma as "an all-Russian comedy," unneeded, since the president decided everything. Inna added, "It seems to me that the Duma is not needed. Not needed because, maybe, there is little power there. They don't make concrete decisions. Everything is transferred elsewhere. Doesn't the president really decide everything? Let him make decisions. Probably that would be handier for him." Even people like Lena, who supported the existence of the Duma, felt that the body could be restricted in some way. Lena said, "The Duma is too inflated. And a lot of money is spent on its upkeep, money that would be better spent, naturally, on the nation."

As a rule, people with a strong sense of social disorder were more concerned with the outputs of government than with the procedures by which those outputs were achieved. If better outputs could be reached with nondemocratic procedures, then democracy was a negotiable value. Ivan Ivanovich summed up the disillusionment of many in this group: "For me as a simple person, the kind of democracy we have now is not useful. I am happy that I was full and safe, that for my work I received an adequate and punctual salary, that I didn't live in want, and that I was not afraid of the streets. The essence of the matter is that there is no power. In places, everything is allowed to run its course, banditism, rackets."

These worried Russians were also on average more skeptical about the value of freedom. More than the wary or relaxed groups, these were people likely to think that Russian society suffered from something of an excess of freedom. For Valentina and Lena, this excess of freedom showed up in daily life—in underdressed youth, public profanity, pornography on the television, and littering on the streets. For most of the other worried Russians, the freedom that troubled them was not their own. Indeed, they did not think they personally had gained much freedom, but they thought that some people had and had used that freedom to harm others. Criminals were freer, many thought, and as a result ordinary citizens hid behind barred windows and triple-locked doors. Government officials and the rich, too, were considered to benefit from relaxed restrictions in ways that ordinary people could not.

Galina Grigor'evna commented, "There's not so much freedom as there is boorishness. There are no controls or limits, so people steal. So the government steals." Ivan Ivanovich agreed, "People don't have too much freedom. Officials have a lot of freedom. Officials have a lot of freedom. They can do whatever they want. . . . So far there's no administrative responsibility for any bureaucrat—either at the local level or the central level—so that they would have to answer for their crimes." Inna concluded, "There are a lot of freedoms, but a certain contingent of people has more money. Even freedom can be bought for money. So for example New Russians can get away with whatever they want. Everything is possible. For instance, related to the police, it's possible to beat someone up and leave, and they won't find him anywhere. . . . I consider that everything is for sale in our country, beginning with the president and ending with freedom."

Since many people in this group associated democracy with greater freedom, their suspicions about the value of freedom were also reflected in their comments about democracy. Zinaida, for instance, defined democracy as whatever was good for people in power, which meant that government officials were free to escape responsibility for their actions and enterprise managers could lavish high salaries on themselves while workers barely earned enough to feed their families. Elena equated democracy with capitalism and capitalism with closed factories; for her, economic freedom brought few benefits. Inna said, "Oy, I don't know what democracy is, but I understand that we got what we wanted. We want to read books, watch movies, go abroad. We got all that. It is possible to say more now on the television, in newspapers, and on the radio. You can say everything. Only there's no work, no money, and soon there won't be anything. Therefore, the word *democracy*—that's when everything is possible, but in the end it turns out you can't do anything." For worried Russians, in a word, freedom had not turned out to be a primary social value.

There were, however, two exceptions to this trend. Both Iosif and Galina Grigor'evna were quite supportive of democracy despite their keen perception of social disorder. What made this stance possible for them, it seems, was that they were more aware than some of their fellows that democracy does not provide a license to do whatever one wants. Iosif noted that democratic procedures and laws limit the arbitrariness of authorities, hence bringing more order. Galina Grigor'evna thought the measured freedom provided by democracy could lead to a general improvement in society. According to her, democracy meant "freedom of speech, freedom of thought, freedom of action, but action within the limits of the law. Not to steal, beat, or kill. Rather, within limits so that the person will be civilized, cultured, so that our nation will be educated. So that institutions will be the possessions of every person, and every person can be educated and be of use to the country."

There were, then, a number of ways that a sense of social disorder undermined support for democracy among most—but not all—of the worried Russians. A strong sense of social disorder made democracy seem pointless, since democratic institutions seemed unable to provide the things people needed. A sense of disorder also made democracy seem dangerous. Diffused power left no one clearly responsible to a troubled public. Freedom provided opportunities to those who would contribute to further disorder but did not seem to help ordinary people take control of the world around them. People with a strong sense of social disorder felt helpless not only before the unpredictability of their lives, but also in the face of a government that they feared would never serve their interests, no matter how supposedly democratic it became.

Order Found

Compared with people who thought they lived in a very disorderly world, more people with a minimal sense of social disorder evaluated Russia's economic situation positively. They felt that some stability had been achieved, at least under Putin, and that there were considerable opportunities for people to improve their circumstances. Dima commented in 2003, "Now, probably in the past several years, literally the last three years, once again a real improvement in welfare can be noticed." Vitya added, "And it has simply become more interesting to live. There's nothing to be afraid of."

Even those who were not so positive as these young men saw the necessity of economic reforms, despite temporarily dislocating consequences. In 1998, Natalia commented, "Changes should have been put forward, maybe more competently, maybe not in the form in which they arrived. I didn't greet everything with a 'hurrah!' We had a distribution of property—everything that had been state property. We had received small salaries. The larger part of our earnings went to the creation of social funds, and suddenly they took all that away from us and we were left with nothing. Nonetheless, it is good that people received the possibility to form their own businesses, to realize themselves. That's good. It is complicated to say in one word how I take it all. It is like we are in a swamp. Although difficult, it is necessary to force one's way forward. It's a natural process, inevitable." Even Olga Iur'evna, who complained that huge pieces of valuable state property were "grabbed up" by suspicious groups, added, "I am not saying that I personally live badly, that I am complaining about something. I don't have any problem with my pay. I think that, if a person has a head, a profession, he can always work."

It was not only in their material lives that relaxed Russians saw some order. They were also able to see sources of predictability in political life. Like worried Russians, many comparatively relaxed citizens criticized Yeltsin. But they were less likely to blame his actions on wholesale criminalization of the executive branch and more likely to attribute his shortcomings to mistakes, age, health, a constitution that gave him too much power, or the complicated nature of the changes he was attempting to execute. Like many in this group, Nadezhda expressed a resigned acceptance of the vagaries of Russian political life. She said of Yeltsin, "All of these repudiations of his own ideas, repudiations of people, various pranks which don't seem appropriate for someone in such a powerful position. There is not a culture of interpersonal relations in politics. It depresses me terribly, although on the other side I understand that it is probably hard to expect better." Expressing the optimism common among young people in the sample, Slava noted that Yeltsin had accomplished much good along with the bad. He summed up, "Life, as they say, is bad, but at the same time it's getting a little better."

Even older respondents in this group showed a fair amount of tolerance for the chaotic conditions of political life in Russia. Marina Aleksandrovna said, "Well, Boris Yeltsin. We voted for Yeltsin. I was in favor. And in that period he was very progressive. He did a lot for the country. If you take a long period—a century—you'd think that of course a lot was accomplished during this short period. Although they yell, 'Bad! It's all bad!' Yes, of course, and it will probably be bad for a long time. But it's not possible to accomplish good in such a short time. Furthermore, it's not good anywhere. There are problems everywhere. The thing is we have such problems that will take a long time to solve."

Most of the more relaxed citizens who were interviewed while Putin held office thought he was making some progress toward solving those problems. Vitya said, "Most of all, it is Putin's activity, his activity and interest in various spheres of life. In the end, it is clear that he is doing something, as opposed to all the previous ones."

Like others in the sample, many people with a minimal sense of social disorder were highly critical of the State Duma. More than others in the sample, though, they were able to see a kind of pattern and purpose to the Duma's actions. In particular, they were more likely to understand how groups in the Duma acted to promote particular interests or to limit the wholesale authority of the president. Kolya commented, "For example, the Union of Rightist Forces. They're not a majority, but they try to push forward the ideas they claim to stand for. . . . In my opinion, many parties act this way. In the end, part of the parties act as they are obliged." Mikhail agreed. Speaking of Yeltsin's ultimately successful efforts to force the Duma to accept Sergei Kirienko as prime minister, he said, "Recent events with the Duma have led the president to understand that he is not all-powerful. I think that—that they can, sometimes, if some kind of conflictual situation arises, limit the activities of the president."

It seems that one of the reasons relaxed Russians were more tolerant of the Duma was because they had a better sense of its role. Of people in the group with a minimal sense of social disorder, nearly two-thirds had either high or moderate support for democracy. Their deeper understanding of democracy, especially regarding the sometimes fractious role of representative institutions, made it easier for people to see a purpose and goal in the actions of the Duma. For instance, Slava commented about representative bodies in the abstract, "I think there should be a duma because there should always be opposition to those in power and probably to avert some incorrect moments in government. I think that all the same the president should pay attention to the opinions of the Duma." Consequently, he was not overly troubled by the actions of the Duma, even though he disagreed with most of them and thought the Duma served as a brake on reforms that needed to be implemented. He commented, "Well, what about the Duma? It's the opposition. Any authorities have their opposition."

Similarly, the relaxed Russians were less likely than more worried Russians to think that democracy implied an excess of freedom that might damage social bonds. They stressed reciprocal obligations that arose with freedoms. Arkadii said that democracy, among other things, included "the right to be a person but not to insult or demean another individual." Nadezhda added, "If you are a free person, a creative person, then you respect yourself and you respect others." Dima defined democracy as "the relationship of the person and society in which the obligations of the person and the obligations of society are clearly stipulated. And these obligations are not violated." As Kolya put it, democracy was the golden mean, between anarchy on the one hand and totalitarianism on the other. For these respondents, democracy signified a kind of order with which they were willing to live.[40]

The relationship between a sense of social disorder and attitudes toward democracy, then, seems to be a two-way street. On the one hand, to people who find their world a relatively predictable place, the uncertainty of democracy is not especially a problem. Opponents can argue. Elected officials will always have their flaws. But society will survive, and democratic processes may ultimately contribute to an improvement in daily conditions. But causation seems to travel in the opposite direction as well. People who better understand the nature of democracy are less troubled by the messiness of political life. For them, plurality and disagreement are not merely indicators, as Oleg put it, of "a lack of discipline." They are evidence of democracy in action.

Order Versus Freedom

Russians vary, then, in how much they are troubled by the fundamental unpredictability of their lives. And the more they worry about that unpredictability, the less they tend to support democracy. It is worth remembering, though, that even the Russians in the sample who are not very supportive of democracy are not necessarily *opposed* to living under democratic institutions. Most of them are inconsistent in their orientations, not hostile to all aspects of democracy. Furthermore, many respondents who rank relatively high in their support for democracy are still troubled by the disorder inherent in daily life or by the potential for political freedoms to increase disorder.[41] Democratic institutions may not adequately address all their concerns. In uncertain conditions, even democrats may choose to surrender liberty for the sake of order. Richard Sakwa has commented, "While in the West politics is formalized, ritualized and conventional, in

40. Tim McDaniel points to the Russian philosopher V. M. Mezhuev's argument that Russians understand only absolute freedom and are not willing to make the pragmatic compromises that life in society requires. That was dramatically not the case with my respondents. See McDaniel, *The Agony of the Russian Idea*, 36.

41. Table 6.2 shows that almost half the respondents with relatively high support for democracy are in either the wary or the worried category. Donna Bahry and her coauthors note that, in Russia, even defenders of democracy are willing to restrict the activities of groups they consider a threat to democracy. See Donna L. Bahry, Cynthia Boaz, and Stacy Burnett Gordon, "Tolerance, Transition, and Support for Civil Liberties in Russia," *Comparative Political Studies* 30, no. 4 (1997): 484–510.

Russia, by contrast, politics is raw, unaggregated and barely mediated by parties, movements or conventions. . . . Thus subjectivity has become a burden which has given rise to 'fear of freedom' and which in Weimar Germany gave rise to support for charismatic leadership."[42]

The relationships traced so far in this chapter, then, have not yet told us enough about the practical choices Russians might make to address their concerns about order. I turn to that question now. In this section, I look more closely at issues surrounding freedom, a value sometimes posited as the opposite of order. In the following section, I examine how concerns about order affect the kinds of political institutions Russians might choose.

Freedom is one of the democratic values with which some observers have argued Russians are uncomfortable. One version of this argument is that Russians understand freedom as the complete absence of any kind of self-control. Hence, freedom is too dangerous, and people who cannot be trusted to police themselves must be subject to outside authority. Leonid Gozman and Alexander Etkind explained the logic: "If people are inclined to exceed the speed limit, traffic police checks are necessary. In a word, a strong regime is needed."[43] An alternative interpretation is that, influenced by Orthodox philosophy, Russians see democratic freedoms as merely formal rights, unconnected to the real freedom of the soul, and hence without great import to their lives.[44] In either interpretation, freedom is something that ordinary Russians might agree to sacrifice. And, indeed, survey results seem to bear that willingness out. Many Russians, even supporters of democracy, when faced with a forced choice between freedom and order, choose order.[45] Does that mean that they are hesitant to accept the personal freedom that underlies democracy?

For some, perhaps yes. I asked respondents to choose between freedom and order, but the open-ended format of the question allowed them to explain their choice or, as sometimes happened, to explain why the forced-choice offered did not apply to their lives.[46] Elena, one of the most worried

---

42. Richard Sakwa, "Subjectivity, Politics, and Order in Russian Political Evolution," *Slavic Review* 54, no. 4 (1995): 963–64.

43. Gozman and Etkind, *Psychology of Post-totalitarianism*, 78.

44. Nelli A. Romanovich, "Demokraticheskie tsennosti i svoboda 'po-russki,'" *Sotsiologicheskie issledovaniia*, no. 8 (2002): 35–39, translated in *Sociological Research* 42, no. 6 (November–December 2003): 62–68.

45. vtsiom, "Informatsiia: Nastroeniia, mneniia i otsenki naseleniia," 52.

46. I asked some of the respondents, "What is better: to live in a society with strict order or to give people so much freedom that they could destroy society?" Of those asked, 64 percent

respondents, said, "We Russians can be accustomed to order because we were enslaved our whole lives; therefore we are used to living with strictness. Therefore order is more important. The Russian Ivan is already used to being under the whip."

For most respondents, though, their understanding of order was more nuanced than Elena's version of "being under the whip." Quite a few preferred a society that guaranteed a minimal level of welfare for all. Among the wary, Vasya said, "They gave us freedom; what were the results? It simply turned out that, if you give a person freedom, and all the same the first necessity of a person is to eat, to dress, to have a place to live, and he can't achieve this, then he will begin to steal. Does freedom exist? It does. But there are no benefits from this freedom." One of the most worried respondents, Lena, said similarly, "Strict order—what is that? If it would include freedom of speech, freedom of the press, financing for medicine, financing for scientific discoveries, if there would be activities for children— if all this would exist, under strict order and there wouldn't be violence in these places against people, then, yes, it is possible to agree with that kind of strictness. And this freedom with raging crime and all the chaos—this is also not needed. Everything should be within reasonable limits."[47]

For many respondents, the type of order they preferred was not obviously inconsistent with the freedoms protected in a democracy. Particularly among people with a heightened sense of social disorder and lower support for democracy, order was often understood to mean that laws applied to everyone, from ordinary people to criminals and all the way to government officials. A member of the work collective interviewed as a group said, "We're all in favor of strong order. But in general strong order is the fulfill-ment of law, the observance of law." She felt that by enforcing law and compelling people to meet their responsibilities, order would provide people

---

preferred "order"; 6 percent chose freedom; 10 percent refused the conditions of the choice, selecting instead some intermediate position. This kind of extreme forced choice is not uncommon in Western surveys. See, for instance, Timothy J. Colton, *Transitional Citizens: Voters and What Influences Them in the New Russia* (Cambridge, MA: Harvard University Press, 2000), 248; Arthur H. Miller, Vicki L. Hesli, and William M. Reisinger, "Reassessing Mass Support for Political and Economic Change in the Former USSR," *American Political Science Review* 88, no. 2 (June 1994): 406.

47. Not surprisingly, Lena did not mention a desire to protect economic freedoms. To get more order, most Russians are apparently relatively willing to forego economic freedoms but not political ones. See Lapkin and Pantin, "Russkii poriadok," 8. Not economic opportunity, but rather material security, seems to be a common feature of Russian views of freedom. See M. A. Shabanova, "Obrazy svobody v reformiruemoi Rossii," *Sotsiologicheskie issledovaniia*, no. 2 (2000): 29–38.

with rights they otherwise lacked. Boris Borisovich agreed. He said, "Here they understand freedom to equate with anarchy. In the democratic socialist countries, freedom is the careful observance of law. I think it's necessary to strive for that."

Clearly, law limits the freedom of lawbreakers, but it does not obviously diminish and may even enhance the liberties that underlie democracy: freedom of speech and assembly do not flourish in a Wild West atmosphere. Thus, a yearning for a law-governed state is hardly a desire to return to the past for most Russians. For Lena, Boris Borisovich, and others like them, freedoms conflict: economic freedom will leave some people so poor that they cannot afford to buy necessary medicine; greater freedom for law-abiding citizens may also mean greater freedom for those who would break laws. Rather than a tradeoff between freedom and autocracy, these respondents saw tradeoffs among a variety of freedoms, which they cannot have in their entirety all at the same time.[48] Their preference for order reflected a willingness to forego some freedoms so that they could enjoy others.

Among people more supportive of democracy, there was also a sense that law provided the foundation for order and that some limitation of freedom is the precondition for life in society.[49] As Dima pointed out, alone on the taiga people can do whatever they want, but freedom cannot be unfettered in urban life. He argued that freedom had to be restrained even as he affirmed freedom as a universal human value. He gave the example of an "unbridled Communist," who "if they arrested him on the street, imagine, and put him in preliminary detention, then he would be in favor of freedom for his struggle, exactly as a democrat would." We all like to be free, but if we are free to do whatever we want then Liuba may be correct about the consequences: "there will be disorder on the streets, fraud everywhere, terrorism, swindlers all around."

That freedoms cannot be unlimited as long as we do not live alone does not mean that the limits are wholly out of the control of the citizen. Although not a particularly strong democrat, Olga Iur'evna recognized this.

---

48. In this way, they are similar to Canadians. See Paul M. Sniderman, Joseph F. Fletcher, Peter H. Russell, and Philip E. Tetlock, *The Clash of Rights: Liberty, Equality, and Legitimacy in Pluralist Democracy* (New Haven: Yale University Press, 1996).

49. This argument is, of course, a staple of democratic theory. See John Locke, *The Second Treatise of Government* [1690] (New York: Macmillan, 1985); Jean-Jacques Rousseau, *The Social Contract and Discourses* [1762], trans. G. D. H. Cole (London: J. M Dent and Sons, Everyman's Library, 1973); John Stuart Mill, *On Liberty* [1859] (New York: Penguin, 1985).

She commented, "I already said that I think that democracy assumes the obeying of the laws that are made by the deputies of the Duma, who in turn were elected by the people. First we elect these people. They make these laws. That means we should strictly observe them. I consider that it is necessary to live in a society, that it is better to live in a society of clear order."

For many of my Russian respondents, the opposite of order is not freedom, but anarchy. For the more worried among them, they have had enough experience with anarchy in their daily lives to prefer any more orderly alternative. But even among more relaxed Russians, anarchy had little appeal. Kolya commented, "If you look at both extremes, in my view the lesser evil is strict order because, all the same, order supports the majority of spheres. But nothing will come of anarchy, which is what you get without order, especially in such a big country."[50] One of the strongest supporters of democracy, Natalia, agreed. She said, "We all want to live in order because for ordinary people it is easier to live in order, when the rules of the game are known, when you know what is demanded of you, what you'll get for that. . . . No one can live in a damaged society." For her, as for many others in the sample, order implied a government based in and bound by law.

That many respondents were willing to limit freedom for the sake of social order did not mean that they were ready to diminish freedom for reasons less crucial to the foundations of communal existence. Many defenders of social order were ready to countenance a free press, for instance, even as they complained about the excess of violent images on television and the tendency for privately owned media outlets to publish the point of view of their owners. Fewer respondents were ready to limit freedom for the purpose of fighting corruption, even if it would bring greater prosperity, than would have limited freedom for the sake of social order.[51] Although

---

50. Kolya seems unwittingly to channel Samuel Huntington, who said, "The primary problem is not liberty but the creation of a legitimate public order. Men may, of course, have order without liberty, but they cannot have liberty without order." See Samuel P. Huntington, *Political Order in Changing Societies* (New Haven: Yale University Press, 1968), 7–8.

51. I asked a question that pressed respondents to choose between individual freedoms, on the one hand, and fighting corruption with the goal of increasing economic prosperity, on the other. The logic behind this question was to put freedom in competition with values less open to interpretation and less fundamental to communal existence than "social order." I chose prosperity and the fight against corruption because they are things about which Russians feel strongly: everyone favors prosperity, and many Russians see corruption as a barrier to prosperity and as a significant contributor to the disorder in their lives. See Lapkin and Pantin, "Russkii poriadok," 76–77.

she had come out in favor of social order, Raisa commented, "We still retain the memory of when there was no freedom, when for any wrong word, they could pick you up, put you in a hospital, and declare that you were psychologically abnormal. We don't want this kind of thing anymore. We want freedom to exist, and problems with corruption can be resolved by a different method, not through limitations of freedom."

This defense of freedom was evident even among respondents who were wary about the disorder in their lives. Andrei Viktorovich said, "I don't think that corruption and freedom stand in antagonistic relationship, that the more freedom there is, the more corruption, and that in order to reduce corruption it is necessary to reduce freedom. I think instead that corruption reduces those freedoms that have been proclaimed for us. It reduces them to nothing. Therefore, the battle against corruption is probably a battle for our freedom." Aleksandra Antonovna added more simply, "We lived for too long in conditions of unfreedom. I would not want to go back to that."

The respondents who were more willing to give up freedom often thought they had very little freedom to start with. Lev allowed that Russians might as well give up freedom to fight corruption, since they did not have much freedom anyway, and life would be better without corruption. Zinaida interpreted her poverty as an obstacle to any claim of freedom. She complained, "In principle, we are not free. We go to work from bell to bell. We spend the whole day at work. We see our kids when we come home tired, sometimes not at all. It's necessary to prepare something to eat. It's necessary all the same to think how we can get out of this situation, how to buy something when there's not enough money to live on. We also have to think how to clean after we've had to economize on soap and detergent. That is, it turns out we have practically no freedom. In what other ways can they take away our freedom?"

Indeed, a survey conducted by the All Russian Center for Public Opinion Research showed that, when asked to rank the importance of various individual rights, around 90 percent of respondents rated "a minimal standard of living" as of the utmost importance, while less than 30 percent gave the same rating to freedom of assembly.[52] In a survey of citizens of the city of Voronezh, 61 percent of respondents expressed themselves willing to give up their freedom for a chance to work; 57 percent were willing to sacrifice

---

52. Teodor P. Gerber and Sara E. Mendel'son, "Grazhdane Rossii o pravakh cheloveka," *Monitoring obshchestvennoe mneniia: Informatsiia analiz*, no. 2, issue 58 (2002): 28.

freedom if they would receive their pay or pension on time.[53] The people in my sample who were more likely to limit freedom in the hope of economic prosperity were those who were less supportive of democracy or more worried about social disorder. Even so, they noted reservations. Evgenii, for instance, said that he did not want to return to gulags.

Freedom's strongest defenders in Russia, then, tend to be among the ranks of democracy's defenders. In my sample, even democrats wary of social disorder were ready to defend freedom against a variety of threats. But Russians who are less vigilant in their defense of freedom often say that they prefer order, law, predictability, and some of the social guarantees they lost with the collapse of the Soviet regime. These preferences do not necessarily limit—and may even enhance—the political freedoms at the heart of democracy. Among those who would sacrifice freedom for other goals, many think they have little freedom to sacrifice. For people such as Zinaida, a sense of incipient social chaos undercuts commitment either to democracy in general or to freedom in particular.

The Political Institutions of Order

If some of Russia's weaker supporters of democracy put the defense of freedom behind the more pressing concerns of a challenging daily life, does that mean they advocate authoritarian institutions as an alternative to the ones that leave them feeling so threatened? In public opinion surveys, Russians have indicated their support for a "strong hand" at the helm of government, but it is not entirely clear what they mean. Igor' Kliamkin, E. Petrenko, and L. Blekher argued, "Russia wants order. But so far she doesn't want dictatorship. Even enlightened."[54] It seemed to them that the leader that most fit their respondents' desires was Margaret Thatcher. I asked my respondents whether they favored a "strong" central government. I also asked them to explain what *strong* meant in that context and to judge whether such a strong government would help people or harm them. This section draws on the responses to those questions.

Answers vary between the more and less democratic respondents and between those more relaxed or more worried in their assessments of social disorder. However, one theme was common in all groups. For many, a "strong" state carries the same connotations as the "order" described above:

---

53. Romanovich, "Demokraticheskie tsennosti."
54. Kliamkin, Petrenko, and Blekher, *Kakim mozhet byt' avtoritarnyi rezhim*, 13.

laws are in place and enforced. One of the most committed democrats commented on this point at length. Marina Aleksandrovna described a strong government as "order, not in the sense of rigid order or something, but the order of laws, the order of certain things under which people live. I know that I can go out and there is order. Because of that, I respect the law. Because of that, I write my declaration and honestly pay my taxes. But the government should at some point protect me. . . . Power should be strong because it's power, but of course, within reasonable limits, not under the gun or the automatic rifle. Otherwise, anarchy will prosper and thieves, and that's all. . . . People now say that in the past we had order, because we were afraid, because an ordinary Communist was afraid of the *raikom*. The *raikom* secretary was afraid of the *obkom*. The *obkom* was afraid of the Central Committee.[55] That's not order. . . . There has to be reasonable, strong power so that the organs of law and order can be organs of law and order. So that I can know that I can approach a policeman and he will defend me. I can complain about some problem and receive help, not a punch in the nose." Iurii agreed that "if people twist and twiddle with the laws and no one can secure their rights, then power is weak."

While people who were not as strong supporters of democracy as Marina Aleksandrovna or Iurii also spoke about the importance of law, they also brought other and more autocratic connotations to the world *strong*. Anna Pavlovna described strong governmental power as the condition under which "he says it and so it is." For Tatiana Mikhailovna, strong power was "the kind of commander who, when he gives an order, everyone salutes." Zinaida used the example of the Stalin period, when people were afraid and felt they had to answer to the country. Compared with more democratic respondents, the sample's weaker democrats talked more often about Russian traditions of concentrated power, of fear and respect for power, and of the need for centralized authority to keep Russia's "empire" intact. Polina said, "You know, at the present moment, I would want that some kind of criminal structure was in power, so that people would be afraid of it. I would even prefer Stalin in this period, only without the gulags, of course. But a strong hand, because everything is too unrestrained, starting from the criminal element and ending even with leaders who don't lead." As far as she was concerned, the stakes were high, and

---

55. Marina Aleksandrovna refers to various levels of Communist Party organization in the Soviet system: the city district committee (*raikom*), the regional *oblast'* committee (*obkom*), and the Central Committee of the Communist Party, the federal party structure.

strong centralized power seemed the way to secure a more contented life. She added, "Powerlessness is chaos. And chaos in a country is criminality. And criminality isn't life, not for yourself, not for your family, not for the future." Like Polina, others among the weaker democrats mentioned Stalin or the czars as a model for strong authority; Grigorii lauded Pinochet.

The people who were most likely to affirm the desirability of autocratic power were people who had both more limited support for democracy and a greater sense of social disorder. The influence of both these orientations can be seen by comparing these people with those who are more democratic or more relaxed about the state of society. People who were similar in their modest support for democracy, but who differed by being less troubled by a sense of imminent social chaos, hinted at autocratic preferences, but less obviously and less often. Sergei, for instance, understood strong power as "might" (moshch'); Nadya referred to military force. But Ruslan talked about the need to limit the power of the president, and Klara was just looking for leaders she could trust.

Among stronger democrats, almost all respondents did not describe strong power in autocratic terms, though they did sometimes refer to Russian traditions of centralized and expansive government. The few democrats who did see strong power in autocratic terms made it clear that they would not favor that type of government. Andrei Viktorovich commented, "The word strong is not entirely clear. Of course, we would want state power to be strong in order to protect our rights, defend them. But if it was 'strong' so to, oppositely, suppress us, then we wouldn't want that." Natalia agreed that strong power might not be what Russians needed. She said, "Oy, we lived the whole time under strong central power, and it didn't help us much. We need not just central power, but power based on a collection of working laws, and a system in which laws are executed and not interpreted for the benefit of a narrow circle of people. Probably, if we had that kind of system, then strong power would not be necessary." Natalia did think that federal power was necessary to offset the ambitions of local authorities who would set themselves up as dictators.

But most of the stronger democrats in the sample did support strong governmental power; they simply were explicit in describing their understanding of strong power as something other than autocracy. Nadezhda said, "Given our anarchistic traditions and such a huge territory, it is impossible to govern such a state without strong power. It's a different thing how strong is understood. Strong isn't the strength of the army. It isn't strength that operates on some kind of violence. Like Marx and

Engels said: the power of authority and the authority of power. It should be strength of authority, the strength of mind, the strength of morals, the strength of law, and not the strength of tanks or the strength of bureaucrats. This is weakness. That is totalitarianism, which I don't support. For me, strong power is power that is able to work and that is effective."

Even among democrats more troubled by social disorder, the same sentiments were expressed. Alla said, "Strong means capable, able to regulate social processes without violence, without bloodshed, without oppression, but holding the reins of government in their hands. . . . Not authoritarian, not totalitarian, not authoritarian. They should depend on information, real information . . . information and flexibility, not threats or bribery. . . . Oy, excuse me, I need to add . . . central power should stop lawbreaking."

Among stronger as well as among weaker democrats, there was considerable agreement that strong government would protect people, make their rights and lives secure, ensure the prosperity of the country, and earn the trust of the population. Perhaps surprisingly given Russian history, ordinary Russians seemed little aware of the danger that strong central government could harm them. There were exceptions, such as Andrei Vikorovich and Natalia, quoted above. In addition, Gennadii recognized that strong power, which he understood as the ability of authorities to make whatever decisions they wanted, without advice, might be simultaneously bad for some people and good for others. He commented, "Strong power, working in the interests of the whole, can bring harm to some part of the population. Well, let's take a classic example. During the epoch of Stalin, one part of the population sat in prisons, in the gulags, and the second part walked free, were happy, and ate red caviar, and there was an abundance of food products in the stores."

But most respondents were certain that a strong government would protect them and ensure their happiness. No doubt this is in part the result of their somewhat casual use of the word *strong* to imply whatever kind of government they liked. It may also be a product of the particular conditions in Russia at the beginning of the twenty-first century. Tolya explained, "What is weak power? It is powerlessness. It is the absence of power. That is, power is the state's ability to manage affairs; that is to say, to control those social relations that are regulated by norms of law or tied to institutions of governmental power. Weak power cannot control these. And who will control them then? Criminals, oligarchs, businessmen— whoever benefits." Or, as Dima pointed out, where mechanisms of popular control over sources of power remain underdeveloped, a centralization of power in the central government is preferable to letting society's mighty overpower the rest.

For respondents who were not especially fervent in their support for democracy and who were troubled by what they saw as the chaos around them, a strong state was one that could keep monsters in line. As Evgenii pointed out, "Our Russian disorderliness, you understand yourself, requires a strong hand." But this was far from the only meaning respondents had in mind when they spoke of—and favored—a strong state. Many of their interpretations were wholly consistent with a democratic government, based in law and responsive to the needs of citizens. This was particularly the case for more democratic citizens, even democrats troubled by the disorder of their lives. Rather than a cultural preference for autocracy, Russians' penchant for "order" and state "strength" may partly reflect a cultural tendency to interpret those words more broadly than observers fear they do.

Americans on Order

If we talk only about Russians, it is tempting to conclude that that there is something distinctive about their preference for order. For perspective, then, it is useful to examine what Americans have to say about order, freedom, and a strong state. It is also useful to listen to Americans because Americans inhabit a different and generally more orderly universe than that occupied by Russians. At the cusp of the twenty-first century, Americans had not recently suffered regime collapse and economic upheaval. For most of them, their jobs and futures were secure and, much as they might complain about government officials, they did not imagine government to be in the grip of bandits and organized crime. Since they were responding to a less disorderly social universe than that dealt with by Russians, we might imagine that Americans would develop different commitments to the value of order.

Compared with the statements made by Russians, the comments of the American respondents showed considerably less concern about social disorder. In particular, the Americans were much less worried about economic dislocation. Harriet, for instance, was a pensioner with a eighth-grade education and a history of unskilled labor—a social profile that in the Russian sample would have predicted a fairly dire outlook on economic life. Yet she had no particular economic worries; in fact, she said she had no worries at all. About the economy, she said, "Right now it's kind of poor. I'm not being benefited by it, that's for sure. Not being harmed by it; it's an even keel. Don't make much difference to me. I'm not working; my husband's on retirement." Others who remarked about economic difficulties saw them as surely temporary and hardly of great concern. After noting that the stock market and consumer confidence were generally down, and that unemployment was the highest it had been in six years, Bill said, "I think we'll come out of it. I think we are coming out of it, slowly. And I have the utmost faith. You know, I have money in the stock market, and I know it's going to be all right. In the long run, it's good. Oh, yeah, we have the greatest economy in the world. If you don't have faith in our economy, then you don't have faith in any economy."

The American respondents as a group were also more satisfied than the Russians with their local police and the management of crime, although this is probably an issue where there is more variability in the American population as a whole. Fred remarked, "You don't really hear, where we're living, of a lot of crime. I mean different things like that. So I assume, since we don't read it in the papers, that we don't have a lot of robberies or a lot of killings or shootings or whatever. I assume the police are doing a good job." The American respondents also did not accuse their political leaders of corruption or radical incompetence. Even in the post-9/11 world, only Leo expressed concerns about terrorism, and he saw that more as a problem that his grandchildren would face. In any case, he thought terrorism was a problem that Americans could solve. He said, "You can dang well see what we do, when we put men on the moon. And you know this country is the greatest country on the face of the earth, and we can do anything we set our mind to."

Using similar measures as with the Russians, I divided the American respondents into groups that were more or less troubled by the disorder of society around them.[56] Here again, it is clear how less worried the Americans were. In the Russian sample, 62 percent of the respondents found their world either moderately or highly disordered. In the American sample, only 29 percent thought their world was disordered, and then only moderately so. Even with these more wary Americans, their worries and concerns were less strongly stated than was true for the Russians.

About the economy, Victoria said, "I think people are in a state of delusion. I mean that. Most simply are barely making it. The rich are getting richer; the poor are getting poorer." But that was it: no complaints about

56. For information on the measure used in the American sample, see Appendix C.

an economic system that had been "pilfered and plundered" or left in a state of "chaos and disorder," as from the Russians. Wary Americans complained more than their relaxed neighbors about crime and the ineffectuality of police, but most of their concerns were fairly personal and sometimes relatively inconsequential. While Adam complained about urban crime rates and Daniel's car had been damaged by a drunk driver whom the police could not catch, Kate was only worried that the police were doing too little to regulate traffic lights. Rick was worried about police procedures, although he was unwilling to condemn the police as a whole. He said, "I'm trying to make a difference between the people who are cops, who are mostly good, and the way that police procedures have become a lot more invasive and a lot more scary." Sam had his own scary story to tell about mistreatment at the hands of a traffic cop, but the outcome was a fine, and he did not generalize much from the experience.

Americans did not vary enough in their support for democracy for connections to be drawn between their support for democracy and their sense of social disorder. And Americans who were more wary of social disorder did not differ substantially from more relaxed Americans in their understanding of democracy or in their preferences for an orderly society or a strong state. As with the Russian respondents, when Americans were faced with a forced choice between freedom and order, most chose order.[57] They tended to qualify their answers, saying that they did not want tyranny, and that personal freedoms were essential, but the American respondents were no more likely than the Russians to imagine that personal freedoms could be unlimited. Fred said, "Even though I think people need their freedoms, there still has to be an orderly society. Otherwise, people just go ramrod everything. There has to be some kind of order, even though it may not be what you want. For example, some people think they should maybe drive faster. But if they did, then we'd have people maybe driving a hundred miles per hour all the time. People would get killed. So there has to be some kind of order even though we may not like it at times."

Leo agreed: "We're creatures of a society that you've got to have laws that people must obey. You cannot have anarchy. If people have so much freedom that they can totally disrupt society all the time, you'll eventually have a breakdown, and then the pendulum could swing the other way.

---

57. In the American sample, 75 percent chose order, 8 percent chose freedom, and 1 percent picked something in the middle. So, a higher percentage of Americans than Russians chose order in a forced choice. The question for American respondents was: "Which is better, to live in an orderly society or to allow people so much freedom that they can become disruptive?"

You would have, rather than all the freedom you want or need, you could end up having none." Sam thought that, without order, "we're all just a bunch of animals." Apparently, like Russians, Americans are willing to limit some freedoms to enable the enjoyment of others. Like Russians, when Americans say they favor "order," they have in mind a police officer at the corner, not a dictatorship of fear.

Public opinion surveys have shown that many Americans are ready to ban books containing dangerous ideas from public school libraries, to limit the rights of unpopular minorities, or to sacrifice the rights of the accused to the fight against crime.[58] In Canada, citizens are prone to place concerns about safety and order above those of free expression, and elites are at least as likely as mass publics to favor restrictions on freedom.[59] My American respondents were no different. They wanted to defend freedom, and most reluctantly granted unpopular minorities the right to say their piece. But quite a few were much less tolerant of disruptive demonstrations. Bill said, "You should be allowed to demonstrate, but not at the expense of other people's freedoms." Fred explained, "The reason why I say no is because it doesn't have to do with the majority of the people, or what our laws . . . dictate. It's against the laws of what we voted for."

In his own interview-based study, the political scientist Robert Lane observed, "Democracy as a popular concept centers in the freedom of the nondeviant individual to do what the majority thinks right."[60] It seems that for most ordinary Americans, as for Russians, the battle for democracy is not fought on the fringes, by extending rights to the very groups that might threaten democracy or by providing so much freedom that the bonds of society are tested. Instead, both groups were more concerned that the freedoms of ordinary, law-abiding citizens not be restricted, so that citizens could live their lives in peace and go about their business in a way that did not interfere with others. When freedoms conflict, some of them may be sacrificed.

Like Russians, the American respondents did not necessarily associate a "strong" state with a tyrannical one. Americans suggested that governmental strength resided in representation, in effective concern for the

58. James W. Prothro and C. W. Grigg, "Fundamental Principles of Democracy: Bases of Agreement and Disagreement," *Journal of Politics* 22 (May 1960): 276–94; William M. Reisinger, Arthur H. Miller, and Vicki L. Hesli, "Russians and the Legal System: Mass Views and Behaviour in the 1990s," *Communist Studies and Transition Politics* 13, no. 3 (1997): 24–55.

59. Sniderman et al., *The Clash of Rights*, 39–41.

60. Robert E. Lane, *Political Ideology: Why the American Common Man Believes What He Does* (New York: The Free Press, 1962), 83.

good of the country, in ethical leadership, in honesty, and in democracy. Ernest described a strong government as one that "can accomplish goals effectively. It has the resources it needs to achieve the goals that it has. It has the confidence of the people. It does its job effectively." Consequently, the American respondents were not inclined to think that strong governmental power would hurt them. More likely, they thought, strong power in the way they described it would give people rights. Even Leo, who identified himself as leaning toward conservative and Republican positions, who worried about government action in Waco and Ruby Ridge, and who said that "having too much freedom is like having a car too fast or a girl too pretty—there ain't such a thing," thought strong governmental power mostly would help people. He said, "Even though there's a lot of times you don't agree with what Congress does and all that, you still need a strong central government. Remember, the purpose of the federal government is to do for people what they can't do for themselves. And so, if you've got a good, strong government doing what they're supposed to do: provide for the national defense, promote general welfare, etc., etc.; they will be doing things to help the people."

In sum, the American respondents do not look all that different from the Russians. Even though the Americans have not experienced the chaotic changes to which Russia has been subjected, they prefer order to unlimited freedom and they favor a strong state, which they do not imagine will hurt them. In comparison with the outlook of these Americans, the concern with social order characteristic of the Russian respondents seems less a unique cultural product than the price of life in community with others.

Conclusion

In some descriptions of the post-Soviet "order," life verges on anarchy. "Black holes" of lawlessness threaten to undermine emerging markets and wobbling democracy.[61] This chapter has shown, though, that ordinary Russian citizens vary in the degree to which they think their country is being consumed by disorder. And that variation is substantially matched by variation in support for democracy. In the Russian sample, people who felt that they lived in the midst of a highly disordered world were more

61. Victor M. Sergeyev, "Organized Crime and Social Instability in Russia: The Alternative State, Deviant Bureaucracy, and Social Black Holes," in *Russia in the New Century: Stability or Disorder?* ed. Victoria E. Bonnell and George W. Breslauer (Boulder, CO: Westview Press, 2001), 158–71.

willing to sacrifice democratic procedures and freedoms—to provide the things people need, to streamline policy making, and to make sure that the guilty would be punished. One member of the work collective particularly captured the sense of a world on edge. She said, "We common people sometimes think that spies have been sent in specially. They entreat us to kneel in order to literally enslave us, turn us into zombies."

It makes sense that, to people who see the world in such apocalyptic terms, democratic methods do not seem the best defense against encroaching disorder. Discussion takes too long, and divided power makes responsibility hard to trace and blame hard to assign. Accordingly, Zinaida complained about democracy, "Well, if you consider that government officials pour dirt on each other and rummage through things that are not their business, don't give us an account of their work, find some kind of flaws in their opponents at work, then, sure, we have a democracy. And the fact that they all the same cannot come to a common opinion, which affects us adversely, is also democracy." She preferred a system in which the president clearly assigned government officials specific tasks and held them accountable for their failures, even if it meant less freedom for everyone. To people such as Zinaida, when freedom seems to be limited to the freedom to lose your job, to fail to provide for your family, and to suffer in fear of crime, then it is easy to forego.

Russians less troubled by social disorder, however, were more consistent in their support for democracy, less willing to sacrifice freedom for other social goals, and more likely to understand a "strong" state in terms consistent with democratic institutions. A sense of greater social predictability apparently made democracy seem less troubling, and a more developed understanding of democracy helped people find order in apparently disorderly conditions. For example, Andrei Viktorovich, a strong democrat despite his moderate sense of social disorder, said about the central government, "This power is not the power of the people, but the power of a narrow group of people, who were chosen, I don't know by whom, and who are trying in this way to solve their own private problems. Some of these affairs they resolve with automatic weapons, Kalashnikovs, contract killings. Some—through government structures. That's better, of course." In other words, to democracy's strongest supporters, democracy provides a mechanism to manage social disorder, as long as people choose to use it. For these Russians, their desire for both order and democracy is based on an interpretation of order that bears little resemblance to the order provided by past regimes but that has a lot in common with Western democracies.

Although Russians in the sample perceived their quotidian environment in more troubled terms than Americans did their own, both groups preferred social order to the kind of freedom than could tear society apart. And both groups favored a strong state. For many, though, "order" meant law, and "strong" power was power that helped people accomplish the things they could not accomplish as individuals. Compared with the Americans, Russians do not seem to have an unusually pronounced cultural commitment to order, even though they may live in peculiarly disordered conditions. Particularly among Russia's democrats, there is little evidence of a "fear of freedom" that would convince democracy's supporters to follow a charismatic leader away from democracy. Among those who might heed the demagogue's call, there is less a fear of freedom than a sense that they have very little freedom to lose.

Even so, in the Russian sample, both the democrats and those with a more authoritarian interpretation of "order" wanted pretty much the same things, and Americans would likely endorse those desires as well. Russians wanted a government that was more responsive to people's needs and social conditions under which their survival would not be threatened. But the democrats imagined that this could be accomplished by democratic institutions. The other group thought more fear and stricter accounting for consequences of actions would help. Both wanted to reduce criminality and corruption in Russia—one group, through openness and a rule of law, and the other, through reducing personal freedom.

The popular sense of social disorder among the Russian respondents is achingly specific. Disorder is the product of closed factories and banks that disappear with account holders' savings. It is the result of wages that are too low to support a family, "guaranteed" benefits that prove difficult to secure, and too many people unconstrained by law or social responsibility. In some ways, this again is good news for those who would like to see democracy flourish in Russia. If daily conditions improve, one source of hostility to democracy should diminish. There is now a home-building supply store in Russia called Perestroika. The fact that "restructuring" now appears to have more to do with rehabbing Soviet-era apartments than with altering Soviet institutions may seem a diminution of Gorbachev's lofty goals. Or maybe all politics in Russia are local, really local. Once daily life—and its kitchens and bathrooms—is put in order, perhaps democracy will have broader appeal to all of Russia's citizens.

Views of Change: The More Things Change, the More They Stay the Same

With the collapse of Communism in the Soviet Union, many things changed. The Communist Party lost its monolithic grip on power. One country became fifteen. In Russia, radical economic reformers grasped the levers that would enable them to dismantle the command economy and begin the transition toward markets. Things changed not only at the systemic level, but also for individuals. Where formerly Russians had been subjects of a regime that claimed to be interested in their welfare but did not think it prudent to give them a choice of candidates at elections, practically overnight they became citizens, endowed with rights and empowered to choose the people who would govern them.[1] For subjects fully to become citizens, however, at some level they have to recognize that political institutions and their relationship to those institutions have both changed.

In this chapter, I examine how Russians interpret the changes that have occurred in their lives since the collapse of Communism. I focus particularly on the degree to which Russians recognize that political institutions based on the popular will, even if imperfectly, are different from the ones they used to have. I also examine the degree to which my respondents feel themselves to be freer than they were under Communism and more empowered to try to influence the choices of those who would govern them. The interviews show that many ordinary Russians do not perceive that much has changed in their political life. Those who do not see much change in institutions remain disaffected and apathetic, unable to act like citizens because they still understand themselves to be subjects.

Letting Russians describe their political world in their own words helps us see how revolutionary changes are translated into a popular idiom and, in that process, diminished. Since

---

1. Timothy J. Colton, *Transitional Citizens: Voters and What Influences Them in the New Russia* (Cambridge, MA: Harvard University Press, 2000), vii.

Americans have not recently experienced the kinds of political changes that Russians have, comments from the American respondents appear only sparingly in this chapter.

Change in Russia

There are conflicting interpretations of the amount of change that occurred in Russia as Communism collapsed. One view is that the changes were essentially revolutionary: what occurred was a rapid, fundamental transformation that left citizens breathless. Not only institutions changed, but also the core principles that informed all political action.[2] Under the Soviet regime, many ordinary Russians had seen their government as a dangerous and predatory force, best avoided, since it could not be controlled. But the end of Communism was supposed to transform the predatory state into one that was responsive to popular demands and respectful of individual freedom. This was more than a "reform" of the Communist system. Victor Sergeyev and Nikolai Biriukov called perestroika "a revolution in the hierarchy of values" and described *glasnost'* as a grand education project aimed at changing the political culture of the country.[3] And the changes of those early years pale in comparison with those that occurred later. In the end and in a manner that mimicked other revolutions, the Soviet state lost effectiveness, alienation and divisions occurred among elites and the population at large, and popular dissatisfaction provided a basis for mass mobilization.[4]

If revolutionary changes occurred, it would seem to follow that ordinary people must have noticed them. Consequently, a considerable body of scholarship has examined how Russians have coped with the fundamental changes in their world. James Alexander remarked, "The tectonic nature of Russian reforms are disrupting Russia at all levels, as society is being overturned in a seemingly headlong rush toward the reconstruction

---

2. Francis Fukuyama, "The End of History?" *National Interest* 16 (1989): 13.

3. Victor Sergeyev and Nikolai Biriukov, *Russia's Road to Democracy: Parliament, Communism, and Traditional Culture* (Brookfield, VT: Edward Elgar/Ashgate, 1993), 13.

4. Jack A. Goldstone, "The Soviet Union: Revolution and Transformation," in *Elites, Crises, and the Origins of Regimes*, ed. Mattei Dogan and John Higley (New York: Rowman and Littlefield, 1998); Vladimir Mau and Irina Starodubrovskaya, *The Challenge of Revolution: Contemporary Russia in Historical Perspective* (New York: Oxford University Press, 2001). Similarly, Jeff Goodwin, *No Other Way Out: States and Revolutionary Movements, 1945–1991* (New York: Cambridge University Press, 2001).

of political and economic institutions."[5] Alexander argued that ordinary Russians were so disoriented by the changes occurring around them and so ill equipped to understand those changes that their attitudes and values had become incoherent, fractured and contradictory, or, as he labeled it, "formless." Similarly, Fran Markowitz argued that Russian adults "felt the impact of these changes as a personally distressing rupture between past and present, stability and disorder, self-assurance and uncertainty, and it has wrecked havoc on their lives."[6]

But not all observers agree that Russia underwent a revolution at the end of the twentieth century. However one might label the events that surrounded the collapse of Communism, they lacked the thoroughness and the cataclysmic destruction of the old system that had marked Russia's revolution at the start of the century. Also, the *process* by which Communism collapsed showed significant differences from what had taken place in earlier revolutions. It was largely nonviolent. While large popular demonstrations, strikes, and nationalist violence occurred, these acts of mass disruption were less a challenge to the old regime than were negotiations among republic leaders. Previous political institutions were not immediately destroyed, since they could function differently once freed from the oversight of the Communist Party.[7]

The *outcomes* of the collapse of Communism, especially in the political sphere, also seem less than revolutionary. Authoritarian elements have crept back into politics, both at the level of Russia's hyperpresidential system and in the behavior of local officials who operate not so differently from the way they did when they were party bosses.[8] In Yurii Luzhkov's Moscow, for instance, opposition groups faced outright persecution; mass media were controlled by the mayor's office; and, between 1993 and 1998, a docile city duma adopted all key laws proposed by the mayor's office, including a new constitution that assigned tremendous authority to

5. James Alexander, *Political Culture in Post-Communist Russia: Formlessness and Recreation in a Traumatic Transition* (New York: St. Martin's Press, 2000), 105.

6. Fran Markowitz, *Coming of Age in Post-Soviet Russia* (Urbana: University of Illinois Press, 2000), 217.

7. Mary McAuley, *Russia's Politics of Uncertainty* (New York: Cambridge University Press, 1997), 3.

8. Peter Reddaway and Dmitri Glinski, *The Tragedy of Russia's Reforms: Market Bolshevism Against Democracy* (Washington, DC: United States Institute of Peace Press, 2001); M. Steven Fish, "The Dynamics of Democratic Erosion," in *Postcommunism and the Theory of Democracy*, ed. Richard D. Anderson Jr., M. Steven Fish, Stephen E. Hanson, and Philip G. Roeder (Princeton:

the mayor.[9] As evidence of a weak rule of law, pervasive corruption also seems to have more in common with the Communist past than with the promised democratic future. As one joke noted, the most apparent change between the old and new regimes was that "the democrats took away all privileges from the communists and took them for themselves."[10] Even at that, there has been considerable carryover of personnel from the old system to the new one.[11]

In this less revolutionary view of the changes that occurred as Communism collapsed in Russia, it is less obvious that citizens would perceive political changes as "a personally distressing rupture between past and present." After all, part of what did not change fundamentally was the way that citizens connect to the state. In the years after the collapse of Communism, mediating institutions such as civil society and political parties did not effectively articulate citizen demands at the levels at which decisions are made.[12] Indeed, citizens across the formerly Communist world complained that at least under Communism wages were paid on time, local services were provided, and ordinary people knew where to complain. In the new world no one listened.[13] As another joke put it, "Earlier the bureaucracy stopped up our mouths; now they cover their own ears."[14] Under these conditions, it would hardly be surprising if

Princeton University Press, 2001), 54–95; V. E. Guliev, "Rossiikaia gosudarstvennost': Sostoianie i tendentsii," in *Politicheskie Problemy Teorii Gosudarstva*, ed. N. N. Deev (Moscow: Institut Gosudarstva i Prava RAN, 1993), 7.

9. James Alexander, Andrei A. Degtyarev, and Vladimir Gel'man, "Democratization Challenged: The Role of Regional Elites," in *Fragmented Space in the Russian Federation*, ed. Blair A. Ruble, Jodi Koehn, and Nancy E. Popson (Washington, DC: Woodrow Wilson Center Press, 2001), 178–87.

10. Iurii Borev, *Istoriia gosudarstva sovetskogo: V predaniiakh i anekdotakh* (Moscow: RITTOL, 1995), 231.

11. Gennadii Ashin, "Smena Elit," *Obshchestvennye nauki i sovremennost'*, no. 1 (1995): 40–50; Olga Kryshtanovskaia and Stephen White, "From Soviet *Nomenklatura* to Russian Elite," *Europe-Asia Studies* 48, no. 5 (1996): 711–33; Eric Shiraev, "The New Nomenclature and Increasing Income Inequality," in *The Russian Transformation: Political, Sociological, and Psychological Aspects*, ed. Betty Glad and Eric Shiraev (New York: St. Martin's Press, 1999), 109–10.

12. Marcia A. Weigle, *Russia's Liberal Project: State-Society Relations in the Transition from Communism* (University Park: Pennsylvania State University Press, 2000); Marc Morje Howard, *The Weakness of Civil Society in Post-Communist Europe* (New York: Cambridge University Press, 2003).

13. Sarah Ashwin, "There's No Joy Any More': The Experience of Reform in a Kuzbass Mining Settlement," *Europe-Asia Studies* 47 (December 1995): 1375–76.

14. Borev, *Istoriia gosudarstva*, 222.

citizens suffered from "apathy born of hopelessness."[15] Nor is it surprising that surveys of Russian citizens showed some to be nostalgic for the past, still afraid of the arbitrariness of authorities, or unenthusiastic about their new political institutions.[16]

Revolutionary Change?

These contrasting views about the degree of change in post-Communist Russia—about whether a revolution has occurred or not—may be partly a function of the amount of change we think revolutions produce. Of course, some theories of revolutionary outcomes predict fundamental transformation as a result of revolution. Marx, after all, described Communism, the social system he believed a proletarian revolution would ultimately produce, as "the *genuine* resolution of the conflict between man and nature and between man and man—the true resolution of the strife between existence and essence, between objectification and self-confirmation, between freedom and necessity, between the individual and the species. Communism is the riddle of history solved, and it knows itself to be this solution."[17] But Marx's apocalyptic vision of revolution has gone largely out of style.

Other theories of revolutionary outcomes predict much less change. Crane Brinton, for instance, observed that revolutions generally end the worst abuses of the old regime and create more efficient and more centralized government, but otherwise they leave more standing than they destroy. The most radical moments of any revolution are generally followed by a return to normalcy, a Thermidorean reaction, when even things that did change go back to the way they were before. While real aspects of society are altered, Brinton observed, "these tangible and useful results look rather petty as measured by the brotherhood of man and the achievement of

15. Tim McDaniel, *The Agony of the Russian Idea* (Princeton: Princeton University Press, 1996), 5.

16. Grigory I. Vainshstein, "Totalitarian Public Consciousness in a Post-totalitarian Society," *Communist and Post-Communist Studies* 27, no. 3 (1994): 247–59; Iurii Levada, Vladimir Shubkin, Grigoriy Kertman, Veronika Ivanova, Vladimir Yadov, and Eric Shiraev, "Russia: Anxiously Surviving," in *Fears in Post-Communist Societies: A Comparative Perspective*, ed. Eric Shiraev and Vladimir Shlapentokh (New York: Palgrave, 2002), 20; Stephen White, Richard Rose, and Ian McAllister, *How Russia Votes* (Chatham, NJ: Chatham House, 1997), 43–56.

17. Karl Marx, "Economic and Philosophic Manuscripts of 1844," in *The Marx-Engels Reader*, ed. Robert C. Tucker, 2d ed. (New York: W. W. Norton, 1978), 84.

justice on earth. The blood of the martyrs seems hardly necessary to establish decimal coinage."[18] Similarly, Shmuel Eisenstadt pointed out that even
in countries where there are great postrevolutionary changes in some
areas, there is also significant continuity in others. In Russia after 1917, for
instance, while symbols of legitimation and institutional systems changed,
there was substantial continuity in cultural codes, center-periphery relations,
patterns of stratification, and tendencies toward political centralization.[19]

Theda Skocpol, one of the most influential figures in the contemporary
study of revolutions, observed that postrevolutionary regimes do not start
with a blank slate. Instead, revolutionary outcomes are constrained by the
need to consolidate state power and by structural conditions inherited from
the past, including the domestic and international problems that challenged
the old regime, as well as by the administrative and institutional weaknesses
that made it difficult for the old regime to respond to challenges.[20] Other
scholars have extended this argument to show how the outcomes of Third
World revolutions in particular were limited both by structural constraints
and by other factors that Skocpol minimized, such as ideology or leadership
abilities.[21] Even as scholars disagreed among themselves about the *reasons*
why revolutionary outcomes fell short of intentions, they agreed that the
change achieved rarely matched the change intended.

Practitioners, as well as scholars, have observed that revolutions change
less than they set out to do. Zhelyu Zhelev, then president of Bulgaria,
observed, "Revolutions, even velvet ones, rarely meet the expectations that
they raise. Disenchantment and pessimism creep in. This is when we realize
that the old regime, whose death knell we have so early sounded, is still very
much alive. The euphoric sense that everything has changed is followed by
the numbing suspicion that nothing has changed."[22] Indeed, democratic

18. Crane Brinton, *The Anatomy of Revolution*, rev. and expanded ed. (New York: Vintage,
1965), 259.

19. Shmuel Noah Eisenstadt, *Revolution and the Transformation of Societies: A Comparative
Study of Civilizations* (New York: Free Press, 1978), 234.

20. Theda Skocpol, *States and Social Revolution: Comparative Analysis of France, Russia, and
China* (Cambridge: Cambridge University Press, 1979).

21. Susan Eckstein, "The Impact of Revolution on Social Welfare in Latin America," *Theory and Society* 11 (1982): 43–49; Farideh Farhi, *States and Urban-Based Revolutions: Iran and
Nicaragua* (Chicago: University of Illinois Press, 1990); John Foran and Jeff Goodwin, "Revolutionary Outcomes in Iran and Nicaragua: Coalition Fragmentation, War, and the Limits of
Social Transformation," *Theory and Society* 22, no. 2 (1993): 209–47.

22. David S. Mason and James R. Kluegel, "Introduction: Public Opinion and Political Change
in the Postcommunist States," in *Marketing Democracy: Changing Opinion About Inequality and*

revolutions may produce less immediately apparent changes than do other kinds of revolutions. If democratic revolutions are less violent than the historical average, then less of the old is likely to be destroyed. Institutions may remain, although they begin to function differently. Old elites survive, and they may be in a position to hold on to pieces of power. The inclusiveness of the democratic project makes it unlikely that people associated with the old regime will all be taken out and shot or denied participation in new structures.

That nothing changes in a revolution, though, is also inaccurate. Theories of revolutionary outcomes consistently predict important changes in less immediately tangible aspects of the processes and understandings that hold political systems together. Revolutions change the values and beliefs that provide legitimation for the political system.[23] They change principles and justifications of political authority and the ways citizens relate to the state.[24] They seem to result in states that are "more centralized, bureaucratic, and autonomously powerful" than was the previous regime.[25] Revolutions leading to the establishment of more *democratic* governments create political systems legitimated by the twin ideas that they represent the popular will and protect the rights of all citizens. Citizens in democratic systems are supposed to recognize their freedoms and to relate to political institutions as vehicles for reflecting the will, potentially, of all citizens, not merely for enacting the personal goals of those who happen to inhabit the offices of power.[26]

Some of these changes are readily perceptible, as new elites replace old, as new symbols are substituted, and as new groups enter politics. But it is easy to imagine that other changes might elude the immediate notice of ordinary citizens. Citizens need to *notice* that they have changed from subjects into citizens for the change to be complete. But we do not generally believe that most ordinary citizens reflect on the fundamental nature

Politics in East Central Europe, ed. David S. Mason and James R. Kluegel (Lanham, MD: Rowman and Littlefield, 2000), 13.

23. Eisenstadt, *Revolution and the Transformation of Societies,* 216–17; Samuel P. Huntington, *Political Order in Changing Societies* (New Haven: Yale University Press, 1968), 308.

24. Chalmers Johnson, *Revolutionary Change,* 2d ed. (Stanford, CA: Stanford University Press, 1982), 1; Jack A. Goldstone, "Toward a Fourth Generation of Revolutionary Theory," *Annual Review of Political Science* 4 (2001): 142.

25. Skocpol, *States and Social Revolutions,* 285.

26. Adam Przeworski et al., *Sustainable Democracy* (New York: Cambridge University Press, 1995), 34–39.

of their government with the insight that noticing such changes may require.[27] Citizens do not mentally inhabit the idealized realm of political theory. Differences that seem stark in theory—such as those between dictatorship and democracy—may be less apparent in the daily life of ordinary citizens.

Some of the distinctions between Communism and the system that followed it may be particularly difficult for the ordinary people who lived under both to see. For ordinary citizens, Communism was neither the perfect utopia that Marx promised and toward which Soviet leaders pretended they were headed, nor was it the evil empire its enemies despised. Communism was a very imperfect system, in which daily life was a challenge. In her anthropological study of the Russian "soul," Dale Pesmen noted that Russia is often "mythologized as a site of ideal disorder and monstrous abomination."[28] For ordinary citizens, disorder characterized the old regime: authorities were arbitrary, government was unreliable, and goods and services were only available on an unpredictable schedule. Revolutions, even mild democratic ones, are unlikely to immediately make the world more orderly. For ordinary Russians, their "democratic revolution" has entailed lost savings, hyperinflation, massive governmental corruption, and the disintegration of their country. The continuity of disorder at the mundane level of daily existence would seem to make it even less likely that citizens will see changes in the ideas that animate political institutions.[29]

Which citizens *are* more likely to perceive the political change produced by transitions out of Communism? If what is at issue is the subtlety of the individual's understanding of the values that structure political relations, then we would expect that *more politically sophisticated* citizens would be more likely to grasp the changes produced by transition out of Communism. Citizens who understand the workings of government at a deeper and more

27. William A. Galston, "Political Knowledge, Political Engagement, and Civic Education," *Annual Review of Political Science* 4 (2001): 218; John R. Zaller, *The Nature and Origins of Mass Opinion* (New York: Cambridge University Press, 1992); David J. Elkins, *Manipulation and Consent: How Voters and Leaders Manage Complexity* (Vancouver: University of British Columbia Press, 1993), 13–16; Philip E. Converse, "The Nature of Belief Systems in Mass Publics," in *Ideology and Discontent*, ed. David E. Apter (New York: Free Press, 1964), 206–61.

28. Dale Pesmen, *Russia and Soul* (Ithaca: Cornell University Press, 2000), 290.

29. That citizens do not understand their political institutions in terms of the ideals on which they are founded can perhaps be illustrated by another joke from the Soviet era: "In a discussion a Russian communist asked a Catholic friend: 'Why do people believe in your heaven but not in ours?' After a moment's thought the Catholic replied, 'We do not show them our heaven.'" John Kolasky, ed. *Laughter Through Tears: Underground Wit, Humor, and Satire in the Soviet Russian Empire* (Bullsbrook, Australia: Veritas, 1985), 59.

fundamental level would be more likely to appreciate the differences between Communist dictatorship and even imperfect democratic institutions. An alternate explanation is that *preferences for the new system* influence the ability to see political change: citizens who approve of the idea of democracy might be more likely to sense how the values underlying protodemocratic systems are different from those that informed institutions in the past.

These are complementary, not directly competing, hypotheses because more politically sophisticated and more democratically oriented groups of citizens are likely to overlap. Since people with more democratic outlooks tend to be younger, more educated, more professional, and more likely to live in large cities, they also have a number of qualities that would lead them to be better students of the political process.[30] Intensive interviews are particularly useful in examining the degree to which respondents recognize the changes occurring around them because interviews can get behind the labels of new institutions to examine how much change those labels imply to the people who use them.

Perceptions of Change

In Chapters 5 and 6, I used a measure of support for democracy to divide respondents into groups to determine how democratic orientations affect other political evaluations, and I use that measure again in this chapter. Here, I also develop a measure of political sophistication. This is an indicator of the quality and thinking behind the answers that respondents provided.[31] People with low political sophistication had trouble answering

30. William M. Reisinger, Arthur L. Miller, and Vicki L. Hesli, "Ideological Divisions and Party-Building Prospects in Post-Soviet Russia," in *Elections and Voters in Post-Communist Russia*, ed. Matthew Wyman, Stephen White, and Sarah Oates (Northampton, MA: Edward Elgar, 1998), 136–66.

31. The measure combines directly observable characteristics, such as education level, with overall assessments of answer quality (a range from monosyllabic to thoughtful), whether respondents show evidence of thinking outside the forced alternatives offered in some of the questions that structured the interview, and a measure of the depth of their understanding of political processes. For more information, see Appendix C.

A more standard measure of sophistication based on correct answers to factual questions was inappropriate for this study because the whole purpose of the intensive interviews was to minimize the impression that respondents were being given a multiple-choice test. (For such a measure, see Colton, *Transitional Citizens*, 2.) The measure I use captures the effects of common elements of measures of political sophistication—such as media exposure, interest in politics, and political knowledge—but in a way suitable for the interview method. (See Zaller, *The Nature and Origins of Mass Opinion*, 331–36.)

questions and provided many monosyllabic or "don't know" responses. Their discussion of politics showed only limited understanding of relevant issues and few concerns beyond their immediate personal situation. People with moderate political sophistication gave longer answers but often veered off subject. They were more apt to talk in clichés. While their understanding of politics extended beyond their own personal situation, it focused more on personalities than on institutional structures. People in the "highly sophisticated" category could speak at length and with subtlety about a variety of political issues. Their understanding of the political system included a grasp of how institutions were supposed to work. And they were more likely to "think outside the box," offering creative responses to forced-choice questions. Faced with two unpalatable—or what they thought were inaccurate—alternatives, they were able to articulate a third.

As Table 7.1 shows, there is some overlap between levels of political sophistication and support for democracy in the sample, with highly politically sophisticated respondents showing overall more support for democracy than the degree shown by less sophisticated respondents.[32] But the two measures are far from identical, and there are a number of individuals with either higher or lower support for democracy than their sophistication level might imply. In the analysis that follows, the attitudes of these individuals in particular will help us understand whether sophistication level or degree of support for democracy seems to have more influence on the ability of ordinary Russians to perceive the changes occurring in their political institutions.

While, as we will see, many Russians intuit changes in their political institutions only dimly, it would be inaccurate to say that they see no change at all in their society. They understand that the collapse of Communism changed their lives fundamentally. It is just that most of the change they see is economic. In regard to their immediate material circumstances, almost all respondents were conscious that much was different from how it used to be and, for many, much was worse. There were, of course, some positive

32. The two measures are correlated at .48, significant at the .001 level. The two measures are substantially different and are largely based on different questions. Part of the political-sophistication measure—degree of political understanding—was based on whether respondents understood how political institutions are supposed to function. One such institution is the Duma, consideration of which was also included in the measure of support for democracy. These two parts of the measures are correlated at .29 (significant at the .05 level). A more important reason for the correlation between sophistication and support for democracy would seem to be the fact that education, part of the sophistication measure, is also a strong predictor of support for democracy.

Table 7.1   Political sophistication and support for democracy among Russian respondents

Low political sophistication	Moderate political sophistication	High political sophistication
High or moderate support for democracy (horizontal) Anya, Ekaterina, Lev, Sonya *(4 respondents)*	Kolya, Misha, Slava, Vitya, Iurii, Konstantin, Mikhail, Oleg, Raisa, Galina Grigor'evna, Liudmilla Vladimirovna *(11 respondents)*	Dima, Raya, Tolya, Alla, Arkadii, Gennadii, Iosif, Nadezhda, Natalia, Svetlana, Aleksandra Antonovna, Marina Aleksandrovna, Andrei Viktorovich *(13 respondents)*
Low or mixed support for democracy (horizontal) Katya, Liuba, Valya, Aleksei, Klara, Pavel, Pelageia, Polina, Sergei, Anna Pavlovna, Vladimir Il'ich, Yegor Yegorovich *(12 respondents)*	Lena, Nadya, Inna, Elena, Evgenii, Grigorii, Sofiia, Kollektiv, Nikolai, Zinaida, Boris Borisovich, Irina L'vovna, Zoia Igorevna, Vilen Nikolaevich *(14 respondents)*	Vasya, Ruslan, Valentina, Ivan Ivanovich, Olga Iur'evna, Tatiana Mikhailovna *(6 respondents)*

assessments of the changes in economic life since Communism, but they did not come particularly from the political sophisticates or from supporters of democracy. Instead, unadulterated positive comments were most frequent at low levels of political sophistication, where the reason may have been a failure to take in much information about the state of the economy. Months before the ruble collapse of 1998, Sergei thought the economy was in fine shape even though he himself was unemployed. Ekaterina, one of the wealthiest of the respondents, exulted, "It has become more interesting to live, more interesting by a lot. In any case, in the sphere of education, in the sphere of commerce, the past five years have had a great influence on stores, on hairdressers, on everything, on sport. For me as a housewife, it is quite pleasant." While the conditions of Ekaterina's life certainly were pleasant, she would not have needed to venture far from her luxurious home to find people who were suffering.

Political sophistication affected the way respondents expressed their dissatisfactions with the economic changes they had endured. At low or moderate levels of political sophistication, the tendency was to complain about a wholesale decline of circumstances. People complained that, although there was more for sale than there had been under Communism, they could not afford to buy anything. Where the Communist government had provided necessities, such as medicines for invalids, now there was nothing. Anna Pavlovna described the differences between life under Communism and in an emerging market: "It seemed to me, we weren't wealthy, but all the same we had tomorrow, as it were. And now I don't know that I will have a tomorrow. . . . I used to consider myself middle class, but now I'm already, well, how can I say? Well, poor and a beggar. I try to work, of course, to be able to buy a few things, but it's still hard. And there are such people among us, oy, how poor! Well, I'm still young. I'm sixty-five years old, but I toil. It is my lot to work and work and work."

Evgenii, unemployed in the new economy, also thought that life had been better under Communism. He said, "Under Communism, under Communism, I could do a lot. I could get any work. They needed workers everywhere. There was stable pay. If you talk about childhood, then, as they say, I went to pioneer camp. The union paid for all of that. It just cost my parents kopecks. Also, they could go to sanatoria, hotels, also paid for by the union. All of that was also very cheap. Then it was better."

Inna worried that her effective salary had been greatly reduced as a result of inflation and now was barely adequate to pay her rent, never mind provide food and transportation for herself and her children. She remarked, "We say that under Communism, under the Communists, under different authorities, we didn't think about all of this. Everyone was paid. Everyone ate. Maybe not as sweetly, like now everything is in the stores. But I assure you, 60 to 70 percent of the population can't buy what they're selling in the stores, can't allow themselves the same smoked sausage that they could have allowed themselves in the past, except it was in deficit." For these respondents, knowing they could afford to buy almost anything that might be available under Communism made up for the fact that there had been little for sale.

While less politically sophisticated respondents complained about the wholesale deterioration of economic conditions since Communism or—more rarely—found the economic picture moderately rosy, the most sophisticated respondents tended to offer mixed responses on economic change. While most of them recognized the need for change overall, many complained about specific problems, policies, or the procedures used to implement reform. They accepted that prices had to rise, but argued that workers still had to be paid and elderly people needed to receive their pensions on time. They complained about the speed of reforms, sometimes arguing that reform lagged too slowly, sometimes that it had been conducted too quickly, needlessly destroying parts of the economy that could have been saved. And they complained about the way privatization was conducted, even if they supported the goal that government property end up in private hands.

Olga Iur'evna commented, "I don't like the fact that, completely independent of the will of the people, huge pieces of property—the oil industry, aluminum—were grabbed up by people who were completely unknown to the country, and that our society was divided into a small group with a lot of property—I don't believe they are people who traded in the market—and citizens were left with very little. . . . We have taken a completely different route of development in which property belongs to a small group of big magnates."

Andrei Viktorovich captured the ambivalence of many in this group when he said, "Economic changes are sufficiently complex that it is hard to say in one word whether they're good or bad. Everyone is happy, and I am in that number, that it is not necessary to stand in lines, that there are more stores and more markets. At the same time, our ability to buy anything in that market has been rather reduced, especially for those who must live on a pension. Beyond that, the situation in the labor market has become quite a bit more complicated. I'm afraid it won't get better, but instead will get worse."

The 2003 respondents gave especially mixed responses, with most expressing mild optimism that economic conditions were improving but nonetheless observing what a wild ride it had been since 1991. Like those interviewed earlier, the 2003 respondents felt that the greater availability of goods was overshadowed by the unaffordable prices.

When we shift our attention from perceptions of economic change to perceptions of political change, strikingly more people comment that little change has occurred, that much more was promised than was ever delivered.

In this regard, the patterns in my sample were similar to those seen in mass surveys. Natal'ia Laidinen observed that only 6.7 percent of respondents in a 2000 ROMIR poll thought that political authorities had become closer to the nation.[33] In other Russian polls, only small minorities thought they could influence political decisions by any means, whether elections, strikes, demonstrations, or personal connections.[34]

In my sample, the tendency to perceive little change was particularly notable for people interviewed while Yeltsin was in power. Boris Borisovich commented about Yeltsin, "I think that he hasn't done a lot that he promised. I don't like that the Communist Party remains in power and that now it is prevailing in places. The main point is that nothing changed in the country." Boris Borisovich was not alone in observing the continued hold on power by Communists. Sergei said, "They used to be Communists, but now they've become democrats. The same people became democrats. . . . It turns out exactly the same. Everything is identical, they just changed the names." Grigorii added, "Unfortunately, I consider that probably all the reforms that have occurred up to now—they were done with post-Communist structures, post-Communist methods, and Communist people. That is, in fact, life in general has really begun to change, cardinally, but at the top the whole government apparatus remains the same." A member of a work collective that was interviewed as group added, "Those who were in power remain in power. It was supposed to be that all Communists were thrown out, but all the Communists remain. All of them. Whoever was in power remains in power."

Others recognized that even if the people in power had changed, the new personnel operated effectively the same as the old. Even before Putin, the new "democrats" had the same tendencies toward absolute power as the old Communists, and citizens were excluded from real influence. Elena commented, "As we were slaves, so we remain slaves." Valentina remarked, "I consider that we are stamping in one place and so far are not going anywhere—neither here nor there. Stagnation." Even some of Yeltsin's supporters commented on the lack of substantive political change. Polina noted, "The ideas are good, and taxes are OK in general, and Yeltsin tried to make different structures, but it didn't come off. Therefore I say, he speaks well, but underneath nothing is happening."

33. Natal'ia Valer'evna Laidinen, "Obraz Rossii v zerkale Rossiiskogo obshchestvennogo mneniia," *Sotsiologicheskie issledovaniia*, no. 4 (2001): 29.

34. M. K. Gorshkov, *Rossiiskoe obshchestvo v usloviiakh transformatsii: Mify i real'nost' (Sotsiologicheskii analiz)* (Moscow: ROSSPEN, 2003), 410.

At the same time that many people complained about the lack of change in political institutions or the people who staff them, some people also pointed out changes that had occurred. Indeed, some of these were the same people who claimed that little had changed. Boris Borisovich, quoted above to the effect that "nothing changed in the country," also noted approvingly that the press had become freer. Marina Aleksandrovna concluded that "a lot has been accomplished": people could travel freely, vote, or say anything they want. They could, notably, meet with American researchers and talk over the kitchen table. That was quite a shift from Grandma's experience with Siberian exile. Not all those who recognized that something had changed in political life thought that the changes were positive. Many commented about the loss of social order or the rise of criminality, including at high governmental levels.

By 2003, after Putin had been in power for a few years, respondents were somewhat more likely to recognize that a political break with the Communist past had occurred, though they thought the break was still incomplete. Liuba, for instance, noted, "There is not now in Russia the kind of prescribed order that there was in Communist times. In my opinion, that is democratic." Yet she qualified her comment by contrasting progress at the national level with a lack of progress in her own city. She said, "I work here in a government institution. Everything is like it was in the past. There is no freedom of speech, freedom of choice. Everything is in the old way." Lena felt that the county was more democratic, but she was so ashamed of the overall decline that Russia had undergone that she found it hard to feel the kind of patriotism she had experienced under Communism. Natalia thought that by 2003 Russia had become a democracy. After all, there were elections and a free press; the problem was simply that democracy had not turned out well for ordinary people. Others continued to see little change. Pelageia commented that life had been hard under Communism, and it was hard still. In her mind, the only difference after Communism was a greater degree of licentiousness, both in the general population and among government officials.

Who Perceives More Political Change?

Even from these brief comments, it is clear that not all Russians see the same degree of political transformation. Some see significant continuities over time, while others are more apt to notice the changes. But what kind of people think that more political change has occurred? To answer this question, I focus on a few specific aspects of political change. In this section of the chapter, I look at whether people see changes in executive institutions. In the following section, I examine how Russians assess the amount of freedom they enjoy compared with under Communism. Following that, I turn to the degree to which citizens think they can influence their new rulers. These are important issues because they concern changes in how key institutions are legitimized and how citizens relate to the government, the kinds of political transformations that revolutions are supposed to bring about.[35]

While Russia's new presidency has been criticized for its authoritarian tendencies, it differs from Communist executive offices insofar as the population elects the president, whose term in power is thus subject to popular approval as well as to constitutional limitations. In other words, the source of legitimation for Russia's president is different from that of Communist Party leaders, who ruled by virtue of a claim to possessing better knowledge of how to bring about Communism. Among the Russian respondents, there was a surprising tendency for people to fail to make distinctions between the executive institutions of a democratic polity and the ones from their Communist or pre-Communist past. Many respondents saw striking similarities between presidents and czars and between mayors and chairpersons of the Communist-era city *ispolkom*. These comments occurred at all levels of political sophistication.

In the low-political-sophistication group, respondents tended to justify the need for a president or a mayor by arguing that it was necessary to have a strong leader, capable of keeping control in unstable circumstances—the same kind of justification that would apply to nonelected executives. Aleksei argued, "In general, there should be an institution like the president so that power will be in one set of hands." Ekaterina added that when power is in a single set of hands, "there will not be discord," to her a positive by-product of centralization. Anya remarked on the need for centralized authority at the local level. She said, "Of course, there has to be a leader in the city, however it's called. I don't know how the institution of the mayor is different from the old *ispolkom*."

In the middle-sophistication group, respondents were more likely to refer back to historical traditions in Russia and to interpret the president as a newfangled czar. Elena argued, "We need a president. We're used to it, because we used to have the czar. We're used to being under someone's

---

35. Eisenstadt, *Revolution and the Transformation of Societies*, 216–19; Huntington, *Political Order*, 308.

authority. We were brought up that way in the spirit of patriotism. What do they say here in Russia? 'Here comes the master. The master will settle our disputes.' We can't get by without a master." Liudmilla Vladimirovna added, "And what difference does it make how it's labeled: president, czar, or monarch? Russia never lived without this."

Even among the most politically sophisticated respondents, a few people remarked on the similarities between presidents and authoritarian political leaders. Tatiana Mikhailovna commented, "Insofar as Russia was always, as they say, inclined toward the little father czar, then probably some kind of post like the presidency is organic for Russia." Similarly, Olga Iur'evna remarked, "Russia is used to autocracy, to undivided authority. The traditions of Russia are czarism. The czar was there, and the Russian people always believed in a kind, good czar. And similarly, in the president they see a person with whom they can trust their faith. Those are the traditions of Russia."

To put these comments in context, it helps to compare them to comments about the presidency made by the American respondents. Rather than seeing the presidency as an office in which power was centralized, people in the American sample were more likely to focus on the role of the president as a spokesperson, a figurehead, a source of unity in a diverse country, a person to set the tone or direction of political life or to balance the power of Congress. Only one of the American respondents compared the president to a monarch, and that was to a modern monarch without real political power. Rick noted that the presidency was "just enough to placate our royalist tendencies to have somebody like that. I mean, even most parliamentary countries have a figurehead royal family."

The view of the presidency among the Russian respondents, then, is distinctive in its implication of autocratic power. No doubt, this is partly a function of the power of the Russian office and of the ways in which its first inhabitants used that power. But frequent comparisons between presidents and czars or Communist Party bosses also indicate that ordinary Russians perceived significant continuities between their political past and present. And it is not only the less politically sophisticated who perceive those continuities.

While political sophistication alone was not sufficient to enable respondents to see how an elected president was different from a czar or a commissar, political sophistication combined with support for democracy made it more likely that a person would see the differences. Even in the middle group in terms of political sophistication, more democratically oriented respondents were less likely to equate presidents with unelected executives. Iurii said, "For Russia, the office of the presidency is not inherent, from the point of view of historical roots." Slava equated the presidency not with Russia's authoritarian traditions, but with the practice of Western democracies. He said, "I think Russia should have a president, like in the whole civilized world." These comments were quite different from those of less democratic people at similar levels of political sophistication, people such as Zoia Igorevna, who defended the presidency on the grounds that "someone should, as they say, keep us in line and in strong hands." Even among democrats in this group, though, there was a tendency to see the president as a boss (*vozhd'*) who could make decisions when a fractious parliament could not.

Compared with respondents in the middle-sophistication group, highly sophisticated respondents were more likely to recognize the *limits* on the power of presidents, that is, to understand the ways in which presidents were functionally different from czars. Even so, they had to admit that those limits did not always obtain in Russia: elections and legislatures curtail the power of presidents only if the elections are free and fair and the constitution gives some power to the legislature. Consequently, while people who were both politically sophisticated and supportive of democracy were the most likely to understand the *significance* of an elected president, their appreciation of the actual change in Russia was somewhat muted.

For instance, Svetlana remarked that since the president is chosen by all the people, the office contributed to the general democratization of society despite, as she put it, mistakes that had been made. Marina Aleksandrovna had some trouble assessing the value of the presidency. She said, "The presidency is an unusual institution for our country and in general there hasn't been much time to analyze it, to tell what's good or bad or might be better." She echoed Slava's comment that Russia might as well have a presidency, since all civilized countries do, and added, "All the same a president has the status to supplement, to balance a normal parliament (not one like ours)." Andrei Viktorovich commented, "Today the situation is like this: parties have little authority insofar as there is little mass support for these parties at this time. . . . And because of this, the parliament made up of these parties is practically independent of the population. But a president who is all the same more or less chosen by the whole people acts as a counterbalance, assuming things work out."

It seems, then, that people who are both politically sophisticated and democratically oriented are more likely to recognize that presidents and czars are different animals, despite the fact that both are executives and that both form, in Russia at least, an overwhelming power base in the political system. These people were also more likely to understand how Russia's institutions only imperfectly embodied the democratic ideal; hence, even if they recognized the changes involved, they were not overly impressed with their extent.

Are Russians More Free?

Even though many of the respondents sensed only minimal—if any—change in executive institutions, one might expect that they would see more change in aspects of the political system that touched them more directly.[36] A person might not worry overly about the source of legitimation for the presidency, but it would be harder to miss the lifting of social fear or greater freedom from arbitrary action by government officials. Indeed it tends to be true that people in my sample noticed that they were freer than they used to be under Communism, at least in some respects. They praised the increased availability of books and movies. They recognized that the fear of arbitrary arrest had lessened, even if it had not entirely evaporated. According to some observers, Putin's efforts to curtail the press and limit the effectiveness (and sometimes the freedom) of his critics have put a chill on the exercise of personal freedom in Russia.[37] But

36. One might expect ordinary people to notice more change in representative institutions, on the principle that they were more likely to have contact with a deputy than with the president, but that expectation was not borne out in the interviews. Just as many respondents thought presidents and tsars occupied roughly equivalent political institutions, a number also compared federal and local dumas to the soviets that existed under the Communist regime and, perhaps more plausibly, to the duma that existed in Russia between the 1905 and 1917 revolutions. These comments were comparatively few, though, so that it was hard to see any patterns in them. This was particularly true, since people with little political sophistication rarely had much to say about representative bodies, claiming not to know enough make any comments. Overall, people were so disillusioned about the way the State Duma functioned and felt so powerless to affect the actions of their representative that the fact that those representatives were chosen in competitive elections did not impress them.

We might also expect people to see more change in local than in federal institutions, again on the principle of greater contact. Here the picture is muddied by the fact that, in many of the regions where interviews were conducted, the methods of local politics had changed *less in fact* than was true for federal institutions. Also, a number of respondents seem to have felt that local institutions were always more responsive to citizen concerns; hence democracy did not necessarily make them more responsive.

37. Lilia Shevtsova, *Putin's Russia* (Washington, DC: Carnegie Endowment for International Peace, 2003), 163–66.

my respondents were too far from the centers of power to feel that chill. People interviewed during the Putin years did not differ substantially in their assessments of personal freedom from people interviewed while Yeltsin was in power. There were, though, some other interesting patterns in comments about freedom.

Among my respondents, *less* politically sophisticated respondents were more likely to think they were *more* free.[38] They did not all think this was a good thing. To Liuba, signs of newfound freedom included "swindlers all around; people do what they want, murder, violence." But Polina was convinced of the benefits of the freedom she now enjoyed. She said, "I consider myself a wholly free person. I am not going abroad, but I am free. I have brothers who have left, and I can meet them without difficulties. They come every year. Earlier, they went to America in 1980, and we were not able to receive a letter until 1991. Not a letter, not a call, nothing. Understand? And now everything is fine." Speaking directly about our interview, she continued, "Before we wouldn't have talked. A KGB agent would have sat across from us and watched us for what we said and what we thought, and God forbid move his hand once."

Some people in the middle group in terms of political sophistication echoed this optimism. Liudmilla Vladimirovna remarked on how people in contemporary Russia had less reason to fear arbitrary action on the part of political authorities than had been the case during her youth when, for instance, she was severely chastised for wrapping the garbage in a piece of newspaper that contained a picture of Stalin. She commented that she only realized late in life how bad things had been during her childhood. Whenever her father was late or missed his train, her mother would stand by the window, afraid that he would never come home. By contrast, Liudmilla Vladimirovna noted, even in an imperfectly democratic Russia people can stand in the middle of the intersection and complain about the bad job authorities are doing. Oleg echoed this same point. He said, "But now the old Communists have rushed to the square with red flags. Then it would not have been permitted; it would have been the opposite. But now, there they stand. You can see them in front of Lenin. They yell and scream there. Well, isn't that freedom? They can express themselves. You can understand that as freedom. And democracy. There it is. Then, they could not express themselves."

---

38. It was also the case that less-democratic respondents were more likely to think they were freer, but that is partially because the measure of support for democracy relies in part on the same question as the assessments of present amounts of freedom.

While some people in the middle-sophistication group lauded their newfound freedom, others were more reticent. Although they might agree with Oleg that they were now free to protest, they were less convinced that the freedom to yell and scream while no one listened was much of an advance over the past. A member of the work collective remarked, "Earlier if someone went out with a flag, oy, I don't know, or with some kind of sign. But now, there they stand every day. That's our freedom. Stand as long as you like." She, like many others, also complained that effective freedom was limited by economic circumstances. She said, "We didn't receive any kind of freedom. Well, truthfully, in the past you could only travel abroad with the permission of the party organization. . . . And now there's no money." Money also figured prominently in Nadya's understanding of the limitations on her freedom. She said, "We do all have some kind of freedom, but freedom is probably all the same power, money. But the majority of the population, including me, live below the minimum necessary for life. A single salary, that is. What kind of freedom is this?" Even a single salary would be better than having none, the fate of those threatened with unemployment. Konstantin said, "It is possible to speak freely, but that's not all there is to freedom. Freedom from what now? Freedom not to work because there are no jobs? That is also not freedom. Little has changed." Zinaida, her own job in a failing factory threatened, summed up the problem: "Only those in power have freedom here."

A couple of respondents stressed the freedoms they had enjoyed under Communism. The moderately sophisticated Galina Grigor'evna proclaimed, "Well, I want to say that earlier we had freedom of speech. I don't know, what was it impossible to say? . . . No one fettered us even under Communism. Our hands weren't tied." As someone who had lived under Stalin and witnessed the destruction of her city at the hands of the invading Nazi army, she did not come to these assessments secondhand. No doubt her sense of personal freedom during these times reflected the conventionality and acceptability of the things she wanted to say. But the gist of her comments was echoed by people much younger than herself, and in the most politically sophisticated category. Raya remarked, "I don't feel that I now have a lot more freedom than under the Communists. I thought I was free then and spoke freely."

Similarly, Gennadii argued that "a kind of hidden ideological hand" operates under democratic conditions, which limits what people can say. He added that, in his opinion, the Soviet shadow economy allowed for greater development of private initiative and entrepreneurialism than the corrupt post-Soviet "free" marketplace. Like many others, Gennadii lamented economic circumstances that restricted effective freedom. He said, "In the Soviet period with all its ideological repression, the average researcher had ten to fifteen business trips a year to different regions of the country. That was very important. Now you can go one to two times, usually, because you have to pay for yourself. Therefore, there has been a significant narrowing of scientific freedom. There is the possibility of access to literature and other things. Politically, we are given scientific freedom and freedom of speech, but freedom is not supported economically. Therefore a paradox arises: in order to do research, I have to undertake nonscientific activities, work somewhere else." Apparently, other Russians share Gennadii's concerns: Eric Shiraev reports that in a July 1995 Vox Populi poll 80 percent of respondents considered that their rights had been better protected under Brezhnev than under Yeltsin.[39]

Revolutions change political institutions and the way people relate to them. It seems from my respondents, however, that not everyone in Russia has noticed the change. To many Russians, new institutions look remarkably like old ones and freedom seems constrained, especially by material circumstances. Political sophistication does not consistently make it more likely that people will appreciate fairly subtle changes. In my sample, political sophisticates were less likely to think they were substantially freer in the post-Communist world. Many political sophisticates failed to distinguish between new executive offices and old ones. Only when political sophistication was combined with support for democracy were respondents more likely to recognize how elected executives differed from the ones in place under Communism. But these respondents were also acutely aware of how little real progress Russians had made in limiting the effective power of their elected officials or in liberating most ordinary, not very prosperous, people.

Making Government Responsive

If many people do not see much change in their political institutions, will they change the way they *act* toward those institutions? Will they regard themselves as democratic citizens, empowered to pressure government officials to respond to their needs? In this section, I examine the effect of

---

39. Eric Shiraev, "Attitudinal Changes During the Transition," in *The Russian Transformation: Political, Sociological, and Psychological Aspects*, ed. Betty Glad and Eric Shiraev (New York: St. Martin's Press, 1999), 157.

political sophistication and attitudes toward democracy on how effective citizens feel in their political life. In particular, I focus on respondents' answers to two questions: whether they feel that authorities care about citizens' opinions and whether they think there is anything that ordinary citizens can do to influence political decisions. This sense of efficacy in political life is a crucial factor distinguishing citizens from subjects.[40] It is also one of the ways observers worry that Russians come up culturally short. Leonid Gozman and Alexander Etkind, for instance, argue that the Soviet period produced in citizens a "learned helplessness" about political life. As a result of their experiences under the Soviet system, Gozman and Etkind argue, Russians are convinced that all political action is doomed to failure.[41]

The overwhelming consensus of my respondents was that people in political office did not care about citizens' opinions and instead thought mostly about their own interests. As Aleksei put it, "They are far from the people, and our opinion in general for them is empty, an empty place." Many felt that in this respect not much had changed since Communism. Formal institutions of democracy did not alter the fact that politicians did what they wanted, not what citizens desired. Comparing the present to the Communist period, Vilen Nikolaevich commented, "Of course, then no one was interested in our opinion, just like now." Irina L'vovna remarked similarly, "In the past they were little interested, but we didn't know it. But now they're little interested and we know it."

Among less politically sophisticated respondents and among those who were more sophisticated but not very democratic, many thought that, far from getting better, the responsiveness of officials had actually declined since the collapse of Communism. Some argued that Communist ideology forced party officials to pay attention to the concerns and opinions of the workers. Olga Iur'eva said, "The Communists were very afraid. They had an ideology. They tried to implant that ideology that interested them, and therefore they were interested that my opinion coincide, that I embraced this ideology, and that all people embraced this ideology. And now there is no ideology, and everyone is indifferent." Olga Iur'evna was not especially troubled that the Communists were more interested in changing her opinion than in listening to it; she liked the fact that they cared about

40. Robert Putnam, *Making Democracy Work: Civic Traditions in Modern Italy* (Princeton: Princeton University Press, 1993), 83–120; Gabriel A. Almond and Sidney Verba, *The Civic Culture: Political Attitudes and Democracy in Five Nations* (Newbury Park, CA: Sage, 1989).

41. Leonid Gozman and Alexander Etkind, *The Psychology of Post-totalitarianism in Russia* (London: Centre for Research into Communist Economies, 1992), 79–83.

what she thought.[42] Sonya similarly felt that ideologically driven concerns led the Communists to serve the needs of ordinary people. She said, "In that time, there was some kind of dialogue, some kind of psychology of everyone. It was in the slogans, in the ideology. It was necessary: the government was obliged to be concerned with the interests of the workers. . . . It seems to me that a lot was actually done in their interests." Apparently, Olga Iur'evna and Sonya are not alone in their impressions. Vladimir Shlapentokh affirms that during Soviet times, a large majority of citizens considered contact with authorities or the media to be an effective way to resolve problems.[43]

Younger respondents, who had not lived under the Soviet regime for much of their lives, cited the social goods provided by government—such as safe streets, guaranteed jobs, and Pioneer palaces—as evidence that Communist officials must have cared about what people wanted. As Arkadii put it, "More came the people's way." Older respondents focused instead on the fact that, under Communism, mechanisms existed through which people could express their opinions. Zoia Igorevna said, "Earlier, Communists, as they say—I was a party member. I could say everything that I thought. And sometimes this was decisive, all the same. And now no one asks our opinions." Ivan Ivanovich stressed the fact that people knew they could meet with Communist officials with their concerns. He said, "Then it was possible to go somewhere and complain. But now there is no one to complain to. Before, for instance, it was possible to go to the party committee or the union committee to complain about the boss. But now business owners, private merchants—where can one go? . . . It debases a person when there is no place he can go to complain. What are you complaining about? Go say something to him, and he'll fire you. And what can be done? So people sit silently."

Comments like these were more common at lower levels of support for democracy than at higher ones. With higher support for democracy, more people in the middle- and high-sophistication groups reasoned that competitive elections made it necessary for elected officials to care about the opinions of the voters. Even if elected officials would have been perfectly happy to ignore the opinions of the people, even if they did so for most of their time in office, the mere fact of competitive elections meant that

42. One respondent put a different spin on the push for ideological conformity under Communism. Sofiia said, "Earlier exactly no one was interested in your opinion, although for the reason that everyone was supposed to think alike."

43. Vladimir Shlapentokh, *A Normal Totalitarian Society: How the Soviet Union Functioned and How It Collapsed* (Armonk, NY: M. E. Sharpe, 2001), 67.

officials were forced to pay some attention to the public. Iurii remarked, "Well, under Communism, those in power were on the whole not interested in us. . . . If earlier, under Communism, we went to the polls only to formally fulfill an obligation, then now we matter. And that means they have to be interested." Raisa warned, "They cannot retain power, if they are going to ignore the opinions of the nation." Tolya cited as evidence of the interest of government officials the various public opinion polls conducted even between elections.

While people at higher levels of support for democracy and political sophistication were more likely than other people to think that officials cared about their opinions to some degree, not all the politically sophisticated democrats were as hopeful as Tolya. Andrei Viktorovich was less convinced that polls proved that his leaders cared what he thought. His take was that "from time to time, the authorities undertake some kind of action that makes it look like they are checking up on how we feel about something." To him, elections were also suspect. He called many of the candidates "demagogues." He elaborated: "They are simply looking for a way to manipulate our emotions, our preferences, nothing more." Similarly, Nadezhda thought that government officials might not care much about her opinion; even so, she thought it was increasingly important that *she* care about and try to influence theirs.

Thinking that people in government might care about one's opinion does not necessarily translate into efforts to influence political officials. Which people were more ready to take action in the political arena? Not surprisingly, less politically sophisticated respondents, who generally felt that government officials had little interest in their opinions, also felt there was little ordinary people could do to influence political decisions. They were ready to vote and mostly thought voting was important. And they held out some hope of influencing local government, but national government remained an impenetrable fortress, with walls they were certain they could never climb. Regarding the federal government, Sergei said, "How can we influence them? We can't influence them in any way. They decide everything by themselves. They decide our, well, our business. Well, not ours, but all of Russia's. And we can't do anything about it."

Polina also noted the difficulty of influencing decisions, especially outside normal election cycles. She said, "Stand in front of the building with a placard—who will read it? This deputy is surrounded by guards; he won't see you. He promises that he'll do everything for the people. But he only works, I don't know, for himself probably. It just doesn't happen.

Good people may be candidates, but within half a year they become deaf.
They only listen to themselves. For that reason, it's completely impossible." This demoralization in the face of authority was also evident in the
more democratically oriented respondents at low levels of political sophistication. Lev noted, "An ordinary person simply can't go to the Duma. No
one will listen."

Similar comments occurred in the middle-sophistication group at lower
levels of support for democracy. People in this group were concerned that
they would not have enough information to effectively influence government. They might not even know if laws detrimental to their interests had
been passed. They had little confidence that they could figure out how to
contact their deputies. Asked what she could do if the Duma made a
harmful law, Zinaida replied, "Absolutely nothing. . . . No, here it isn't that
simple. First, deputies have particular hours, say, days. They're available
on particular days. Say, I write something. I even go to him. But he turns
out to be in Moscow today. Tomorrow he'll be in the district. The day after
tomorrow, he'll be somewhere else. I don't have the spare time to go. If I
work, I work from bell to bell. I can't call anywhere."

Even when people in this category thought that some officials might be
open to addressing their needs, they feared that those officials would be
powerless to help them. Elena said, "All the means they gave us for social
welfare were divided up earlier. There's nothing left. And who will give
anything now? You can't generally do much just on enthusiasm." Nadya
was afraid that even if she tried to act, no one else would. She lamented,
"Now it is possible to raise prices for utilities, but everyone is silent. They
pay out of their last money but are silent. This is only possible in Russia,
nowhere else. Therefore, to go alone and cry that I disagree?" Between the
feeling that most elected officials were more concerned about their own
welfare than the welfare of the people, that there were not many ways that
citizens could get effective messages to their leaders, and that resources
were scant in any case, many of the less democratic, less sophisticated
respondents were very discouraged about their ability to have any influence in political life. As one woman in the work collective commented, "A
lot depends on us. But no one asks us and no one notices us." And so, as
Ivan Ivanovich said, "people sit silently."

Even at high levels of political sophistication, the less democratically
oriented respondents echoed this despair. Ruslan commented, "Heavens!
The miners strike and strike. All completely without effect. Everyone is

busy with their own affairs." Olga Iur'evna noted, "I think the only way to influence the federal government is through elections. That is the only way. There are no other ways. . . . Unfortunately, our mass media is only interested in the opinions of a narrow group of people. . . . I think that Russia is very rich in people, rich in talented, intelligent people, but that there are not channels to put all this potential to use. It directly weakens the situation in Russia. We received this freedom to express our opinions, but it has not been realized. I can go out and talk, but no one will hear me." The problem, as Vasya put it, is that "I am too small."

Higher levels of support for democracy, especially when combined with middle to high political sophistication, made it more likely that respondents would express the feeling—maybe only the hope—that they could do something. Perhaps their votes sent a message to people in power. Perhaps the right people read the reports or letters they wrote, and action was taken. Raya said, "We should certainly participate in elections, choose those parties that we consider will best represent our interests in the government. We must not surrender this power passively. That is, we should participate in various meetings, write letters, sign petitions." She had confidence even in the potential responsiveness of the system, at least at the level of the local duma. She said, "There are always people in the city duma who reflect the interests of ordinary people, and they can protest against the harmful law. . . . Simple people like me can also step forward. Things can somehow be resolved in a peaceful way. Well, again to sign something, attend a meeting with the mayor, in the end they will listen."

Galina Grigor'evna agreed that a united people could address local problems and maybe even issues on the national level. About whether ordinary people could influence the federal government, she said, "We can. We can, because if we also unite and make demands, we are many." She felt that the united people could respond even to a State Duma making harmful laws: everyone would have to get together and demand that a new Duma be elected. Kolya agreed. He said, "But if I considered that a law was not only against me but against the majority, in my opinion we should one way or another fight against it with various types of methods, even through the representatives we elected to the Duma. We must fight against those laws that are opposed by the majority of the population."

At the highest levels of political sophistication, many of democracy's defenders tried to reconcile this sense of what the people should be able to do with the recognition that the population was not organized in such a way that they could wield their potential political power with much effectiveness.[44] These respondents argued that much in political life was hidden from ordinary people, leaving the public without the knowledge necessary for influence. They noted also the weak ties between citizens and political institutions, making it easier for elected officials to ignore the population than to listen to their concerns. Some complained that, while voting was the main way for most people to make their opinions known, the electoral system left voters without the means to make an informed choice.

Natalia commented, "I consider that it is important to vote because if people don't go to the polls, don't express their evident opinions toward what the deputies propose, then they create the opportunities for people who will pursue their own egoistic interests. However, the information about each participant in the electoral campaign is very little. We all vote by intuition: do we like or not like the candidate? There is only indirect information that arrives through unofficial routes—rumors, conversations. It's clearly insufficient to make an aware choice." In this regard, she echoed some of the less sophisticated, less democratic respondents. Zinaida, for instance, similarly remarked, "Of course, it's important to vote, only how do we vote? We vote with closed eyes. . . . We don't drink tea with him at the same table, as they say."

Even if they thought government might be predisposed not to listen, though, the politically sophisticated, democratic-leaning respondents could conceive of other ways to affect social outcomes. Gennadii was involved in the production of a policy journal aimed at influencing public opinion. Despite a lack of confidence in her ability to influence those in power directly, Nadezhda thought her work as a teacher gave her influence over other people and the opinions they began to form. Arkadii considered that it was probably necessary to organize social protests, although he felt that the time was not ripe. He said, "We don't put together protests. I consider this is a bad thing. . . . But society has to mature. And that maturation can

44. The doubts expressed by this group mirror those uncovered in some mass surveys. In Russia, groups that in other countries would be *more* likely to be politically involved are less likely to be so. For instance, high-income, high-status groups show up in some surveys as less likely to vote. Donna L. Bahry and Lucan Way, "Citizen Activism in the Russian Transition," *Post-Soviet Affairs* 10, no. 4 (1994): 330–66; Ralph S. Clem and Peter R. Craumer, "Regional Patterns of Voter Turnout in Russian Elections, 1993–1996," in *Elections and Voters in Post-Communist Russia*, ed. Matthew Wyman, Stephen White, and Sarah Oates (Northampton, MA: Edward Elgar, 1998), 67.

only occur with some kind of natural transition to something. Now is the time for balance." Andrei Viktorovich was active in a political group and believed that, through organization, people could have a kind of power. He said, "In what sense can people like me have any influence? If by the route of election—every one, four, or five years—then under present conditions, in my opinion, very little. However, if we were better organized, then it would be possible that that influence would be quite a bit more. If we talk about daily politics, daily events, then again everything depends on our organization, intelligence."

In this sample, then, people who were both relatively politically sophisticated and also supportive of democracy were more likely to think that their opinions mattered and to have confidence that they could affect political outcomes. But even their confidence was undermined by an awareness of the continued unresponsiveness of government and the difficulties of popular action. Although they are the *most* hopeful group in the sample, they are not very hopeful on average. The overriding feeling of the people in my sample was that there was little they could do to influence government, and in that sense little had changed. Olga Shevchenko has argued that Russians did not actively resist some of the unpleasant changes in their lives because they feared that political action might make things worse.[45] For many of my respondents, it seems, rather, that the main impediment to political activism was a sense that, at least in terms of government responsiveness, not much had got better.

Conclusion

The collapse of Communism brought monumental changes to Russia. What is striking, however, is the degree to which many Russian citizens have not internalized those changes. In some respects, of course, ordinary Russian people are vitally aware that their lives have changed. Particularly as regards their daily lives of work and leisure, of providing for families and establishing their children in independent lives, ordinary Russians have noticed—and often bemoaned—the effects of change. For most people in this sample, economic life has become less secure. Wages barely cover necessities. Work remains a necessity for people who had expected to

45. Olga Shevchenko, "Bread and Circuses: Shifting Frames and Changing References in Ordinary Muscovites' Political Talk," *Communist and Post-Communist Studies* 34, no. 1 (March 2001): 77–90.

retire. And the opportunities that change was supposed to bring seem to be largely reserved for someone else.

But political changes in Russia have also been significant. Elements of democracy—competitive elections, representative institutions, constitutionally protected individual rights—have been introduced, and in principle ordinary Russians have begun the transition from subjects to citizens. The only problem is that many of them seem not to have noticed. As Elena remarked, "As we were slaves, so we remain slaves." Many Russian citizens fail to perceive that their new political institutions are in some ways fundamentally different from their old ones. Presidents seem a lot like czars or general secretaries. Government officials, even if elected by the people, seem unapproachable and uninterested in the lives of ordinary people. The rights and obligations of citizens mean little to people who still see themselves as subjects, without the means to connect to those in power, and without an effective claim on their attention. Granted, the operation of new Russian institutions provides plenty of grounds for complaint, but many of my respondents seem not even to have noticed the limited changes that have occurred.

But in this respect, not all Russian citizens are the same. In this sample, more politically sophisticated and more democratically oriented respondents were generally more likely to think that changes had occurred and to recognize the opportunities these changes provided for ordinary citizens to affect political outcomes. This was not true in terms of assessments of freedom: here, *less* sophisticated respondents thought they were freer. But more sophisticated, more democratic respondents were more likely to recognize how presidents differed from nonelected executives and to think they might be able to influence political decisions. This is not to say that they were rosy-eyed optimists. They considered that their new institutions did not always work well, that even democratically elected presidents could wield close to absolute power when legislatures were too weak to confront them, that structures linking the population to centers of power were nearly nonexistent, that the freedoms they had received still left a lot to be desired. But their more nuanced understanding of political institutions helped them to see the changes that had occurred and to recognize the potential for further improvements under pressure from an active citizenry.

To put Russians' sense of how much their government cares about their opinions in context, it is useful briefly to compare the Russian responses to the American sample. The American respondents were much more likely than the Russians to think that government officials cared about their opinions. This was particularly true among the more sophisticated respondents.[46] Ernest commented, "You know, one thing people scoff at is how poll conscious the politicians are, but in a way that is in the best tradition of democracy, to take the pulse of the people. So, yeah, I think they care, I don't think that George Bush gives a hoot about me personally, but I think he cares about what—and his pollsters care a whole lot—about what people like me are thinking."

The American respondents were also more likely to think that ordinary people could influence decisions made in the federal government. They were aware of the obstacles. Like Zinaida, Victoria complained that it was too difficult to meet with members of Congress: their offices were too far away, and the average person did not have the free time. Ted thought that well-funded special interest groups had a better chance of being heard, while "the ordinary guy is swept under the carpet." But a number of the American respondents, especially the more politically sophisticated ones, thought these obstacles could be overcome if citizens tried hard enough. Adam said, "I think, if I personally just went up to my congressman and started talking to him, I don't think it would do anything. But I have the power to get people behind me. And if I get a large enough group, then I think my congressman will listen." Leo added, "I have to tell you, sometimes I think no, but then at other times you see where people decide they're going to do something about it. It's a difficult situation to do. They really have to bust their buns, so to speak, to get something done. But it can be done, but it's a pretty tall job to do."

Compared with the Russian respondents, the Americans had more confidence in their ability to influence government decisions but little more interest in trying to do so. As Ted said, "I really don't want that part. There are a thousand decisions made every day that affect our lives, directly or indirectly. That's a job I'll leave to them. I'll just trust in them to make the right decisions." Most of the respondents were similarly reluctant to become politically involved. Some averred that, should the situation become critical enough, they would consider taking action, but most of the time they did not feel that their interests were sufficiently threatened. So while Americans may have quite a bit more confidence in the responsiveness of their government and faith in their abilities as

---

46. The political-sophistication measure used to categorize the Americans was similar to the measure used for the Russians. It was based on education levels, length and quality of answers, and overall understanding of political life. See Appendix C.

citizens, their behavior may not be very different from that of the largely disillusioned Russians with whom I spoke. But Americans enjoy a more stable political system.

Revolutions change the world, but it seems they do not change it quickly, neatly, and in ways that ordinary people necessarily understand. The full consolidation of Russia's democratic revolution requires a change in popular political culture, a change in the long-standing "cultural idioms" people use to understand politics and the ways in which they relate to governmental power.[47] To become democratic citizens, ordinary Russians need to see government institutions as something that can serve and advance their needs. The prevailing cultural response to government— the less contact with it the better—needs to be replaced with the idea that citizens can influence political outcomes. Without that transformation, citizens will remain passive, government will likely be unresponsive, and the legitimizing principles of democratic power will be undermined. The Russian voices that have informed this chapter, though, provide evidence that this change has not yet taken place. For many ordinary Russians, their image of their government was not fundamentally transformed by the collapse of Communism. The predatory state may have retracted its claws, but life on the whole remained scary. The threat of economic loss and the danger of social criminality left citizens feeling little safer. And as far as they could see, government remained largely unresponsive to their concerns. As Inna said, "They sit by themselves high above us. They don't come down here to us. They don't ask what hurts us, what kind of problems we have. No one is interested in that."

Rather than an image of citizens left breathless by the pace of transformation, perhaps we should have an image of citizens waiting for real change to begin—in Russia, as in many postrevolutionary contexts. Political change, it seems, is particularly hard for many people to see. Institutions may be altered, but for people who understand politics primarily as a clash of personalities, those changes may be wholly below the radar.

---

47. The phrase is Skocpol's. See Theda Skocpol, "Cultural Idioms and Political Ideologies in the Revolutionary Reconstruction of State Power: A Rejoinder to Sewell," *Social Revolutions in the Modern World* (New York: Cambridge University Press, 1994), 199–209. On the importance of political culture in revolution, see also John Foran, "Discourse and Social Forces: The Role of Culture and Cultural Studies in Understanding Revolutions," in *Theorizing Revolutions,* ed. John Foran (New York: Routledge, 1997), 203–26; Eric Selbin, "Revolutions in the Real World: Bringing Agency Back In," in *Theorizing Revolutions,* ed. John Foran (New York: Routledge, 1997), 123–36; Jeff Goodwin, "Toward a New Sociology of Revolution," *Theory and Society* 23, no. 6 (1994): 759–60.

Opportunities for political action may expand, but people who do not see those opportunities will not take advantage of them. Democratic revolutions can transform subjects into citizens, but they may not have the power to change the way people understand their governments, their roles, and the possibilities inherent in a transformed world.

What Russians Want

In previous chapters, we have examined Russians' opinions about democracy, markets, and the degree to which political institutions had changed. We have seen why order is for many Russians such a compelling social value. But the most crucial questions may be more basic: What do Russians want from government? Do they support the government they have? What would they change about it if they could? These questions are addressed in this chapter. This chapter, thus, moves beyond more specific questions of support for democracy and capitalism to more fundamental issues concerning the relationship between Russian citizens and their government. In plumbing this relationship, we touch on the issue of political legitimacy, or the "sense of what is right and proper in the political sphere."[1]

The interviews show that support for the existing political system is not related to whether people favor democracy or markets. Nor is support significantly predicted by the demographic attributes of respondents, at least in this sample. Support is, however, related to perceptions that the regime has been successful in creating an orderly and predictable environment. Respondents who are troubled by what they perceive as the "disorder" in their society are more likely to feel that those in power rule in their own personal interest, not for the public good. Although there is considerable dissatisfaction with the existing system among some parts of the sample, there is very little enthusiasm for change. The prevailing sense among my Russian respondents is that their political institutions are more or less appropriate; they just do not work very well.

In the American sample, by contrast, there is both a stronger sense that the existing institutions are the right ones and more apparent willingness to contemplate changing them. At first glance, this might look like a culturally rooted

---

1. David Easton, *A Systems Analysis of Political Life* (New York: John Wiley and Sons, 1965), 278.

difference, with Russian quiescence in the face of dissatisfaction the result of centuries of life under oppressive regimes. And it would be hard to deny that Russians today are influenced at least by their immediate past. The experience of Soviet power no doubt produced lasting expectations about what government should do and what citizens could do about governments that failed their expectations.

But there is more beneath the surface, as well. To a significant extent, the comparative reluctance of Russians to contemplate political change appears to be rooted in the context in which they find themselves. Given recent political and economic upheavals and continuing material insecurity, at the moment change seems to many Russians to be too risky. Furthermore, the ties between citizens and officials remain badly developed in Russia, making it difficult for ordinary people to imagine that they have the power to remake their government. As a result, Russians are both allegiant to existing institutions—in that they do not want to change them—and alienated from those same institutions, insofar as those institutions fail to serve popular needs.

The result is a political passivity that gives leaders space to make mistakes without fear of immediate public backlash. This passivity also provides leaders with room to shape structures to fit their own desires, desires that could lead institutions even farther from what ordinary Russians want.

Legitimacy and the Russian State

Rousseau observed that "the strongest is never strong enough to be always the master, unless he transforms strength into right, and obedience into duty."[2] Every government aims to effect that transformation, to instill in citizens a sense that they are obliged to obey laws, to pay their taxes, and in the last instance to lay down their lives in defense of their country. Rule based only on coercion is too costly and not especially durable. Rule based on a perception of right is less taxing on rulers and less threatened with disruption. When citizens generally believe that political institutions are founded on *right* and *duty*, those institutions can be called legitimate.

Seymour Martin Lipset defined legitimacy as being conferred by the popular belief that existing political institutions are the most appropriate ones for the society.[3] With somewhat different language but the same

2. Jean-Jacques Rousseau, *The Social Contract and Discourses* [1762], trans. G. D. H. Cole (London: J. M Dent and Sons, Everyman's Library, 1973), 168.

3. Seymour Martin Lipset, *Political Man: The Social Bases of Politics* [1959], expanded ed. (Baltimore: Johns Hopkins University Press, 1981), 64.

underlying meaning, David Easton talked about "diffuse support," the "inner conviction of the moral validity of the authorities or regime" and the sense that the regime "conform[s] to [the individual's] own moral principles, his own sense of what is right and proper in the political sphere."[4] Robert Lane referred to "allegiance," to the belief that government functions on behalf of the citizens, that the rules of the game are fair, that government is effective and "given" in the nature of things; the opposite of allegiance is alienation.[5] Similarly, Gramsci wrote of "hegemony," the social construction of the ideas that keep rulers in power and make their rule seem inevitable. All these conceptualizations have in common the idea that popular beliefs about how government is supposed to function and what it is supposed to do sometimes do and sometimes do not align with actual political practices. When the population believes that government practices do align with their expectations, we can call that political system legitimate.

Legitimacy is, thus, an elusive attribute. If popular expectations change, governments can lose legitimacy without changing their behavior. Conversely, under some circumstances governments may remain highly legitimate in the eyes of their citizens even as they fail to meet citizens' basic needs or the expectations of outside observers. Legitimacy is also elusive because it is hard to measure. It depends on evaluations made by ordinary citizens, who may have trouble reporting their own "inner conviction of the moral validity" of the regime or articulating "what is right and proper in the political sphere."

Despite its elusiveness, legitimacy would seem to provide a number of advantages. For one thing, it may make government more effective. It seems that citizens more likely will comply with the directives produced by government structures they consider right and proper. Hence, legitimate regimes should be better positioned to take on large and complicated processes, such as social modernization, market reform, or even democratization.[6] Force can compel citizens *not* to do something, but legitimate

4. Easton, *A Systems Analysis*, 278; see also David Easton, "A Re-assessment of the Concept of Political Support," *British Journal of Political Science* 5 (1975): 435–57.

5. Robert E. Lane, *Political Ideology: Why the American Common Man Believes What He Does* (New York: Free Press, 1962), 176.

6. Michael Mann, "The Autonomous Power of the State: Its Origins, Mechanisms and Results," in *States in History*, ed. John A. Hall (Oxford, U.K.: Basil Blackwell, 1986), 109–36; Joel S. Migdal, *State in Society: Studying How States and Societies Transform and Constitute One Another* (New York: Cambridge University Press, 2001); Tim McDaniel, *Autocracy, Modernization, and Revolution in Russia and Iran* (Princeton: Princeton University Press, 1991).

regimes may inspire citizens to act positively on behalf of the political community, thereby removing the need to resort to force or other costly types of social control.[7] Legitimate regimes also may be better able to weather temporary difficulties, such as war or economic recession. Gramsci argued that hegemony functions as a bulwark that protects the state, while states that do not have the advantage of conforming to their citizens' expectations topple readily in the face of relatively small threats. Comparing Western European governments with the czarist regime that collapsed in 1917, Gramsci observed, "In the West, there was a proper relation between State and civil society, and when the State trembled a sturdy structure of civil society was at once revealed. The State was only the outer ditch, behind which there stood a powerful system of fortresses and earthworks."[8] Legitimacy provides that powerful system of fortresses, and hence is an attribute that rulers covet and may feel compelled to claim, even given evidence to the contrary.

To be accepted as legitimate is a goal of any ruler, but legitimacy is of particular importance for Russia's post-Communist government. For one thing, the Russian government is new, and any new government lacks the implicit acceptance that comes from having been in place for as long as citizens can remember. New institutions also tend to work less well than those that have been around for a while and that are staffed by skilled bureaucrats following predictable procedures. In Russia, new institutions have functioned poorly, as shown by problems with tax collection, crime control, corruption, irregularities in the privatization process, and more generally the disobedience of bureaucrats in the face of commands from their superiors.[9] This institutional incapacity was especially problematic because the post-Soviet Russian government took on huge tasks, particularly the transformation of the socialist economy, and these tasks have entailed huge costs for many citizens. Consequently, one possible source of government legitimacy—the welfare of the population—was seriously compromised in the early stages of economic reform. Lipset argues that when the position of a major, conservative class is threatened, the system's

---

7. Robert W. Jackman, *Power Without Force: The Political Capacity of Nation-States* (Ann Arbor: University of Michigan Press, 1993); William A. Gamson, *Power and Discontent* (Homewood, IL: Dorsey Press, 1968), 128–35.

8. Antonio Gramsci, *Prison Notebooks: Selections*, trans. Quinton Hoare and Geoffrey Smith (New York: International, 1971), 238.

9. L. I. Nikovskaia, "Politika i Ekonomika v Sovremennoi Rossii: Konflikt na pereput'e (Kruglyi Stol)," *Sotsiologicheskie issledovaniia*, no. 2 (2000): 87–100.

legitimacy will be in question,[10] and that was precisely the situation in Russia in the first decades after Communism. The working majority lost social guarantees without yet gaining much wealth or many opportunities.

In addition, building popular consent is especially important for Russian institutions because they are being constructed on such infertile ground. Going back to czarist times, Russia suffered under a "predatory state" that sucked available wealth out of society while serving only the barest social needs.[11] The Soviet state may have earned some approval based on generally popular social welfare provisions, but Soviet rule also reinforced the vast gulf between ordinary people and the state. Few think that gulf has been bridged in the post-Soviet era. As Vladimir Shlapentokh remarked, "Russians trust nothing and nobody, and react indifferently to almost any public issue."[12] Trust in political institutions is low.[13] Apathy is high.[14] And little in the way the Russian government operates—with its patronage, corruption, and enduring battles over the spoils of power—is likely to inspire popular support.

What Inspires Support?

But what *is* likely to inspire popular support? The prevailing arguments are relatively few but nonetheless contested. One common explanation is that government *effectiveness* builds support. Citizens are presumed to support governments that do well by them, for instance, by protecting freedom, defending security, and promoting prosperity. Following the

10. Lipset, *Political Man*, 65–67.

11. John P. LeDonne, "The Ruling Class: Tsarist Model," *International Social Science Journal* (May 1993): 285–300.

12. Vladimir E. Shlapentokh, "Early Feudalism: The Best Parallel for Contemporary Russia," *Europe-Asia Studies* 48 (May 1996): 396.

13. See Richard Rose, "Postcommunism and the Problem of Trust," *Journal of Democracy* 5 (July 1994): 26; Richard Rose, "Russia as an Hour-Glass Society: A Constitution Without Citizens," *East European Constitutional Review* 4, no. 3 (1995): 36–44; M. K. Gorshkov, *Rossiiskoe obshchestvo v usloviiakh transformatsii: Mify i real'nost' (Sotsiologicheskii analiz)* (Moscow: ROSSPEN, 2003), 469. Western publics are also cynical about political institutions. See Peter A. Hall, "Social Capital in Britain," *British Journal of Political Science* 29 (1999): 417–61.

14. Eric Shiraev, "Attitudinal Changes During the Transition," in *The Russian Transformation: Political, Sociological, and Psychological Aspects*, ed. Betty Glad and Eric Shiraev (New York: St. Martin's Press, 1999), 158; Vladimir Mau and Irina Starodubrovskaya, *The Challenge of Revolution: Contemporary Russia in Historical Perspective* (New York: Oxford University Press, 2001), 162, 175; Dmitry Oreshkin, "The Silence of the Oligarchs," *Moscow News*, no. 28, 23–29 July 2003, 5.

same logic, a "crisis of legitimacy" is predicted when government performance is compromised, whether for reasons implicit in the development of advanced capitalism, as Jürgen Habermas argued, or because of
expanding popular demands, as Samuel Huntington and others predicted
in the 1970s.[15]

That citizens approve of governments that perform well and doubt governments that do not has considerable plausibility, and there is evidence
to support this argument. Using data from the 1995–97 World Values
Surveys, for instance, William Mishler and Richard Rose found that
regime performance was the chief predictor of political support in the
thirty-eight countries included in their study.[16] For the twelve countries in
the International Social Justice Project survey, David Mason concluded,
"Economic concerns, whether they be macrolevel (concern over growth of
poverty) or microlevel (concern over one's own standard of living), loom
large in the explanation of political satisfaction or dissatisfaction."[17]
Russian surveys also show much more positive evaluations of government during the Putin years than under Yeltsin; and it is probably not
irrelevant that the economy has been growing since Putin took office and
that a greater portion of the population thinks the country is headed in
the right direction.[18] Overall, there is more evidence that government
effectiveness encourages support than that ineffectiveness causes citizens

15. Jürgen Habermas, *Legitimation Crisis* (Boston: Beacon Press, 1975); Michael J. Crozier,
Samuel P. Huntington, and Joji Watanuki, *The Crisis of Democracy: Report on the Governability
of Democracies to the Trilateral Commission* (New York: New York University Press, 1975).

16. William Mishler and and Richard Rose, "Political Support for Incomplete Democracies:
Realist vs. Idealist Theories and Measures," *International Political Science Review* 22, no. 4 (2001):
303–20; William Mishler and Richard Rose, "Trajectories of Fear and Hope: Support for Democ-
racy in Post-Communist Europe," *Comparative Political Studies* 28 (January 1996): 553–81;
William Mishler and Richard Rose, "Learning and Re-learning Regime Support: The Dynamics
of Post-Communist Regimes," *European Journal of Political Research* 41 (January 2002): 5–36;
Richard Rose and William T. Mishler, "Mass Reaction to Regime Change in Eastern Europe:
Polarization or Leaders and Laggards?" *British Journal of Political Science* 24 (April 1994): 159–82.

17. David S. Mason, "Justice, Socialism, and Participation in the Postcommunist States,"
in *Social Justice and Political Change: Public Opinion in Capitalist and Post-Communist States*, ed.
James R. Kluegel, David S. Mason, and Bernd Wegener (Hawthorne, NY: Aldine De Gruyter,
1995), 71.

18. Boris Dubin, "Model'nye instituty i simvolicheskii poriadok: Elementarnye formy
sotsial'nosti v sovremennom rossiiskom obshchestve," *Monitoring obshchestvennoe mneniia:
Informatsiia analiz*, no. 1, issue 57 (2002): 14–19; E. B. Shestopal, "Ustanovki rossiiskikh grazhdan
na vlast' kak pokazatel' kachestva demokratii (Po dannym politiko-psikhologicheskogo issledovaniia 1993–2003)," *Politiia*, no. 2, issue 29 (2003): 32–53; VTSIOM, "Monitoring peremen:
Osnovnye tendentsii," *Monitoring obshchestvennoe mneniia: Informatsiia analiz*, no. 2, issue 58
(2002): 3–8.

to withdraw their support. At least it seems that governments that have popular support can weather short-term lapses in performance.[19]

A second explanation focuses on *procedures* instead of performance. The idea here is that citizens support governments based on *how* they make decisions, on the political *process*, rather than on any particular outcomes. If citizens think that political procedures are largely fair, they will support the government. Fair procedures are those that are neutral, unbiased, and honest and that respect the rights of citizens.[20] But exactly which procedures are considered fair will vary given the structure of society. In highly segmented societies, for instance, majoritarian procedures seem to discriminate against minorities, and procedures based on proportionality may appear to be fairer.[21] However fairness is understood in the specific instance, fair procedures give everyone a chance to affect outcomes. Players do not need to win in order to agree to keep playing. They need only the confidence that they may be able to win in the future. Frederick Weil argued, "If democracy is a game among players, the players are unlikely to reject the game solely because of its outcome, but rather because its rules are not working as designed."[22]

Again, there is evidence to support this interpretation. Weil's study demonstrated that confidence in political institutions increased given a responsive opposition structure, particularly one in which parties were not too factionalized or polarized. Hibbing and Theiss-Morse have shown that Americans are dissatisfied with their government institutions because of what they see as problems with procedures. Americans dislike Congress because it seems to them to be inefficient and inequitable.[23] In the United

19. Edward N. Muller and Thomas O. Jukam, "On the Meaning of Political Support," *American Political Science Review* 71 (1977): 1561–95; Mitchell A. Seligson and Edward N. Muller, "Democratic Stability and Economic Crisis: Costa Rica, 1978–1983," *International Studies Quarterly* 31 (1987): 301–26; Frederick D. Weil, "The Sources and Structure of Legitimation in Western Democracies: A Consolidated Model Tested with Time-Series Data in Six Countries Since World War II," *American Sociological Review* 54 (October 1989): 682–706. Some scholars use indicators of government performance as measures of legitimacy. See M. Stephen Weatherford, "Measuring Political Legitimacy," *American Political Science Review* 86 (March 1992): 149–66. I follow Lipset (*Political Man*, 64) in separating performance from the conclusions citizens draw as a result of that performance.

20. Tom R. Tyler, *Why People Obey the Law* (New Haven: Yale University Press, 1990).

21. Ronald Rogowski, *Rational Legitimacy: A Theory of Political Support* (Princeton: Princeton University Press, 1974), 165.

22. Weil, "Sources and Structure of Legitimation," 697.

23. John R. Hibbing and Elizabeth Theiss-Morse, *Congress as Public Enemy: Public Attitudes Toward American Political Institutions* (New York: Cambridge University Press, 1995).

States, evaluations of political processes affect approval of the federal government and assessments of whether people should obey the law.[24]

A third explanation for political support focuses on *values* held by citizens, arguing that citizens support governments that fit the values they have. Inglehart, for instance, has argued that popular expectations of government change as processes of modernization affect citizens' dominant values.[25] Putnam identified the specific values of social trust and civic engagement as the foundations of support for government.[26] Others look at the particular values present in a specific culture. In the Russian case, for instance, Tim McDaniel has argued that only a government dedicated to some form of the Russian Idea will be "truly legitimate in the eyes of the Russian people."[27] According to McDaniel, the Russian Idea encompasses a commitment to utopian goals, intensive community, equality of material outcomes, and paternalistic government.

In addition to debates about what causes citizens to support government, there is some disagreement about how legitimacy is most usefully understood and measured. Explanations based on legitimacy have a tendency to become circular, with contributing factors or products hard to distinguish from legitimacy itself.[28] For instance, if legitimacy is thought to promote regime stability or citizen compliance with law, then those features cannot be part of the definition of legitimacy or the means through which legitimacy is measured. In this chapter, legitimacy is understood as the subjective acceptance of existing political structures as the proper ones for the society, as directly expressed by popular attitudes, not behavior. Legitimacy is not understood to be synonymous with regime survival, although some implications for regime survival are examined in the final

24. John R. Hibbing and Elizabeth Theiss-Morse, "Process Preference and American Politics: What the People Want Government to Be," *American Political Science Review* 95, no. 1 (March 2001): 145–53.

25. Ronald Inglehart, *Culture Shift in Advanced Industrial Society* (Princeton: Princeton University Press, 1990).

26. Robert Putnam, *Making Democracy Work: Civic Traditions in Modern Italy* (Princeton: Princeton University Press, 1993).

27. Tim McDaniel, *The Agony of the Russian Idea* (Princeton: Princeton University Press, 1996) 33. Similarly, see Duane F. Alwin et al., "Comparative Referential Structures, System Legitimacy, and Justice Sentiments: An International Comparison," in *Social Justice and Political Change: Public Opinion in Capitalist and Post-Communist States*, ed. James R. Kluegel, David S. Mason, and Bernd Wegener (Hawthorne, NY: Aldine De Gruyter, 1995), 109–30.

28. See Rosemary H. T. O'Kane, "Against Legitimacy," *Political Studies* 41 (1993): 471–87.

section of this chapter. The primary focus of this chapter is on which factors might encourage governmental legitimacy or, in other words, what might inspire citizens to believe that the government they have is the one they want.

Measuring legitimacy is complicated by the need to tap into feelings about government that are not dependent on the individuals who happen to be in office, feelings that are relatively constant and that touch on support for institutional structures and for the ideas behind those structures.[29] In this chapter, I begin with a measure of support for incumbents and examine the factors that seem to contribute to such support in Russia. To move past evaluations of current officeholders and to try to tap the degree to which respondents think that present institutions are the right ones for Russia, I employ a series of questions about how respondents would change existing institutions, what they value in the institutions they have, and whether they can imagine institutions that would better fit their needs. To better see the patterns in the Russian answers, I compare them to answers from the American respondents.

Support for Incumbents: The Overall Picture

While there are difficulties measuring support for the political system as a whole—Easton's "diffuse" support, or legitimacy—it is not problematical to measure support for incumbents. Such direct evaluations of people and policies are not overly challenging for respondents; indeed, they are staples of public opinion research. I divided the Russian respondents into three groups characterized by increasing support for existing authorities, based on their answers to three questions on whether the president, the State Duma, and their mayors work in the interest of the majority of citizens.[30] This is not a measure of legitimacy, but it is a first step in helping us understand how Russians evaluate their government.

Table 8.1 summarizes demographic features of the respondents in each category. Too much significance should not be given to the *number* of

29. To support for political actors, regime institutions, and regime principles, Pippa Norris adds two more dimensions: support for the political community and support for regime performance. See Pippa Norris, "Introduction: The Growth of Critical Citizens?" in *Critical Citizens: Global Support for Democratic Government*, ed. Pippa Norris (New York: Oxford University Press, 1999), 1–27.

30. See Appendix C for information on the incumbent support measure.

Table 8.1   Demographic factors related to support for incumbents (Russian respondents, $N = 60$)

Low support for incumbents (24 respondents)	Moderate support for incumbents (15 respondents)	High support for incumbents (21 respondents)
14 interviewed in 1998, 5 in 2000, 5 in 2003	6 interviewed in 1998, 6 interviewed in 2000, 3 in 2003	10 interviewed in 1998, 3 in 2000, 8 in 2003
16 female, 8 male	7 female, 8 male	9 female, 12 male
3 under 30, 7 over 60	1 under 30, 6 over 60	10 under 30, 2 over 60
7 from Siberia, 7 from Moscow, 10 from European Russia	1 from Siberia, 7 from Moscow, 7 from European Russia	None from Siberia, 5 from Moscow, 16 from European Russia
3 with less than secondary education, 12 with higher education	1 with less than secondary education, 5 with higher education	1 with less than secondary education, 11 with higher education

respondents in each category, since the size of each group would have been different under different decision rules.[31] The purpose of the categories is to enable comparisons across groups and to provide a picture of the distribution of support in the sample, not to count the number of respondents in each group or generalize the configuration of support to the population of Russia.

Table 8.1 suggests some patterns in the configuration of support. Support for incumbents was higher among respondents interviewed in 2003. This probably reflects in part the comparative popularity of Vladimir Putin and consistent economic growth during the time he was in office. Whereas Yeltsin's approval ratings in his last years in office rarely topped 30 percent; Putin's have only on unusual occasions dropped below 70 percent.[32] From Boris Dubin's work, it appears that assessments of the president significantly

31. For instance, with cutoffs of 1.5 and 2.5, there would be 11 people in the "low" group, 7 in the "high" group; and 42 in the middle category.

32. For useful summaries of vtsiom polls, see Stephen White, Richard Rose, and Ian McAllister, *How Russia Votes* (Chatham, NJ: Chatham House, 1997), 169; Richard Rose and Neil Munro, *Elections Without Order: Russia's Challenge to Vladimir Putin* (New York: Cambridge University Press, 2002), 86, 190; and www.russiavotes.org.

drive overall assessment of government.[33] Support for incumbents was also higher among younger respondents, probably a result of the fact that younger Russians are generally more supportive of reform and less likely to look back nostalgically at the past.[34] In my sample, respondents from Siberia also tended to show lower support for incumbents than did respondents in other parts of the country, probably a product of particular pressures on Siberian regions: distance from the center, limited economic opportunities, widespread decline in material welfare, and a relatively high proportion of uncompetitive industries. Education level, profession, and gender did not have much impact on support for incumbents in my sample.[35]

Statistical analysis confirmed these findings, as reported in Table 8.2. The only significant demographic predictors of support were age, respondents' evaluation of their economic situations, and residence in Siberia, although for the first two variables the correlation was not particularly strong. Younger and better-off respondents in European Russia were more likely to think that the people in power operated in the interests of the majority. Correlations were also calculated with the sample split between respondents from 1998, when Yeltsin was president, and later respondents, when Putin had replaced Yeltsin. Only residence in Siberia was significant in 1998, perhaps a reflection of the generalized distain in which Yeltsin was held by that time. In the two later interview years, younger, more educated, better-off individuals were more supportive of government incumbents. Again, my purpose in this limited statistical analysis is to share patterns in my sample with readers. While my group of respondents is much smaller than the average sample for nationally representative surveys, the group is nonetheless large enough that patterns of support do not emerge directly from the texts of the interviews themselves.

Table 8.2 also shows correlations between support for policy makers and the political orientations discussed in previous chapters. Here again, what is most striking is the lack of significant correlations. Supporters of democracy are not more or less supportive of public officials. Market

33. Dubin, "Model'nye instituty," 16.
34. The fact that more of the younger respondents were interviewed in 2003 makes it hard to disentangle the effects of youth and time. Iurii Levada has shown that younger Russians have been more effective at adapting to and thriving in the new Russia. Iurii Levada, "Varianty adaptivnogo povedeniia," *Monitoring obshchestvennoe mneniia: Informatsiia analiz*, no. 1, issue 57 (2002): 7–13.
35. This is consistent with previous studies. See Mishler and Rose, "Political Support for Incomplete Democracies"; Mishler and Rose, "Trajectories of Fear and Hope."

Table 8.2   Explaining support for public officials (Russian respondents, $N = 60$)

	Incumbent support all years ($N = 60$)	Incumbent support 1998 ($N = 30$)	Incumbent support 2000, 2003 ($N = 30$)
Age (high = older)	−.323* .012	−.092 .627	−.473** .008
Education	.071 .592	−.199 .291	.384* .036
Personal economic assessment (high = better)	.274* .034	.199 .291	.463* .010
Sex (high = male)	.187 .153	.194 .305	.184 .330
Live in Siberia? (high = yes)	−.361** .005	−.450* .013	−.241 .200
Support for democracy	−.146 .265	−.149 .432	−.090 .635
Support for markets	.225 .084	.152 .422	.376* .041
Political sophistication	−.144 .273	−.358 .052	.117 .538
Sense of social disorder	−.381** .003	−.290 .120	−.505** .004

NOTE: The upper number in each box is the Pearson correlation coefficient between incumbent support and the variable to the left. The lower number is the 2-tailed significance. A single asterisk indicates correlations significant at the .05 level (2-tailed). Double asterisks indicate correlations significant at the .01 level (2-tailed). Except where indicated, measures are ordered so that higher values indicate more (more education, more support, and so on).

supporters were more likely to think that public officials worked for the majority during the Putin presidency, but not during the Yeltsin years, and even where there is a correlation it is not especially strong. Political sophistication also does not have an effect. The only political attitude that is fairly consistently correlated with support for incumbents is the sense of social disorder examined in Chapter 6. People with a high sense of social disorder were less likely to think that officials work in the interests of the majority. Table 8.3 shows how the Russian respondents were distributed according to their support for incumbents and perceptions of social disorder. This table may be useful to readers trying to keep the various voices straight as we turn to the comments of individual respondents.

The Importance of Performance

If we look more closely at the comments that people made in assessing government officials, we can see that when respondents perceived that the actions of officials increased the difficulty and unpredictability of their own lives, then they did not think that officials worked in the interest of the majority, which they assumed to be made up of people like themselves. That is to say, *government performance* appears to be a major contributor to incumbent support. Similar relationships show up in mass surveys. Vladimir Mokryi, for instance, shows a sharp decline in support for the president and cabinet after the 1998 financial crisis.[36]

My respondents were concerned about major macroeconomic adjustments, of course, but their complaints regarding government performance often dealt with the immediate and mundane circumstance of their lives. Valentina, for instance, complained that the mayor of her city did nothing about the filth in the streets and could not understand the daily problems of ordinary people because he never walked on the ground but only traveled by car. She said, "Judging by the fact that the city is very disorderly, I am not satisfied. I would like that our mayor became for a week an ordinary person and had to walk around like the rest of us, go around the city and see what kind of city he has." Galina Grigor'evna's immediate concerns were also quite close to home. She said, "The mayor should concern himself with everything in the city, with the streets, and with garbage, and with water and heat and, it's the same thing, gas, with everything. And he does this badly. Our streets are not cleaned. Garbage lies about in containers. They turn off the water without warning."

For many, it was poor economic performance, closed factories, and missing paychecks that provided evidence that officials did not have the interests of the majority at heart. Andrei Viktorovich had a more complicated view of what the interests of the people and the predictability of

36. Vladimir Semenovich Mokryi, "Dinamika sotsial'no-politicheskikh orientatsii elektorata v usloviiakh finansovo-ekonomicheskogo krizisa," *Sotsiologicheskie issledovaniia,* no. 8 (1999): 23.

Table 8.3   Perceptions of social disorder and support for incumbents among Russian respondents

	Low sense of disorder	Moderate sense of disorder	High sense of disorder
High support for incumbents	Katya, Ekaterina, Iurii, Kolya, Liuba, Mikhail, Nadya, Pavel, Raisa, Ruslan, Sergei, Slava, Vitya *(13 respondents)*	Anna Pavlovna, Gennadii, Irina L'vovna, Raya, Tolya, Valya, Vasya *(7 respondents)*	Iosif *(1 respondent)*
Moderate support	Arkadii, Dima, Klara, Nadezhda, Oleg, Olga Iur'evna *(6 respondents)*	Aleksandra Antonova, Evgenii, Nikolai, Polina, Vilen Nikolaevich *(5 respondents)*	Inna, Vladimir Il'ich, Yegor Yegorovich, Zoia Igorevna *(4 respondents)*
Low support	Anya, Marina Aleksandrovna, Misha, Natalia *(4 respondents)*	Alla, Andrei Viktorovich, Boris Borisovich, Grigorii, Konstantin, Lev, Liudmilla Vladimirovna, Sofiia, Sonya, Svetlana, Tatiana Mikhailovna *(11 respondents)*	Aleksei, Elena, Galina Grigor'evna, Ivan Ivanovich, Kollektiv, Lena, Pelageia, Valentina, Zinaida *(9 respondents)*

their lives might entail, but like the others, he refused to support officials who did not advance those interests. He said of Yeltsin, "It seems to me that he had opportunities to further the construction of reforms, but he didn't realize those possibilities. Besides that, by the constitution, he plays the role of guarantor of our rights, and again he didn't fulfill this, or didn't always fulfill it at least on important questions." In Chapter 6, we saw how strong feelings that society was becoming unhinged undermined support for democracy. Here we see how those perceptions of social disorder also weaken support for incumbents, whether incumbents are seen as democrats or not.

Conversely, people who supported public officials tended to think that life was pretty predictable and social circumstances were manageable. Of her mayor, Liuba said, "I am satisfied because the city is clean, in the end. No kind of unusual incidents occur, no fights; there aren't drunks walking in the street; the police work well." She continued about the city legislative body, "I am satisfied because the city soviet doesn't especially interfere with us. They make normal kinds of laws and try to make sure people are paid on time." Raisa was satisfied with her mayor because "we in our city like order, clean streets, flowers, green spaces. He tries to understand all questions. He is himself from our city. He's one of us, local. He knows all our enterprises, all problems." The mayor she liked so well was also the person who had been mayor, as she put it, "under Soviet power." He was "well, a fine person, a Communist." By contrast, the "mayor-democrat" the town had during perestroika "mainly went abroad. He went himself. He took his family. He took his assistants," all while Raisa's husband was collecting potatoes overlooked in a nearby collective farm's harvest, which he was forced to do because neither he nor Raisa were receiving their paychecks.

Given that Raisa was a strong advocate for markets, not Communism, it is notable that her desire for a well-run city overrode ideological concerns. Her comments, like those of the others, show that it is not just any kind of government performance that encourages support for incumbents in Russia, but specifically effectiveness in creating a stable, predictable existence. Generally, people who were critical of public officials were concerned about the conditions of daily life: roads, sidewalks, transport, crime, whether anyone was picking up the trash. They also looked for performance in the economic sphere. Their complaints were not about their own individual economic circumstances, which in most cases they reported to be fine or at least adequate. Rather, they were concerned about the overall economic situation, whether factories were operating, people could find jobs, and there was hope for tomorrow.

Why did some respondents think these conditions were better than others, with the result that they supported public officials more? Of course, one reason is that people's immediate experiences varied, particularly in terms of the quality of local government. Vitya, from the same town in Moscow Oblast as Raisa, was equally enthusiastic about the mayor. And Alla generally agreed with Valentina's negative assessment of their mayor, only adding the caveat that he needed greater financial resources. Then, she thought, he would be harder to bribe and might serve the interests of the majority more often. Some individuals also were doing better themselves. Almost half the respondents who highly supported public officials evaluated their own personal circumstances as fine, and none were wholly overwhelmed. Among respondents who ranked low in support for officials, less than a third felt they were doing fine and a quarter felt overwhelmed. But there is more to the difference in perceptions of these two groups than differences in their own circumstances.

For one thing, people who were more supportive of incumbents tended to expect somewhat different things from government. In some cases, these were things that were more readily provided than the economic prosperity that concerned respondents who were hostile to public officials. Iurii, for instance, looked to the government to create the conditions under which people could work for themselves. He did not expect, as he guessed some of his fellow citizens did, that "a real czar will come and give us everything on a platter." Other of the more supportive respondents expressed appreciation for the greater freedom they had since the collapse of the Soviet Union, the fact that they could travel to other countries, or the fact that reforms were proceeding, even if palpable benefits were still somewhat in the distance. Freedom is easier than abundant jobs and clean streets for governments to provide, since all the authorities have to do is not get in the way.

Not only did the more supportive respondents expect different things from government, they were also more willing to wait for them. As a group, they were more optimistic than the government's critics that things would be better in the future. Pavel said that he trusted Putin because "I live fine. I work. Well, I think that in the future everything will be good here. I'm an optimist." Tolya said, "In general, I would like to think, of course, that we are going in the progressive, correct direction. I wouldn't want to be a pessimist in this regard. I think that eventually everything will be fine." Tolya also believed that since the constitution stipulated that the president act in the interests of the whole population, it must be the case that he did so. Indeed, only three of the strong supporters of public officials doubted that Russia was headed in the right direction.[37] By contrast, nearly all the respondents in the low-support group had doubts about the direction in which Russia was heading. Even if they considered the direction generally correct, which only four did, they doubted whether much progress was being made. As Misha said, "They are going in the right direction, but not the right way." Others were bolder. Konstantin said, "There is

37. Most of the respondents were asked whether they thought Russia was headed in the right direction, a common question on standardized surveys.

hope that maybe it will be better, but so far I don't see it. It seems to me that so far disintegration is occurring. How can this be the right direction?"

It is very difficult to discern the roots of the optimism and pessimism that distinguish government supporters from those with less confidence in public officials. The roots of optimism do not lie solely in personal circumstances. When they were interviewed, Sergei and Slava were unemployed; Raya, Tolya, Liuba, and Mikhail were *budzhetniki,* that is, their wages were dependent on the budgets of local governments;[38] Kolya had cut his education short to support his family. Yet all these people expressed confidence that Russia was headed in the right direction and government officials had the interests of the majority at heart. By contrast, Grigorii and his wife were both employed in private business and owned a home and a car; but Grigorii feared that Russia was headed in the wrong direction and officials had little concern for the damage their policies were doing. He said, "Our prime minister is a puppet. Here they are all puppets. We have a single czar, as it were, like a single god. That's the president. . . . Even if something is done which is not acceptable to Yeltsin, he will use it in his own kind of personal, mercenary interests. He wants to get rid of someone to accomplish some kind of goals, not state goals but goals related to internal political games. This is clear to practically the whole people."

The internal politics of the Yeltsin regime indeed were fairly obvious toward the end of Yeltsin's term. But still they did not impair the optimism of some respondents. Some of the optimists simply were not very well informed. Valya, Katya, and Ekaterina had trouble finding much to say about their government at all, yet they were confident that officials had their best interests in mind. People certain that Russia was heading in the right direction and that officials served the majority were more likely than not to be advocates of free markets. In Russia, confidence in free markets is more a sign of faith in the future than of any concrete accomplishment. One is tempted to conclude that some people are simply more optimistic by nature, and that this optimism spills over into the rest of their opinions.[39] These hopeful souls are more likely to see the good in what government

38. This category includes not only people who work for local governments directly, but also teachers and doctors. Respondents regularly complained that this group was seriously underpaid. In the latter 1990s, this was the group most likely to suffer wage arrears.

39. John R. Alford and John R. Hibbing suggest that the origins of some political orientations may be genetic. See John R. Alford and John R. Hibbing, "The Origins of Politics: An Evolutionary Theory of Political Behavior," *Perspectives on Politics* 2, no. 4 (December 2004): 707–23.

accomplishes, and they are more confident about the goodwill of officials even when performance is lacking.

In any case, positive assessments of government performance seem to be an important source of support for incumbents. Specifically, respondents who saw their immediate environment as an orderly and predictable place were more likely to have confidence that government officials operated with the interests of the majority in mind. Some of what people saw, though, seems to have depended on what they were predisposed to see. Beyond innate optimism, values appeared to play a decidedly lesser role in my respondents' evaluation of incumbents. Democratic values did not influence support for incumbents in my Russian sample. Nor did respondents express a yearning for a utopian vision of social equality and meaningful community, as they might have had they wanted incumbents to act more in line with traditional Russian values. While respondents who criticized incumbents spoke of jobs and paychecks, they seem to have wanted macroeconomic stability more than a return to Soviet-style socialism.

In some ways, though, it is difficult to disentangle comments about performance from the values held by the people making the comments. My respondents' assessments of government performance were influenced by what they expected government to do. If they expected a strong economy, they were more disappointed than if they expected the right to travel abroad. It may also be the case that ordinary citizens may speak more readily the language of performance, as opposed to values. It is easier for most people to talk about whether the snow is cleared from the streets than about whether government conforms to their deepest desires.

It is probably also easier for most people to talk about performance than about procedures. Indeed, government procedures mattered in assessments of incumbents, but comments about procedures and performance were interrelated, making it difficult to separate their effects.[40] The chief complaints about procedures were the same ones we have heard in earlier chapters: that government officials paid too much attention to their own interests or to the demands of influential friends. Andrei Viktorovich complained that existing political institutions could only operate "as far as they can orient themselves or agree to work in the interests of big firms and companies." Valya observed that her mayor "took the money with

---

40. Indicators for procedural concerns (the undue influence of specific groups and individuals) and for support for incumbents (whether incumbents work for the good of the majority) were similar enough to make the relationship nearly tautological; therefore, I do not want to overemphasize its importance.

him in a purse, in his pockets, and left." That there were no jobs in town and that young people like her were forced to migrate to Moscow were problems a mayor more focused on the good of his city and less on his own pockets might have addressed. Apparently, the logic of the link between procedures and performance in Russia is that officials overly beholden to a few powerful and wealthy supporters or only interested only in their own welfare produce outcomes counter to the common good. Where the rules of the game benefit the few, the many lose.

Consequently, we can conclude that government performance contributes to incumbent support among the Russian respondents, apparently directly and without much interpretation. But values and procedures seem to play at least an indirect role as well.

Advocates for Change

The disdain with which many respondents held those who governed them was palpable. Echoing Valya, Pelageia described the series of mayors of her city: "One left, the second left, the third left. One stuffed his pockets, then left. The second stuffed his pockets, then left. Everyone says it." Dima complained of "corruption in the State Duma, lobbying by large-scale owners and various economic groups and by criminal groups." He thought officials engaged in intrigues and defended the interests "not of the majority of the population, but of exactly some kind of group." In this section, I examine the degree to which criticisms of incumbents extend to fundamental dissatisfaction with political institutions or the political system as a whole. Do Russians who are alienated from their present government want to replace it with something completely different?

Using comments about possible changes to government is a different approach from that used in most studies of political support or legitimacy.[41]

---

41. I asked respondents whether they thought it would be possible to create new political structures that would be better than the ones that already existed. I also asked more specific questions about suggestions they would make to improve the Duma or the work of the president. And I asked more general questions about what the leaders of the country do that is important or necessary and what emotions respondents felt when they thought about government. Answers to all those questions inform this section and the following one.

Some of the standard practices developed by public opinion researchers to encourage survey participants to think about institutions rather than individuals may not do so in fact. One common approach is to focus on "trust" or "confidence" in government to do the right thing. But studies indicate that respondents in Western surveys have in mind particular office-holders and current policies when they answer questions about "trust" in institutions. See Jack

But it is a way to encourage respondents to talk about areas of dissatisfaction and aspects of government that they like. This approach establishes a minimal condition of legitimacy—whether government institutions should continue to exist as constituted—and allows respondents to elaborate on that condition. As it turned out, asking respondents to talk about what they would change in their government was an effective way of getting them to think about what they wanted from government and the degree to which the existing system satisfied those demands.

This was an instance of how intensive interviews provide opportunities to tap the opinions of ordinary citizens in ways that standardized surveys usually do not. In particular, in intensive interviews it is possible to ask people how they would change existing institutions or what they would prefer to see in their stead without providing preselected alternatives. This gives respondents the freedom to come up with unexpected suggestions, and it also ensures that they will not be counted as agreeing with an alternative that had not occurred to them independently, as can happen when people respond to preselected choices. The disadvantage, of course, is that most citizens do not think about political institutions—and how to perfect them—in their spare time. Consequently, asking people to imagine alternatives is asking them to stretch the usual limits of the ways they think about politics. Even that disadvantage is somewhat reduced by the context of intensive interviews, which push respondents to articulate opinions

---

Citrin, "Comment: The Political Relevance of Trust in Government," *American Political Science Review* 68 (1974): 973–88; Jack Citrin and Donald Green, "Presidential Leadership and Trust in Government," *British Journal of Political Science* 16 (1986): 431–53; William Mishler and Richard Rose, "Trust, Distrust, and Skepticism: Popular Evaluations of Civil and Political Institutions in Post-Communist Societies," *Journal of Politics* 59, no. 2 (May 1997): 422. My own respondents found it difficult to talk about "trust" in terms of individuals they had never met in person, or, as they put it, whose hand they had not held or with whom they had not drunk tea. Many found it impossible to conceive what it might mean to trust an institution. Ruslan said about the Duma, "Insofar as there are so many people there, I can say that the people for whom I voted, by the information I have, arouse trust. But for the rest, there's not even enough information." Similarly, see Russell Hardin, "Do We Want Trust in Government?" in *Democracy and Trust*, ed. Mark E. Warren (New York: Cambridge University Press, 1999), 22–41.

Another effort to bypass discussion of incumbents relies on questions about how well democracy is functioning. The problem here is that democracy means different things to different people—abstract principles for some, the performance of incumbents for others. Answers to such questions, then, are almost impossible to interpret. See Damarys Canache, Jeffrey J. Mondak, and Mitchell A. Seligson, "Meaning and Measurement in Cross-National Research on Satisfaction with Democracy," *Public Opinion Quarterly* 65, no. 4 (2001): 525.

throughout the interview process. As a result, by the time respondents get to the hard questions, they have already had a lot of practice organizing and explaining their ideas about political life.

It is therefore notable that, despite often raw criticism of government officials, there were relatively few suggestions for radical change in Russia's institutional structures. Grigorii argued that it was necessary to "wholly change the entire governing structure and all incumbents." More specifically, he added that "maybe, now in this period of our historical-economic development, we need serious presidential power and some kind of, simply, structures, let's say, organs, having the function of enabling the more optimal execution of the president's decisions in life and control over their implementation." A couple of other respondents suggested that Russia might benefit from a monarchy. As Lena noted, "It would be cleaner." But most who thought they might like a czar did not think that monarchy was a viable option for Russia in the post-Soviet world. And most respondents thought that the point was not to come up with new institutions but to fix the ones that existed.

For instance, Raya said, "It seems to me that our apparatus, our institutions, are sufficient. It is simply necessary to try to instill new meaning in them, that is, to make the Duma work better, to make the government work better, to create associations so that these parties can better reflect the interests of the people, to demand from the Duma and government the best solutions to problems. But to create new institutions is not necessary." Raya was a relatively strong supporter of incumbents, but even among those with much-diminished support, there was little taste for wholesale change of institutions. Valentina, for instance, said, "Oy, no, in my opinion it is not necessary to construct anything. We've had enough experiments! It's necessary to improve what already exists. Enough! I don't think that something else will be better." For most respondents, wholesale change was out of the question, but piecemeal solutions to specific problems might still be on the agenda.

While there was a slight tendency for people who showed little support for incumbents also to be more likely to advocate widespread change of the political system, so few respondents suggested fundamental changes that this tendency should not be overemphasized. Many more respondents favored smaller alterations in the structures of power, but respondents seemed as likely to favor small-scale changes and to favor many of the same changes whether they were very supportive of incumbents or not.

The kinds of changes people advocated did, however, vary with the depth of their support for democracy.[42] Less democratic respondents were more likely to suggest changes to existing institutions that would make institutions function less democratically, such as giving more power to the president and less to the Duma or toughening up the behavior of individual leaders. Zoia Igorevna, for instance, said, "In the present moment, I would say that Vladimir Putin needs to have the steadfastness of Stalin, his steadfastness. And maybe his power should be tough. Crimes are committed. Punish them to keep others from doing the same. The president is too soft. A steadier hand is needed, more resolute, as they say." She did not imagine, however, that a steadier hand at the helm required changes in institutional structures. She said, "In my opinion, there is no use in creating new institutions. It is simply necessary to fix the old ones. Give them, as they say, strength so that they can function correctly." Vladimir Il'ich similarly recommended a strong fist in the interest of greater order, and he was open to the idea of eliminating the Duma.[43]

By contrast, democratically oriented respondents were more likely to recommend changes to deepen the democratic nature of the Russian system. Some of them recommended reducing the power of the president so that the president and Duma would be more equally balanced. In 1998, Konstantin said, "The constitution that we have was written under Yeltsin and all the trouble lies there. When they created this constitution, they said that our president was so good, honest, respectable that it was possible, so to speak, to give him power." But now, he continued, "we have in effect a presidential republic. The State Duma is like a consulting voice. All power is concentrated in the president. For that reason, I consider that the president's power is sufficient, even more than sufficient. Some kind of control over power is needed."

Strong supporters of democracy were also more likely to recommend changes that would improve the way government institutions were connected to the people. Tolya commented, "The Duma is not only an organ that makes laws. It is also one of the democratic institutions, that is, an

42. Here, as elsewhere in this book, support for democracy is based on the measure first used in Chapter 5 and explained in Appendix C.

43. Less democratic respondents are by definition more likely to approve eliminating the Duma, since willingness to eliminate the Duma was one of the criteria by which support for democracy was determined. That, however, is not the only way their suggestions for revisions to existing institutions work against democracy.

organ of representative power, where people could come, voters with their problems. I think that now it would make sense to work on the State Duma in exactly this direction, so that there would be ties back and forth with the people, with the voters. Now there aren't any. That is, it is not possible to be limited to lawmaking. It is necessary to meet more with people and live with their problems, with those problems with which they live. There, 450 people meet and discuss some problems in isolation from the people. You can't do it like that."

Some suggestions for changing existing institutions were common to people at all levels of support for democracy and at all levels of support for incumbents. Many respondents felt that they did not have enough information to make informed votes, especially in Duma elections. They complained that there were too many parties for people to know what they stood for, that party-list voting resulted in candidates with little responsibility to the population, and that little information was available during elections that would enable voters to make intelligent choices. Vilen Nikolaevich complained, "All these programs are sufficiently slippery, sufficiently simplified, that you can't tell who wants what and who knows what. Or what anyone will do." Some less democratic respondents suggested closing down some parties to create a simpler political landscape for voters. More democratic respondents suggested that deputies should report to voters on what the legislature had accomplished, and voters should have the right to recall deputies if they were not satisfied with their work.

Another suggestion that turned up across all levels of support for democracy or incumbents was that government officials should think less about themselves and more about the people. Iurii commented, "Now I don't see any people there who have turned their faces toward me. I see people expressing their political ambitions, desiring something for themselves to insure against some or another situation." Raisa agreed. She said, "There is too large a gap between the lifestyle, how they live and how the nation lives. Sometimes they are simply, it seems to me, far away and don't understand the interests of the nation." In order to encourage deputies to turn their faces toward the population, some people thought that more ordinary people should be in power. Vasya said about the Duma, "There should be people who rub shoulders with the people . . . people who constantly are surrounded by people, who know the problems of the people and what is necessary to make life better. Because, in my opinion, the fundamental task of the Duma is to improve the welfare of the population." No matter how it was accomplished, most respondents agreed that if Russians could somehow manage to elect more honest, energetic, and knowledgeable people to the Duma, everything would be fine.

On the whole, then, it seems that many of the Russian respondents wanted the same thing: a government oriented toward serving the needs of the country. They differed on how that goal could be accomplished. More democratically oriented respondents suggested improving the electoral system and links between elected officials and citizens. Less democratic respondents preferred executive efforts to manage the competition between parties. More rarely, some of the less democratic respondents suggest a stronger hand at the helm and the elimination of the unsatisfactory Duma. Respondents who were more supportive of incumbents were not less likely to suggest changes to existing institutions, although the very few respondents who would totally eliminate the existing system did tend to show relatively little support for incumbents.

All this indicates that support for incumbents is not a good measure of acceptance of existing institutions. Even people such as Tolya, Vasya and Raisa, who had high support for incumbents, suggested changes in the ways in which government operates. Even respondents (for example, Valentina or Konstantin) with low support for incumbents would leave existing institutions more or less in place. The paradox is this: Russians widely complain about how government officials service the latter's own interests rather than the public good, regularly chastise Duma deputies for talking too much and accomplishing too little, and think their mayors are stuffing their pockets with the proceeds of the public till and skipping out of town, and yet these same Russians want to leave existing institutions more or less in place. Why?

Why Tolerate Government Failure?

One reason that Russians might be willing to leave imperfect government institutions in place is that they have trouble conceiving of alternatives. Even though she had no difficulty coming up with specific suggestions about how institutions might be improved, when faced with a question of whether wholly new institutions were needed in Russia, Raisa responded, "No, I have trouble answering. It seems to me that what now exists is fine." Most respondents thought it was necessary to have some kind of executive headed by a single person who could keep everyone on target and serve as a human face on power for the population. Few thought a single person could make all the laws that Russia needed, or should be trusted to do so, so they also thought that there was no way of getting around having some kind of legislature, probably elected. Tatiana Mikhailovna remarked about the Duma, "Let them be. And if they didn't exist, then what would be in their place? It's not important what you call it, all the same there has to be some kind of council of officials."

As we saw in the previous chapter, many of the respondents were not especially sensitive to the distinctions between democratic and nondemocratic versions of common political practices: to them, presidents looked a lot like czars, and the State Duma was the newly renamed Supreme Soviet. The issue seems to be less an inability to *articulate* alternatives to existing institutions than insensitivity to significant differences. Galina Grigor'evna, for instance, though otherwise quite supportive of democratic practices, suggested that Russians might get better presidents if the president was appointed rather than elected, as was the case under Soviet power. She said, "I lived through the old way, when we never elected a president. Yeltsin was the first, for almost two terms, and then there will be Putin. But the people, we people don't know candidates by their qualities, by their work, by their quality, by their ability, by their knowledge, by their intellect. We don't know them. It seems to me it would be better if they were appointed. Or elected by the circle around them, parliament or whoever they are." As a result of this relative insensitivity to the particulars of institutional structures, respondents tended to advocate leaving the institutions as they were and just changing the people in them. As Irina L'vovna remarked, "The Duma would work better if there were more people there who knew the business to which they were called." Or as Zinaida said, new institutions were not needed, "it's simply that people should all the same be at a civilized level."

Another reason Russians might be willing to leave imperfect government institutions in place is that they despair of being able to change them, even if they could conceive of a preferred alternative. On the subject of new people, for instance, people who would be honest and competent and get existing structures to work, a number of respondents doubted that new people could actually be found. Svetlana, for instance, compared the search for new political leaders to a recently aired television talent search. Although the contestants who won had good voices, the producers made them sound small. Similarly, political structures might drain desirable qualities out of new candidates. Dima suggested that only time would address the problems in Russian political institutions. He said, "Probably to change the situation we should replace one generation of people with the next in line. But things will change themselves over time. And now we have what we have, and it is difficult to change the situation with merely organizational methods." Thinking along the same lines, Boris Borisovich worried that the new leaders Russia needed were probably still in kindergarten.

Others suggested that the barriers to change lay in a power structure under the sway of big money. Speaking of Yeltsin, Polina said, "At the present moment, there is no way to improve the president's work. It's like in Sicily—the mafia is higher than the government structure. I'm afraid it's already too late. Either that or it's necessary to break up everything in some kind of revolution from below, in principle like in 1917, in order to put a cook or someone in power. . . . Now it's impossible to impose it. Money makes power. Already it's not the government that is power, but money that is power." A few respondents saw a barrier to change in their fellow citizens. Sofiia said, "There is an expression that a country has the sort of government that it deserves. . . . We ourselves chose the representatives in this Duma." Among more educated respondents, the reluctance to advocate radical change was expressed as a rejection of "Bolshevik methods," a recognition of the dangers of trying to remake the future according to a theoretical plan instead of being limited by the practical possibilities inherent in the present.

Faced with the unlikelihood of change, many respondents opted for accepting what existed. Regarding the Duma, Galina Grigor'evna said, "And what else can I do? Only trust them. I can't do anything to change them." Speaking of the presidency, Alla argued that nothing better could be expected. She said, "Of course, given all the unhappy events that have occurred in Russia, the presidency is the lesser evil. . . . Probably, the best path for Russia was monarchy, but we can't bring that back to life now. There remains only party power, the power of a single party—and that also isn't any good. The power of a single parliament is also bad. So the president is the lesser evil." Tatiana Mikhailovna expressed the fatalism of many of the respondents when she said, "There is no way to improve the actions of the president. And why bother? Just let them be to occupy themselves with their own affairs, so they'll trouble us less."

This sentiment that ordinary people would be better off if they just let government be has the effect of transforming widespread dissatisfaction with existing political institutions into grudging acceptance. But is readiness to let institutions be—*pust' oni budut* in Russian—anything like support? Many of the respondents who were particularly disillusioned about the possibilities of change—including Alla, Sofiia, Svetlana, Galina Grigor'evna, Boris Borisovich, and Tatiana Mikhailovna, all of whose comments we heard in this section—also expressed little support for incumbents. That is to say, many of the people unhappiest with the way things are were also unlikely to think things could change. While lack of hope for change is short of positive support, it has the same effect of leaving existing institutions in place.

There is a third reason that people might leave flawed institutions in place: what many Russians want from their government is not something that can be accomplished by eliminating it. If we look at the portion of the sample that is more troubled by social disorder, we find that what they want from government is stability, jobs, a functioning system of law, and attention to the pressing problems of the day. They want government officials who are honest, not corrupt, and who are conscientious and respectable.

Alla, for instance, said, "I would want government officials to recognize, to understand, that society is in crisis. And the economy is in crisis. All of society is in systemic crisis, especially moral and economic. The government needs to understand that and develop a program to lead the country out of crisis. That is, they have to think about saving society and not about their own welfare." Tolya added, "Well, in the global sense, I would like that in the end we get closer to a law-governed state, that all social relations, all processes that occur here, will proceed within the bounds of law, so that more than anything the corruption that troubles us would vanish. Well, and that as a result of that the well-being of the nation would improve, wages would rise, the nation would begin to receive, people would begin to receive exactly the pay that they deserve." Svetlana's concerns were more modest: she just wanted the government to do its job better, so she could ignore it.[44]

None of these desires are for things that could be accomplished in the absence of government or in the midst of radical institutional change. And again, since the people most dissatisfied with incumbents are those with the strongest fear of social disorder, the desire for order undercuts desires for even positive change. Even people not very troubled by social disorder wanted a more normal and predictable political system. Marina Aleksandrovna said, "I would like my country, where I live, to have a normal

44. Svetlana's desires were remarkably similar to those of Hibbing and Theiss-Morse's American respondents. See John R. Hibbing and Elizabeth Theiss-Morse, *Stealth Democracy: Americans' Beliefs About How Government Should Work* (New York: Cambridge University Press, 2002).

government, a normal president. Well, what is normal? Normal is one I wouldn't have to think about and I could concern myself with my own affairs. One that would protect me when I was old and sick, after I'd worked for forty years, or thirty, like in a normal country." Dima said he would want "predictability of power. Predictability. And correspondingly, so that I can construct my plans in relation to the situation, in order to be able to predict the situation, there should be predictable power."

If legitimacy is the sense that the existing institutions are the appropriate ones for the society, then Russian political institutions may be said to be fairly legitimate in the eyes of most respondents.[45] While many respondents criticize the way in which institutions or the people in them operate, few advocate significant changes in institutional structures. The cause behind their criticisms is the same as the reason they are reluctant to advocate change: social disorder is taken as evidence that government is not doing its job and also as evidence that government has a crucial job to do. In difficult conditions, the job of government is too crucial to permit significant alterations in institutional structures. For many of the Russian respondents, government is legitimate simply because it is there and has a function to fulfill. Insofar as they value the function, they accept the structures empowered to perform it.

Are Americans Different?

There is reason to think that Russians might be distinctive in their readiness to accept political institutions that do not serve their needs well. After all, that is the sort of institutions they have tended to have. Russians' experiences under Soviet power would not have left them with much confidence that citizens could shape government to serve popular desires better. By

---

45. Other definitions of legitimacy also support this conclusion. Dieter Fuchs and Hans-Dieter Klingemann distinguish between congruence at the level of political processes, when government gives citizens what they want (responsiveness), and congruence at the level of formal structures, when citizens perceive these structures as commensurate with generally accepted values and norms (legitimacy). Russian institutions are legitimate by this definition, since institutions are perceived to be commensurate with the value of social order. See Dieter Fuchs and Hans-Dieter Klingemann, "Citizens and the State: A Changing Relationship?" in *Citizens and the State*, ed. Hans-Dieter Klingemann and Dieter Fuchs, Beliefs in Government, vol. 1 (New York: Oxford University Press, 1995), 3. David Held argues that legitimacy is based on normative agreement or the belief that the institutions that exist are right for the circumstances, if not ideal. Russians imply theirs are the best possible institutions, despite their shortcomings. See David Held, *Models of Democracy* (Stanford: Stanford University Press, 1987), 238, 182.

contrast, Americans are supposed to share an optimistic belief that anything can be fixed. Americans may also have different expectations of government, since they are thought to prefer small government that does not get too much in their way. Americans also have not suffered the same kinds of social disorder and wrenching dislocations that Russians did in the transition from Communism. The United States is more stably prosperous; the Constitution has been in place for centuries. Consequently, it would be logical to expect that Americans would show quite different structures of support for government than we saw among the Russian respondents. In order to determine how distinctive are the grounds for Russian acceptance of their political system, I turn now to analysis of the American interviews.

As with the Russian sample, I divided the American sample into groups with differing levels of support for incumbents, based on questions about whether the respondents thought the president, members of Congress, and local mayors acted in the interests of the majority of the population. (See Appendix C.)

Using the same cutoffs as in the Russian sample, American respondents expressed more support for incumbents than did Russians. More than half the American respondents ended up in the "high" support category, compared with about a third of the Russians. Less than a quarter of the American sample showed "low" support, compared with 40 percent of Russians. As with the Russians, most demographic characteristics had little effect on support for incumbents, although there was a slight tendency for Americans who felt that their own economic situation was good to be more likely to support incumbents.[46] Also as with the Russian sample, there was a tendency for people with a higher sense that daily life was disorderly and unpredictable to be less supportive of incumbents. Among Americans, however, this relationship appears in attenuated form, at least partly because the American respondents perceived much less social disorder than did the Russians. (See Table 8.4.)

Despite this attenuation, Americans' comments provide evidence of the link between satisfaction with political officials and satisfaction with the way life is going in general. Like Russians, the American respondents were happy with their local mayors when streets were clean, snow was

---

46. Most American respondents were satisfied but not overjoyed with their own economic situation. Of the five who labeled their situation considerably better than satisfactory, four were in the high-support group. Only one American respondent found his situation highly dissatisfactory. He was in the low-support group.

Table 8.4   Perceptions of social disorder and support for incumbents among American respondents

	Low sense of disorder	Moderate sense of disorder	High sense of disorder
High support for incumbents	Betty, Bill, Chris, Emily, Ernest, Harriet, Jacob, Jane, Jean, Leo, Trish *(11 respondents)*		
Moderate support	Grace, Ted *(2 respondents)*	Daniel, Kate, Rick *(3 respondents)*	
Low support	Caroline, Fred *(2 respondents)*	Adam, Sam, Victoria *(3 respondents)*	

removed, and citizen concerns received responses. People interviewed during the administration of President Bill Clinton observed that the jobless rate was down and the market was up, and those accomplishments were a source of satisfaction. Jean said of Clinton, "I think he's doing a good job. Because the economy is good and we're pretty much at peace." Like many of the respondents, she was reluctant to endorse Clinton fully because of his lapses in upholding his marriage vows, but she added, "I trust him when it comes to looking after our country and to do good, to benefit our country, but if I was Hillary I wouldn't trust him when it came to personal issues."

With terrorist attacks, war, and economic recession, the world was an apparently less orderly place during the administration of George W. Bush, but at least in late 2001 many of the American respondents still felt that their lives were relatively stable and predictable, and many supported Bush in his efforts to preserve their security. Betty said, "He's doing what needs to be done. And he's doing it now." Bill thought that Bush was correctly addressing economic difficulties. He said, "I think Bush thinks by helping big business he helps the little guy, and I agree with that, too. So yeah, I think he acts in the interests of everybody, the majority." This support even surfaced in people predisposed not to like Bush, people who had not voted for him and who identified themselves as Democrats. Ernest said of Bush, "He certainly puts on a better show of working in the interests of the majority. I thought it was admirable, for example, that he went to the mosques and made such a point of emphasizing tolerance after the September 11 attacks. So in many ways he is the most inclusive Republican president that we have had, at least that I can recall in my lifetime."

Among Americans with few worries about social disorder, even criticisms of public officials were temperate. Mayors were accused of being overly consumed with commercial development. Clinton, of course, was criticized for his marital lapses, but usually not for the policies he advocated. Congress was recognized as an inefficient body and members of Congress were seen as overly partisan, but the benefits of the resulting divisions were also noted. Bill, for instance, observed that institutional checks and balances prevented any one office from having too much power or getting too much done, adding that "too much legislation in the long run would be a bad thing."

American respondents with a greater sense of the problematical nature of daily life were more fundamentally critical of incumbents. In their disgust with the way politics operates and their sense of the unresponsiveness of power, they sounded much more like the Russian respondents. Victoria complained about Congress, "They spend far too much time on topics that are not at all important. They are far too accessible to lobbying groups. And this whole campaign issue, campaign finance is costing so much money. I mean the average Joe Blow cannot go out and run for something; he couldn't afford it. That's like not being able to go to church. . . . I think the poor people are getting ignored because they can't contribute to campaigns." Victoria also thought her mayor worked primarily in the interests of white people and business interests, and she was a member of neither group.

American respondents with a stronger sense of social disorder were more likely to complain that public officials worked toward the latter's own good, and not the good of the country, and that elected officials had to preserve the favor of major campaign donors, making them unresponsive to the concerns of ordinary people. Adam thought that Congress was riddled with corruption and should be completely revamped. He sounded much like the Russian respondents when he said, "I think they squabble too much over things. It seems like all the Congressmen are interested in doing is grandstanding. They all just want to make a name for themselves. . . . They all try to line their pockets, and I hate that. I think a lot of them should be gotten rid of." Rick complained that policies that many Americans seemed to favor did not seem to survive congressional procedures. While Rick thought that Congress failed to serve the interests of the population because it was beholden to "money and big business," Ted blamed dependence on "specific interest groups . . . all the minorities, the minority of the population, the racial groups, women." Others thought the problem was that politicians put the interests of their parties above the interests of their constituents.

In any event, like Russians, Americans evaluated those who ruled them based on what these lawmakers accomplished, on their effectiveness, together with an eye to procedures, particularly whether certain groups received more attention than others. In their assessments of incumbents, comments about values were much less common.

Among some of the American respondents, support for public officials was influenced by party affiliations, with Democrats more likely to think that Democratic presidents served the interests of the majority, and Republicans more likely to have confidence in Republican presidents. But the effect here was not especially strong. Republicans interviewed during the Clinton years noted the positive state of the economy as reason enough to think that Clinton served the interests of the majority. Some Democrats were happy with Bush's war on terror, even if they did not think much of his domestic policies. In any case, these partisan concerns mostly did not extend to Congress or local mayors.

As with the Russians, an optimistic outlook tended to bolster support for elected officials. This was particularly apparent with respondents interviewed during the Bush administration. People with strong confidence in free markets supported Bush even in the face of economic recession: their confidence that markets would fix themselves kept them from blaming Bush for the economic downturn. Those less supportive of incumbents were more likely to think the country was heading in the wrong direction. Rick said, "I think, well, domestically, it's not heading anywhere. I think it's just stagnant, there's no movement in any direction. And if you try and gauge public opinion or you try and gauge the general sense of the country, it's almost like it's cacophonous. There's no general sense of the country. . . . In terms of foreign affairs, I think we're going in the wrong direction, too. We're kind of using a lot of force, using a lot of our clout right now, which we can get away with in the short run. But in the long run it might hurt us."

Unlike Russians, who tended to shy away from institutional changes even when they were convinced that their country was hurtling toward an abyss, Americans unhappy with incumbents were more likely to suggest fairly fundamental changes in existing institutions. Although he was alone in his suggestion, Sam advocated a shift toward dictatorship and suggested Richard Nixon as someone who would have been good at the job. He said, "It's the most efficient form of leadership there ever has been. I mean total control. The only problem with a dictatorship is who is to succeed. . . . But he's got to have power, and he shouldn't be questioned." Sam was also ready to outlaw lobbyists. Daniel suggested eliminating the presidency, arguing that by including both Democrats and Republicans the Congress did a better job representing the varied will of the American people. Fred spoke at length about the desirability of eliminating political parties, which he felt forced his representatives to vote against their consciences and his interests. Victoria said she would run government "more like a business" and would split up the major institutions and spread them across the country. Her logic was that if the Supreme Court met in Mexico (the name of a town in Missouri), for instance, it would be more accountable to citizens.

These were minority suggestions. Although Fred was not alone in his dislike of political parties, no one but Daniel questioned the existence of the presidency. Even Sam, flirting as he was with dictatorship, implied that he would leave Congress in place. But it is nonetheless interesting that Americans who were unhappy with incumbents were more likely than Russians to advocate fundamental structural changes. Americans were less likely than Russians to despair of the possibility of change, less likely to think that flawed structures could not be fixed, and less worried about the social upheavals that might accompany alterations in political institutions. This willingness to contemplate change can be seen as representing underlying confidence in the way things are. In a world that works, government is not the last defense against social chaos.

Most of the American respondents, relatively happy with public officials, relatively secure in the stability of their daily lives, thought existing political institutions were fine as they were. They lived, as many commented, in the best country in the world, and they thought some of the credit was due to political structures. Unlike Russians, many of the American respondents, even those unhappy with incumbents or with the conditions of their lives, expressed pride in the country and their government. Ted said, "It's the best government on the planet. Took two hundred years to become the number one power in the world. We did it by our government. Our constitution is so brilliantly written that it covered all the bases—with the amendments. It hasn't let us down in the past, and probably not in the future." Even Adam, who had plenty of criticisms of the way government worked, said, "No, I don't hate the government. I like it. I really get upset when people bad-mouth the U.S. government. I don't know. Like I just think that we've got the best government in the world, when it's working right."

Leo, whose own life story epitomized the can-do spirit behind the American dream, was particularly effusive but not alone in the gist of his sentiments. He said, "I'm damn lucky and damn proud to be born and raised in this country, as all of us should be. And we need to wake up every day and just realize, as you look around the world, how lucky we are to be where we are. And we haven't arrived. We're not Shangri-La, still got many problems, but we're working on it."

Certainly, not all the respondents were as positive as Leo, but even the unhappy ones tended to feel irritation or indifference toward the government, not the rank disgust characteristic of many Russians. The American respondents wanted many of the same things from government that the Russians wanted. They wanted honest and energetic leaders, who tried to do well by the people who elected them. They wanted peace, economic prosperity, social assistance for the elderly, and good schools for their kids. Despite intermittent complaints, the American respondents were more or less satisfied that government provided these things.[47]

The evidence presented here suggests that, where the Russian government enjoys a kind of legitimacy by default—because any political order is better than chaos—the American political system enjoys a deeper legitimacy. Despite growing evidence of declining trust in government in the United States, when pushed to talk about it Americans do not merely tolerate government; they praise it.[48] Government performance seems to play an important role here, as was the case regarding support for incumbents.

But democratic values and procedures also contribute to the support the American respondents expressed for their government. When pushed to consider the value of various institutions, they suggested that democracy

---

47. Analysis of national surveys of Americans confirms the connection between positive government outcomes, specifically a prosperous economy, and support for government. See Jack Citrin and Samantha Luks, "Political Trust Revisited: Déjà Vu All Over Again?" in *What Is It About Government That Americans Dislike?* ed. John R. Hibbing and Elizabeth Theiss-Morse (New York: Cambridge University Press, 2001), 9–27.

48. On declining trust in government in the Western democracies, see Susan J. Pharr and Robert D. Putnam, eds., *Disaffected Democracies: What's Troubling the Trilateral Countries?* (Princeton: Princeton University Press, 2000); Pippa Norris, ed., *Critical Citizens: Global Support for Democratic Governance* (New York: Oxford University Press, 1999); Joseph S. Nye Jr., Philip D. Zelikow, and David C. King, eds., *Why People Don't Trust Government* (Cambridge, MA: Harvard University Press, 1997).

was the best form of government, that democracy required representative, deliberative bodies such as Congress, and therefore justified even a Congress no one loved. They spoke with authority about the role of checks and balances in preserving liberty and averting tyranny. Rick said, "You need a deliberative body in a democracy. I mean, come on, that's what it's all about, really. Because there's a multiplicity of viewpoints and a multiplicity of interests within the country, and the only way that you can closely synthesize or bring forth those multiplicities is through a deliberative body, deliberate representative body of some sort." Less eloquently but still to the point, one of the fiercest critics of incumbents, Grace, added, "I have to say, it sounds all negative, but the thing that I have to say is that, in my limited knowledge—and it is limited—democracy is still the best system that is available. I guess it's the checks and balances that can be healthy."

Conclusion

We have seen, then, that among both Russians and Americans, people who are distressed by the vagaries of daily existence are less likely to believe that government officials have their best interests in mind. Among the Russian respondents, however, this lack of support for government officials does not make respondents any more likely to recommend fundamental change in institutional structures. The same things that make Russians unhappy with government officials—the failure to provide conditions for a predictable existence—also keep Russians from thinking that institutional change might help. Daily life is too precarious to contemplate the possible disruptive consequences of political transformation. So my respondents shrug and say, "Let them be." This is very different from the reactions of American respondents. American respondents who were unhappy with incumbents and with the security and predictability of daily life were quite ready to offer suggestions for fundamental institutional change. They were much more ready to think that flawed structures could be made better. They were less likely to "let them be."

One reason for the different responses of Russians and Americans seems to be the different contexts in which they find themselves—the relative disorder of post-Soviet Russia versus the relative order of American prosperity. But comparing the responses of these two groups helps us see other factors as well. The American commitment to democratic procedures, even when actual practice is somewhat unsavory, is not as obvious among the Russians. Russian appreciation of the democratic process might improve with time and practice. In the meantime, the legitimacy of Russian government rests more on fear of any alternative than on a positive commitment to the institutions that exist.

What are the potential consequences of these different patterns of support? On the one hand, the Russian government wins a little wiggle room. Short of an unexpected economic miracle, most Russians probably will not be stably prosperous in the near future, but their daily dissatisfactions are not likely to lead them to advocate institutional change. They will certainly vote incumbents out of office, but they are not likely to clamor for a new constitution—or for disregard of the present one. The fear of change and the weariness with instability expressed by many of my Russian respondents is thus a source of stability and of space for new governments to grow into their tasks.

On the other hand, my respondents' distrust of institutional change might also inadvertently provide permission for those who might try to change institutions slowly, from within, for the kind of creeping authoritarianism with which Putin is associated. Citizens who expect little that is positive from their government and who believe that any government is better than the chaos around the corner are not likely immediately to become aroused as their rights are curtailed. Indeed, concentration of power in an executive branch that took steps to make life better would probably make sense to many of my Russian respondents.

Although unhappy Americans were more likely to suggest institutional changes, the structure of support for government institutions in the United States also militates against change. In my admittedly small American sample, fewer of the respondents were unhappy with incumbents or distressed about the state of social order. The dissatisfied American respondents suggested wildly disparate types of change, from concentrating power in the presidency to eliminating the office. There is hardly the basis for a social movement in their differing visions of change.

More significant, even many of the dissatisfied Americans expressed what practically none of the Russians did: a sense of pride in their government, a confidence that they lived in the best country on earth. That underlying confidence, wholly missing in the Russian sample, is both a strong expression of fundamental legitimacy and a source of stability. As Bill said about the American political system, "If it's not broke, don't fix it. I'm sure ideally you probably could fine-tune it, but you never know. So I wouldn't trust myself or any of my peers to mess around with something that's worked so well for so long." Both Russians and Americans seem to want the same things from government—a predictable daily existence and the hope that someone in power will respond to them in their time of need. The difference is that Americans largely get what they want, and Russians do not.

A great deal of the information about how people feel about their government occurred between the lines. All the American respondents and some of the Russians were asked what feelings arose when they thought about their government. Americans were quite animated in response and offered up many of the comments that affirmed their underlying pride and satisfaction. Russians fell silent, groped for words, and talked about very different things, from what it used to feel like to see the red flag with hammer and sickle raised at the Olympic games, to their embarrassment at a landscape littered with closed factories, to their fears for the welfare of the Russian nation. During my conversations with Russians, the silence that often followed my question about what government does that is useful and important was more eloquent than some of the answers. A few of the Russian respondents grew more and more despondent as the interview proceeded and they put together the story of how deeply government failed their expectations.

The Russian language sets up a barrier for researchers interested in government legitimacy because of the absence of a word for *government* that nearly matches the English-language usage. That my respondents overcome this barrier by talking about "them"—just as they referred to Communism as "then"—hinted at the distance they perceived between themselves and their government. Russians use the possessive *our* more regularly than do Americans, referring to "our people," "our Russia"—or, as the staff in the hotel in Voronezh referred to my husband and me, "our foreigners." But they do not tend to convey that sense of ownership or complicity when talking about their government. And they certainly did not interject the comment, as the American respondents regularly did, that deep down, despite their complaints about specific individuals or unpopular policies, everything really was OK.

Conclusion

More than a decade after the collapse of Communism, the prospects for full democracy in Russia remained obscure. While people were freer than they had been under the Soviet regime and leaders were constrained, even if only imperfectly, by elections and law, democracy's success was far from certain. The general consensus was that Vladimir Putin was moving the country away from democracy rather than toward it, and ordinary Russians were doing little to stop the slide. Although electoral revolts in Georgia, Ukraine, and even Kyrgyzstan provided evidence of a population ready to defend its democratic freedoms, Russian citizens remained largely quiescent. Indeed, Putin's continued popularity in the face of his restrictions on democratic freedoms led some observers to conclude that ordinary Russians actively supported his autocratic intentions. But is that the picture painted in the extended conversations with Russians that form the backbone of this book?

Not exactly. This chapter starts with a summary of the findings of previous chapters, describing first the findings that indicate considerable support for democratic and market institutions and, second, findings that hint at areas of difficulty. After that, some broader conclusions are drawn about the sources of Russian citizens' support for Putin. I end with some implications about the importance of cultural traditions in the construction of democracy.

Can Russians Be Democrats?

The conversations I had with Russians between 1998 and 2003 provided evidence of some widely shared orientations conducive to democracy. Most of the Russian citizens interviewed for this book were strongly committed to the idea that government officials ought to be responsive to the demands of citizens: they thought that officeholders should care about the opinions of constituents, strive their best to serve the interests of the population, and be informed by and subject to the electorate's will. These ordinary Russians were also highly protective of the personal and political freedoms they had gained since the collapse of Communism. They greatly appreciated the freer exchange of information begun under Gorbachev and enjoyed the availability of books and music from around the world; they did not want to lose the opportunity to travel abroad. They wanted to vote and to be able to criticize their government without fear of reprisals.

While it is true that some of my respondents might have been convinced to curtail their new freedoms in the hope of greater social order, this reflected less a low value placed on freedom than awareness that personal freedoms can hardly be practiced in a lawless environment, where the weak are at the mercy of the strong, the wealthy, or the person who happens to hold a gun. Aside from a few mild references to the desirability of a monarchy (which, after all, exists in a number of European democracies), the Russian respondents showed no enthusiasm for a wholesale alteration of their political structures. Compared with the American respondents, fewer of the Russians spoke of the virtue of checks and balances or separation of powers, but the difference here was one more of degree than of kind. Many of the Russian respondents did understand that a fractious parliament, even if it does not seem to be getting much done, might be a useful fetter on the power of the executive. On the whole, my respondents' understanding of democratic practices was surprisingly good, even if still imperfect. There were many ways that the Russians respondents did not differ very much from Americans, and many ways in which they had the right ideas to be democrats.

Similarly, there were a number of ways in which many of the Russian respondents had the right ideas to live and function effectively in a market economy. Most did not favor an equal distribution of wealth. Most thought that some people deserved greater material rewards than did others—because they worked harder, were more creative, or made greater contributions to the welfare of society. The Russian respondents largely did see a productive role for government in the economy, but their expectations of government were not so different from those expressed by the American respondents. My Russian respondents wanted government to ensure the essential prosperity of the country, to establish conditions under which people could find jobs and work for their own advancement. Like many Americans, the Russians believed that some people did have a claim on government resources, especially the elderly and people too ill to work, but most people could fend for themselves as long as economic conditions provided sufficient opportunities. Some observers have argued that Russians are overly dependent on government, carrying over paternalistic views from their recent past.[1] But that dependence was not particularly observable among my respondents. Olga Iur'evna said about the government, "They don't have to do anything for me. I myself should build my own life. I am not one of those people who are waiting for something, demanding, begging. I consider that every person is the master of his own life." Indeed, some of the Russian respondents only hoped that the people in power would not meddle too much in their lives. Asked what government did that was useful, Polina replied, "Well, of course it is important that there is peace, first of all. All the rest we do for ourselves, as long as they leave us alone."

These generally democratic and promarket leanings were not merely artifacts of the approach used in this book—reliance on intensive interviews with a comparatively small number of Russians. Mass surveys have also shown substantial support for democratic values and somewhat more limited support for capitalism among ordinary Russians, at least until the questions become more pointed.[2] The particular contribution of the intensive interviews lay in illuminating the reasons behind some of the apparently *less* democratic answers that Russians have given in mass surveys. For instance, mass surveys have shown Russians to be slow to trust representative institutions.[3] When given the opportunity to explain *why* they were unconvinced about the efficacy of representation, the Russian respondents made it clear that their complaint was not with the ideal of a representative legislature, but rather with the form that that ideal had taken in Russia, particularly with the State Duma. As we saw in Chapter 4, the Russian respondents complained that the Duma failed in its representative functions. They called the deputies mercenaries or "gangs of swindlers" and accused them of serving their own personal interests at

1. See, for instance, Rudra Sil and Cheng Chen, "State Legitimacy and the (In)significance of Democracy in Post-Communist Russia," *Europe-Asia Studies* 56, no. 3 (2004): 347–68; Tim McDaniel, *The Agony of the Russian Idea* (Princeton: Princeton University Press, 1996), 32–46; Grigory I. Vainshstein, "Totalitarian Public Consciousness in a Post-totalitarian Society," *Communist and Post-Communist Studies* 27, no. 3 (1994): 247–59.

2. For survey findings, see the discussion in Chapter 2. Shevtsova cites polls that show that 33 percent of the Russian population fully supports the liberal democratic agenda, and 37 percent is inclined to support it. See Lilia Shevtsova, *Putin's Russia* (Washington, DC: Carnegie Endowment for International Peace, 2003).

3. Richard Rose and Doh Chull Shin, "Democratization Backwards: The Problem of Third-Wave Democracies," *British Journal of Political Science* 31 (2001): 331–54; Richard Rose and Neil Munro, *Elections Without Order: Russia's Challenge to Vladimir Putin* (New York: Cambridge University Press, 2002), 226; Stephen White, "Russia's Disempowered Electorate," in *Russian Politics Under Putin*, ed. Cameron Ross (New York: Manchester University Press, 2004), 78.

the expense of the nation. But my respondents wanted more and better representation, not less. It is true that the Russian respondents also showed only limited tolerance for the messiness of the day-to-day work of legislative institutions, preferring less fractiousness and political posturing, but in this they were similar to Americans.[4]

Allowing Russians to explain their opinions made it clear that apparently undemocratic orientations to a meaningful degree were *products* of institutions that were supposed to be exemplars of democracy but that were not. That is to say, imperfect support for democracy was partly caused by imperfect institutions on the ground. This was true in terms of attitudes toward representative institutions and also toward the police. My respondents had little confidence in the effectiveness or professionalism of law enforcement in Russia, and hence some hinted that law was not a valuable means of regulating behavior. But most advocated *stricter* enforcement of existing law. That is to say, they were ready to put their faith in law, as long as law enforcement agencies did their job. As with representative bodies, the reasons for uncertainty about the role of law lay in how institutions operated, not with the democratic ideal of a law-governed society.

The imperfections of existing institutions also provided an explanation for Russians' reluctance to get more involved in political life. As far as they were concerned, the structures that might connect ordinary citizens to their government simply did not exist. Andrei Viktorovich explained, "Russia does not have the tradition of fighting for your rights that exists in the West. There are no labor unions that could defend the interests of their members. The courts are not ready for this. There is no judicial system that could guarantee this." In any case, my Russian respondents were highly doubtful that anyone would listen if they did try to talk to the people in power. Asked about her ability to influence the government, Inna responded, "I think that nobody thinks about us. In this I'm simply certain. Thanks to God, I am forty-six years old; and I don't remember a time when the government cared about its people. How many times did they fleece us? How many times did they leave us without money, without the means for survival? People trust in government, in the strongest institution. But in terms of protection, we look not to them—only, as we say, to ourselves alone."

4. This was true both for my own American respondents and in other scholars' work on American attitudes toward Congress. See particularly John R. Hibbing and Elizabeth Theiss-Morse, *Congress as Public Enemy: Public Attitudes Toward American Political Institutions* (New York: Cambridge University Press, 1995).

Just as some of the Russians' apparently undemocratic orientations could be explained as responses to purportedly democratic institutions that worked poorly, a substantial amount of hostility to capitalism seemed to stem from the chaotic, robber baron type of capitalism that had evolved in Russia. As we saw in Chapter 5, the respondents who were less supportive of capitalism listed flaws in Russian-style capitalism as the reason: in Russia, markets did not provide opportunities for most people; the people who earned more were not the ones who worked harder or contributed more to the good of society.

Most mass surveys of Russians have turned up a significant portion of the population who appear to support democracy but are suspicious of markets.[5] Whether a truly liberal democratic system can develop in Russia seems to hinge on these market-skeptical democrats. Here again the intensive interviews were useful in extracting the reasons for hostility to capitalism among some of Russia's democrats. Like Russia's liberal democrats, market-skeptical democrats did not advocate an equal distribution of wealth. They thought that economic life should be governed by principles of desert and that not all people deserved exactly the same things. Compared with Russia's liberal democrats, though, market-skeptical democrats were much more alarmed by the shortcomings of Russian capitalism. As with the imperfections in democratic institutions, recognition of imperfections in Russian markets did not necessarily imply a desire to return to socialism. Rather, many respondents simply wanted Russian capitalism to work better, to provide more widely the opportunities that it theoretically promised.

In sum, ordinary Russians share many values and orientations that enable them to support democratic institutions and market structures. And where their support falls short, it often can be explained at least partly by inadequacies of the progress in Russia so far. From the standpoint of efforts to encourage liberal democracy in Russia, these are positive findings. A populace with the wrong ideas is not one of the obstacles that democracy has to scale in Russia. Many Russians are at least warily ready to support a market democracy; they just doubt that they yet have one. Their skepticism could even make a positive contribution if it provided the rationale for deepening democracy and encouraging the growth of a substantial middle class.

5. See, for instance, Judith S. Kullberg and William Zimmerman, "Liberal Elites, Socialist Masses, and Problems of Democracy," *World Politics* 51 (April 1999): 323–58; Robert J. Brym, "Re-evaluating Mass Support for Political and Economic Change in Russia," *Europe-Asia Studies* 48 (July 1996): 751–66.

Cautionary Notes

But there were also ideas expressed by my Russian respondents that may not encourage liberal democracy. One problem lies in the desire for order. Just as my respondents' preferences and values reflected the imperfect political and economic institutions under which they found themselves, their political leanings were affected by the degree to which they perceived their environment as, on the one hand, predictable and orderly or, on the other, as on the brink of chaos. As we saw in Chapter 6, respondents varied in terms of their perceptions of social order. The disorderliness of democracy was not troubling to respondents for whom social life seemed to work—those who thought that people could find jobs, that the police would arrest criminals, and that government officials tried their best to improve the conditions of daily life. While they might still choose "order" over apparently more democratic alternatives, the order they had in mind involved the adequate implementation of laws made by representative bodies. That is to say, what they understood as order was wholly consistent with democracy. But for those who sensed themselves to be on the brink of social collapse, democracy had far less appeal. The problems they saw—closed factories, street crime, corrupt officials, the raw unpredictability of life on the edge—seemed to demand authoritarian solutions. These people were suspicious of democratic institutions and leaders, contemptuous of market reforms, ready to hand over freedoms from which they could see no benefits, and willing to submit to the strong hand of authority.

Michael Ignatieff implies that a sensitivity to social dysfunctionality is the real legacy of the Soviet system. Ignatieff said, "The yoke they wear but do not talk about is the whole weight of Soviet civilization, which can be measured in its totality only in the details: the lifts that do not work, the buses held together by bits of wire and string, the windows everywhere smeared with dirt, the casual brutality of all officialdom, the constant humiliation of workers in a workers' state."[6] For Russians sensitive to this social disorder, democratic procedures do not seem to be solutions, and indeed they may even contribute to the problem. These Russians especially miss those elements of stability that the Soviet system was able to provide: stable prices and jobs. If economic conditions continue to

---

6. Michael Ignatieff, *Blood and Belonging: Journeys into the New Nationalism* (New York: Farrar, Straus, and Giroux, 1994), 141. Ignatieff was referring to Ukrainians, but conditions were the same in Russia.

improve in Russia, perhaps fears of social disorder will diminish, and with them one element potentially undermining democracy.

In some parts of Russia, the disorder of the Soviet past seems to be yielding to a brighter and more functional future. In the center of Moscow, for instance, windows are no longer "everywhere smeared with dirt," neon advertisements for products that are actually for sale have replaced red signs urging the world's workers to unite, and new construction offers Western-style amenities. But, as Svetlana liked to say, "Moscow is not Russia." For many of the Russians I interviewed, daily life has not changed fundamentally with the rise of the post-Communist system. They live in the same apartments and ride the same rickety buses, "held together by bits of wire and string," to the same jobs they used to hold. Their paychecks simply buy less. As we saw in Chapter 7, some think they are ruled by effectively the same government.

That many ordinary Russians are not highly sensitive to the differences between even imperfectly democratic and wholly nondemocratic institutions is another cause for concern. To many of my Russian respondents, the difference between a president and a czar or a Communist commissar was not immediately clear. Nor were they convinced that their roles as citizens had changed substantially. In this regard, Russians are probably not unique. The American respondents also drew odd parallels between democratic and nondemocratic institutions. For instance, Victoria's recommendation that government be run more like a business is not one that suggests sensitivity to the requirements of democracy, common though that comment is in the American context. In the United States, or in other stable democracies, it may matter less that citizens are not finely attuned to the niceties of democratic practice, because those practices will most likely continue in any case. But in the Russian context, with threats of creeping authoritarianism on the part of government officials, it is a problem if some citizens cannot recognize the changes as they are occurring. As Chapter 7 demonstrated, the Russian respondents who were less likely to be sensitive to the practical dimensions of democracy were less politically sophisticated and less democratically oriented. These same people, however, may be no less likely to vote.[7]

A final cause for concern for the prospects of democracy in Russia is the fact that many respondents continue to see government as a distant

7. Donna L. Bahry and Lucan Way, "Citizen Activism in the Russian Transition," *Post-Soviet Affairs* 10, no. 4 (1994): 330–66; Stephen White, Richard Rose, and Ian McAllister, *How Russia Votes* (Chatham, NJ: Chatham House, 1997), 120–21.

and unresponsive force. As their comments in Chapter 8 indicated, many of the Russian respondents have little confidence in those who rule them and little hope that things will ever improve. Nadezhda said that the primary emotional response that she had to government was one of alienation. She added, "I feel that the state has its own interests that are different from my interests. And often my interests are wholly foreign to it." Similarly, Valentina confided that she felt like "a forgotten stowaway," since the Yeltsin government showed such utter disregard for her or her family's welfare. Asked what the government did that was useful to him, Yegor Yegorovich replied, "I consider that they do nothing. Maybe a little, how can I say? I consider that they do almost nothing. It will always be such." This alienation from government is particularly alarming because it is often combined with a feeling that there is nothing that ordinary people can do about the unresponsiveness of government. If citizens do not expect government to serve their needs and are not willing to force it do so, then surely it will not.

In the final account, the story told by my Russian respondents is a complicated and multifaceted one. In some ways—their preference for taking charge of their own fates, their readiness to participate in elections, their willingness to rely on law as a means to regulate an imperfect society, their attachment to freedom—they have the right ideas to be democrats. And even where they do not seem to have quite the right ideas—for instance, suspicions about the fairness of market rewards or the effectiveness of contentious legislatures—their opinions seem to be reflections of poorly functioning systems. Should those systems function better, popular ideas would likely adjust. But in other ways, some of my Russian respondents also held ideas likely to undermine the development of democracy in challenging circumstances.

Concerns about order, inattention to the qualities that separate demo-cratic and nondemocratic governments, and very low expectations about what government can do may prevent my respondents from being vigilant protectors of imperiled democracy. Instead, my respondents are likely to be defenders of the status quo, not because they particularly like the government they have, but because they think it is better than the chaos that might surround change. In 1994, Gennady Burbulis, a Yeltsin advisor, spoke about the usefulness of popular apathy. He said, "Most people have stopped needing the authorities and the government. No one listens to the opposition anymore. The indifference of the masses is useful; it is even stabilizing. This indifference is a protection against rebellion, as it were."[8] If Russian leaders were trying to construct a liberal democratic system and were worried about popular resistance to short-term costs, then this stabilizing indifference would be a force for democracy. However, if Russian leaders are moving away from democracy, an indifferent public will not stand in their way. The question is, which way are Russian leaders tending?

Tolerance for President Putin

Under President Vladimir Putin, Russia seemed to be slipping away from democracy.[9] Personal and political freedoms were curtailed. Opposition parties withered. And Putin strove to create a "power vertical" with himself at the top. While all this was occurring, ordinary Russians put up little fuss. How do the intensive interviews in this book help us understand their reluctance to complain?

One thing that was clear from my Russian respondents was that, as far as they were concerned, Putin had earned some latitude because he was so much better liked than his predecessor, Boris Yeltsin. For people who did not live in Russia during the 1990s, Yeltsin retains something of a heroic aspect. He stood before the tanks in August 1991 and ushered in an era of greater freedom. He disassembled the Communist system and began construction of a new Russia. Most of my Russian respondents granted Yeltsin those accomplishments, but they credited him with others as well. In their interpretation, Yeltsin had delivered them freedoms they could not use in a lawless environment where rights meant little without a gun to enforce them. Yeltsin had ushered in a form of capitalism that offered few people meaningful opportunities, while at the same time leaving them less secure and considerably poorer. He had governed in such a way that it was hard to know who would be in charge from one day to the next or how much one's money would be worth. And he had stayed in power too long, past the point where he could be effective, which left him open to the kinds of jokes that had been told about Brezhnev.

8. Quoted in McDaniel, *The Agony of the Russian Idea*, 177. Similarly, see Dmitry Oreshkin, "The Silence of the Oligarchs," *Moscow News*, no. 28 (23–29 July 2003), 5.

9. Michael McFaul, Nikolai Petrov, and Andrei Ryabov, *Between Dictatorship and Democracy: Russian Post-Communist Political Reform* (Washington, DC: Carnegie Endowment for International Peace, 2004); Steven Lee Myers, "Using Power, Losing Favor: Putin Falters on World Stage," *New York Times*, 10 December 2004, A1, A8; Ol'ga Kryshtanovskaia, "Vybor patriotov: Bednost' ili rakety?" *Argumenty i Fakty*, no. 30 (July 2003): 3.

Although my respondents would not have come up with the label, there was much about the Yeltsin period characteristic of a neopatrimonial regime.[10] Power was concentrated in the executive, while the legislature held a primarily symbolic role. Politics was a contest over spoils between well-connected cliques, and the winners quickly became very wealthy while ordinary citizens watched their savings evaporate. Authorities worried about pacifying the elites, who had enough power to threaten the government, and ignored the rest of the population.

For my Russian respondents, Putin was preferable to Yeltsin for a number of reasons. They lauded his personal qualities. Whereas Yeltsin's reputation by the end of his reign figured him as an inarticulate and barely competent gasbag, Putin seemed to be intelligent, sober, thoughtful, and decisive. Putin seemed less intent on securing a personal fortune for himself or, as Lena put it, on pulling everything to his side of the blanket. Speaking on the cusp of Putin's first election, Inna remarked that the only thing she wanted from the leaders of Russia was honesty. She said, "Honesty, just honesty. There's nothing more because, when a person is honest, everything else follows: respectability, the lack of a desire to hurt anyone. . . . If you already have a high position, you should devote yourself to it and not, excuse me, stuff your pockets with money and set your family up with this money for the next hundred years." At that point in time, Russians were already tired of news reports on the degree to which the Yeltsin family and close colleagues had profited from Boris Yeltsin's time in office.

Beyond personal qualities, Putin also seemed much more effective than Yeltsin at improving the daily conditions of life for many Russian citizens. The Russian economy grew steadily after 1999, leaving most Russians better off than they had been under Yeltsin. Political life under Putin seemed less of a free-for-all, particularly as politicians increasingly signed on to the parliamentary party that supported Putin, and a fractious opposition became a thing of the past. By 2003, Russians had some confidence in tomorrow, some sense they would survive and maybe eventually prosper. Earlier, that confidence had been almost entirely missing. The elemental

---

10. See Shmuel Noah Eisenstadt, *Revolution and the Transformation of Societies: A Comparative Study of Civilizations* (New York: Free Press, 1978), 277; Vladimir Mau and Irina Starodubrovskaya, *The Challenge of Revolution: Contemporary Russia in Historical Perspective* (New York: Oxford University Press, 2001), 338.

stability of life that Putin's government had begun to provide is the foundation of the "order" that Russians value. Evgenii remarked that all he wanted from government was the prospect of stable work. "Then, after work, would be a secure old age, as they say, a pension, a normal life for the person who gave his strength and, you could say, years to the flourishing of the country. That they would value this." In Putin, many Russians felt they had finally found a leader with his face turned toward them, who meant to help them improve their lives.

As indicated in Chapter 4, effectiveness—not careful attention to democratic procedures—is the criterion that matters to Russians in evaluating their leaders.[11] That said, it is not obvious that my respondents would interpret many of Putin's actions as necessarily hostile to democracy. For instance, the Western press presented legal prosecution of the oligarchs under Putin as an effort to undermine capitalism, private property, free enterprise, and by association democracy.[12] But it is unlikely that many of my Russian respondents would interpret events the same way. While they might agree that political considerations had motivated the prosecution of one or another individual, they were highly unlikely to think that any oligarch was actually innocent. There was, most thought, no way to make that much money in so little time by legal means. Furthermore, it was doubtful that the very rich were paying all their taxes, as ordinary people were expected to do. If oligarchs had become wealthy by skirting the law, then the orderly implementation of law would necessarily put some of them in jail.

Before the Russian government had begun to take action against the oligarchs, Ivan Ivanovich said that what he wanted from Putin's new government was that "laws will be followed from the bottom to the top, . . . that the law would be for all, for rich and poor, for the bosses and the simple people. That punishment would be inevitable after any kind of crime. Whoever is there, regardless of their social position. That's what I want, that laws

11. On this point, see also Richard Rose, Neil Munro, and William Mishler, "Resigned Acceptance of an Incomplete Democracy: Russia's Political Equilibrium," *Post-Soviet Affairs* 20, no. 3 (2004): 195–218; Shevtsova, in *Putin's Russia*, 259, cites poll results that show that 78 percent of the population of Russia desires a country that is convenient to live in and where the interests of people are the priority.

12. Michael McFaul, "Reengaging Russia: A New Agenda," *Current History* 103, 675 (October 2004): 307–13; Steven Lee Myers, "Old Kremlin, New Kremlin: It's Still a Big Secret," *New York Times*, 27 August 2003, A4; Therese Raphael, "Commentary: Business as Usual," *Wall Street Journal*, 31 October 2003.

would be observed here in Russia." Restraining the abuses of the oligarchs, thus, could be seen as a way to *strengthen* the rule of law and, with it, property rights of ordinary people.[13] Some observers have argued that the ultimate goal of some oligarchs was to diminish presidential power so that wealthy Russians could control political outcomes through large donations to parliamentary parties.[14] My respondents would not have seen that outcome as a more democratic option than strong presidential power.

Putin also took a number of steps that seemed to threaten the status of elections in Russia. Here again, my respondents' comments indicate that these actions might not be understood as hostile to democracy. For one thing, Putin sent to the Duma legislation to eliminate elections for regional governors. My respondents, especially those in Siberia, felt that greater control over governors might be a good thing. In their opinion, Yeltsin had given local officials too much leeway, allowing officials who were in his good graces to run their territories like little fiefdoms. As a result, some respondents feared that Russia was in danger of fracturing, much as the Soviet Union had, since some governors had begun to treat regional borders like borders of countries and had put into place laws that contradicted federal laws. Anya remarked, "I think that it is important to preserve the territorial integrity of Russia. Otherwise the country will splinter into little cities, as it was in the past, and nothing good will come of it." My respondents also expressed considerable skepticism about standards of democratic procedure in some regional elections. Faced with the choice between appointed governors or governors who had managed to buy their way into office or intimidated their political opponents by force, presidential appointment might not seem such a bad option.

Similarly, Putin's move to replace Russia's split electoral system with one based only on party-list voting probably would not seem to be a straightforward challenge to democracy to most of my respondents. Indeed, party-list voting is the standard in many stable democratic systems. The only reason party-list voting would be likely to have undemocratic consequences in

13. On this point, see also Peter Lavelle, "What Does Putin Want?" *Current History* 103, no. 675 (2004): 314–18. Lavelle argues that Putin intends to create a modern and diversified economy and ensure that Russia's energy resources are used for the good of the nation as a whole. This is likely to be good for ordinary Russians and possibly even democratic institutions, even if it is bad for Russia's oligarchs.

14. Centre TV, "Russian Think-Tank Says Big Business Is Plotting to Change State System," BBC Worldwide Monitoring, 7 June 2003.

Russia is that Edinaia Rossiia, the parliamentary party that supports Putin, would be likely to sweep the elections, at least at first. But understanding how electoral systems affect prospects for democracy in particular circumstances requires a more sophisticated analysis of the consequences of election rules than most ordinary citizens are likely to be able to conduct. Furthermore, voting in the single-member elections was more challenging for most of my informants than was making choices in the party-list part of the election. Most people had a reasonably good understanding of the differences between the parties—or at least thought they knew what the differences were and could make choices based on those opinions. But the candidates for the single-member districts often flew so completely under the radar that my respondents had no idea who they were. With so little information about candidates, citizens had no choice but to "vote with closed eyes," as Zinaida noted in Chapter 7. Consequently, having only party-list elections, again, would not seem to my respondents to be a big step away from democratic procedures.

The same is true about the consolidation of parties into larger electoral blocs and the decline of some opposition parties, notably those on the most liberal side of the spectrum. While my respondents had no great love for Edinaia Rossiia, they also had little regard for the smaller opposition parties. The issue here was not a lack of sympathy for shared goals. Dima thought that none of the opposition parties really wanted to hold power. Svetlana thought they were more interested in self-promotion than in the good of the country. The leaders of the liberal parties came in for particular criticism, more for what were seen as failings in the personalities of their leaders than for reasons of ideology. All this is not to say that my respondents would have actively supported Putin's efforts to deny media exposure to opposition parties, but it is not clear whether more exposure to other candidates would have affected their votes.

Putin is also sometimes accused of bringing back to the fore Russia's imperial aspirations, trying to pressure former Soviet republics to return to Russian domination, or being opposed to orienting Russia toward Europe.[15] Most of my respondents showed little interest in foreign policy,

15. Maria Lipman, "How Russia Is Not Ukraine: The Closing of Russian Civil Society," *Carnegie Endowment for International Peace Policy Outlook,* January 2005, http://www. CarnegieEndowment.org; Steven Lee Myers, "Putin Backs Ukrainian Leader, Dismissing Calls for New Runoff," *New York Times,* 3 December 2004, A1, A12; Erin E. Arvedlund, "Russian Talk on Ukraine Recalls Cold War," *New York Times,* 2 December 2004, A14.

but they were concerned that Russia had been weakened in the transition away from Communism. Consequently, they would be likely to support efforts to strengthen the country and return pride to the population.

Many respondents were unhappy with the reduced circumstances into which they felt Russia had fallen. In 1998, Grigorii said, "It used to be that when we watched television and our flag was raised, whether at a political debate or the Olympic games, then the sensation of the state, of its strength, of the authorities, was completely different, stronger than now. Now, I really don't know. Now it's hard to think about it. The state is sick, and it needs medicine." By 2003, Lena's assessment was not much better. She said, "Well, they don't talk about patriotism in general, because now there is corruption everywhere. What kind of patriotism can there be? Earlier there was. Yes, under Communism, that's how we were brought up. Those of us older than thirty or thirty-five, well twenty-eight, let's say, still have it. Patriotism—it is a shame for our motherland. That's all, yes? That our government became like it did." To the degree that Putin is seen as standing up for Russia's interests and dignity, then my respon-dents would likely think he was doing the right thing. It might be a while before Russians could assert that their country was the best country in the world, as the American respondents often affirmed, but at least Putin held out the hope that it could be better than it had become.

Nonetheless, my respondents showed very mixed assessments of the war in Chechnya. While many asserted that the Russian people had to defend themselves against terrorists, they were also reluctant to risk the lives of Russian soldiers to hold the country together by force. Sonya remarked that she hoped Russian territorial integrity could be preserved, "but only if it is possible without some kind of war. If it's a question of war to preserve territory, then we need to find a way to let them go peace-fully." Konstantin agreed: "The question of Chechnya shows that force doesn't work." My respondents mourned the end of the Soviet Union, but more from a sense of inconvenience than because of a loss of empire. Because of the collapse of the Soviet Union, families had been torn apart, and travel had become difficult. Many people knew ethnic Russians who felt pressured to leave their homes in parts of the former Soviet Union. Most of my respondents would have been happy enough to see the Soviet Union reconstituted, but they had no illusions that that day would ever come. Most also had a fairly expansive view of Russian nationalism: they felt that Russians were bound by culture and language more than by ethnic heritage or bloodlines.[16] Consequently, anyone who wanted to could become a Russian. This idea has got Russians into trouble in the past; indeed, most of my respondents had no idea why people in the former Soviet republics would not have welcomed the opportunity to become Russians. But it is not a sound basis for wars of domination, and if that is what Putin intends by his commitment to the strength of Russia, then my respondents are unlikely to follow along.

On the whole, my respondents did not favor a return to the past and did not see Putin leading them backward. About the Communists, Natalia said, "That train has left." Tatiana Mikhailovna called the Communists "poor little ones" and noted that they were more unassuming and modest than they had been when in power and consequently now caused little trouble. Certainly the Communist Party had its supporters. Many of my older respondents admitted that they had been Communists their whole lives; some still voted Communist if only out of nostalgia and melancholy over what had been lost,[17] mostly not with the confidence that the Communist Party, if in power, would make their lives any better. As Zoia Igorevna, a lifelong party member, remarked, "They also came to naught." For most of my respondents, a return to Communism was no longer a question of any interest. As far as they were concerned, Putin was taking them somewhere else. The destination might not be perfect, but it was surely different from what had existed in the past.

Hundreds of thousands of Ukrainians demonstrated against rigged elections in fall 2004. Reports are that they saw in opposition leader Viktor Yushchenko a cleaner and more competent leader who would lead the country out of endemic corruption and into the "civilized" world.[18] My Russian respondents may be wrong, but many of them are of the opinion that this is the leader they already have in Vladimir Putin. Putin's high approval ratings indicate his citizens' unwillingness to give up on this hope.

The Verdict on Culture

This book began as an effort to examine presumptions about Russian political culture, particularly the idea that today's Russians inherited a set

---

16. Similarly, see Fran Markowitz, *Coming of Age in Post-Soviet Russia* (Urbana: University of Illinois Press, 2000), 145–60.

17. This phrase is from Dima's comments.

18. Adrian Karatnycky, "Ukraine's Orange Revolution," *Foreign Affairs* 84, no. 2 (2005): 35–52.

of ideas and values from their own past that made Russia's citizens obstacles to the deepening of democracy. The verdict from the interviews is that inherited attitudes are *not* a major obstacle to building democracy in Russia. For one thing, the interviews provide little evidence of some of the traits often used to characterize Russian political culture: my respondents were not especially authoritarian, egalitarian, messianic, or utopian. They did not show a preference for extremes over moderation. They were not waiting for government to take care of them. Most appreciated the value of law as a means to regulate an imperfect society, and none craved the reinstitution of a totalitarian political order.[19]

It is true, though, that some other aspects of traditional Russian political culture still seem current today. In particular, my respondents are attracted to the ideal of social order, although they do not all mean the same thing when they talk about "order." In addition, my respondents were fairly cynical about government and about their own ability to influence their rulers. Most of them felt that the gap between ordinary people and those who led them was huge and, at least for now, insurmountable. For many, the only ray of hope was that Vladimir Putin seemed to have their long-run interests at heart, or at least he performed much better than any of his predecessors in this regard.

What I have tried to show in this book is that, even though many Russians respond to their government in ways characteristic of traditional Russian political culture, this is not necessarily because they inherited orientations that make it hard for them to trust either those who govern them or one another. The intensive interviews on which this book is based provide considerable evidence that present attitudes are reflections of present conditions. Russian citizens are cynical about government because their government has done little to respond to their needs. They are slow to engage in the sustained political activity that might raise the profile of their demands because they lack confidence that the payoff would be worth their effort. And besides, with the few opportunities provided by Russia's cutthroat capitalism, ordinary Russians must devote considerable attention to just getting by. Theirs is an unpredictable and challenging

---

19. For these traits of Russian political culture, see McDaniel, *The Agony of the Russian Idea*, 32–46; Frederic J. Fleron Jr. "Congruence Theory Applied: Democratization in Russia," in *Can Democracy Take Root in Post-Soviet Russia? Explorations in State-Society Relations*, ed. Harry Eckstein, Frederic J. Fleron Jr., Erik Hoffmann, and William Reisinger (New York: Rowman and Littlefield, 1998), 36; Vainshstein, "Totalitarian Public Consciousness," 256.

world, perhaps slowly becoming more orderly under the guidance of Vladimir Putin.

Particularly in terms of the ways in which they relate to government, though, it is also clear that Russians today carry some heavy baggage left over from the Soviet period. For all but the youngest of my respondents, their views of government were formed under Soviet power, and the basic substance of those views has changed little since the collapse of Communist rule. From their perspective, there has been little reason to change how they relate to government, since much of the time government continues to act like a hostile, alien force. But as long as citizens do not change, as long as they do not object to their government's compromises of democratic practice and tendency to ignore the needs of the population, they must bear a portion of the responsibility for the fate of democracy in Russia.

Given the context in which Russians form their attitudes about government, it is hardly surprising that many Russian citizens expect little from their government and feel powerless to change it, that they fail to endorse every particular of the new political and economic systems that have not yet greatly improved their lives. But it also seems certain that these people who managed to survive the Soviet system, its collapse, and the messy restructuring of their whole society could also adjust to democracy. If only the people who rule them choose to allow it.

Appendix A: Demographic Characteristics of the Russian Respondents

Assigned name	Year of interview	Support for democracy	Support for markets	Sense of disorder	Sex	Age in 2000	Area of residence	Education level[a]	Profession
Aleksandra Antonovna	1998	Moderate	High	Moderate	Female	Over 60	Moscow	Higher	Pensioner/professional
Aleksei	1998	Low	Low	High	Male	46–60	Moscow	Specialized secondary	Worker
Alla	1998	Moderate	Low	Moderate	Female	46–60	Siberia	Higher	Professional
Andrei Viktorovich	1998	High	Mixed	Moderate	Male	Over 60	Siberia	Higher	Pensioner/professional
Anna Pavlovna	1998	Mixed	Low	Moderate	Female	Over 60	Moscow oblast'	Less than secondary	Pensioner/worker
Anya	1998	Moderate	Mixed	Low	Female	31–45	European Russia	Specialized secondary	Skilled worker
Arkadii	1998	High	Low	Low	Male	46–60	Siberia	Higher	Professional
Boris Borisovich	1998	Mixed	High	Moderate	Male	Over 60	Moscow	Specialized secondary	Skilled worker

APPENDIXES

Assigned name	Year of interview	Support for democracy	Support for markets	Sense of disorder	Sex	Age in 2000	Area of residence	Education level[a]	Profession
Dima	2003	High	Mixed	Low	Male	30 or under	European Russia	Higher	Professional
Ekaterina	1998	Moderate	High	Low	Female	46–60	Moscow	Higher	Housewife
Elena	2000	Mixed	Low	High	Female	46–60	Siberia	Specialized secondary	Skilled worker
Evgenii	2000	Low	Low	Moderate	Male	31–45	Moscow	Specialized secondary	Unemployed
Galina Grigor'evna	2000	Moderate	Low	High	Female	Over 60	European Russia	Less than secondary	Pensioner/worker
Gennadii	2000	High	Low	Moderate	Male	31–45	European Russia	Higher	Professional
Grigorii	1998	Mixed	Mixed	Moderate	Male	31–45	Siberia	Higher	Private business
Inna	2000	Low	Low	High	Female	46–60	Moscow	Secondary	Worker
Iosif	1998	High	Low	High	Male	31–45	European Russia	Higher	Professional
Irina L'vovna	1998	Mixed	Low	Moderate	Female	Over 60	Moscow oblast'	Higher	Pensioner/professional
Iurii	1998	Moderate	High	Low	Male	46–60	Moscow	Higher	Professional
Ivan Ivanovich	2000	Mixed	Low	High	Male	Over 60	Siberia	Specialized secondary	Professional
Katya	1998	Mixed	Mixed	Low	Female	30 or under	European Russia	Secondary	Student

Assigned name	Year of interview	Support for democracy	Support for markets	Sense of disorder	Sex	Age in 2000	Area of residence	Education level[a]	Profession
Klara	2000	Mixed	Mixed	Low	Female	31–45	Moscow	Specialized secondary	Worker
Kollektiv (group interview)	2000	Mixed	Low	High	Female	46–60	Siberia	Higher	Professional
Kolya	2000	Moderate	High	Low	Male	30 or under	European Russia	Secondary	Worker
Konstantin	1998	High	Low	Moderate	Male	46–60	Moscow	Specialized secondary	Pensioner/worker
Lena	2003	Mixed	Mixed	High	Female	30 or under	Moscow oblast'	Specialized secondary	Worker
Lev	2003	Moderate	Low	Moderate	Male	46–60	Moscow oblast'	Secondary	Worker
Liuba	2003	Mixed	High	Low	Female	30 or under	European Russia	Specialized secondary	Worker
Liudmilla Vladimirovna	1998	High	High	Moderate	Female	Over 60	Moscow oblast'	Higher	Pensioner/worker
Marina Aleksandrovna	1998	High	High	Low	Female	Over 60	Moscow	Higher	Private business
Mikhail	1998	Moderate	Mixed	Low	Male	31–45	Moscow	Higher	Professional
Misha	2003	High	High	Low	Male	30 or under	European Russia	Specialized secondary	Worker
Nadezhda	1998	High	Mixed	Low	Female	31–45	European Russia	Higher	Professional

Assigned name	Year of interview	Support for democracy	Support for markets	Sense of disorder	Sex	Age in 2000	Area of residence	Education level[a]	Profession
Nadya	2003	Mixed	Low	Low	Female	30 or under	European Russia	Specialized secondary	Worker
Natalia	All three years	High	Mixed	Low	Female	46–60	Moscow	Higher	Professional
Nikolai	1998	Mixed	Mixed	Moderate	Male	31–45	Moscow	Specialized secondary	Skilled worker
Oleg	2000	High	High	Low	Male	46–60	European Russia	Secondary	Skilled worker
Olga Iur'evna	2000	Mixed	Low	Low	Female	Over 60	Moscow	Higher	Professional
Pavel	2003	Mixed	Mixed	Low	Male	46–60	European Russia	Specialized secondary	Worker
Pelageia	2003	Mixed	Low	High	Female	46–60	European Russia	Less than secondary	Pensioner/worker
Polina	1998 and 2000	Mixed	High	Moderate	Female	31–45	Moscow	Secondary	Worker
Raisa	2003	Moderate	High	Low	Female	46–60	Moscow oblast'	Higher	Professional
Raya	2000	Moderate	Low	Moderate	Female	30 or under	European Russia	Higher	Professional
Ruslan	1998	Mixed	Mixed	Low	Male	46–60	Moscow	Specialized secondary	Private business
Sergei	1998	Mixed	Mixed	Low	Male	46–60	Moscow oblast'	Specialized secondary	Unemployed/worker
Slava	1998	Moderate	High	Low	Male	30 or under	Moscow	Specialized secondary	Unemployed

Assigned name	Year of interview	Support for democracy	Support for markets	Sense of disorder	Sex	Age in 2000	Area of residence	Education level[a]	Profession
Sofiia	2003	Mixed	High	Moderate	Female	31–45	European Russia	Higher	Professional
Sonya	1998	Moderate	Mixed	Moderate	Female	30 or under	European Russia	Higher	Student
Svetlana	All three years	Moderate	High	Moderate	Female	31–45	Moscow	Higher	Professional
Tatiana Mikhailovna	1998	Low	Mixed	Moderate	Female	Over 60	Moscow	Higher	Pensioner/professional
Tolya	2003	Standard	Mixed	Moderate	Male	30 or under	European Russia	Higher	Professional
Valentina	1998	Mixed	Mixed	High	Female	31–45	Siberia	Higher	Professional
Valya	2003	Low	Low	Moderate	Female	30 or under	Moscow Oblast'	Secondary	Worker
Vasya	2003	Mixed	High	Moderate	Male	30 or under	European Russia	Higher	Professional
Vilen Nikolaevich	2000	Mixed	Mixed	Moderate	Male	Over 60	European Russia	Secondary	Pensioner/worker
Vitya	2003	Moderate	High	Low	Male	30 or under	Moscow oblast'	Higher	Professional
Vladimir Il'ich	1998	Low	Low	High	Male	Over 60	Near Russia	Specialized secondary	Pensioner/worker
Yegor Yegorovich	2003	Mixed	Low	High	Male	Over 60	European Russia	Less than secondary	Worker
Zinaida	2000	Mixed	Low	High	Female	31–45	European Russia	Less than secondary	Worker

Assigned name	Year of interview	Support for democracy	Support for markets	Sense of disorder	Sex	Age in 2000	Area of residence	Education level[a]	Profession
Zoia Igorevna	2003	Mixed	Mixed	High	Female	Over 60	Moscow oblast'	Secondary	Worker

[a] Less than secondary: The respondent completed fewer than eleven grades.
Secondary: The respondent completed all eleven grades.
Specialized secondary: The respondent attended some variety of technical school, PTU (*professional'no-tekhnicheskoe uchilishche* [trade school]), or *tekhnikum* (school for skilled technical training).
Higher: The respondent completed study at a university or academic institute.

Appendix B: Demographic Characteristics of the American Respondents

Assigned name	Year of interview	Sex	Age in 2000	Education	Profession	Party affiliation
Adam	1999	Male	30 or under	Some college	Student	Democrat
Betty	2002	Female	Over 60	Higher	Retired professional	Republican
Bill	2001	Male	30 or under	Some college	Student	Republican
Caroline	1998	Female	46–60	Higher	Professional	None
Chris	1998	Male	30 or under	Higher	Professional	Independent
Daniel	2001	Male	30 or under	Secondary	Worker	Democrat
Emily	1998	Female	Over 60	Secondary	Retired	Democrat
Ernest	2002	Male	46–60	Higher	Professional	Democrat
Fred	2001	Male	46–60	Some college	Own business	Independent
Grace	1999	Female	46–60	Secondary	Homemaker	Republican
Harriet	2001	Female	Over 60	Less than secondary	Retired worker	Democrat
Jacob	1998	Male	Over 60	Less than secondary	Retired	Independent
Jane	1999	Female	31–45	Some college	Professional	Democrat
Jean	1998	Female	31–45	Secondary	Own business	None
Kate	1998	Female	30 or under	Some college	Student	Democrat
Leo	2001	Male	Over 60	Higher	Retired professional	Republican
Rick	2001	Male	30 or under	Higher	Professional	Democrat
Sam	2001	Male	46–60	Secondary	Professional	Republican
Ted	1998	Male	30 or under	Some college	Student	Republican
Trish	1998	Female	30 or under	Some college	Student	Republican
Victoria	1998	Female	31–45	Higher	Professional	Neutral

Appendix C: Measures Used in the Analysis

In order to analyze the answers that the respondents provided, it was often helpful to divide the respondents into groups according to some set of shared orientations. This was accomplished by creating measures based on respondents' answers to certain questions. For the purposes of creating measures, I numerically coded each respondent's answers to relevant questions. As described below, I either added or averaged these numbers to produce a metric by which to categorize respondents. Where possible, similar measures were used for both the Russians and the Americans. When a measure analogous to the one developed for use with the Russian respondents did not seem to meaningfully categorize the American respondents, Americans were not divided into groups. This appendix describes the measures used to divide respondents into groups.

Support for Democracy

This measure categorizes the Russian respondents according to their degree of support for democratic values. It was first used in Chapter 5, and it was used in most of the subsequent chapters as well. The measure was based on five questions. I relied particularly on those parts of the answers that expressed general values rather than assessment of particular existing institutions. For the purposes of creating the measure, answers were coded as shown below:

"In general, do you think there should be an institution like the State Duma, or is such an institution unnecessary?"

    0—The respondent expressed the idea that representative institutions have no value even in principle, not just in Russia.

    1—The respondent expressed support with qualifications. For instance, perhaps he or she thought a representative body had some value but not in all conditions or contexts. Or the respondent could not articulate why representative bodies were worth having.

    2—Answers showed an explicit understanding of the role representative institutions play in a democratic system.

"How important is it to vote in presidential elections, in State Duma elections, and in local elections?"

    0—The respondent indicated that voting was worthless.

    1—The respondent expressed some ambivalence, perhaps noting that it is worthwhile to vote in some elections but not others or commenting that voting had some but not a great deal of importance.

2—The respondent thought it was important to vote in all elections.

"Should the people in power care about what people like you think?"

0—The respondent thought the people in power should not care about the opinions of ordinary people.

1—The respondent thought people in government should care about the opinions of ordinary people.

"What in your opinion does the word *democracy* mean?"

0—The definition of democracy offered by the respondent focused on a negative aspect, such as growing disorder or criminality.

1—The definition focused on a single, unelaborated aspect of democracy, such as *freedom.*

2—The definition was nuanced or included multiple aspects of democracy.

"Do you think that there is too much freedom today?"

0—The respondent indicated that some restriction on the amount of freedom would be a good thing.

1—The respondent expressed no dissatisfaction with the level of freedom available.

2—The respondent argued that there was no such thing as too much freedom or noted that there was insufficient freedom in Russia.

Responses were added across five questions. There were no missing responses. Possible scores varied between 0 and 9. Respondents with scores 4 or below were categorized as having *low* support for democracy. Scores of 5 or 6 indicated *mixed* support. Those with scores of 7 were labeled *moderate* supporters of democracy. Scores of 8 or 9 earned the *high support* designation. In much of the analysis, the *moderate* and *high support* groups are combined.

The American respondents were not divided into groups according to support for democracy, because there was too little variation in their answers to produce meaningful groups.

Support for Market Reform

This measure was used in Chapter 5 to divide the Russian respondents according to their degree of support for market reform. The measure is based on answers to the question "How do you feel about the economic changes that have occurred in Russia in the past years?" The 2003 version of the question asked about the "past fifteen years." Responses were coded on a five-point scale:

     1—Comments were uniformly negative. There was nothing about market reforms that the respondent supported.

     2—Comments were mixed, but more negative than positive.

     3—Comments were evenly mixed. The respondent could see positive and negative aspects of market reforms.

     4—Comments were mixed, but more positive than negative.

     5—Comments were uniformly positive.

For Table 5.1, the five-point measure was used. For Table 5.2, the comments were coded as follows:

     1—Comments were overwhelmingly, but not exclusively, negative.

     2—Comments were mixed.

     3—Comments were overwhelmingly, but not exclusively, positive.

The American respondents were not divided into groups according to their support for market reform, because the United States has not experienced a recent move toward markets, as has Russia.

Sense of Social Disorder

This measure appears in Chapters 6 and 8. The measure is based on multiple questions, collapsed into three items. For the Russians, they are coded as shown below:

"Tell me, please, how much are you satisfied with the activities of the police? Why?"

     0—The respondent expressed satisfaction with the police. Some remarked that the police were doing as well as could be expected under the circumstances.

     1—The respondent praised some aspects of the work of the police and criticized others.

     2—The respondent mentioned fear of crime, corruption, or the incompetence of the police.

"How did you survive economic changes?" "To what degree are you satisfied with your material circumstances?" Answers were coded as follows:

     0—The respondent expressed little worry about economic conditions. He or she thought the economy was improving and that conditions were fine.

1—The respondent considered that there were economic problems but that people would manage.

2—The respondent thought that the economy was falling apart and wondered how people would survive.

In coding answers to these two questions, I used the parts of the answers that focused on the economic situation in the country as a whole, not reflections on personal circumstances. Personal assessments did not always seem related to actual conditions. Indeed, some of the better-off respondents were the most dissatisfied with their present economic situation.

The measure also included answers to questions about government, coded as shown below:

"To what degree are you satisfied with the activities of the president [either Yeltsin or Putin]?" "To what degree are you satisfied with the activities of the State Duma?"

0—The respondent did not mention corruption, links to criminals, or flagrant incompetence.

1—There was some mention of corruption, criminality, or incompetence, but not in the form of condemnation of the whole government.

2—The respondent made strong negative statements about corruption, criminality, internal conflict, or the flagrant pursuit of self-interest by government officials.

Answers about the police, economic situation, and satisfaction with government were summed to produce a measure that ranged from 0 to 6. Respondents with scores 5 or 6 were categorized as having a *strong* sense of social disorder. Scores of 3 or 4 indicated a *moderate* sense of disorder. People with scores 2 and below were labeled as having a *minimal* sense of disorder.

A comparable measure was developed for the American sample, with two minor differences. Americans were asked about the satisfaction with economic conditions, but not how they survived economic reform. In the third part, Americans were asked about Clinton or Bush and the Congress. For the Americans, 0 or 1 indicated minimal concerns for social disorder and 2 or 3 indicated moderate concern. No one in the American sample had a score above 3.

Political Sophistication

This measure appears in Chapter 7. It was based on four items, coded as follows:

Respondent's educational attainment

  1—less than secondary

  2—secondary

  3—higher

An overall assessment of the quality of answers offered throughout the interview.

  1—Answers were very short, monosyllabic, or close to it, with many "don't know" responses.

  2—A mix of answers characterized the interview. Some were monosyllabic, while others were more thoughtful. Respondents sometimes gave longer answers but often veered off subject. Phrasing relied heavily on clichés.

  3—The answers were all thoughtful, with some detail offered.

An overall assessment of the political understanding expressed throughout the interview, especially in discussion of institutions and parties.

  1—The respondent showed limited understanding of issues and few concerns beyond his or her immediate personal situation. (For instance, the respondent might think that the Duma was not doing its job because he or she had lost a job.)

  2—The respondent was able to talk about political personalities, but not about policies or processes.

  3—The respondent could speak at length and with subtlety about a variety of political issues. He or she had a good understanding of what institutions existed and what they did, including at the local level. He or she had accurate knowledge about the orientation of political parties and could discuss at least some government policies.

In the Russian interviews, respondents were asked three forced-choice questions. They were asked whether they would sacrifice individual freedom in the fight against corruption, whether it was better to live in a society of strict order or give people so much freedom that they might tear society apart, and whether things in Russia were heading in the right or the wrong direction. Here, respondents were coded on whether they were able to "think outside the box" and articulate a creative response to replace two unpalatable—or inaccurate—choices. Responses were coded as follows:

  0—No additional answers offered.

  1—At least one refusal to accept the forced choice, with an alternative formulation suggested.

The items were summed, with a resulting measure that ranged from 3 to 10. Respondents who scored 3 to 5 were considered to show *low* political sophistication. Scores of 6 to 8 were in the *moderate* category; and scores of 9 or 10 ranked *high*.

A similar measure was developed for the American respondents, but there were some modifications. The forced-choice questions were not asked of the American respondents. Consequently, the American political-sophistication measure was based only on education, answer quality, and political understanding. Education was coded in four categories (1—less than secondary; 2—secondary; 3—some college; 4—higher). The measure ranged from 3 to 10, and the same cutoffs were used as for the Russians.

Incumbent Support

This measure appears in Chapter 8 and divides the Russian respondents according to their support for government incumbents. It is based on three questions: "Do you consider that Putin [the State Duma, the mayor of the respondent's city] acts in the interests of the majority of the citizens of Russia or in the interests of a small group of people?" Each question was coded as follows:

> 1—The respondent felt that the official did not serve the interests of the majority.
>
> 2—The respondent expressed considerable ambivalence about whether the interests of the majority were served or not.
>
> 3—The respondent believed that the official largely did serve the interests of the majority.

The average across the three questions was computed. If the respondent answered only one or two of the questions, those answers were used to compute the average. Averages below 2 were labeled *low support*. Answers above 2 were labeled *high support*. A 2 average indicated *moderate support*.

Support varied by institution. As to whether the president acted for the benefit of the majority, 35 percent of the respondents said that he did not, 30 percent that he only partly acted in the benefit of the majority. The remaining 35 percent thought the president did act to advance the majority's interests. For the State Duma, 57 percent believed that Duma deputies were unconcerned about the needs of the majority; 32 percent thought they were somewhat concerned; only 10 percent felt that Duma deputies acted in the interest of the majority. (One person did not answer.) Mayors enjoyed the greatest popular confidence. Eighteen percent of the respondents thought mayors did not act for the good of the majority of the city; 22 thought this was somewhat the case; 50 percent were certain that mayors acted to advance the majority's interests. (Ten percent did not answer.)

A similar measure was developed for the American respondents, except that Americans were asked about the president, Congress, and their local mayor. The same coding and cutoffs were used.

Akheizer, Aleksandr S."Dezorganizatsiia kak kategoriia obshchestven-noi nauki" [Disorganization as a Category of Social Science]. *Obshchestvennye nauki i sovremennost'*, no. 6 (1995): 42–52.

———. "Krizis liberalizma v sovremennoi Rossii." *Liberalizm i demokratiia: Opyt Zapada i perspektivy Rossii.* Moscow: International Fund for Socio-economic and Political Research (Gorbachev Fund), 1992.

Aleksandrov, Aleksei. "Korruptsiia trebuet zhertv." *Argumenty i Fakty,* no. 9 (February 1998): 2.

Alexander, James. *Political Culture in Post-Communist Russia: Formlessness and Recreation in a Traumatic Transition.* New York: St. Martin's Press, 2000.

Alexander, James, Andrei A. Degtyarev, and Vladimir Gel'man. "Democratization Challenged: The Role of Regional Elites." In *Fragmented Space in the Russian Federation,* edited by Blair A. Ruble, Jodi Koehn, and Nancy E. Popson. Washington, DC: Woodrow Wilson Center Press, 2001.

Alford, John R., and John R. Hibbing. "The Origins of Politics: An Evolutionary Theory of Political Behavior." *Perspectives on Politics* 2, no. 4 (2004): 707–23.

Allina-Pisano, Jessica. "Reorganization and Its Discontents: A Case Study in Voronezh Oblast." In *Rural Reform in Post-Soviet Russia,* edited by David J. O'Brien and Stephen K. Wegren. Washington, DC: Woodrow Wilson Center Press, 2002.

Almond, Gabriel A. *A Discipline Divided: Schools and Sects in Political Science.* Newbury Park, CA: Sage, 1990.

Almond, Gabriel A., and Sidney Verba. *The Civic Culture: Political Attitudes and Democracy in Five Nations.* Newbury Park, CA: Sage, 1989.

Alvarez, R. Michael, and John Brehm. *Hard Choices, Easy Answers: Values, Information, and American Public Opinion.* Princeton: Princeton University Press, 2002.

Alwin, Duane F., Galin Gornev, and Ludmila Khakhulina, with the collaboration of Vojko Antončič, Wil Arts, Bogdan Cichomski, and Piet Hermkens."Comparative Referential Structures, System Legitimacy, and Justice Sentiments: An International Comparison." In *Social Justice and Political Change: Public Opinion in Capitalist and Post-Communist States,* edited by James R. Kluegel, David S. Mason, and Bernd Wegener. Hawthorne, NY: Aldine De Gruyter, 1995.

Andreenkov, V. G., and Aleksandr Zhavoronkov. *Katalog peremennykh bazy sotsiologicheskikh dannykh po problemam izucheniia ideologicheskogo protsessa.* 4 vols. Moscow: Institut Sotsiologicheskikh Issledovaniia AN SSSR, 1988.

Andrews, Josephine. *When Majorities Fail: The Russian Parliament, 1990–1993.* New York: Cambridge University Press, 2002.

Aristotle. *The Politics*. Edited and translated by Ernest Barker. New York: Oxford University Press, 1958.

Arvedlund, Erin E. "Russian Talk on Ukraine Recalls Cold War." *New York Times*, 2 December 2004, A14.

Ashin, Gennadii. "Smena Elit." *Obshchestvennye nauki i sovremennost'*, no. 1 (1995): 40–50.

Ashwin, Sarah. "Endless Patience: Explaining Soviet and Post-Soviet Social Stability." *Communist and Post-Communist Studies* 31, no. 2 (1998): 187–98.

———. "There's No Joy Any More': The Experience of Reform in a Kuzbass Mining Settlement." *Europe-Asia Studies* 47 (December 1995): 1367–81.

Bahry, Donna L. "Comrades into Citizens? Russian Political Culture and Public Support for the Transition." *Slavic Review* 58 (Winter 1999): 841–53.

———. "Society Transformed? Rethinking the Social Roots of Perestroika." *Slavic Review* 52 (Fall 1993): 512–54.

Bahry, Donna L., Cynthia Boaz, and Stacy Burnett Gordon. "Tolerance, Transition, and Support for Civil Liberties in Russia." *Comparative Political Studies* 30 (August 1997): 484–510.

Bahry, Donna L., and Brian D. Silver. "Intimidation and the Symbolic Uses of Terror in the USSR." *American Political Science Review* 81 (1987): 1061–98.

Bahry, Donna L., and Lucan Way. "Citizen Activism in the Russian Transition." *Post-Soviet Affairs* 10, no. 4 (1994): 330–66.

Barber, Benjamin R. *Strong Democracy: Participatory Politics for a New Age*. Berkeley and Los Angeles: University of California Press, 1984.

Basina, E. Z. "Individualizm i kollektivizm v postsovetskom obshchestve: Differentsiatsiia sotsial'nykh ustanovok." In *Chelovek v perekhodnom obshchestve: Sotsiologicheskie i sotsial'no-psikhologicheskie issledovaniia*, edited by G. G. Diligenskii. Moscow: Institute of World Economics and International Relations, 1998.

Belin, Laura. "Lebed's Presidential Campaign: His Most Enduring Legacy." *RFE/RL Russian Political Weekly* 2, no. 14 (2002), www.rferl.org.

Belin, Laura, and Robert W. Orttung. *The Russian Parliamentary Elections of 1995: The Battle for the Duma*. Armonk, NY: M. E. Sharpe, 1997.

Belson, William. *Validity in Survey Research*. Aldershot, England: Gower, 1986.

Bennett, Stephen E. "Know-Nothings' Revisited: The Meaning of Political Ignorance Today." *Social Science Quarterly* 69 (1988): 476–90.

Berdiaev, Nikolai. *The Russian Idea*. Hudson, NY: Lindisfarne Press, 1992.

Berdiaev, Nikolai, Sergei Bulgakov, Mikhail Gershenzon, A. S. Izgoev, Bogdan Kistiakovskii, Petr Struve, and Semen Frank. *Vekhi* [Landmarks]. Translated and edited by Marshall S. Shatz and Judith E. Zimmerman. Armonk, NY: M. E. Sharpe, 1994.

Berezovskii, V. N., and N. I. Krotov. *Neformal'naia Rossiia: O neformal'nykh politizirovannykh dvizheniia i gruppakh v rfsfr (opyt spravochnika)*. Moscow: Molodaia Gvardiia, 1990.

Bikmetov, Rustam Muratovich. "Izbiratel'nyi protsess, vlast' i oppozitsiia v Ul'ianovskoi oblasti." *Polis: Politicheskie Issledovaniia*, no. 3 (1999): 7119–30.

Blee, Kathleen M., and Verta Taylor. "Semi-structured Interviewing in Social Movement Research." In *Methods of Social Movement Research*, edited by Bert Klandermans and Suzanne Staggenborg. Social Movement, Protest, and Contention, vol. 16. Minneapolis: University of Minnesota Press, 2002.

Boeva, Irina, and Viacheslav Shironin. "Russians Between State and Market: The Generations Compared." *Studies in Public Policy*, no. 205. Glasgow: University of Strathclyde, Centre for the Study of Public Policy, 1992.

Bogomolova, Tat'iana Iu., and Vera S. Tapilina. "Ekonomicheskaia stratifikatsiia naseleniia Rossii v 90-e gody." *Sotsiologicheskie issledovaniia*, no. 6 (2001): 32–43.

———. "Mobil'nost' naseleniia po material'nomy polozheniiu: Sub"ektivnyi aspekt." *Sotsiologicheskie issledovaniia*, no. 12 (1998): 28–37.

Borev, Iurii. *Istoriia gosudarstva sovetskogo: V predaniiakh i anekdotakh.* Moscow: RITTOL, 1995.

Bourdieu, Pierre. "The Forms of Capital." In *Handbook of Theory and Research for the Sociology of Education*, edited by John G. Richardson. New York: Greenwood Press, 1986.

Bova, Russell. "Democracy and Liberty: The Cultural Connection." In *The Global Divergence of Democracies*, edited by Larry Diamond and Marc F. Plattner. Baltimore: Johns Hopkins University Press, 2001.

———. "Political Culture, Authority Patterns, and the Architecture of the New Russian Democracy." In *Can Democracy Take Root in Post-Soviet Russia? Explorations in State-Society Relations*, edited by Harry Eckstein, Frederic J. Fleron Jr., Erik Hoffmann, and William Reisinger. New York: Rowman and Littlefield, 1998.

Brader, Ted, and Joshua A. Tucker. "The Emergence of Mass Partisanship in Russia, 1993–1996." *American Journal of Political Science* 45 (January 2001): 69–83.

Brady, Rose. *Kapitalizm: Russia's Struggle to Free Its Economy.* New Haven: Yale University Press, 1999.

Brehm, John, and Wendy Rahn. "Individual-Level Evidence for the Causes and Consequences of Social Capital." *American Journal of Political Science* 4 (July 1997): 999–1023.

Brinton, Crane. *The Anatomy of Revolution.* Revised and expanded edition. New York: Vintage, 1965.

Brown, Archie. "From Democratization to 'Guided Democracy.'" *Journal of Democracy* 12, no. 4 (2001): 35–41.

———. "Ideology and Political Culture." In *Politics, Society, and Nationality Inside Gorbachev's Russia*, edited by Seweryn Bialer. Boulder, CO: Westview Press, 1989.

Brym, Robert J. "Re-evaluating Mass Support for Political and Economic Change in Russia." *Europe-Asia Studies* 48 (July 1996): 751–66.

Brzezinski, Zbigniew K. "Soviet Politics: From the Future to the Past?" In *The Soviet Polity in the Modern Era*, edited by Erik P. Hoffmann and Robbin Laird. New York: Aldine, 1984.

Bunce, Valerie. *Subversive Institutions: The Design and Destruction of Socialism and the State.* New York: Cambridge University Press, 1999.

Burawoy, Michael, and Katherine Verdery. Introduction to *Uncertain Transition: Ethnographies of Change in the Postsocialist World*, edited by Michael Burawoy and Katherine Verdery. New York: Rowman and Littlefield, 1999.

Burlatsky, Feodor. "Democratization Is a Long March." In *Voices of Glasnost: Interview with Gorbachev's Reformers,* edited by Stephen F. Cohen and Katrina vanden Heuvel. New York: W. W. Norton, 1989.

Byzov, Leontii Georgievich. "Pervye kontury 'postperekhodnoi epokhi.'" *Sotsiologicheskie issledovaniia,* no. 4 (2001): 3–15.

Canache, Damarys, Jeffrey J. Mondak, and Mitchell A. Seligson. "Meaning and Measurement in Cross-National Research on Satisfaction with Democracy." *Public Opinion Quarterly* 65, no. 4 (2001): 506–28.

Carnaghan, Ellen. "Alienation, Apathy, or Ambivalence? 'Don't Knows' and Democracy in Russia." *Slavic Review* 55, no. 2 (1996): 325–63.

———. "A Revolution in Mind: Russian Political Attitudes and the Origins of Democratization under Gorbachev." PhD diss., New York University, 1992.

———. "Thinking About Democracy: Interviews with Russian Citizens." *Slavic Review* 60, no. 2 (2001): 336–66.

Centre TV. "Russian Think-Tank Says Big Business Is Plotting to Change State System." BBC Worldwide Monitoring, 7 June 2003.

Citrin, Jack. "Comment: The Political Relevance of Trust in Government." *American Political Science Review* 68 (1974): 973–88.

Citrin, Jack, and Donald Green. "Presidential Leadership and Trust in Government." *British Journal of Political Science* 16 (1986): 431–53.

Citrin, Jack, and Samatha Luks. "Political Trust Revisited: Déjà Vu All Over Again?" In *What Is It About Government That Americans Dislike?* edited by John R. Hibbing and Elizabeth Theiss-Morse. New York: Cambridge University Press, 2001.

Clark, Terry D., and Ernest Goss, and Larisa B. Kosova. "Economic Well-Being and Popular Support for Market Reform in Russia." *Economic Development and Cultural Change* 51, no. 3 (2003): 753–68.

Clem, Ralph S., and Peter R. Craumer. "A Rayon-Level Analysis of the Russian Election and Constitutional Plebiscite of December 1993." *Post-Soviet Geography* 36 (October 1995): 459–75.

———. "The Regional Dimension." In *The Russian Parliamentary Elections of 1995: The Battle for the Duma,* edited by Laura Belin and Robert W. Orttung. Armonk, NY: M. E. Sharpe, 1997.

———. "Regional Patterns of Voter Turnout in Russian Elections, 1993–1996." In *Elections and Voters in Post-Communist Russia,* edited by Matthew Wyman, Stephen White, and Sarah Oates. Northampton, MA: Edward Elgar, 1998.

———. "Urban and Rural Effects on Party Preference in Russia: New Evidence from the Recent Duma Election." *Post-Soviet Geography and Economics* 43, no. 1 (2002): 1–12.

Coleman, James S. "Social Capital and the Creation of Human Capital." *American Journal of Sociology,* supplement ("Organizations and Institutions: Sociological and Economic Approaches to the Analysis of Social Structure"), 94 (1988): S95–S120.

Colton, Timothy J. "Determinants of the Party Vote." In *Growing Pains: Russian Democracy and the Election of 1993,* edited by Timothy J. Colton and Jerry F. Hough. Washington, DC: Brookings Institution, 1998.

———. "Economics and Voting in Russia." *Post-Soviet Affairs* 12, no. 4 (1996): 289–317.

————. *Moscow: Governing the Socialist Metropolis.* Cambridge, MA: Belknap Press of Harvard University Press, 1995.

————. *Transitional Citizens: Voters and What Influences Them in the New Russia.* Cambridge, MA: Harvard University Press, 2000.

Colton, Timothy J., and Jerry F. Hough, eds. *Growing Pains: Russian Democracy and the Election of 1993.* Washington, DC: Brookings Institution, 1998.

Colton, Timothy J., and Michael McFaul. *Popular Choice and Managed Democracy: The Russian Elections, 1999 and 2000.* Washington, DC: Brookings Institution, 2003.

————. "Are Russians Undemocratic?" Carnegie Endowment Working Papers, no. 20 (June). Washington, DC: Carnegie Endowment for International Peace, 2001.

Converse, Jean M. "Predicting No Opinion in the Polls." *Public Opinion Quarterly* 40 (1976): 515–30.

Converse, Jean M., and Stanley Presser. *Survey Questions: Handcrafting the Standardized Questionnaire.* Newbury Park, CA: Sage, 1986.

Converse, Philip E. "The Nature of Belief Systems in Mass Publics." In *Ideology and Discontent,* edited by David E. Apter. New York: Free Press, 1964.

Crozier, Michael J., Samuel P. Huntington, and Joji Watanuki. *The Crisis of Democracy: Report on the Governability of Democracies to the Trilateral Commission.* New York: New York University Press, 1975.

Dahl, Robert A. *Democracy and Its Critics.* New Haven: Yale University Press, 1989.

————. *Polyarchy: Participation and Opposition.* New Haven: Yale University Press, 1971.

————. *A Preface to Democratic Theory.* Chicago: University of Chicago Press, 1956.

————. *Who Governs? Democracy and Power in an American City.* New Haven: Yale University Press, 1961.

Denisovskii, G. M., and Polina M. Kozyreva. *Politicheskaia tolerantnost' v reformiruemom Rossiiskom obshchestve vtoroi poloviny 90-kh godov.* Moscow: Institut Sotsiologii Rossiiskoi Akademii Nauk, Tsentr Obshchechelovecheskikh Tsennostei, 2002.

Di Palma, Guiseppe. *To Craft Democracies: An Essay on Democratic Transitions.* Berkeley and Los Angeles: University of California Press, 1990.

Dryzek, John S., and Leslie Holmes. *Post-Communist Democratization: Political Discourses Across Thirteen Countries.* New York: Cambridge University Press, 2002.

Dubin, Boris. "Model'nye instituty i simvolicheskii poriadok: Elementarnye formy sotsial'nosti v sovremennom rossiiskom obshchestve." *Monitoring obshchestvennoe mneniia: Informatsiia analiz,* no. 1, issue 57 (2002): 14–19.

————. "Zapad, granitsa, osobyi put': Simvolika 'drugogo' v politicheskoi mifologii sovremennoi Rossii." *Monitoring obshchestvennoe mneniia: Informatsiia analiz,* no. 6, issue 50 (2000): 25–34.

Duch, Raymond M. "Economic Chaos and the Fragility of Democratic Transition in Former Communist Regimes." *Journal of Politics* 57 (February 1995): 121–58.

————. "Tolerating Economic Reform: Popular Support for Transition to a Free Market in the Former Soviet Union." *American Political Science Review* 87 (September 1993): 590–608.

Dugin, Aleksandr G. *Russkaia Veshch': Ocherki natsional'noi filosofii.* 2 vols. Moscow: Arktogeia, 2001.

Dunn, Elizabeth. "Slick Salesmen and Simple People: Negotiated Capitalism in a Privatized Polish Firm." In *Uncertain Transition: Ethnographies of Change in the Postsocialist World,* edited by Michael Burawoy and Katherine Verdery. New York: Rowman and Littlefield, 1999.

Easton, David. "A Re-assessment of the Concept of Political Support." *British Journal of Political Science* 5 (1975): 435–57.

———. *A Systems Analysis of Political Life.* New York: John Wiley and Sons, 1965.

Eckstein, Harry. "A Culturalist Theory of Political Change." *American Political Science Review* 82 (September 1988): 789–804.

Eckstein, Harry, Frederic J. Fleron Jr., Erik Hoffmann, and William Reisinger, eds. *Can Democracy Take Root in Post-Soviet Russia? Explorations in State-Society Relations.* New York: Rowman and Littlefield, 1998.

Eckstein, Susan. "The Impact of Revolution on Social Welfare in Latin America." *Theory and Society* 11 (1982): 43–49.

Eisenstadt, Shmuel Noah. *Revolution and the Transformation of Societies: A Comparative Study of Civilizations.* New York: Free Press, 1978.

Elkins, David J. *Manipulation and Consent: How Voters and Leaders Manage Complexity.* Vancouver: University of British Columbia Press, 1993.

Elster, Jon, Claus Offe, and Ulrich K. Preuss. *Institutional Design in Post-Communist Societies: Rebuilding the Ship at Sea.* New York: Cambridge University Press, 1998.

Faibisovich, Semen. *Russkie novye i nenovye: Esse o glavnom.* Moscow: Novoe Literaturnoe Obozrenie, 1999.

Farhi, Farideh. *States and Urban-Based Revolutions: Iran and Nicaragua.* Chicago: University of Illinois Press, 1990.

Fazullina, Guzel. "Ulyanovsk Hovers on the Brink of Change." *Moscow News,* no. 39 (9–15 October 1996), 3.

Finifter, Ada, and Ellen Mickiewicz. "Redefining the Political System of the USSR: Mass Support for Political Change." *American Political Science Review* 186 (December 1992): 857–74.

Fish, M. Steven. *Democracy from Scratch: Opposition and Regime in the New Russian Revolution.* Princeton: Princeton University Press, 1995.

———. "The Dynamics of Democratic Erosion." In *Postcommunism and the Theory of Democracy,* edited by Richard D. Anderson Jr., M. Steven Fish, Stephen E. Hanson, and Philip G. Roeder. Princeton: Princeton University Press, 2001.

Fitzpatrick, Sheila. *Everyday Stalinism: Ordinary Life in Extraordinary Times; Soviet Russia in the 1930s.* New York: Oxford University Press, 1999.

———. *Stalin's Peasants: Resistance and Survival in the Russian Village After Collectivization.* New York: Oxford University Press, 1994.

Fleron, Frederic J., Jr. "Congruence Theory Applied: Democratization in Russia." In *Can Democracy Take Root in Post-Soviet Russia? Explorations in State-Society Relations,* edited by Harry Eckstein, Frederic J. Fleron Jr., Erik Hoffmann, and William Reisinger. New York: Rowman and Littlefield, 1998.

———. "Post-Soviet Political Culture in Russia: An Assessment of Recent Empirical Investigations." *Europe-Asia Studies* 48 (March 1996): 225–60.

Fleron, Frederic J., Jr., and Richard Ahl. "Does the Public Matter for Democratization in Russia? What We Have Learned from 'Third Wave' Transitions and

Public Opinion Surveys." In *Can Democracy Take Root in Post-Soviet Russia? Explorations in State-Society Relations*, edited by Harry Eckstein, Frederic J. Fleron Jr., Erik Hoffmann, and William Reisinger. New York: Rowman and Littlefield, 1998.

Foran, John. "Discourse and Social Forces: The Role of Culture and Cultural Studies in Understanding Revolutions." In *Theorizing Revolutions*, edited by John Foran. New York: Routledge, 1997.

Foran, John, and Jeff Goodwin. "Revolutionary Outcomes in Iran and Nicaragua: Coalition Fragmentation, War, and the Limits of Social Transformation." *Theory and Society* 22 (April 1993): 209–47.

Francis, Joe D., and Lawrence Busch. "What We Know About 'I Don't Knows.'" *Public Opinion Quarterly* 39 (1975): 207–18.

Fuchs, Dieter, and Hans-Dieter Klingemann. "Citizens and the State: A Changing Relationship?" In *Citizens and the State*, edited by Hans-Dieter Klingemann and Dieter Fuchs. Beliefs in Government, vol. 1. New York: Oxford University Press, 1995.

Fukuyama, Francis. "The End of History?" *National Interest* 16 (1989): 3–18.

———. "The Primacy of Culture." In *The Global Resurgence of Democracy*, edited by Larry Diamond and Marc F. Plattner. Baltimore: Johns Hopkins University Press, 1996.

———. *Trust: The Social Virtues and the Creation of Prosperity.* New York: Free Press, 1995.

Galston, William A. "Political Knowledge, Political Engagement, and Civic Education." *Annual Review of Political Science* 4 (2001): 217–34.

Gamson, William A. *Power and Discontent.* Homewood, IL: Dorsey Press, 1968.

Gel'man, Vladimir, Sergei Ryzhenko, Michael Brie, with Vladimir Avdonin, Boris Ovchinnikov, and Igor' Semenov. *Making and Breaking Democratic Transitions: The Comparative Politics of Russia's Regions.* New York: Rowman and Littlefield, 2003.

Gerber, Teodor P., and Sara E. Mendel'son. "Grazhdane Rossii o pravakh cheloveka." *Monitoring obshchestvennoe mneniia: informatsiia analiz*, no. 2, issue 58 (March–April 2002): 26–32.

Gerth, Hans, and C. Wright Mills, eds. and trans. *From Max Weber: Essays in Sociology.* New York: Oxford University Press, 1946.

Gibson, James L. "Mass Opposition to the Soviet Putsch of August 1991: Collective Action, Rational Choice, and Democratic Values in the Former Soviet Union." *American Political Science Review* 91, no. 3 (1997): 671–84.

———. "A Mile Wide but an Inch Deep (?): The Structure of Democratic Commitments in the Former USSR." *American Journal of Political Science* 40 (May 1996): 396–420.

———. "Political and Economic Markets: Changes in the Connections Between Attitudes Toward Political Democracy and a Market Economy Within the Mass Culture of Russia and Ukraine." *Journal of Politics* 58 (November 1996): 954–84.

———. "Putting Up with Fellow Russians: An Analysis of Political Tolerance in the Fledgling Russian Democracy." *Political Research Quarterly* 51 (March 1998): 37–68.

———. "A Sober Second Thought: An Experiment in Persuading Russians to Tolerate." *American Journal of Political Science* 42, no. 3 (1998): 819–50.

———. "The Struggle Between Order and Liberty in Contemporary Russian Political Culture." *Australian Journal of Political Science* 32, no. 2 (1997): 271–90.

———. "The Russian Dance with Democracy." *Post-Soviet Affairs* 17, no. 2 (2001): 101–28.

Gibson, James L., and Gregory A. Caldeira. "Defenders of Democracy? Legitimacy, Popular Acceptance, and the South African Constitutional Court." *Journal of Politics* 65, no. 1 (2003): 1–30.

Gibson, James L., and Raymond M. Duch. "Postmaterialism and the Emerging Soviet Democracy." *Political Research Quarterly* 47 (1994): 5–39.

Gibson, James L., Raymond M. Duch, and Kent L. Tedin. "Democratic Values and the Transformation of the Soviet Union." *Journal of Politics* 54 (May 1992): 329–71.

Gill, Graeme, and Roger D. Markwick. *Russia's Stillborn Democracy? From Gorbachev to Yeltsin.* New York: Oxford University Press, 2000.

Gleason, Abbott. *Young Russia: The Genesis of Russian Radicalism in the 1860s.* New York: Viking Press, 1980.

Glinkina, Svetlana P., Andrei Grigoriev, and Vakhtang Yakobidze. "Crime and Corruption." In *The New Russia: Transition Gone Awry,* edited by Lawrence R. Klein and Marshall Pomer. Stanford: Stanford University Press, 2001.

Goldman, Marshall. *The Piratization of Russia.* New York: Routledge, 2003.

Goldstone, Jack A. "The Soviet Union: Revolution and Transformation." In *Elites, Crises, and the Origins of Regimes,* edited by Mattei Dogan and John Higley. New York: Rowman and Littlefield, 1998.

———. "Toward a Fourth Generation of Revolutionary Theory." *Annual Review of Political Science* 4 (2001): 139–87.

Golenkova, Zinaida T., Viktor V. Vitiuk, Iurii V. Gridchin, Alla I. Chernykh, and Larisa M. Romanenko. "Stanovlenie grazhdanskogo obshchestva i sotial'naia stratifikatsiia" [The Formation of Civil Society and Social Stratification]. *Sotsiologicheskie issledovaniia,* no. 6 (1995): 14–24.

Goodwin, Jeff. *No Other Way Out: States and Revolutionary Movements, 1945–1991.* New York: Cambridge University Press, 2001.

———. "Toward a New Sociology of Revolution." *Theory and Society* 23 (December 1994): 731–66.

Goodwin, Jeff, and James M. Jasper. "Caught in a Winding, Snarling Vine: The Structural Bias of Political Process Theory." In *Rethinking Social Movements: Structure, Meaning, and Emotion,* edited by Jeff Goodwin and James M. Jasper. New York: Rowman and Littlefield, 2004.

Gordon, Leonid A., A. Terekhin, and Ie. Bubilova. *Monitoring obshchestvennoe mneniia: Ekonomicheskie i sotsial'nye peremeny; Informatsionnyi biulleten',* no. 2 (1998): 18.

Gorshkov, M. K. *Rossiiskoe obshchestvo v usloviiakh transformatsii: Mify i real'nost' (Sotsiologicheskii analiz).* Moscow: ROSSPEN, 2003.

Gozman, Leonid, and Alexander Etkind. *The Psychology of Post-totalitarianism in Russia.* London: Centre for Research into Communist Economies, 1992.

Gramsci, Antonio. *Prison Notebooks: Selections.* Translated by Quinton Hoare and Geoffrey Smith. New York: International, 1971.

Grishaev, Sergei Vasil'evich. "Dinamika sotsial'noi struktury Krasnoiarskogo regiona." *Sotsiologicheskie issledovaniia*, no. 2 (2001): 117–20.

Grossman, Vasilii. *Forever Flowing*. Translated by Thomas P. Whitney. New York: Harper and Row, 1972.

Grushin, Boris Andreevich. "Est'li u nas obshchestvennoe mnenie?" Interview with Boris Balkarei. *Novoe Vremia*, no. 30 (1988): 29–31.

Grushin, Boris Andreevich, and L. A. Onikov. *Massovaia informatsiia v sovetskom promyshlennom gorode: Opyt kompleksnogo sotsiologicheskogo issledovaniia*. Moscow: Izdatel'stvo Politicheskoi Literatury, 1980.

Guliev, V. E. "Rossiiskaia gosudarstvennost': Sostoianie i tendentsii." In *Politicheskie Problemy Teorii Gosudarstva*, edited by N. N. Deev. Moscow: Institut Gosudarstva i Prava RAN, 1993.

Gumilev, Lev. *Chtoby svecha ne pogasla: Sbornik esse, interv'iu, stikhotvorenii, perevodov*. Moscow: Airis Press, 2002.

Habermas, Jürgen. *Legitimation Crisis*. Boston: Beacon Press, 1975.

Hahn, Jeffrey W. "Changes in Contemporary Russian Political Culture." In *Political Culture and Civil Society in Russia and the New States of Eurasia*, edited by Vladimir Tismaneanu. Armonk, NY: M. E. Sharpe, 1995.

———. "Continuity and Change in Russian Political Culture." *British Journal of Political Science* 21, no. 4 (1991): 393–41.

Hall, Peter A. "Social Capital in Britain." *British Journal of Political Science* 29 (1999): 417–61.

Hamilton, Alexander, James Madison, and John Jay. *The Federalist Papers*. New York: New American Library, 1961.

Hardin, Russell. "Do We Want Trust in Government?" In *Democracy and Trust*, edited by Mark E. Warren. New York: Cambridge University Press, 1999.

Harrison, Lawrence E., and Samuel Huntington, eds. *Culture Matters: How Values Shape Human Progress*. New York: Basic Books, 2000.

Hartz, Louis. *The Liberal Tradition in America*. New York: Harcourt Brace Jovanovich, 1955.

Havel, Václav. "The Power of the Powerless." In *Without Force or Lies: Voices from the Revolution of Central Europe in 1989–90*, edited by William M. Brinton and Alan Rinzler. San Francisco: Mercury House, 1990.

Hayek, Friedrich. *The Road to Serfdom*. Chicago: Chicago University Press, 1944.

Held, David. *Models of Democracy*. Stanford: Stanford University Press, 1987.

Helmer, John. "Communist Reform: A Success Story." *The Russian*, November 1997.

Hesli, Vicki L., and Elena Bashkirova. "The Impact of Time and Economic Circumstances on Popular Evaluations of Russia's President." *International Political Science Review* 22, no. 4 (2001): 379–98.

Hibbing, John R., and Elizabeth Theiss-Morse. *Congress as Public Enemy: Public Attitudes Toward American Political Institutions*. New York: Cambridge University Press, 1995.

———. "Democrats or Anti-democrats? Americans' Preferences for Governmental Processes." Paper presented at the annual meeting of the Midwest Political Science Association, Chicago, April 1999.

———. "Process Preference and American Politics: What the People Want Government to Be." *American Political Science Review* 95, no. 1 (2001): 145–53.

————. *Stealth Democracy: Americans' Beliefs About How Government Should Work.* New York: Cambridge University Press, 2002.

Hochschild, Jennifer. *What's Fair? Americans' Attitudes Toward Distributive Justice.* Cambridge, MA: Harvard University Press, 1981.

Horowitz, Donald L. "Comparing Democratic Systems." In *The Global Resurgence of Democracy,* edited by Larry Diamond and Marc F. Plattner. 2d ed. Baltimore: Johns Hopkins University Press, 1996.

Hough, Jerry F. "The Russian Election of 1993: Public Attitudes Toward Economic Reform and Democratization." *Post-Soviet Affairs* 10, no. 1 (1994): 1–37.

————. *Democratization and Revolution in the USSR, 1985–1991.* Washington, DC: Brookings Institution, 1997.

Hough, Jerry F., Evelyn Davidheiser, and Susan Goodrich Lehmann. *The 1996 Russian Presidential Election.* Washington, DC: Brookings Institution, 1996.

Howard, Marc Morje. *The Weakness of Civil Society in Post-Communist Europe.* New York: Cambridge University Press, 2003.

Huntington, Samuel P. *The Clash of Civilizations and the Remaking of World Order.* New York: Touchstone, 1996.

————. *Political Order in Changing Societies.* New Haven: Yale University Press, 1968.

Iakovlev, A. N. "Ot proshlogo k budushchemu: liberalizm i demokratiia v kontse XX veka." *Liberalizm i demokratiia: Opyt Zapada i perspektivy Rossii.* Moscow: International Fund for Socio-economic and Political Research (Gorbachev Fund), 1992.

Ignatieff, Michael. *Blood and Belonging: Journeys into the New Nationalism.* New York: Farrar, Straus, and Giroux, 1994.

Inglehart, Ronald. *Culture Shift in Advanced Industrial Society.* Princeton: Princeton University Press, 1990.

————. *The Silent Revolution: Changing Values and Political Styles Among Western Publics.* Princeton: Princeton University Press, 1977.

Ioffe, Grigory, Olga L. Medvedkov, Yuri Medvedkov, Tatiana Nefordova, and Natalia Vlasova. "Russia's Fragmented Space." In *Fragmented Space in the Russian Federation,* edited by Blair A. Ruble, Jodi Koehn, and Nancy E. Popson. Washington, DC: Woodrow Wilson Center Press, 2001.

Isaev, I. A. *Puti Evrazii: Russkaia intelligentsiia i sud'by Rossii.* Moscow: Russkaia Kniga, 1992.

Jackman, Robert W. *Power Without Force: The Political Capacity of Nation-States.* Ann Arbor: University of Michigan Press, 1993.

Javeline, Debra. *Protest and the Politics of Blame: The Russian Response to Unpaid Wages.* Ann Arbor: University of Michigan Press, 2003.

————. "Response Effects in Polite Cultures: A Test of Acquiescence in Kazakhstan." *Public Opinion Quarterly* 63, no. 1 (1999): 1–28.

Johnson, Chalmers. *Revolutionary Change.* 2d ed. Stanford: Stanford University Press, 1982.

Jowitt, Kenneth. "The New World Disorder." In *The Global Resurgence of Democracy,* edited by Larry Diamond and Marc F. Plattner. 2d ed. Baltimore: Johns Hopkins University Press, 1996.

Kachanovskii, Ivan. "Budushchee liberal'noi demokratii v Rossii." *Obshchestvennye nauki i sovremennost'*, no. 2 (1995): 52–56.

Kagarlitsky, Boris. *The Thinking Reed: Intellectuals and the Soviet State, 1917 to the Present.* Translated by Brian Pearce. New York: Verso, 1988.

Karatnycky, Adrian. "Ukraine's Orange Revolution." *Foreign Affairs* 84 (March/April 2005): 35–52.

Kazintsev, Aleksandr. "Na pereput'e. Vybornoe shou i glubinnaia zhizn' Rossii." *Nash sovremennik*, no. 2 (1994): 112–28.

Keane, John. *Democracy and Civil Society: On the Predicaments of European Socialism, the Prospects for Democracy, and the Problem of Controlling Social and Political Power.* London: Verso, 1988.

Keenan, Edward L. "Muscovite Political Folkways." *Russian Review* 45 (April 1986): 115–81.

Kelley, Jonathan, and M. D. R. Evans. "The Legitimation of Inequality: Occupational Earnings in Nine Nations." *American Journal of Sociology* 99, no. 1 (1993): 75–125.

Kharkhordin, Oleg. *The Collective and the Individual in Russia: A Study of Practices.* Berkeley and Los Angeles: University of California Press, 1999.

Khenkin, S. M. "Potensial massovogo protesta v usloviiakh protivorechivykh peremen." *Politiia*, no. 2, issue 8 (1998): 129–46.

Kim, Kyung-won. "Marx, Schumpeter, and the East Asian Experience." *Journal of Democracy* 3 (July 1992): 17–31.

Kinder, Donald R., and D. Roderick Kiewiet. "Sociotropic Politics: The American Case." *British Journal of Political Science* 11 (1981): 129–61.

Klebnikov, Paul. "The Khodorkovsky Affair." *Wall Street Journal*, 17 November, 2003, A20.

Kliamkin, Igor' Moiseevich, E. Petrenko, and L. Blekher. *Kakim mozhet byt' avtoritarnyi rezhim v Rossii?* Seriia issledovanii Narod i politika, vypusk 5/5. Moscow: Fond "Obshchestvennoe mnenie," 1993.

Kliamkin, Igor' Moiseevich, Vladimir Valentinovich Lapkin, and V. I. Pantin. "Mezhdu avtoritarizmom i demokratiei." *Polis* 2, no. 26 (1995): 57–87.

Klingemann, Hans-Dieter, and Dieter Fuchs, eds. *Citizens and the State.* New York: Oxford University Press, 1995.

Kluegel, James R., Gyorgy Csepeli, Tamas Kolosi, Antal Orkeny, and Maria Nemenyi. "Accounting for the Rich and the Poor: Existential Justice in Comparative Perspective." In *Social Justice and Political Change: Public Opinion in Capitalist and Post-Communist States*, edited by James R. Kluegel, David S. Mason, and Bernd Wegener. Hawthorne, NY: Aldine De Gruyter, 1995.

Kluegel, James R., and David S. Mason. "Market Justice in Transition." In *Marketing Democracy: Changing Opinion About Inequality and Politics in East Central Europe*, edited by David S. Mason and James R. Kluegel. Lanham, MD: Rowman and Littlefield, 2000.

Kluegel, James R., and Petr Mateju. "Egalitarian vs. Inegalitarian Principles of Distributive Justice." In *Social Justice and Political Change: Public Opinion in Capitalist and Post-Communist States*, edited by James R. Kluegel, David S. Mason, and Bernd Wegener. Hawthorne, NY: Aldine De Gruyter, 1995.

Kluegel, James R., and Eliot R. Smith. *Beliefs About Inequality: Americans' Views of What Is and What Ought to Be.* Hawthorne, NY: Aldine De Gruyter, 1986.

Kolasky, John, ed. *Laughter Through Tears: Underground Wit, Humor and Satire in the Soviet Russian Empire.* Bullsbrook, Australia: Veritas, 1985.

Krasnikov, Viktor. "Krasnoiarskii krai." In *Regiony Rossii v 1999 g.,* edited by Nikolai Petrov. Moscow: Gendal'f, 2001.

Krasil'nikova, Oksana Viacheslavovna. "Politicheskie predpochteniia vozrastnykh grupp." *Sotsiologicheskie issledovaniia,* no. 9 (2000): 49–52.

Kryshtanovskaia, Ol'ga. "Vybor patriotov: Bednost' ili rakety?" *Argumenty i Fakty,* no. 30 (July 2003): 3.

Kryshtanovskaia, Ol'ga, and Stephen White. "From Soviet *Nomenklatura* to Russia Elite." *Europe-Asia Studies* 48, no. 5 (1996): 711–33.

Kullberg, Judith S. "Preserving the Radical Stronghold: The Election in Moscow." In *Growing Pains: Russian Democracy and the Election of 1993,* edited by Timothy J. Colton and Jerry F. Hough. Washington, DC: Brookings Institution, 1998.

Kullberg, Judith S., and William Zimmerman. "Liberal Elites, Socialist Masses, and Problems of Democracy." *World Politics* 51 (April 1999): 323–58.

Kuns, Brian. "Old Corruption in the New Russia." In *The Russian Transformation: Political, Sociological, and Psychological Aspects,* edited by Betty Glad and Eric Shiraev. New York: St. Martin's Press, 1999.

Ladd, Everett Carll, and Karlyn H. Bowman. *Attitudes Toward Economic Inequality.* Washington, DC: American Enterprise Institute Press, 1998.

Laidinen, Natal'ia Valer'evna. "Obraz Rossii v zerkale Rossiiskogo obshchestvennogo mneniia." *Sotsiologicheskie issledovaniia,* no. 4 (2001): 27–31.

Laitin, David D. "The Civic Culture at 30." *American Political Science Review* 89, no. 1 (1995): 168–73.

Lallemand, Jean-Charles. "Who Rules Smolensk Oblast." *EWI Russian Regional Report* 3, no. 40 (8 October 1998). http://wwwceri-sciencespo.com/archive/october/artjcl.pdf.

Lane, Robert E. "Market Justice, Political Justice." *American Political Science Review* 80 (1986): 383–402.

———. *Political Ideology: Why the American Common Man Believes What He Does.* New York: Free Press, 1962.

———. *Political Man.* New York: Free Press, 1972.

Lapin, N. I. *Puti Rossii: Sotsiokul'turnye transformatsii.* Moscow: Rossiiskaia Akademiia Nauk, Institut Filosofii, 2000.

Lapkin, Vladimir Valentinovich. "Prezhde chem vypisyvat' retsept, trebuetsia utochnit' diagnoz." *Polis: Politicheskie Issledovaniia,* no. 4 (1999): 73–76.

Lapkin, Vladimir Valentinovich, and V. I. Pantin. "Russkii poriadok." *Politicheskie issledovaniia,* no. 3 (1997): 74–88.

———. "Tsennosti postsovetskogo cheloveka." In *Chelovek v perekhodnom obshchestve: Sotsiologicheskie i sotsial'no-psikhologicheskie issledovaniia,* edited by G. G. Diligenskii. Moscow: Institute of World Economics and International Relations, 1998.

Lardeyret, Guy. "The Problem with PR." In *The Global Resurgence of Democracy,* edited by Larry Diamond and Marc F. Plattner. Baltimore: Johns Hopkins University Press, 1996.

Lavelle, Peter. "What Does Putin Want?" *Current History* 103, no. 675 (2004): 314–18.

LeDonne, John P. "The Ruling Class: Tsarist Model." *International Social Science Journal* 45, no. 2 (1993): 285–300.

Levada, Iurii. "'Chelovek sovetskii' piat' let spustia: 1989–1994 (predvaritel'nye itogi sravnitel'nogo issledovaniia)." *Monitoring obshchestvennoe mneniia: Ekonomicheskie i sotsial'nye peremeny: Informatsionnyi biulleten'* 1 (January–February 1995): 9–14.

———. "Kompleksy obshchestvennogo mneniia (stat'ia vtoraia)." *Monitoring obshchestvennoe mneniia: Ekonomicheskie i sotsial'nye peremeny: Informatsionnyi biulleten'* 1 (January-February 1997): 7–12.

———. "Koordinaty cheloveka i itogam izucheniia 'cheloveka sovetskogo.'" *Monitoring obshchestvennoe mneniia: Informatsiia analiz,* no. 1, issue 51 (2001): 7–15.

———. "Varianty adaptivnogo povedeniia." *Monitoring obshchestvennoe mneniia: Informatsiia analiz,* no. 1, issue 57 (2002): 7–13.

Levada, Iurii, Vladimir Shubkin, Grigoriy Kertman, Veronika Ivanova, Vladimir Yadov, and Eric Shiraev. "Russia: Anxiously Surviving." In *Fears in Post-Communist Societies: A Comparative Perspective,* edited by Eric Shiraev and Vladimir Shlapentokh. New York: Palgrave, 2002.

Levitsky, Steven, and Lucan A. Way. "Elections Without Democracy: The Rise of Competitive Authoritarianism." *Journal of Democracy* 13, no. 2 (2002): 51–65.

Lijphart, Arend. "Constitutional Choices for New Democracies." In *The Global Resurgence of Democracy,* edited by Larry Diamond and Marc F. Plattner. Baltimore: Johns Hopkins University Press, 1996.

Linz, Juan J. "The Perils of Presidentialism." In *The Global Resurgence of Democracy,* edited by Larry Diamond and Marc F. Plattner. Baltimore: Johns Hopkins University Press, 1996.

Lipman, Maria. "How Russia Is Not Ukraine: The Closing of Russian Civil Society." *Carnegie Endowment for International Peace Policy Outlook,* January 2005. http://www.CarnegieEndowment.org.

Lipset, Seymour Martin. *Political Man: The Social Bases of Politics.* 1959. Expanded edition. Baltimore: Johns Hopkins University Press, 1981.

Locke, John. *The Second Treatise of Government.* 1690. New York: Macmillan, 1985.

Lukin, Alexander. *The Political Culture of the Russian "Democrats."* New York: Oxford University Press, 2000.

Luong, Pauline Jones. "Tatarstan: Elite Bargaining and Ethnic Separatism." In *Growing Pains: Russian Democracy and the Election of 1993,* edited by Timothy J. Colton and Jerry F. Hough. Washington, DC: Brookings Institution, 1998.

Magomedov, Arbakhan. "Ul'ianovskaia oblast': Khronika politicheskikh sobytii (1990–1998)." In *Nizhegorodskaia oblast', Ul'ianovskaia oblast'.* Regiony Rossii: Khronika i rukovoditeli, edited by K. Matsuzato and A. B. Shatilov, vol. 6. Sapporo, Japan: Slavic Research Center, Hokkaido University, 1999.

Mann, Michael. "The Autonomous Power of the State: Its Origins, Mechanisms and Results." In *States in History,* edited by John A. Hall. Oxford, U.K.: Basil Blackwell, 1986.

March, James G., and Johan P. Olsen. "The New Institutionalism: Organizational Factors in Political Life." *American Political Science Review* 78 (1984): 734–49.

————. *Rediscovering Institutions: The Organizational Basis of Politics*. New York: Free Press, 1989.

Markovitz, Irving Leonard. "Constitutions, the Federalist Papers, and the Transition to Democracy." In *Transitions to Democracy*, edited by Lisa Anderson. New York: Columbia University Press, 1999.

Markowitz, Fran. *Coming of Age in Post-Soviet Russia*. Urbana: University of Illinois Press, 2000.

Marsh, Christopher. *Russia at the Polls: Voters, Elections, and Democratization*. Washington, DC: CQ Press, 2002.

Marx, Karl. "Economic and Philosophic Manuscripts of 1844." In *The Marx-Engels Reader*, edited by Robert C. Tucker. 2d ed. New York: W. W. Norton, 1978.

Mason, David S. "Attitudes Toward the Market and Political Participation in the Post-Communist States." *Slavic Review* 54 (Summer 1995): 385–406.

————. "Justice, Socialism, and Participation in the Postcommunist States." In *Social Justice and Political Change: Public Opinion in Capitalist and Post-Communist States*, edited by James R. Kluegel, David S. Mason, and Bernd Wegener. Hawthorne, NY: Aldine De Gruyter, 1995.

Mason, David S., and James R. Kluegel. "Introduction: Public Opinion and Political Change in the Postcommunist States." In *Marketing Democracy: Changing Opinion About Inequality and Politics in East Central Europe*, edited by David S. Mason and James R. Kluegel. Lanham, MD: Rowman and Littlefield, 2000.

Mason, David S., and James R. Kluegel, with Ludmilla Khakhulina, Petr Mateju, Antal Orkeny, Alexander Stoyanov, and Bernd Wegener. *Marketing Democracy: Changing Opinion About Inequality and Politics in East Central Europe*. New York: Rowman and Littlefield, 2000.

Mau, Vladimir, and Irina Starodubrovskaya. *The Challenge of Revolution: Contemporary Russia in Historical Perspective*. New York: Oxford University Press, 2001.

McAuley, Mary. "Political Culture and Communist Politics: One Step Forward, Two Steps Back." In *Political Culture and Communist Studies*, edited by Archie Brown. Armonk, NY: M. E. Sharpe, 1984.

————. *Russia's Politics of Uncertainty*. New York: Cambridge University Press, 1997.

McClosky, Herbert, and John Zaller. *The American Ethos: Public Attitudes Toward Capitalism and Democracy*. Cambridge, MA: Harvard University Press, 1984.

McDaniel, Tim. *The Agony of the Russian Idea*. Princeton: Princeton University Press, 1996.

————. *Autocracy, Modernization, and Revolution in Russia and Iran*. Princeton: Princeton University Press, 1991.

McFaul, Michael. "Reengaging Russia: A New Agenda." *Current History* 103 (October 2004): 307–13.

————. *Russia's Unfinished Revolution: Political Change from Gorbachev to Putin*. Ithaca: Cornell University Press, 2001.

McFaul, Michael, Nikolai Petrov and Andrei Ryabov. *Between Dictatorship and Democracy: Russian Post-Communist Political Reform*. Washington, DC: Carnegie Endowment for International Peace, 2004.

McIntosh, Mary E., Martha Abele MacIver, Daniel G. Abele, and Dina Smeltz. "Publics Meet Market Democracy in Central and East Europe, 1991–1993." *Slavic Review* 53 (Summer 1994): 483–512.

Meleshkina, Elena Iur'evna. "Perspektivy i ogranicheniia politicheskoi reformy." *Polis: Politicheskie Issledovaniia*, no. 4 (1999): 85–87.

Michelbach, Philip A., John T. Scott, Richard E. Matland, and Brian H. Bornstein. "Doing Rawls Justice: An Experimental Study of Income Distribution Norms." *American Journal of Political Science* 47, no. 3 (2003): 523–39.

Migdal, Joel S. *State in Society: Studying How States and Societies Transform and Constitute One Another*. New York: Cambridge University Press, 2001.

Migranian, Andranik. "Dolgii put' k evropeiskomu domu." *Novyi Mir* 7 (July 1989): 166–84.

———. "On Historical Parallels." *Literaturnaia Gazeta*, no. 1 (1990): 9.

Mikhalev, Vladimir. "Poverty and Social Assistance." In *The New Russia: Transition Gone Awry*, edited by Lawrence R. Klein and Marshall Pomer. Stanford: Stanford University Press, 2001.

Mill, John Stuart. *On Liberty*. New York: Penguin, 1985.

Miller, Arthur H., and Thomas F. Klobucar. "The Development of Party Identification in Post-Soviet Societies." *American Journal of Political Science* 44 (October 2000): 667–86.

Miller, Arthur H., Vicki L. Hesli, and William M. Reisinger. "Conceptions of Democracy Among Mass and Elite in Post-Soviet Societies." *British Journal of Political Science* 27 (1997): 157–90.

———. "Reassessing Mass Support for Political and Economic Change in the Former USSR." *American Political Science Review* 88, no. 2 (1994): 399–411.

———. "Understanding Political Change in Post-Soviet Societies: A Further Commentary on Finifer and Mickiewicz." *American Political Science Review* 90 (March 1996): 153–66.

Miller, David. *Principles of Social Justice*. Cambridge, MA: Harvard University Press, 1999.

Mishler, William, and Richard Rose. "Learning and Re-learning Regime Support: The Dynamics of Post-Communist Regimes." *European Journal of Political Research* 41 (January 2002): 5–36.

———. "Political Support for Incomplete Democracies: Realist vs. Idealist Theories and Measures." *International Political Science Review* 22, no. 4 (2001): 303–20.

———. "Trajectories of Fear and Hope: Support for Democracy in Post-Communist Europe." *Comparative Political Studies* 28 (January 1996): 553–81.

———. "Trust, Distrust, and Skepticism: Popular Evaluations of Civil and Political Institutions in Post-Communist Societies." *Journal of Politics* 59, no. 2 (1997): 418–51.

———. "What Are the Origins of Political Trust? Testing Institutional and Cultural Theories in Post-Communist Societies." *Comparative Political Studies* 34, no. 1 (2001): 30–62.

Mitev, Petr-Emil, Veronika Alekseevna Ivanova, and Vladimir Nikolaevich Shubkin. "Katastroficheskoe soznanie v Bolgarii i Rossii." *Sotsiologicheskie issledovaniia*, no. 10 (1998): 111–17.

Mokryi, Vladimir Semenovich. "Dinamika sotsial'no-politicheskikh orientatsii elek-torata v usloviiakh finansovo-ekonomicheskogo krizisa." *Sotsiologicheskie issle-dovaniia*, no. 8 (1999): 20–25.

Montesquieu, Charles. *The Spirit of the Laws*. Birmingham, AL: Legal Classics Library, 1984.

Moore, Barrington, Jr. *Social Origins of Dictatorship and Democracy: Lord and Peasant in the Making of the Modern World*. Boston: Beacon Press, 1966.

Mueller, John. *Capitalism, Democracy, and Ralph's Pretty Good Grocery*. Princeton: Princeton University Press, 1999.

Muller, Edward N., and Thomas O. Jukam. "On the Meaning of Political Support." *American Political Science Review* 71 (1977): 1561–95.

Muller, Edward N., and Mitchell A. Seligson. "Civic Culture and Democracy: The Question of Causal Relationships." *American Political Science Review* 88, no. 3 (1994): 635–52.

Myers, Steven Lee. "Old Kremlin, New Kremlin: It's Still a Big Secret." *New York Times*, 27 August 2003, A4.

———. "Putin Backs Ukrainian Leader, Dismissing Calls for New Runoff." *New York Times*, 3 December 2004, A1, A12.

———. "Putin Revels in Election, but Others Cite Flaws." *New York Times*, 9 December 2003, A1, A8.

———. "Using Power, Losing Favor: Putin Falters on World Stage." *New York Times*, 10 December 2004, A1, A8.

Nachmias, David, and Chava Nachmias. *Research Methods in the Social Sciences*. 3d ed. New York: St. Martin's Press, 1987.

Naumova, Nina F. "Sotsial'naia politika v usloviiakh zapazdyvaiushchei modern-izatsii." *Sotsiologicheskii Zhurnal*, no. 1 (1994): 6–21.

Nemirovskii, V. G. "Sibiriaki: Dinamika sotsial'no-politicheskikh orientatsii." *Sotsi-ologicheskie issledovaniia*, no. 8 (1999): 25–31.

Nemtsov, Boris. "Boris Nemtsov o presidentstve, bogatstve i Chubaise." *Argumenty i Fakty*, no. 12 (March 1998): 3.

Newton, Kenneth. "Social and Political Trust in Established Democracies." In *Critical Citizens: Global Support for Democratic Government*, edited by Pippa Norris. New York: Oxford University Press, 1999.

Nikitinskii, Leonid. "'Million terzanii' zabludshego intelligenta (popravki k para-digme)." *Obshchestvennye nauki i sovremennost'*, no. 2 (1995): 110–20.

Nikovskaia, L. I. "Politika i ekonomika v sovremennoi Rossii: Konflikt na pereput'e (kruglyi stol)." *Sotsiologicheskie issledovaniia*, no. 2 (2000): 87–100.

Norris, Pippa, ed. *Critical Citizens: Global Support for Democratic Governance*. New York: Oxford University Press, 1999.

———. "Introduction: The Growth of Critical Citizens?" In *Critical Citizens: Global Support for Democratic Government*, edited by Pippa Norris. New York: Oxford University Press, 1999.

Nye, Joseph S., Jr., Philip D. Zelikow, and David C. King, eds. *Why People Don't Trust Government*. Cambridge, MA: Harvard University Press, 1997.

O'Donnell, Guillermo. "Delegative Democracy." *Journal of Democracy* 5 (January 1994): 55–69.

O'Donnell, Guillermo, and Philippe C. Schmitter. *Transitions from Authoritarian Rule: Tentative Conclusions About Uncertain Democracies.* Baltimore: Johns Hopkins University Press, 1986.

O'Kane, Rosemary H. T. "Against Legitimacy." *Political Studies* 41 (1993): 471–87.

Olekh, Grigory L. "Novosibirsk Oblast: Problems of Globalization and Regionalization." Regionalization of Russian Foreign Policy and Security Policy, Working Paper no. 9. Zurich: Center for Security Studies and Conflict Research, 2001.

Olson, Mancur. *Power and Prosperity: Outgrowing Communist and Capitalist Dictatorship.* New York: Basic Books / Perseus, 2000.

Oreshkin, Dmitry. "The Silence of the Oligarchs." *Moscow News,* no. 28 (23–29 July 2003), 5.

Ostrom, Elinor. *Governing the Commons: The Evolution of Institutions for Collective Action.* New York: Cambridge University Press, 1990.

Patrushev, S. V., S. G. Aivazova, G. L. Kertman, L. Ia. Mashezerskaia, T. V. Pavlova, and A. D. Khlopin. "Vlast' i narod v Rossii: Povsedevnye praktiki i problema universalizatsii institutsional'nogo poriadka." *Politiia,* no. 2, issue 29 (Summer 2003): 54–79.

Pelevin, Victor. *Homo Zapiens.* New York: Viking, 1999.

Pesmen, Dale. *Russia and Soul.* Ithaca: Cornell University Press, 2000.

Petro, Nikolai. *The Rebirth of Russian Democracy: An Interpretation of Political Culture.* Cambridge, MA: Harvard University Press, 1995.

Petrov, Nikolai. "Vybory gubernatora Krasnoiarskogo Kraia." In *Regiony Rossii v 1998,* edited by Nikolai Petrov. Moscow: Gendal'f, 1999.

Pharr, Susan J., and Robert D. Putnam, eds. *Disaffected Democracies: What's Troubling the Trilateral Countries?* Princeton: Princeton University Press, 2000.

Plattner, Marc F. "From Liberalism to Liberal Democracy." In *The Global Divergence of Democracies,* edited by Larry Diamond and Marc F. Plattner. Baltimore: Johns Hopkins University Press, 2001.

Popper, Karl R. *The Open Society and Its Enemies.* 4th ed. Princeton: Princeton University Press, 1963.

Powers, Denise V. "Understanding Reactions to Post-Communist Transitions: Conception of Self, Political Attitudes, and Democratic Consolidation." Paper presented at the annual meeting of the American Association for the Advancement of Slavic Studies, Boca Raton, Florida, September 1998.

Prothro, James W., and C. W. Grigg. "Fundamental Principles of Democracy: Bases of Agreement and Disagreement." *Journal of Politics* 22 (May 1960): 276–94.

Przeworski, Adam. *Democracy and the Market: Political and Economic Reforms in Eastern Europe and Latin America.* New York: Cambridge University Press, 1991.

———. "Some Problems in the Study of the Transition to Democracy." In *Transitions from Authoritarian Rule: Comparative Perspectives,* edited by Guillermo O'Donnell, Philippe C. Schmitter, and Laurence Whitehead. Baltimore: Johns Hopkins University Press, 1986.

Przeworski, Adam, Michael E. Alvarez, Jose Antonio Cheibub, and Fernando Limongi. *Democracy and Development: Political Institutions and Well-Being in the World, 1950–1990.* New York: Cambridge University Press, 2000.

Przeworski, Adam, et al. *Sustainable Democracy.* New York: Cambridge University Press, 1995.

Putnam, Robert. *Making Democracy Work: Civic Traditions in Modern Italy.* Princeton: Princeton University Press, 1993.

Pye, Lucian W. "Culture and Political Science: Problems in the Evaluation of the Concept of Political Culture." In *The Idea of Culture in the Social Sciences,* edited by Louis Schneider and Charles M. Bonjean. Cambridge: Cambridge University Press, 1973.

Quade, Quentin. "PR and Democratic Statecraft." In *The Global Resurgence of Democracy,* edited by Larry Diamond and Marc F. Plattner. Baltimore: Johns Hopkins University Press, 1996.

Rancour-Laferriere, Daniel. *The Slave Soul of Russia: Moral Masochism and the Cult of Suffering.* New York: New York University Press, 1995.

Raphael, Therese. "Business as Usual." *Wall Street Journal,* 31 October 2003, A12.

Rawls, John. *Justice as Fairness: A Restatement.* Edited by Erin Kelly. Cambridge, MA: Belknap Press of Harvard University Press, 2001.

Reddaway, Peter, and Dmitri Glinski. *The Tragedy of Russia's Reforms: Market Bolshevism Against Democracy.* Washington, DC: United States Institute of Peace Press, 2001.

Reisinger, William M. "The Renaissance of a Rubric: Political Culture as Concept and Theory." *International Journal of Public Opinion Research* 7, no. 4 (1995): 328–52.

———. "Survey Research and Authority Patterns in Contemporary Russia." In *Can Democracy Take Root in Post-Soviet Russia? Explorations in State-Society Relations,* edited by Harry Eckstein, Frederic J. Fleron Jr., Erik Hoffmann, and William Reisinger. New York: Rowman and Littlefield, 1998.

Reisinger, William M., Arthur L. Miller, and Vicki L. Hesli. "Ideological Divisions and Party-Building Prospects in Post-Soviet Russia." In *Elections and Voters in Post-Communist Russia,* edited by Matthew Wyman, Stephen White, and Sarah Oates. Northampton, MA: Edward Elgar, 1998.

———. "Political Norms in Rural Russia: Evidence from Public Attitudes." *Europe-Asia Studies* 47 (September 1995): 1025–42.

———. "Public Behavior and Political Change in Post-Soviet States." *Journal of Politics* 57, no. 4 (1995): 941–70.

———. "Russians and the Legal System: Mass Views and Behaviour in the 1990s." *Communist Studies and Transition Politics* 13, no. 3 (1997): 24–55.

Reisinger, William M., Arthur H. Miller, Vicki L. Hesli, and Kristen Hill Maher. "Political Values in Russia, Ukraine, and Lithuania: Sources and Implications for Democracy." *British Journal of Political Science* 24 (April 1994): 183–223.

Ries, Nancy. *Russian Talk: Culture and Conversation During Perestroika.* Ithaca: Cornell University Press, 1997.

Rivera, Sharon Werning, Polina M. Kozyreva, and Eduard G. Sarovskii. "Interviewing Political Elites: Lessons from Russia." *PS: Political Science and Politics* 35, no. 4 (2002): 683–88.

Roeder, Philip G. "Transitions from Communism: State-Centered Approaches." In *Can Democracy Take Root in Post-Soviet Russia? Explorations in State-Society*

Relations, edited by Harry Eckstein, Frederic J. Fleron Jr., Erik Hoffmann, and William Reisinger. New York: Rowman and Littlefield, 1998.

———. "Varieties of Post-Soviet Authoritarian Regimes." *Post-Soviet Affairs* 10, no. 1 (1994): 61–101.

Rogowski, Ronald. *Rational Legitimacy: A Theory of Political Support.* Princeton: Princeton University Press, 1974.

Romanovich, Nelli A. "Demokraticheskie tsennosti i svoboda 'po-russki.'" *Sotsiologicheskie issledovaniia,* no. 8 (2002): 35–39. Translated in *Sociological Research* 42, no. 6 (2003): 62–68.

Rose, Richard. "Living in an Antimodern Society." *East European Constitutional Review* 8, nos. 1/2 (1999): 68–75.

———. "Postcommunism and the Problem of Trust." *Journal of Democracy* 5 (July 1994): 18–30.

———. "Russia as an Hour-Glass Society: A Constitution Without Citizens." *East European Constitutional Review* 4, no. 3 (1995): 36–44.

Rose, Richard, and Doh Chull Shin. "Democratization Backwards: The Problem of Third-Wave Democracies." *British Journal of Political Science* 31 (2001): 331–54.

Rose, Richard, and Ellen Carnaghan. "Generational Effects on Attitudes to Communist Regimes: A Comparative Analysis." *Post-Soviet Affairs* 11 (January–March 1995): 28–56.

Rose, Richard, and William T. Mishler. "Mass Reaction to Regime Change in Eastern Europe: Polarization or Leaders and Laggards?" *British Journal of Political Science* 24 (April 1994): 159–82.

Rose, Richard, William Mishler, and Christian Haerpfer. *Democracy and Its Alternatives: Understanding Post-Communist Societies.* Baltimore: Johns Hopkins University Press, 1998.

Rose, Richard, and Neil Munro. *Elections Without Order: Russia's Challenge to Vladimir Putin.* New York: Cambridge University Press, 2002.

Rose, Richard, Neil Munro, and William Mishler. "Resigned Acceptance of an Incomplete Democracy: Russia's Political Equilibrium." *Post-Soviet Affairs* 20, no. 3 (July–September 2004): 195–218.

Rousseau, Jean-Jacques. *The Social Contract and Discourses.* 1762. Translated by G. D. H. Cole. Reprint. London: J. M. Dent and Sons, Everyman's Library, 1973.

Rustow, Dankwart A. "Transition to Democracy: Towards a Dynamic Model." *Comparative Politics* 2, no. 2 (1970): 337–63.

Ryvkina, R. V. "Politika i ekonomika v sovremennoi Rossii: Konflikt na pereput'e (Kruglyi Stol)." *Sotsiologicheskie issledovaniia* no. 2 (2000): 87–100.

Sabine, George H. "The Two Democratic Traditions." *Philosophical Review* 61 (October 1952): 451–74.

Sakwa, Richard. "Subjectivity, Politics, and Order in Russian Political Evolution." *Slavic Review* 54, no. 4 (1995): 943–64.

Satter, David. *Darkness at Dawn: The Rise of the Russian Criminal State.* New Haven: Yale University Press, 2003.

Schober, Michael F., and Frederick G. Conrad. "Does Conversational Interviewing Reduce Survey Measurement Error?" *Public Opinion Quarterly* 61 (Winter 1997): 576–602.

Schumpeter, Joseph A. *Capitalism, Socialism, and Democracy.* 3d ed. New York: Harper and Row, 1950.

Scott, James C. *Domination and the Arts of Resistance: Hidden Transcripts.* New Haven: Yale University Press, 1990.

Selbin, Eric. "Revolutions in the Real World: Bringing Agency Back In." In *Theorizing Revolutions,* edited by John Foran. New York: Routledge, 1997.

Seligson, Mitchell A., and Edward N. Muller. "Democratic Stability and Economic Crisis: Costa Rica, 1978–1983." *International Studies Quarterly* 31 (1987): 301–26.

Sen, Amartya. *Inequality Reexamined.* New York: Russell Sage Foundation, 1992.

Sergeyev, Victor M. "Organized Crime and Social Instability in Russia: The Alternative State, Deviant Bureaucracy, and Social Black Holes." In *Russia in the New Century: Stability or Disorder?* edited by Victoria E. Bonnell and George W. Breslauer. Boulder, CO: Westview Press, 2001.

Sergeyev, Victor, and Nikolai Biriukov. *Russia's Road to Democracy: Parliament, Communism, and Traditional Culture.* Brookfield, VT: Edward Elgar /Ashgat, 1993.

Shabanova, M. A. "Obrazy svobody v reformiruemoi Rossii." *Sotsiologicheskie issledovaniia,* no. 2 (2000): 29–38.

Shenfield, Stephen D. *Russian Fascism: Traditions, Tendencies, Movements.* Armonk, NY: M. E. Sharpe, 2001.

Shestopal, E. B. "Perspektivy demokratii v soznanii rossiian." *Obshchestvennye nauki i sovremennost',* no. 2 (1996): 45–60.

———. "Ustanovki rossiiskikh grazhdan na vlast' kak pokazatel' kachestva demokratii (Po dannym politiko-psikhologicheskogo issledovaniia 1993–2003)." *Politiia,* no. 2, issue 29 (2003): 32–53.

Shevchenko, Olga. "Bread and Circuses: Shifting Frames and Changing References in Ordinary Muscovites' Political Talk." *Communist and Post-Communist Studies* 34, no. 1 (2001): 77–90.

Shevtsova, Lilia. *Putin's Russia.* Washington, DC: Carnegie Endowment for International Peace, 2003.

Shiraev, Eric. "Attitudinal Changes During the Transition." In *The Russian Transformation: Political, Sociological, and Psychological Aspects,* edited by Betty Glad and Eric Shiraev. New York: St. Martin's Press, 1999.

———. "The New Nomenclature and Increasing Income Inequality." In *The Russian Transformation: Political, Sociological, and Psychological Aspects,* edited by Betty Glad and Eric Shiraev. New York: St. Martin's Press, 1999.

Shiraev, Eric, and Betty Glad. "Generational Adaptations to the Transition." In *The Russian Transformation: Political, Sociological, and Psychological Aspects,* edited by Betty Glad and Eric Shiraev. New York: St. Martin's Press, 1999.

Shlapentokh, Vladimir E. "Early Feudalism: The Best Parallel for Contemporary Russia." *Europe-Asia Studies* 48 (May): 393–411.

———. *A Normal Totalitarian Society: How the Soviet Union Functioned and How It Collapsed.* Armonk, NY: M. E. Sharpe, 2001.

———. "Two Levels of Public Opinion: The Soviet Case." *Public Opinion Quarterly* 49 (Winter 1985): 443–59.

Shlapentokh, Vladimir E., Roman Levita, and Mikhail Loiberg. *From Submission to Rebellion: The Provinces Versus the Center in Russia.* Boulder, CO: Westview Press, 1997.

Shturman, D. "Razmyshleniia o liberalisme." *Novyi Mir,* no. 4 (1995): 159–68.

Shugart, Matthew Soberg, and John Carey. "Presidents and Assemblies." In *The Democracy Sourcebook,* edited by Robert A. Dahl, Ian Shapiro, and Jose Antonio Cheibub. Cambridge, MA: MIT Press, 2003.

Sil, Rudra, and Cheng Chen. "State Legitimacy and the (In)significance of Democracy in Post-Communist Russia." *Europe-Asia Studies* 56, no. 3 (2004): 347–68.

Silver, Brian D. "Political Beliefs of the Soviet Citizen: Sources of Support for Regime Norms." In *Politics, Work, and Daily Life in the USSR: A Survey of Former Soviet Citizens,* edited by James R. Millar. New York: Cambridge University Press, 1987.

Simis, Konstantin M. *USSR: The Corrupt Society; The Secret World of Soviet Capitalism.* New York: Simon and Schuster, 1982.

Skocpol, Theda. "Cultural Idioms and Political Ideologies in the Revolutionary Reconstruction of State Power: A Rejoinder to Sewell." *Social Revolutions in the Modern World.* New York: Cambridge University Press, 1994.

———. *States and Social Revolution: Comparative Analysis of France, Russia, and China.* Cambridge: Cambridge University Press, 1979.

Sniderman, Paul M., Joseph F. Fletcher, Peter H. Russell, and Philip E. Tetlock. *The Clash of Rights: Liberty, Equality, and Legitimacy in Pluralist Democracy.* New Haven: Yale University Press, 1996.

Solnick, Steven L. *Stealing the State: Control and Collapse in Soviet Institutions.* Cambridge, MA: Harvard University Press, 1998.

Sorenson, Georg. *Democracy and Democratization.* Boulder, CO: Westview Press, 1993.

Spradley, James P. *The Ethnographic Interview.* New York: Harcourt Brace Jovanovich, 1979.

Stepanov, E. I. "Politika i Ekonomika v Sovremennoi Rossii: Konflikt na pereput'e (Kruglye Stol)." *Sotsiologicheskie issledovaniia,* no. 2 (2000): 87–100.

Stephenson, Svetlana, and Ludmila Khakhulina. "Russia: Changing Perceptions of Social Justice." In *Marketing Democracy: Changing Opinion About Inequality and Politics in East Central Europe,* edited by David S. Mason and James R. Kluegel. Lanham, MD: Rowman and Littlefield, 2000.

Stoner-Weiss, Kathryn. *Local Heroes: The Political Economy of Russian Regional Governance.* Princeton: Princeton University Press, 1997.

Suchman, Lucy, and Brigitte Jordan. "Validity and the Collaborative Construction of Meaning in Face-to-Face Surveys." In *Questions About Questions: Inquiries into the Cognitive Bases of Surveys,* edited by Judith M. Tanur. New York: Russell Sage Foundation, 1992.

Sukhovol'skii, V. G. "A. Lebed' v Krasnoiarskom krae: Elektoral'nye uspekhi i politicheskie porazheniia." *Politiia,* no.1, issue 11 (1999): 95–109.

Tarasov, Alexei. "'Legal Corruption' Deeply Rooted in Krasnoyarsk." *Moscow News,* no. 27 (16–22 July 2003), 5.

Tarrow, Sidney. *Power in Movement: Social Movements, Collective Action, and Politics.* New York: Cambridge University Press, 1994.

Tedin, Kent L. "Popular Support for Competitive Elections in the Soviet Union." *Comparative Political Studies* 27 (July 1991): 241–71.

The Territories of the Russian Federation. 2d ed. London: Europa, 2001.

Titkov, Aleksei. "Obrazy regionov v rossiiskom massovom soznanii." *Polis*, no. 3 (1999): 61–73.

Titma, Mikk. "Videt' dal'she, chem na khod vpered." Interview. *Sovetskaia Kul'tura*, 10 November 1990, 4.

Tocqueville, Alexis de. *Democracy in America*. New York: New American Library, 1956.

Tsipko, Aleksandr. "The Roots of Stalinism, Essay No. 3: The Egocentricity of Dreamers." *Nauka i Zhizn* 1 (January 1989): 46–56.

Tucker, Robert C. *The Soviet Political Mind*. Revised edition. New York: W. W. Norton, 1971.

Turchin, Valentine. *The Inertia of Fear and the Scientific Worldview*. Translated by Guy Daniels. New York: Columbia University Press, 1981.

Turovskii, R. F. "Otnosheniia 'tsentr-regiony' v 1997–1998 gg.: Mezhdu konfliktom i konsensusom." *Politiia*, no. 1 (Spring 1998): 5–32.

Tyler, Tom R. *Why People Obey the Law*. New Haven: Yale University Press, 1990.

Vainshstein, Grigory I. "Obshchestvennoe soznanie i institutsional'nye peremeny." In *Chelovek v perekhodnom obshchestve: Sotsiologicheskie i sotsial'no-psikhologicheskie issledovaniia*, edited by G. G. Diligenskii. Moscow: Institute of World Economics and International Relations, 1998.

———. "Totalitarian Public Consciousness in a Post-totalitarian Society." *Communist and Post-Communist Studies* 27, no. 3 (1994): 247–59.

Vaksberg, Arkady. *The Soviet Mafia*. Translated by John and Elizabeth Roberts. New York: St. Martin's Press, 1991.

Verba, Sidney. "Comparative Political Culture." In *Political Culture and Political Development*, edited by Lucian W. Pye and Sidney Verba. Princeton: Princeton University Press, 1965.

Verba, Sidney, Norman H. Nie, and Jae-on Kim. *Participation and Political Equality: A Seven-Nation Comparison*. New York: Cambridge University Press, 1978.

Viola, Lynn. *Peasant Rebels Under Stalin: Collectivization and the Culture of Peasant Resistance*. New York: Oxford University Press, 1996.

Vodolazov, Grigorii, et al. "Demokratiya v Rossii: Samokritika i perspektivy." *Obshchestvennye nauki i sovremennost'* (roundtable), no. 2 (1995): 40–51.

Volkov, Vadim. *Violent Entrepreneurs: The Use of Force in the Making of Russian Capitalism*. Ithaca: Cornell University Press, 2002.

VTSIOM. "Informatsiia." *Monitoring obshchestvennoe mneniia: Informatsiia analiz*, no. 2, issue 58 (2002): 67–81.

———. "Informatsiia: Nastroeniia, mneniia i otsenki naseleniia." *Monitoring obshchestvennoe mneniia: Ekonomicheskie i sotsial'nye peremeny: Informatsionnyi biulleten'*, no. 1 (1997): 49–58.

———. "Informatsiia: Resul'taty oprosov." *Monitoring obshchestvennoe mneniia: Informatsiia analiz*, no. 1, issue 51 (1997): 64–94.

———. "Monitoring peremen: Osnovnye tendentsii." *Monitoring obshchestvennoe mneniia: Informatsiia analiz*, no. 2, issue 58 (March–April 2002): 3–8.

Walicki, Andrzej. *A History of Russian Thought: From the Enlightenment to Marxism*. Translated by Hilda Andrews-Rusiecki. Stanford: Stanford University Press, 1979.

Warren, Mark E., ed. *Democracy and Trust*. New York: Cambridge University Press, 1999.

Weatherford, M. Stephen. "Measuring Political Legitimacy." *American Political Science Review* 86 (March 1992): 149–66.

Weigle, Marcia A. *Russia's Liberal Project: State-Society Relations in the Transition from Communism*. University Park: Pennsylvania State University Press, 2000.

Weil, Frederick D. "The Sources and Structure of Legitimation in Western Democracies: A Consolidated Model Tested with Time-Series Data in Six Countries Since World War II." *American Sociological Review* 54 (October 1989): 682–706.

Weiss, Robert S. *Learning from Strangers: The Art and Method of Qualitative Interview Studies*. New York: Free Press, 1994.

Welch, Stephen. "Review Article: Issues in the Study of Political Culture; The Example of Communist Party States." *British Journal of Political Science* 17, no. 4 (1987): 479–500.

White, Stephen. "Political Culture in Communist States: Some Problems of Theory and Method." *Comparative Politics* 16 (April 1984): 351–65.

———. "Russia's Disempowered Electorate." In *Russian Politics Under Putin*, edited by Cameron Ross. New York: Manchester University Press, 2004.

Whitefield, Stephen, and Geoffrey Evans. "The Russian Election of 1993: Public Opinion and the Transition Experience." *Post-Soviet Affairs* 10, no. 1 (1994): 38–60.

———. "Support for Democracy and Political Opposition in Russia, 1993–1995." *Post-Soviet Affairs* 12 (July–September 1996): 218–42.

White, Stephen, Richard Rose, and Ian McAllister. *How Russia Votes*. Chatham, NJ: Chatham House, 1997.

Wines, Michael. "In Russia's Far East, a Region Freezes in the Dark." *New York Times*, 12 February 2001, A6.

Wyman, Matthew. "Russian Political Culture: Evidence from Public Opinion Surveys." *Journal of Communist Studies and Transition Politics* 10, no. 1 (1994): 25–54.

Yavlinskii, Grigorii. "Periferiinyi kapitalizm." *Moskovskie Novosti*, no. 18, issue 1187 (2003): 10–12.

Yorke, Andrew. "Business and Politics in Krasnoyarsk *Krai*." *Europe-Asia Studies* 55, no. 2 (2003): 241–62.

Zaller, John R. *The Nature and Origins of Mass Opinion*. New York: Cambridge University Press, 1992.

Zaller, John R., and Stanley Feldman. "A Simple Theory of the Survey Response: Answering Questions Versus Revealing Preferences." *American Journal of Political Science* 36 (1992): 579–616.

Zarakhovich, Yuri. "A Russian's Lament: Democracy Must Mean More Than Sausage." *Time*, 21 September 1998, 76.

Zaslavskaia, Tatiana I. "Biznes-sloi rossiiskogo obshchestva: Sushchnost', struktura, status." *Obshchestvennye nauki i sovremennost'*, no. 1 (1995): 17–32.

Zhavoronkov, Aleksandr V. "Nekotorye izmeneniia v strukture informatsionnoi i obshchestvenno-politicheskoi deiatel'nosti naseleniia Taganroga za 10 let (1969–1979 gg.)." *Problemy sovershenstvovaniia deiatel'nosti sredstv massovoi informatsii i propagandy v gorode*. Moscow: Institut Sotsiologicheskikh Issledovaniia AN SSSR, 1988.

Zimmerman, William. "Synoptic Thinking and Political Culture in Post-Soviet Russia."
    Slavic Review 54 (Fall 1995): 630–41.
Zubkova, Elena. *Poslevoenno sovetskoe obshchestvo: Politika i povsednevnost'. 1945–1953.*
    Moscow: ROSSPEN, 2000.